D0759405
LIBRARY

The British General Election of 1931

THE BRITISH GENERAL ELECTION OF 1931

ANDREW THORPE

CLARENDON PRESS · OXFORD
1991

Oxford University Press, Walton Street, Oxford OX2 6DP
Oxford New York Toronto
Delhi Bombay Calcutta Madras Karachi
Petaling Jaya Singapore Hong Kong Tokyo
Nairobi Dar es Salaam Cape Town
Melbourne Auckland
and associated companies in
Berlin Ibadan

Oxford is a trade mark of Oxford University Press

Published in the United States
by Oxford University Press, New York

British Library Cataloguing in Publication Data
Thorpe, Andrew
The British general election of 1931.
1. Great Britain. Parliament. House of commons. Members.
General election history
I. Title
324.941
ISBN 0–19–820218–0

Library of Congress Cataloging in Publication Data
Thorpe, Andrew.
The British general election of 1931/Andrew Thorpe.
p. cm.
Includes bibliographical references and index.
1. Great Britain. Parliament—Elections, 1931. 2. Elections—Great Britain. 3. Great Britain—Politics and government—1910–1936. I. Title.
JN955.T48 1991
324.941'083—dc20 90–47266
ISBN 0–19–820218–0

Typeset by Cambrian Typesetters, Frimley, Surrey
Printed and bound in
Great Britain by Bookcraft Ltd,
Midsomer Norton, Bath

To My Parents
Chris and Shirley Thorpe

ACKNOWLEDGEMENTS

IT is at once humbling and reassuring to write these acknowledgements, for it shows to what extent I have depended on the efforts of others for success or failure. In writing this book I have, certainly, incurred many debts. The British Academy, through a Major State Studentship, and, on a lesser but still valued scale, the University of Sheffield, through its Crewe Awards, provided the financial assistance without which it could never have been written. On this score I am also eternally grateful to my parents, whose very real help, toleration, and encouragement were invaluable. The debt I owe them is recorded in the dedication. Dr John Stevenson, my supervisor at Sheffield, helped immeasurably in transforming this project from the vague notion of a local government clerk into, first, a thesis, and then, a book. He was the ideal supervisor, always full of ideas and ready to discuss all areas of the twentieth century, reminding me that there is more to history than 1931. My former tutors at Birmingham, Professor R. H. C. Davis and the late Mr Richard Shackleton, were a source of great assistance and encouragement when I decided to return to academic pursuits, and, in the latter case, this extended to allowing me to try out some of my ideas on his Special Subject class. Richard was always a great influence on me and my greatest regret is that he did not live to see this and future books published. Dr Philip Williamson was generous in his encouragement throughout; I also gained much from discussions with Dr Stuart Ball. Dr Ross McKibbin and Dr David Close were kind enough to answer postal enquiries at an early stage in the research. Professor David Marquand and Dr Michael Bentley, my examiners, were very helpful; in the latter case, throughout my period at Sheffield. I am also grateful to my colleagues at Exeter, both for employing me in the first place and then, particularly in the persons of Dr John Critchley, Dr Michael Duffy, and Professor Colin Jones, encouraging me when the book's prospects did not look too bright. My Special Subject students at Exeter have given ideas and considerable encouragement: one could not ask for better. My editor at OUP, Anthony Morris, was always encouraging and enthusiastic; to him I owe an immense debt of gratitude. The comments of two anonymous OUP readers helped me to tighten up the arguments in places and generally improve upon the first draft. The librarians and archivists of the repositories I used were unfailingly helpful; in particular, though, I would like to thank the staff of Sheffield University Library, where most of the thesis on which this book is based was drafted, for their assistance. Finally, I would like to thank Jody, for reminding me, when perhaps I had begun to forget, that there is more to life than history.

I would like to acknowledge the gracious permission of Her Majesty the Queen for the publication and republication of material which is subject to copyright. Crown-copyright material in the Public Record Office is reproduced by permission of the Controller of Her Majesty's Stationery Office.

I would also like to thank the following for allowing me to reproduce copyright material of individuals (name of correspondent or collection involved follows in brackets): Rt. Hon. Julian Amery, MP (L. S. Amery); the Bodleian Library (Geoffrey Dawson); Lord Bonham-Carter (Margot Asquith); the Librarian, British Library of Political and Economic Science (Hugh Dalton, Lord Passfield, and Beatrice Webb); Baron Citrine (Walter Citrine); Sir John Cripps (Sir Stafford Cripps); Baron Croft (Sir Henry Page Croft); Baron Denman (R. D. Denman); Baroness Elliot (Walter Elliot); Baron Hankey (Sir Maurice Hankey); Baron Harlech (William Ormsby-Gore); Clerk of Records, House of Lords Record Office (Samuel and Lloyd George papers); Lord Kennet (Sir Edward Hilton-Young); the County Archivist, Kent (J. H. Thomas); the Earl of Kintore (Lord Stonehaven); Marquess of Lothian (Lord Lothian); Mrs Sheila Lochhead (Ramsay MacDonald); Mr A. D. Maclean (Sir Donald Maclean); Baron Mottistone (J. E. B. Seely); the Librarian, National Library of Wales (Lloyd George papers); Mr F. Noel-Baker (Philip Noel-Baker); Mr F. P. U. Phillips (Sir Henry Morris-Jones); Marquess of Reading (Lord Reading); Viscount Runciman (Walter Runciman); David, Viscount Samuel (Sir Herbert Samuel); Lord Shuttleworth (1st Lord Shuttleworth); Hon. Mrs Stacey (Lord Bridgeman); Baron Strauss; Earl Swinton (Sir Philip Cunliffe-Lister); Mr A. J. Sylvester (Sylvester diaries); Viscount Thurso and Dr G. De Groot (Thurso papers); University of Birmingham (Chamberlain papers).

I am grateful to the following organizations for allowing me to reproduce copyright material (if the name has changed, the name in 1931 is given in brackets): the Conservative Party and Conservative Research Department; the Labour Party; the Trades Union Congress; the Transport and General Workers' Union; Cities of London and

Westminster CA (City of London CA); Birmingham CA; Cambridgeshire County Labour Party; Leeds District Labour Party; the Liberal Party, Yorkshire region; Social and Liberal Democrats, Greater Manchester region (LCNWLF); Bury South CA, and Heywood and Middleton CA (Middleton and Prestwich CA); Crosby CA (Waterloo CA papers); Ealing Southall CA (South Ealing CA); West Dorset CA.

Permission was given to use quotations taken from the following periodicals: *Daily Express*; *Daily Mail*; *Daily Mirror*; *Daily Telegraph*; *Daily Worker* (*Morning Star*); *Liberal Magazine* (Social and Liberal Democrats); *Locomotive Journal* (ASLEF); *Manchester Guardian* (*The Guardian*); *New Dawn* (Union of Shop, Distributive and Allied Workers); the *Observer*; the *Spectator*. *The Times* refused permission to quote editorials except in full; I am grateful to it for thereby forcing me to remove all direct quotations, which has greatly improved the quality of this book.

I am grateful to Dr Mark Pegg for allowing me to use the figures for radio licences and audiences which form the basis of Table 9.10, and to the following publishers for permission to quote from published works: Constable (H. Nicolson, *King George the Fifth*); Curtis Brown and Farrer & Co. (C. Stuart (ed.), *The Reith Diaries*); Longman (J. Ramsden, *The Age of Balfour and Baldwin*, and M. I. Cole, introduction to volume 2 of *The Beatrice Webb Diaries*); Macmillan (D. Butler and D. Kavanagh, *The British General Election of 1983*); Methuen (C. L. Mowat, *Britain between the Wars, 1918–1940*).

If I have inadvertently infringed copyright in any way, I offer my sincere apologies.

CONTENTS

LIST OF TABLES

ABBREVIATIONS

ASLEF	Amalgamated Society of Locomotive Engineers and Firemen
ASW	Amalgamated Society of Woodworkers
BLP	Borough Labour Party
BUF	British Union of Fascists
CA	Conservative Association
CEC	Cabinet Economy Committee
CPGB	Communist Party of Great Britain
CRD	Conservative Research Department
DLP	Divisional Labour Party
EAC	Economic Advisory Council
EIA	Empire Industries Association
FRB	Federal Reserve Bank
ILP	Independent Labour Party
LA	Liberal Association
LCC	London County Council
LCNWLF	Lancashire, Cheshire and North-Western Liberal Federation
LF	Liberal Federation
LPP	Liberal Parliamentary Party
MFGB	Miners' Federation of Great Britain
NDP	National Democratic Party
NEC	National Executive Committee (Labour Party)
NLF	National Liberal Federation
NUDAW	National Union of Distributive and Allied Workers
NUR	National Union of Railwaymen
NUWM	National Unemployed Workers' Movement
PLP	Parliamentary Labour Party
PPS	Parliamentary Private Secretary
PR	proportional representation
RCA	Railway Clerks' Association
TCLP	Trades Council and Labour Party
TGWU	Transport and General Workers' Union
TUC	Trades Union Congress

INTRODUCTION

BRITAIN in the years after the First World War was a country searching for solutions in a political landscape much changed since 1914. The Liberal Party had split and fallen into decline and been replaced by 1924, if not sooner, by the Labour Party as the main Opposition party to the Conservatives. The removal of the Irish MPs due to the creation of the Irish Free State had altered the parliamentary balance significantly in favour of the Tories. Finally, the extension of the franchise to all men over 21 and women over 30 in 1918, and to women over 21 ten years later, had created a mass electorate which seemed to be less predictable than had been the old, more restricted one. Combined with this was a change in the policy agenda. Social welfare politics assumed a new centrality, especially for example after the extension of unemployment insurance to most manual workers in 1920 and 1921. The imperial commitment was expanded as new 'mandated' territories, especially in the Middle East, fell under British control. And economic problems were to assume a political centrality they had rarely had in pre-war Britain. It must be said that in finding a solution to its problems during the 1920s, Britain was by no means successful: well has it been described as a 'chequered decade'.[1]

The search for solutions led to all sorts of political combinations being tried. None seems to have satisfied the electorate. By 1931 two of the three major parties had run out of practicable ideas as to how to deal with the problems of Britain and its ailing economy. Only one party, the Conservatives, had a definite policy, and they seemed to be heading for a decisive electoral victory. Ultimately it came about in an unexpected manner, in combination with the Liberals and under the leadership of Ramsay MacDonald, the erstwhile head of the Labour Party. The search for solutions had produced a sweeping victory for a National Government, and left the Labour Party in Opposition for many years to come.

In the immediate aftermath of victory in 1918, few Britons would have

[1] D. H. Aldcroft, *The British Economy, Vol. 1: The Years of Turmoil, 1920–1951* (Brighton, 1986), 1.

anticipated such events. An economic boom and, that December, the electoral triumph of the Conservative-dominated Lloyd George coalition seemed to some to have established a new stability or 'normalcy'. Such people were soon to be disabused. In late 1920 the boom broke; by the following June there were 2,171,288 (17.8 per cent of) insured workers unemployed. For the rest of the inter-war period the figure would remain above one million. Then, in October 1922, the coalition was destroyed when Conservative MPs voted, against the advice of their leader, Austen Chamberlain, to fight the next election as a separate party. Andrew Bonar Law took over as leader, formed a party Government without most of the coalitionists, and won a commanding majority at the general election of November 1922. Law had avoided the thorny problem of trade policy by pledging that no general tariff would be introduced without a second election. Ostensibly, Law's Government would last until 1926 at least; but he was fatally ill and resigned in May 1923, to be succeeded by Stanley Baldwin. Within months, the latter had declared for protection; and, in keeping with Law's pledge, an election was called. The Tories lost numerous seats and their overall majority and, while remaining the largest party, were voted out of office when Parliament met. The Liberals decided to support a minority Labour administration instead.

Labour had advanced steadily since 1918, though it was hindered in Parliament until 1922 by the absence or preoccupation with union or party matters of most of its leading figures. But in 1922 the leaders returned, MacDonald immediately ousting J. R. Clynes as party leader. By then, too, industrial militancy was on the wane, enabling Labour to project a more 'respectable' image. All this helped it to advance to 191 seats and—somewhat fortuitously—office in 1924. The first Labour Government lasted nine months, before it was defeated by the Liberals and Conservatives in the Commons. The ensuing election saw a Conservative landslide. Labour lost 40 seats, but the real losers were the Liberals, who were reduced to a rump of 40 MPs.

Nineteen twenty-four saw a number of developments which seemed to signify a return to two-party politics. Labour in office passed some useful reforms, and could blame its minority position for its failure to do more, and although sceptics might have pointed to a lack of detailed policy proposals it had at least shown many people that it was 'fit to govern'. Meanwhile, by the end of the year the leading former coalitionists were back in the Tory fold, with Austen Chamberlain,

Winston Churchill, and Lords Balfour and Birkenhead all in the Cabinet. And finally, the Liberals had been reduced to seeming insignificance, having been able to nominate only 339 candidates at the election and, as stated above, winning only 40 seats.

The second Baldwin Government (1924–9) seemed to continue this reversion to stability. True, there was the General Strike (1926), but that only lasted nine days, and ended with total defeat for the unions. Thereafter, the TUC moved towards corporatism, holding a series of discussions with employers' organizations in 1927 and 1928. In foreign affairs, the Locarno Treaties (1925), on top of the earlier renegotiation of reparations, seemed to signify a new spirit of co-operation in Europe. And in 1925 Britain symbolically restored 'normalcy' by returning to the gold standard at the pre-war parity.

For all that, Baldwin's Government was not felt, by the end of its term, to have been wholly successful. Despite numerous valuable reforms, unemployment remained stubbornly above a million at a time when other countries, most notably the USA, were experiencing unprecedented prosperity. Some ministers, like the Colonial and Dominions Secretary, L. S. Amery, felt the figure could be reduced by protective tariffs, but the renewal of Law's pledge by Baldwin in 1924, allied to the presence of the free trader Churchill at the Treasury, meant little could be done. Some industries like motor-car manufacturing were protected by the restoration of the McKenna duties on luxury imports; others like lace-making were 'safeguarded' against unfair foreign competition; but the pleas of others, notably iron and steel, went unheeded. Baldwin felt caution would see the return of prosperity, hence the use of the slogan 'Safety First' in 1929. Both Labour and the Liberals said more could be done. Labour's 1928 programme, *Labour and the Nation*, stated, as did its 1929 manifesto, that in Government it would have little difficulty in cutting unemployment. The Liberals were more specific, advocating a scheme of major loan-financed public works to reduce the jobless total. In the first British election fought on universal adult suffrage Labour emerged, for the first time, as the largest party, with 287 seats to the Conservatives' 260 and the Liberals' 59, although the Tories had won slightly more votes. MacDonald became Labour Prime Minister for the second time.

As will be seen, the new administration started brightly but was soon weighed down by world depression and inexorably rising unemployment. Soon the party was faring disastrously at by-elections. If anything the Liberals did even worse. By contrast, the Conservatives, it will be argued, despite severe internecine strife until March 1931, were, by the middle of that year, well placed to repeat their success of 1924 on a fully protectionist platform.

It was then that the political crisis of 1931 occurred. In August, faced with a flight from sterling, the Labour Cabinet was forced to consider demands for reductions in public expenditure. Ultimately it could not agree to cut unemployment benefits by 10 per cent, and so had to resign. However, MacDonald stayed on as head of a National Government, comprising a few Labourites plus the Conservative and Liberal Parties. Initially, the administration was meant to be temporary, but within six weeks it had decided to fight an election, at which it won the most sweeping victory in modern British history, obtaining 554 seats (of which the Conservatives won 470) to Labour's 46.

Ostensibly, therefore, the 1931 election was a great triumph for the National Government, and especially the Conservatives; and, conversely, a disaster for Labour. Certainly the latter party was to win only 154 seats at the next election, in 1935, and there is very little evidence to suggest that it could have won the subsequent election due before the end of 1940, had not the Second World War intervened. It will be argued here, in fact, that the 1931 election marked a decisive and long-term shift against Labour, and that only the impact of the Second World War made possible its great victory in 1945. Yet few historians have seen the 1931 general election in quite this light.

At the front of G. D. H. Cole's *History of the Labour Party from 1914* (1948) there is a graph showing the number of votes Labour obtained at every general election between 1906 and 1945.[2] The overall trend was distinctly upward; there was, indeed, only one recession, in 1931, when the party's vote fell back to the 1924 level after the peak of 1929. However, this was followed by increases in 1935 and, of course, 1945, when the party had been able to form its first majority administration. Here, in a chart, was implied the 'fact' that gradualism had been inevitable after all. Another Labourite, Francis Williams, wrote the following year that history had 'fully live[d] up to its spectacular possibilities'.[3] Viewed in this light, 1931 had been an aberration, brought about by treacherous leaders and dishonourable opponents.

[2] G. D. H. Cole, *A History of the Labour Party from 1914* (London, 1948), x.
[3] F. Williams, *Fifty Years' March: The Rise of the Labour Party* (London, 1949), 9.

The 1930s were regarded as a decade of 'tragedy'[4] and the National Governments had been very largely to blame. In particular, by trickery, by duping the electorate, and by seducing—or allowing themselves to be seduced by—Labour's erstwhile leader, MacDonald, the Conservatives had foisted themselves onto an unwilling country. But in 1945 they had finally paid the price: the people had finally seen through them and done what, in their hearts, they had wanted to do all along—elect a Labour Government. Thus the 1931 election was part and parcel of the view of the 1930s as 'the Devil's decade'. This view of the 1930s has long since been challenged by economic and social historians like Derek Aldcroft and John Stevenson, although the work of the 'new pessimists' like Charles Webster and Forrest Capie serves to warn against taking too rosy a view.[5]

A countervailing view was slow to materialize. After all, the leaders of the National Governments had been responsible, not only for domestic, but also for foreign and defence policies during the 1930s. The Second World War saw the eclipse of most of these politicians—for example, Chamberlain and Hoare—and their replacement at the head of the Conservative Party by two men, Churchill and Anthony Eden, who had spent most or some of the 'Devil's decade' dissenting on the back benches. As few were ready to defend the foreign and defence policies of Baldwin and Chamberlain, so few would be prepared to argue vehemently against the Labourite view of 1931. In his book on the 1930s, *The Gathering Storm* (1948), Churchill merely praised the patriotism of the nation at that election, while lamenting that it had enthroned the National Government in power. He had no wish to try to rehabilitate his party, the Government, or their leaderships for their conduct during the crisis and the election. Then, in 1955, C. L. Mowat largely endorsed the orthodox Labour view in the first scholarly account of the inter-war period to be published.

It was largely Mowat's version of the 1931 crisis which led Reginald Bassett to produce *Nineteen Thirty-One: Political Crisis* in 1958. This was a weighty study, written, as might have been expected from someone who had resigned as a Labour candidate in order

[4] Cole, *Labour Party*, 343.

[5] Aldcroft, *The British Economy*, 44–163; J. Stevenson and C. Cook, *The Slump: Society and Politics during the Depression* (London, 1977); C. Webster, 'Healthy or Hungry Thirties?', *History Workshop*, 13 (1982), 111–25, and 'Health, Welfare and Unemployment during the Depression', *Past and Present*, 109 (1985), 204–29; F. Capie and M. Collins, 'The Extent of British Economic Recovery in the 1930s', *Economy and History*, 23 (1980), 40–60.

to support the National Government, in a pro-MacDonald and anti-Labour tone. It was valuable both in studying the subject in depth, and in establishing a coherent non-Labour view of the events of that year. Succeeding decades have seen further erosion of the once-established orthodoxy regarding 1931. The opening of archival sources and the dying down of passions (not least because of the death of most of the surviving participants) have led to more sober accounts, such as those in the biographies of MacDonald, Baldwin, and Herbert Morrison. However, in the thirty years since Bassett published, there has been no attempt to reassess the crisis and, in particular, the election as a whole, despite the availability of vast amounts of archival material and despite the advances made by numerous scholars in various areas relating to the subject. In addition, as Bassett himself acknowledged, he was writing at a time of an established two-party system and of economic prosperity, when political flux and economic crisis seemed aberrant. The experience of Britain in the 1970s and 1980s, especially for a young Labour supporter living and writing in a once heavily industrialized area, suggests, in fact, that neither prosperity nor the two-party system is as typical of Britain as might have been thought in the two decades after the Second World War; in particular, it could be argued that the only thing which was 'inevitable' about the Labour Party in the 1980s was its presence on the Opposition benches in the House of Commons. Indeed, from the perspective of the early 1990s it is 1945–70 which seems the aberrant period in electoral terms.

There exist, therefore, powerful arguments in favour of a new analysis of the general election of 1931 and the events leading to it, and the present study attempts to provide it by explaining the causes and consequences of the events of August to October 1931. In Chapters 1 to 3 the fortunes of each of the three major parties from the aftermath of the 1929 election to the early summer of 1931 are examined broadly. There then follow three chapters analysing the fall of the Labour Government, the first National Government and the decision to call the election, and the Labour Party in Opposition prior to the dissolution. Inevitably, these chapters tend towards 'high' politics, but they do not eschew discussion of the wider factors involved. The politicians have not been treated as mere actors, but a close study of individual motivation has at times been essential in establishing why certain courses were followed. The next four chapters cover the election campaign. In Chapter 7 I discuss the respective parties' election programmes, and in Chapter 8 analyse relations between the various National parties during the campaign. Chapter 9 follows with an in-depth discussion of the means by which the election was carried to the electors—party electioneering and the mass media: some established, like newspapers, others more novel, like radio and film. Chapter 10 takes an issue-by-issue look at the campaign. Finally, in a chapter on the results, I look at reactions, offer deeper analysis, and place the outcome in a wider context.

'No matter how often it is told, the story remains fantastic,' wrote Margaret Cole of the 1931 crisis a quarter of a century after it had happened.[6] Now, more than thirty years after that, the time has come to treat the crisis and especially the election historically rather than polemically. In fact, it will be argued, much of what happened in 1931 was perfectly logical given the events of the preceding years. This study will show that little about the events of 1931 should be regarded as 'fantastic' today.

[6] M. I. Cole (ed.), *Beatrice Webb's Diaries 1924–1932* (London, 1956), xiv.

1

FROM ELATION TO DESPAIR: LABOUR 1929–1931

RARELY if ever in British political history has a Government which started out with such high hopes and keen support come to grief so ignominiously as did the second Labour administration of Ramsay MacDonald. The dramatic nature of Labour's demise in August–October 1931 should not be allowed to mask the fact that, by the early summer of that year, the party was facing a heavy defeat whenever and however the next general election might be fought. Nor should the immense difficulties which faced the Government after its brief honeymoon period be permitted to disguise the initial enthusiasm with which the Labour movement greeted the party's success at the polls in May 1929. Then, Labour won 287 seats to the Conservatives' 260 and so formed its second minority administration, for the first time as the largest party in Parliament, although still dependent on Liberal support.[1]

I

The initial euphoria permeated almost all sections of the Labour movement. The bulk of the parliamentary Labour party (PLP) was 'elated'.[2] The trade unions were also delighted: W. A. Robinson, political general secretary of the National Union of Distributive and Allied Workers (NUDAW) emphasized the overwhelming need for loyalty, and added that he had 'never at any time moved about in such an atmosphere of enthusiasm'.[3] The party activists reflected this mood; York divisional Labour Party (DLP) 'congratulate[d] the Working Class on at last becoming the Ruling Class'.[4] Even the more cautious were optimistic. The *Monthly Journal* of the Amalgamated

[1] For an example of the 'all-gloom' approach, see M. G. Bondfield, *A Life's Work* (London, n.d. [1948]), 276.

[2] C. J. Simmons, *Soap-Box Evangelist* (Chichester, 1972), 79.

[3] *New Dawn*, 6 July 1929.

[4] York DLP, delegate meeting 17 July 1929 (York Archives Office, York Labour Party papers, Acc. 196/1/4, f. 157).

Society of Woodworkers (ASW) pointed out that the Government would be hampered by its minority position; even so, it could do much useful work, before calling another election at which it could win a majority for 'root changes in ownership and control'.[5] Even the left-wingers in the Independent Labour Party (ILP) were hopeful; of the leadership, only John Wheatley opposed the decision to take office; his colleagues hoped that the Government would make a bold attack on unemployment. If Labour were defeated in Parliament on a bold programme, they argued, it need have no fear of the result of the ensuing general election.[6]

The next election was not something that worried many Labourites at this time. Many believed that it would yield, ineluctably, an overall Labour majority. The chairman of Glasgow Labour Party, for example, after referring to the seats won in the city, added that 'he had no doubt that those seats which had not been won . . . would be won by Labour at the next election'.[7] Presumably this included constituencies like Hillhead and Pollok, with Conservative majorities over Labour (in straight fights) of 7,330 and 12,392 respectively.

The problem with such euphoria was that it tended to mask the harsh realities by which seats were won and lost, although it should be added that the state of psephological study in inter-war Britain was so poor that few could see this at the time. Labour, although winning more seats than the Conservatives, had obtained only 8,370,417 votes (37.1 per cent of the poll) to the latters' 8,656,225 (38.1 per cent). Labour had won 287 seats; for a bare overall majority it needed 308, or 21 more. A uniform swing of 3 per cent from the leading party to Labour after the 1929 election would have resulted in 18 gains from the Conservatives and 3 from the Liberals. But the conditions of the 1929 election could not be repeated. Although in the summer some Conservatives feared a 'snap' election, the mood soon passed, and from February 1930 onwards by-elections went steadily against Labour and towards the Conservatives. The difficulties of minority Government in general, and Labour's failure to deal with unemployment and economic crisis in particular, meant that Labour would be more likely to lose than to gain ground at a subsequent election, especially if, as seemed increasingly likely, the Liberals fought on a

[5] ASW, *Monthly Journal*, July 1929.

[6] R. E. Dowse, *Left in the Centre: The Independent Labour Party, 1893–1940* (London, 1966), 152.

[7] Glasgow trades council and borough Labour Party, meeting 5 June 1929 (Glasgow TCBLP papers, on microfilm at Birmingham Reference Library).

much narrower front than in 1929. This also made the 123 seats Labour won on minority votes in three-cornered contests look especially vulnerable. Indeed, many of the party's seats were held by narrow margins over the Tories: 21 with a majority of 2 per cent or less, and a further 35 by between 2.1 and 6 per cent. Thus 56 seats were susceptible to a 'swing' of 3 per cent or more. Thus Labour's hold in over one-fifth of its seats was extremely tenuous. On the other hand, it would be difficult further to 'squeeze' the Conservative vote and gain further seats from that party. Hence the purely psephological position made Labour especially vulnerable in an adverse political climate.

In the summer of 1929, however, the initial success of MacDonald's administration did little to dispel its supporters' early optimism. Unemployment rose slightly, to over 1,200,000, but it did not seem out of hand, and MacDonald had appointed to deal with the problem one of his ablest colleagues, J. H. Thomas, as Lord Privy Seal at the head of a strong team comprising George Lansbury, the First Commissioner of Works, and two non-Cabinet Ministers, Sir Oswald Mosley (Chancellor of the Duchy of Lancaster) and Thomas Johnston (Under-Secretary of State for Scotland). In the mean time, the administration of unemployment benefit and pensions was liberalized somewhat. Foreign policy seemed like one long string of successes, be it Arthur Henderson, the Foreign Secretary, over Egypt in July; Philip Snowden, the Chancellor of the Exchequer, over reparations in September; or MacDonald's triumphal visit to the United States in October, when he became the first British premier to address Congress. These successes were crowned with 'respectability' when Prime Minister and Chancellor were awarded the freedom of the City of London.

The party remained suitably contented. MacDonald, never one for light-hearted optimism, noted on 26 September that if it was not for the 'industrial condition' the Government 'look[ed] as if it would live for ever'.[8] The party conference was told by that year's chairman, Herbert Morrison, that Labour was 'the miracle of politics'. Morrison added that Labour had won the first election fought on adult suffrage, a clear hint that 'the inevitability of gradualism' was manifesting itself.[9] At the end of the year, the ILP-sponsored MP, Alfred Salter, was

[8] MacDonald diary, 26 Sept. 1929 (Public Record Office, MacDonald papers, PRO 30/69/1753).

[9] Labour Party, *Annual Report, 1929* (London, 1929), 150–3.

arguing that on all questions except unemployment benefit the Government's record was 'brilliant beyond precedent'.[10]

II

Precedents were soon to be broken in the opposite direction, however. While foreign policy under Henderson continued to be a matter for pride, with a number of steps being taken to fulfil Labour's programme—most notably in the progress made towards convening the world disarmament conference, of which Henderson himself was elected president in May 1931—domestic affairs were paramount in the eyes of most electors. And here the Government's record became, after its early successes, increasingly barren. The prime issue was unemployment. Labour had given 'an unqualified pledge to deal immediately and practically with this question'.[11] However, after a slight dip in June 1929, the figure began to rise in August. The total number registered at the employment exchanges rose above 1,200,000 in September, and above 1,300,000 two months later. By January 1930 it stood at 1,534,000, with one-eighth of the insured work-force unemployed. Even so, this was only 100,000 more than a year earlier. The real crisis came in the spring of 1930, when the full effects of the Wall Street crash of October 1929 and ensuing American Depression began to be felt in Britain. Instead of taking the usual seasonal downturn, the figure continued inexorably to rise, exceeding 2,000,000 in June 1930 and reaching 2,725,000 by December, when one in five of the insured population was out of work. Although unemployment fell in January, March, and April 1931, it was only by 54,000, 39,000, and 61,000 respectively; the overall trend remained upwards, and by the end of July 22 per cent of the insured population (2,783,000) was out of work.[12]

In the face of such difficulties, Thomas was completely out of his depth, although, to be fair, so too were most of his colleagues and many economists. Thomas's own ideas—a limited scheme of public works, colonial development, and the 'rationalization' of industry—were of little short-term utility in the face of such a crisis, with rationalization in particular liable to increase the numbers out of work. It would not be going too far to say, in fact, that his most memorable

[10] A. F. Brockway, *Bermondsey Story: The Life of Alfred Salter* (London, 1949), 144.
[11] 'Labour's Appeal to the Nation' (1929 election manifesto).
[12] *Ministry of Labour Gazette*, Feb. 1930, Feb. 1931, Feb. 1932.

act as Lord Privy Seal was describing his dingy office as 'a bloody hawful 'ole, more Privy than Seal about it'.[13] He rarely met his colleagues in the ministerial team, and they, not surprisingly, went behind his back to collaborate on the so-called Mosley memorandum, which was sent direct to MacDonald in January 1930. This advocated economic expansion through public works, a move towards imperial autarky, and the diminution of the labour market through increased pensions and the raising of the school-leaving age, under the direction of a small executive like Lloyd George's War Cabinet. After some consideration it was rejected, primarily on the advice of Thomas and Snowden, prompting Mosley's resignation in May 1930. Thomas was switched to the Dominions Office, and Vernon Hartshorn succeeded him, although MacDonald took over control of unemployment policy himself. It made no difference; there was no change of policy.

The second Labour Government's failure to solve the problem of unemployment has been much debated, and much of the debate remains inconclusive.[14] Few people today would give unqualified support to the view that governmental action could have made considerable inroads into the level of unemployment. And, as Ross McKibbin has shown, there was a lack of examples for Labour to follow. Indeed, he goes so far as to argue that, by drifting rather than furiously deflating, the Government was more radical than most of its foreign counterparts. There were Mosley's suggestions, but MacDonald and Snowden clearly believed that there were worse things for the people they represented than unemployment—for example, a crisis of confidence leading to devaluation and the kind of hyperinflation which had afflicted Germany as recently as 1923. And they would have argued that in a country like Britain, importing most of its food requirements, the collapse of sterling would lead to starvation among the British people. Snowden's line of keeping the house in order and waiting for better times was certainly endorsed by the Cabinet and the bulk of the PLP.

[13] G. Blaxland, *J. H. Thomas: A Life for Unity* (London, 1964), 224.

[14] For the view that alternative policies were available, and that Labour could have implemented them with Liberal support, see R. Skidelsky, *Politicians and the Slump: The Labour Government of 1929–1931* (London, 1967), and *Oswald Mosley* (London, 1975). For alternative views, see R. I. McKibbin, 'The Economic Policy of the Second Labour Government, 1929–1931', *Past and Present*, 68 (1975), 95–123; J. A. Roberts, 'Economic Aspects of the Unemployment Policy of the Government, 1929–1931', Ph.D. thesis (London, 1977); A. Booth and M. Pack, *Employment, Capital and Economic Policy in Great Britain, 1918–1939* (Oxford, 1985).

Labour's failure, however, raised difficult questions about the ideology of the party which caused great disquiet to leaders and followers alike. MacDonald and Snowden had always believed that socialism would be paid for by the surplus of a successful capitalism. Thus their philosophy had no serious response to capitalism in crisis, other than to restore it to health as best they knew how while avoiding 'palliatives' as far as possible. Indeed, Snowden advocated the restriction of wages and social expenditure, and opposed shorter working hours, in order that British industry should be allowed to reinvest its profits in bringing its old-fashioned plant up-to-date.[15] As he told Parliament in his 1930 budget speech, 'I abate not one jot or tittle of my lifelong advocacy of great schemes of social reform and national reconstruction, but our immediate concern is to make these things ultimately possible out of a revived and prosperous industry.'[16] This was genuinely felt, but it was bound to affect the morale of socialists high and low.

The failure over jobs also exposed a lack of leadership and, some argued, courage, which did the party little credit. And for that lack of leadership, the leader must take much of the responsibility. Always a moderate, keen to prove Labour's respectability, MacDonald was now shorn of much of his ideological coat, tired, and more suspicious of his colleagues, especially Henderson, than ever.[17] He took an uncomfortably prominent role in foreign policy, especially in Anglo–American relations. In domestic affairs, MacDonald was too ready to let matters drift. He was not indolent, but his activity was often unchannelled, involving little more than interference in the work of other ministers. And this prevented him from exerting himself as co-ordinator and leader. From early 1930, for example, he favoured a revenue tariff to help balance the budget, maintain social services, and promote economic recovery. However, when he raised the matter in Cabinet, he failed to give a strong enough lead, and was defeated.[18] Snowden, an adamantine free trader, might have resigned, but had MacDonald himself threatened resignation, he should have been able to isolate the Chancellor, who was losing his old popularity within the PLP. MacDonald must be criticized for failing to take a risk on so

[15] Beatrice Webb diary, 3 Aug. 1930 (British Library of Political and Economic Science, Passfield papers).

[16] *Parl. Deb.*, 5th ser., 237, 14 Apr. 1930.

[17] D. Marquand, *Ramsay MacDonald* (London, 1977), 493–4.

[18] Ibid. 555–6, 564.

important an issue. In addition, his belief in consensus led the Government to institute a plethora of enquiries and royal commissions and, most spectacularly, to create the Economic Advisory Council (EAC), comprising economists, businessmen, and trade unionists, in January 1930. This might not have been as futile as it has sometimes been portrayed, but it was a fairly ineffective body in which to formulate a response to the slump.

This is not to claim that MacDonald was the flood barrier against which the thrusting intellectual tide of his colleagues broke. The rest of the Cabinet opposed the Mosley memorandum, as did the PLP and, more narrowly, the party conference. MacDonald remained 'the leader'. Only Henderson, whose prestige rose due to his conduct of foreign affairs, was a conceivable successor, since the reputations of the others of the 'big five' inner Cabinet Ministers (Snowden, Thomas, and the Home Secretary, J. R. Clynes) all suffered and none of the younger men looked ready, as yet. But Henderson still regarded MacDonald as the only possible leader, smothering back-bench intrigues which sought to make him, Henderson, leader in late 1930 and the spring of 1931.[19] In addition, MacDonald was still able to use his oratory to swing the party activists behind him, as he showed at the 1930 conference. One appalled critic wrote that 'Mr MacDonald was to most delegates what the grown-up is to the child of three.'[20]

Even a child of three might have noticed that employment was not the only area of domestic policy where the Government lacked success. In February 1931, its efforts to increase the school-leaving age to fifteen were thwarted by a combination of the House of Lords and its own Catholic back-benchers. In housing, there was more success, with slum clearance legislation being passed, but even here sections of the movement wanted a more positive programme.[21]

III

Discontent came especially from the unions, and these years witnessed a steady and grave decline in relations between the political and industrial wings of the Labour movement. This took many forms. First, there was no formal machinery for consultation, such as many

[19] Beatrice Webb diary, 2 Dec. 1929 (Passfield papers); M. A. Hamilton, *Arthur Henderson: A Biography* (London, 1938), 353; J. M. Kenworthy, *Sailors, Statesmen—and Others: An Autobiography* (London, 1933), 270–1.

[20] J. Scanlon, *Decline and Fall of the Labour Party* (London, n.d. [1931]), 192.

[21] ASW, *Monthly Journal*, Aug. 1929.

union leaders, especially the TUC general secretary, Walter Citrine, wanted. It did not augur well for relations when, against Citrine's strong objections, Margaret Bondfield was appointed Minister of Labour.[22] There were some contacts, but they were intermittent and often ineffectual. Only once did the TUC general council meet Thomas regarding unemployment, in November 1929. There were further meetings with MacDonald in January 1930 and in January, April, and June 1931; but such events were generally about such single issues as the repeal of the Trade Disputes and Trade Union Act, 1927, which, as well as outlawing general strikes and forbidding trade unionism among civil servants, had substituted 'contracting in' for 'contracting out' of the trade-union political levy, and so reduced the income of unions' political funds and therefore of the party.

Even when contact did take place, it often served only to incense trade unionists. In July 1929 the general council expressed disquiet about the fact that the Government had made direct approaches to Arthur Pugh and Ernest Bevin to serve on the colonial development committee, instead of observing the established protocol whereby the council was asked as a body to nominate representatives.[23] High-handed behaviour by ministers like Bondfield and Clynes also exacerbated the situation. By mid-1930 both ministers, former union officials themselves, were arousing trade-union anger by not receiving TUC deputations personally.[24] The greatest crisis came in December 1930, when the Royal Commission on Unemployment Insurance was set up. Its brief was, basically, to make economies: there was no reference to Labour's supposed policy of improving benefits and extending the insurance scheme to all workers. These terms of reference, and Bondfield's offhand manner in presenting them to the council, brought matters to a head.[25] On 17 December, the council decided to protest directly to MacDonald, and Citrine let loose his ire on the premier, saying that after 'a number of incidents' which had 'caused perplexity and uneasiness to the General Council' they felt they could remain silent no longer.[26] It took a long discussion with the

[22] 'Cabinet Making', 5 June 1929 (British Library of Political and Economic Science, Citrine papers, 7/8).

[23] TUC general council minutes, 24 July 1929 (Modern Records Centre, TUC papers).

[24] TUC general council minutes, 23 July 1930 (TUC papers).

[25] H. A. Clegg, *A History of British Trade Unions since 1889. Vol. 2: 1911–33* (Oxford, 1985), 505–6.

[26] Citrine to MacDonald, 18 Dec. 1930, TUC general council minutes, 17 Dec. 1930 (TUC papers).

premier to get the council to agree, still under protest, to give evidence to the commission.[27]

The general performance of the Government did little to stimulate union goodwill. In August 1930, the general secretary of the Transport and General Workers' Union (TGWU), Ernest Bevin, told his executive committee that the economic situation warranted a state of national emergency.[28] However, the idea that nothing could be done short of socialism, which a minority Government could not introduce, remained persuasive. The 1930 TUC regretted the Government's failure to reduce unemployment, but added that it could not be expected to introduce socialist remedies, which were the only solution.[29]

The Government's failure to deliver union demands for legislation was, perhaps, more serious. It is revealing to note that, of fourteen such demands identified by Citrine in January 1930, only one—regarding housing and slum clearance—was enacted by the administration.[30] The Trade Disputes Act was not repealed; the attempt was not even made until the 1930–1 session of Parliament, despite the fact that the Labour Party's finances were handicapped by the 1927 law. When the attempt finally was made, the bill was amended into oblivion by the Liberals, an action seen as 'a declaration of war' by the general council.[31] The Government's lack of enthusiasm and failure to treat the bill as a matter of confidence—which might have swung the votes of Liberal MPs anxious to avoid a general election in the spring of 1931—served further to dishearten trade unionists. At least the effort had been made, however. The unions' demands for the ratification of the Washington hours convention and for new workmen's compensation legislation did not even get that far.

The Government also let down individual unions. Despite party policy, no attempt was made to abolish tied cottages or to extend unemployment insurance to agricultural workers. The Coal Mines Act, 1930, replaced the eight-hour day, not with the seven hours demanded by party and Miners' Federation of Great Britain (MFGB) policy, but with seven-and-a-half hours. The 1930 woollen textile

[27] TUC general council minutes, 28 Jan. 1931 (TUC papers).

[28] General secretary's report, TGWU executive minutes, 19 Aug. 1930 (Modern Records Centre, TGWU papers, MSS 126/T&G/1/1/8).

[29] TUC, *Report*, 1930, 287.

[30] 'Points which the general council desire to raise with the Prime Minister', 16 Jan. 1930 (Citrine papers, III/1/13).

[31] TUC general council minutes, 25 Feb. 1931 (TUC papers).

lock-out was settled with the help of the Government, but only at the expense of heavy wage cuts. And no concession was made to the demands of unions in steel, textiles, hosiery, or lace, as well as DLPs in some agricultural areas, for a measure of protection even against the most blatant foreign dumping.[32]

It should have been little wonder, then, that leading trade unionists became increasingly disillusioned with, and almost hostile towards, the Government. As early as February 1930 Citrine was saying privately that he was 'disillusioned with the Labour world' and believed that 'the other side "[was] far abler"'.[33] John Bromley, leader of the train drivers' union, ASLEF, and MP for Barrow, had been very enthusiastic in June 1929. But by March 1931 he had decided to retire from Parliament at the next election, writing that 'the Government . . . [would] either have to go to the country or die like a sick sheep under the hedge.'[34]

IV

Bromley's attitude was symptomatic, not only of the disillusionment of trade unionists, but also of the increasing alienation of left-wing elements within the Labour Party. In 1929, as already stated, the ILP leadership had favoured, broadly, the formation of a second Labour Government, but on condition that it mounted a bold attack on unemployment. Thus the ultra-moderation of the Cabinet and its policies were certain to lead to discontent. This culminated in the decision of the 1930 ILP conference that the party's MPs were to give ILP policy precedence over Government policy. There were 142 ILP members in Parliament, but only 18 accepted this directive. They now formed a quasi-independent group under the leadership of the Glaswegian, James Maxton, and at the Labour Party conference in October, he moved an amendment criticizing the administration for its 'timidity and vacillation in refusing to apply Socialist remedies'.[35] Negotiations between Henderson and Maxton to settle the anomalous position of the ILP MPs were inconclusive, and ILP candidates were not given official Labour Party endorsement unless they signed a

[32] Cambridgeshire TCLP, executive committee 4 July 1931 (Cambs. Record Office, Cambs. Labour Party papers, 416/0/4).
[33] Beatrice Webb diary, 5 Feb. 1930 (Passfield papers).
[34] *Locomotive Journal*, Apr. 1931.
[35] Dowse, *Left in the Centre*, 152, 161, 165; Cole, *Labour Party*, 239.

pledge whose effect was to negate the decision of the ILP conference. The nadir was reached on 15 July 1931, when the ILP group forced an all-night sitting against the Unemployment (No. 3), or anomalies, Bill, which the Government hoped would prevent 'abuses' of the unemployment insurance scheme. The ILPers claimed that their motives were honourable, but to the bulk of the PLP, which also disliked the bill but wanted still more to be loyal to the Government, they were being fractious for the sake of it. One senior back-bencher described it as 'the most disgraceful scene of humiliation that the Labour Party [had] ever had to submit to', adding ominously that '[t]he position [could] not continue as it [was]'.[36]

Another group had already left. In May 1930 Mosley had resigned from the Government, making a devastating attack on what he saw as the inactivity of the Cabinet. Proof of Mosley's popularity among Labour activists came from the large number of DLPs which purchased multiple copies of his speech for propaganda purposes.[37] Defeated in the PLP, he was far closer to success at the 1930 party conference.[38] He was narrowly defeated, but won a great ovation and was elected to the national executive committee (NEC) in place of Thomas. In December he issued the Mosley manifesto with the signatures of seventeen MPs plus the secretary of the MFGB, A. J. Cook. Mosley, however, was frustrated by his lack of progress, and decided that a new departure was needed. In February 1931 he launched his New Party, but only four Labour MPs, plus one Conservative, followed him. On 10 March he was expelled, with his followers, from the Labour Party for 'gross disloyalty'.[39] No DLPs followed his lead, but the loss of five MPs directly because of the perceived lethargy of the Cabinet was not an encouraging sign. Nor was the loss of a man who, though certainly not without faults, possessed great ability and drive.

There was left-wing disquiet at higher levels, too. In March 1931

[36] Marion Phillips to George Ford (her agent), 20 July 1931 (Labour Party library, Phillips papers, MP 1/323).

[37] Doncaster DLP, executive committee, 25 June 1930 (Doncaster Archives Dept., Doncaster Labour Party papers, DS 7/1/4, f. 237); Cambridge TCLP, executive committee, 30 June 1930 (Cambridgeshire Record Office, Cambridge Labour Party papers, 634/07, f. 77); York DLP, delegate meeting, 18 June 1930 (York Labour Party papers, Acc. 196/1/5, f. 29).

[38] The votes were 202:29 in the PLP and 1,251,000:1,046,000 at conference. Cole, *Labour Party*, 241.

[39] Labour Party NEC minutes, 10 Mar. 1931 (Labour Party library, Labour Party papers).

Sir Charles Trevelyan resigned as President of the Board of Education, making it clear that the defeat of his Education Bill was the occasion rather than the cause of his departure. At a meeting of the PLP he launched a strong attack on MacDonald and stressed the need for a change of leadership, but his words were met with a hostile silence.[40]

V

The loyalty of the bulk of the parliamentary party was reflected in the party in the country, where critics often found themselves isolated among party members for whom, very often, the mere fact of a Labour Government after years of effort excused a great deal.[41] But if on the whole DLPs' loyalty gave party headquarters at Transport House little cause for concern, their organizational and financial difficulties more than made up for it. By February 1931 the official paper, *Labour Organiser*, was complaining about the 'state of unpreparedness' of many DLPs.[42] In fact, some were quite well organized. But Labour, lacking extensive financial resources, relied heavily on voluntary help and here, unemployment and general disillusionment with the Government had a deleterious effect. Although officially individual membership rose, these figures have always been very inaccurate, and many DLPs in important areas reported falling rolls. In Central Leeds, for example, membership fell by around 10 per cent between 1929 and 1930. In January 1931 South Nottingham reported a loss of membership in all wards.[43] The decision of the NEC in June 1931 to hold a special membership campaign in September betrayed the growing disquiet of party officials and leaders.[44]

Finance, however, was the bugbear for most divisional parties. Reading their minutes, one is struck again and again by the increasing impoverishment of DLPs as the tenure of the second Labour

[40] A. J. A. Morris, *C. P. Trevelyan, 1870–1958: Portrait of a Radical* (Belfast, 1977), 184.

[41] See e.g. Wansbeck DLP papers, annual meeting, 19 Apr. 1930 (Northumberland Record Office, NRO 527/A/2).

[42] *Labour Organiser*, Feb. 1931.

[43] Labour Party, *Annual Report*, 1929, 1930, 1931. Cf. Central Leeds DLP, annual meeting, 29 Jan. 1931 (West Yorkshire Archive Service, Central Leeds Labour Party papers, 63/3); South Nottingham DLP, annual meeting, 11 Jan. 1931 (Notts. Record Office, South Nottingham Labour Party papers, DDPP 7/1, f. 194).

[44] Labour Party NEC minutes, 23 June 1931 (Labour Party papers).

Government progressed. By November 1930, for example, Newport DLP was finding difficulty in sending its usual donations to by-election funds, and by the following June its finances were 'in a bad way'; in September 1929 North Lambeth DLP had to borrow £75 from its MP in order to ease bank pressure for repayment of an overdraft of £108.[45] This naturally affected propaganda work and organizational efficiency.

VI

Party headquarters also faced difficulties, many caused, paradoxically, by Labour's success at the 1929 election. Henderson's appointment as Foreign Secretary meant that he could no longer act as party general secretary. He became honorary secretary and his assistant, James Middleton, took on the role of acting general secretary. Henderson continued to take an active part, spending at least an hour a day on party business, but his wider duties inhibited his impact at Transport House. Middleton, though worthy, was no adequate replacement. The electoral success of key party officials—such as Henderson's son, William, who was head of the party's press and publicity department, and Dr Marion Phillips, the chief woman officer—meant that they were unable to devote sufficient time to their work at Transport House. The problems created were so great that, in January 1930, the NEC decided that in future no member of the staff except the general secretary would be allowed to stand for Parliament, although those who were already MPs would be allowed to remain such so long as they retained their present seats.[46]

Head office also faced financial difficulties. Due to the slump, the 1927 Act, and in some cases, a falling proportion of contracted-in membership,[47] trade unions were finding it increasingly difficult to help the party. In 1930 the party's deficit was £466; the estimated

[45] Newport DLP, executive committee, 5 Nov. 1930, 1 June 1931 (South Wales Coalfield Archive, Newport Labour Party papers, A.6, ff. 60, 107); North Lambeth DLP, executive committee, 13 Sept. 1929 (British Library of Political and Economic Science, North Lambeth Labour Party papers, 1/1, f. 55).

[46] E. A. Jenkins, *From Foundry to Foreign Office: The Romantic Life-Story of the Rt. Hon. Arthur Henderson, MP* (London, 1933), 168; Labour Party NEC minutes, 22 Jan. 1930 (Labour Party papers). After Henderson was forcibly retired in 1934, this provision was made to cover the general secretary also.

[47] Untitled, undated memoranda by A. G. Walkden (Modern Records Centre, Railway Clerks' Association papers, MSS 55B/3/WEH/1/58/6, 7 and 9).

deficit for 1931 was £8,500, which was 'extremely serious'.[48] On 23 June 1931 Henderson, who had succeeded MacDonald as treasurer a year earlier, told the NEC that the party was in dire financial straits due to the trade depression. The 1929 conference had refused to increase the political levy from 3d per member per annum, but had accepted a special levy of 2d per member spread over three years. Now, said Henderson, that money was 'practically exhausted'.[49] In July 1931 it was decided to ask the party conference that October for an increase of affiliation fees to 4d or, failing that, a repetition of the special levy.[50] It is an open question, given the extent of union dissatisfaction with the Government, whether either proposal would have been accepted had the administration survived until then.

VII

However long the Government might last, it became increasingly clear that it would be defeated at the next general election. The by-elections of 1929 went quite well, with two largely technical gains, from the Liberals at Preston and the Irish Nationalists at Liverpool Scotland, and improved showings in the Tory-held seats of Twickenham and Tamworth. But the Sheffield Brightside by-election of February 1930 began a disastrous run which continued until the Government's demise. During this period, Labour lost four seats to the Conservatives: West Fulham (May 1930), Shipley (November 1930), Sunderland (March 1931), and Ashton-under-Lyne (April 1931). It lost, respectively, majorities of 2,211, 4,961, 1,905, and 3,407 to small Tory pluralities on swings of 3.4, 7.6, 1.9, and 8.3 per cent.[51] In addition, and equally seriously in the long run, Labour held a number of seats on sharply reduced majorities, caused by a mixture of apathy and switching. A few examples are given in Table 1.1. At a general election this might have been reduced, but not obliterated. Results like Gateshead showed that Liberal withdrawals damaged Labour; the Tory poll share rose from 21.5 to 48.4 per cent in a straight fight, as opposed to a four-cornered fight in 1929, whereas the Labour share

[48] Labour Party, *Annual Report, 1931* (London, 1931), 79.
[49] Labour Party NEC minutes, 23 June 1931 (Labour Party papers).
[50] Labour Party NEC minutes, 20 Aug. 1931 (Labour Party papers).
[51] Butler swing is a simple means of expressing changes in the poll shares attained by the two leading parties at two successive elections. The swing from A to B is worked out by adding the increase in B's share to the decrease in A's share, and then dividing by two.

Table 1.1. *Reduced Labour majorities, 1930–1931*

	Date	% Majority	
		1929	By-election
Glasgow, Shettleston	June 1930	20.8	1.7
Stepney, Whitechapel	Dec 1930	42.4	5.1
East Woolwich	Apr 1931	26.4	13.4
Glasgow, St Rollox	May 1931	25.5	6.2
Gateshead	June 1931	31.1	3.2
Manchester, Ardwick	June 1931	20.6	1.0

fell one point to 51.6. The results at East Bristol and Pontypridd in January and March 1931 were more cheering, with both seats being retained but, generally, it was a bleak picture, and, after Twickenham in August 1929, Labour was never close to gaining a seat at a by-election. The pattern which would so damage it at the 1931 general election—collapsing support, a surge of backing for the Conservatives, frequent Liberal withdrawals which damaged Labour, and Labour with no real prospect of gains from the Conservatives—was already being set by the by-elections of the 1929 Parliament. Nor did municipal elections provide any comfort. After advancing steadily for eight years, Labour fell back sharply, losing many seats in the elections of November 1930.

Labour's electoral performance in 1930 and 1931 was so generally bad that it could not and cannot be explained away as 'mid-term blues'. The swing towards the Conservatives at by-elections approached that against them in the darkest days of the Lloyd George coalition, as Table 1.2 demonstrates. The more serious factors causing these swings were unlikely to have been remedied by the time MacDonald decided, or was forced, to call a general election. Two issues above all damaged Labour. First, the slump: at the Brightside by-election in February 1930, unemployment consequent on rationalization—Thomas's vogue word at the time, incidentally—was exploited by the Communists and helped substantially to reduce the Labour vote.[52] Later in the year, Labour's losses in the municipal elections were

[52] Labour Party NEC minutes, 26–7 Feb. 1930 (Labour Party papers).

Table 1.2. *Mean by-election swing to the Conservatives, 1919–1931*

Year	Government	% Swing to Cons
1919	Coalition	−12.0
1920		− 7.9
1921		−11.2
1922		−11.9
1922–3	Conservative	− 3.0
1924	Labour	− 0.2
1925	Conservative	− 4.9
1926		− 6.9
1927		− 5.8
1928		− 7.6
1929		−12.9
1929	Labour	− 2.5
1930		+ 6.9
1931		+10.1

Source: C. Cook and J. Ramsden (eds.), *By-Elections in British Politics* (London, 1973), 387.

attributed by Henderson to unemployment, and in the Bromley by-election, activists refused to help the Labour candidate as a protest against the Government's failure to deal with the problem.[53] The continuing failure of the administration here suggested that, whenever an election came, Labour would lose votes and some activist support on the issue.

If anything, though, the party officials were more worried about the issues surrounding the Education Bill. This caused hostility towards the Government because of the instinctive working-class dislike of the idea of raising the school-leaving age as impoverishing the family economy. It also aroused the ire of the Roman Catholic Church, which saw the bill as an attempt to secularize religious schools. The first aspect damaged Labour in the 1930 municipal and March 1931 London County Council elections; the second caused it serious difficulties in by-elections during 1931, and Henderson, alive to the potential danger, asked Bevin to sound out Catholic friends on the

[53] Labour Party NEC minutes, 25–6 Nov. 1930, 29 Aug. 1930 (Labour Party papers).

issue.[54] R. D. Denman, the MP for Central Leeds, was criticized severely by members of his divisional executive for supporting the Bill.[55] At almost every by-election from late 1930 onwards, in a seat with a fair proportion of Catholics, the issue damaged Labour. 'There can be no question', reported the national agent, G. R. Shepherd, after the Ashton by-election in April, 'that we lost ground owing to the Catholic Schools issue. Our candidate was himself a Catholic but he had to meet the antagonism of his Church and violent attacks by certain Catholic newspapers.'[56] At St Rollox in May, the issue also cost votes, and at Ardwick in June, '[a]lthough it [was] not a subject of public discussion the vital issue [was] the Catholic Schools question.'[57]

By-election campaigns also suffered from the general scarcity of finance. Adequate campaigns could be fought where there was trade-union sponsorship or a wealthy candidate, but in areas where the movement was weak—cities like Liverpool, rural areas like Salisbury, or where the dominant union was in financial difficulties, as at Ogmore—it was at least a contributory factor in Labour's poor showing.[58] Yet many of these seats were just those in which Labour would need to improve its performance in order to win an overall majority at the next election. Meanwhile, social changes within certain constituencies also worked to Labour's disadvantage. In March 1931 North Lambeth DLP claimed that the removal of their supporters from slums to other areas outside the division had contributed to their poor showing in the LCC elections. Two months later, at the Rutherglen (Lanarkshire) by-election, Shepherd attributed the swing to the Conservatives—which almost resulted in the loss of the seat—to new middle-class housing in the constituency. If, as is thought today to be the case, working-class voters thus displaced are less likely than their middle-class counterparts to retain their old loyalties, then such

[54] Labour Party NEC minutes, 25–6 Nov. 1930 (Labour Party papers); North Lambeth DLP, 'Report on the LCC elections, presented to & adopted by the general council', 13 Mar. 1931 (North Lambeth Labour Party papers, 1/1); Bevin to Henderson (replying), 31 Dec. 1930 (Modern Records Centre, Bevin papers, MSS 126/EB/MV/1, f. 4).

[55] Central Leeds DLP executive committee, 11 Feb. 1931 (Central Leeds Labour Party papers, 63/3).

[56] Labour Party NEC minutes, 23 June 1931 (Labour Party papers).

[57] Ibid.

[58] Labour Party NEC minutes, 28–9 Jan. 1931, 21 Apr. 1931, 20 Aug. 1931 (Labour Party papers); A. Townley to H. E. Rogers, undated [*c.* May 1931] (Bristol City Record Office, East Bristol Labour Party papers, 39035/60).

shifts might well have worked disproportionately to the disadvantage of Labour.[59]

The overwhelming impression which emerged from Labour's by-election fights, however, was one of apathy. Reluctance of activists to canvass was a regular complaint from September 1930 onwards. At the Labour marginal of East Islington in February 1931, for example, 'apart from a few very enthusiastic members of the Party there was an almost entire lack of canvassers'.[60] Shepherd felt it was a cause for concern, because '[a]part from the general disinclination to canvass, which ha[d] existed for many years past, there [was] now a distinct objection to the work involved, owing to the parliamentary situation.'[61] This is not to suggest that only a scarcity of canvassers stood between Labour and success. At Ashton in April 1931 there was a thorough canvass and an intensive campaign, but the seat was still lost; while at Ardwick two months later, the Labour vote collapsed despite a 'big effort' involving an influx of outside agents.[62]

Perhaps the best indication of the party officials' sense of impending electoral doom was the outrageous manner in which they played up Labour's slightest by-election success. The loss of one of the Sunderland seats, in March 1931, admittedly by a narrow margin, was a serious blow which hardly justified the near jubilation of Shepherd, who reported that it was 'a matter of congratulation that in this somewhat fickle Division the Labour vote [had] so closely reached the figure at the General Election'.[63] On the basis of a rise of 324 in the Labour vote, and a Conservative fall of only 59, *Labour Organiser* went into raptures over the result in the safe Tory seat of Stroud in May 1931, saying that it proved that the party had improved its electoral position and that there was 'a good deal of evidence to show that not only [had] the bottom been touched, but the Labour prospects [were] distinctly on the upgrade'.[64] What it did not say was that, while the Labour share had increased from 26.1 to 30.0 per cent, the

[59] North Lambeth DLP, 'Report on the LCC elections, . . .', 13 Mar. 1931 (North Lambeth DLP papers, 1/1); Labour Party NEC minutes, 23 Jun. 1931 (Labour Party papers); see e.g. R. J. Johnston, *The Geography of English Politics: The 1983 General Election* (London, 1985), 18.

[60] Labour Party NEC minutes, 29 Aug., 25–6 Nov. 1930, 24 Feb., 23 June 1931 (Labour Party papers).

[61] Labour Party NEC minutes, 24 Feb. 1931 (Labour Party papers).

[62] Labour Party NEC minutes, 23 June, 20 Aug. 1931 (Labour Party papers).

[63] Labour Party NEC minutes, 21 Apr. 1931 (Labour Party papers).

[64] *Labour Organiser*, June 1931.

Conservative share had risen from 44.4 to 49.6 per cent. Indeed, to maintain its joyful tone, *Labour Organiser* had to ignore the fact that on the same day Labour's majority at Rutherglen had been cut from 15.7 to 2.8 per cent.

VIII

The ability of Shepherd and *Labour Organiser* to remain cheerful during the developing debacle showed, if little else, an admirable strength of morale which was almost completely lacking from the rest of the party by mid-1931. Beatrice Webb had noted a year earlier:

> [D]iscontent and disillusionment grow within the Parliamentary Labour Party and throughout the movement in the country. The Front Bench is strangled by the multitudinous and complicated issues raised in government departments, and by the alarming gravity of . . . the continuous and increasing unemployment. The Labour government will be kept in office by the other two parties, because neither Baldwin or [*sic*] Lloyd George want [*sic*] an immediate general election. . . . But it is rather a humiliating position for the genuine socialist of the movement.[65]

The extent of this decline in morale among trade unionists has already been noted. It was no less serious among Cabinet Ministers and MPs.

By mid-1931 MacDonald was a tired and ageing premier presiding over an ill, not infrequently incompetent and often acrimonious Cabinet. As early as August 1930 Lord Passfield (age 72) was ready to retire, and by the spring of 1931 he was becoming desperate to do so. Parmoor, Labour's leader in the House of Lords, was ill for most of the first half of 1931 and, at the age of 79, could not be expected to go on much longer.[66] And senior figures in the Lower House were also pondering their futures. In early March 1931 Snowden was taken critically ill and had to have a prostate gland operation, which kept him out of action for seven weeks. This led to speculation about his future, and Passfield expected to be succeeded as Colonial Secretary in the Lords by him.[67] In April 1931, Henderson told MacDonald that he wanted to go to the House of Lords; he was 68, in indifferent health, and wanted to be able to devote more time to the Foreign Office and

[65] Beatrice Webb diary, 1 July 1930 (Passfield papers).
[66] Ibid. 2 Aug. 1930; Lord Passfield to Beatrice Webb, 11 June 1931 (Passfield papers, II 3(1)27, f. 64, and ff. 1–22, *passim*).
[67] C. Cross, *Philip Snowden* (London, 1966), 268–9.

Transport House.[68] MacDonald and his senior colleagues rejected the request, arguing that the party could not afford to lose his services in the Commons.[69] The premier did little, though, to reduce the average age of his Cabinet; although he brought in two of the brighter young stars in the Labour firmament, Thomas Johnston and Herbert Morrison, in March 1931, he had replaced the 55-year-old Lord Thomson as Air Secretary on his death the previous October with the septugenarian Lord Amulree.

It was also an acrimonious Cabinet. MacDonald and Snowden had, for many years, cordially despised each other.[70] The premier's attitude towards Henderson is difficult to describe·short of hatred: in every move of the latter, especially his election to the presidency of the world disarmament conference, he believed he saw Henderson's desire to supplant him as leader. Henderson, in fact, was loyal, but resented what he saw as MacDonald's ingratitude. By the early summer of 1931, after two years of clashes—mainly on foreign policy—the two men were barely on speaking terms.[71] Relations between Snowden and Thomas were not of the best, either. The Chancellor's obsession with budget secrecy stemmed, partly at least, from his belief that if he revealed his proposals to the Cabinet in advance, Thomas would use the information for stock exchange speculation. During Snowden's illness, Thomas made little secret of his desire to take over at the Treasury, saying that the crippled Snowden was 'ill in the head as well as in the balls', which charming observation found its way to Mrs Snowden, if not to the Chancellor himself.[72] Lower down the scale, Christopher Addison, Minister of Agriculture, had a very low regard for Bondfield and Thomas. No wonder a leading civil servant said it was the worst Cabinet he had known for bad relations among ministers.[73]

[68] Dalton diary, 16 Apr. 1931 (British Library of Political and Economic Science, Dalton papers); MacDonald diary, 16 Apr. 1931 (Public Record Office, MacDonald papers, PRO 30/69/1753).

[69] Ibid. 11 June 1931; Philip, Viscount Snowden, *An Autobiography* (2 vols.; London, 1934), ii. 925–6.

[70] See e.g. E. Shinwell, *Conflict without Malice* (London, 1955), 112–13.

[71] D. Carlton, *MacDonald versus Henderson: The Foreign Policy of the Second Labour Government* (London, 1970), *passim*; Marquand, *MacDonald* 576; Hamilton, *Henderson*, 353; A. J. Thorpe, 'Arthur Henderson and the British Political Crisis of 1931', *Historical Journal*, 31 (1988), 117–39; H. Dalton, *Call Back Yesterday: Memoirs, 1887–1931* (London, 1953), 326.

[72] Dalton diary, 29 Sept., 3 Nov. 1931 (Dalton papers).

[73] K. O. and J. Morgan, *Portrait of a Progressive: The Political Career of Christopher, Viscount Addison* (Oxford, 1980), 181–2.

The morale of individual ministers cracked. By the end of 1929 Thomas was 'almost hysterical' in his self-pity and 'bordering on lunacy'. This was due partly to his failure to reduce unemployment, but also to the fact that, as a stock exchange speculator, he was terrified by the collapse in share values following the Wall Street crash.[74] Early in 1930 the First Lord of the Admiralty, A. V. Alexander, was 'most depressed'.[75] By October 1930 MacDonald was 'dog tired' and appeared to want to leave office; three months later he was telling Citrine that he hoped to retire quite soon.[76] He had grown increasingly pessimistic, doubting that 'anything of a very drastic character' could be done about unemployment.[77] Even the eternal optimist, Lansbury, was hit by the gloom, so much so that he appealed to Lloyd George to join the Labour Party.[78] Shortly afterwards, Sir Charles Trevelyan resigned. And in May 1931 MacDonald complained to his old friend, Middleton, that if only he could see a clear successor he would retire because after 'two years of heavy drudgery' he was 'more tired in body & mind than anybody knows'.[79]

The parliamentary party was no more immune to pessimism and disillusionment. The high hopes of 1929 had been dashed, and electoral defeat consequent on the Government's poor performance was staring many Labour MPs in the face. Thus when Leah Manning entered Parliament 'fresh and euphoric from a totally unexpected by-election victory' in February 1931 she found an atmosphere 'which stung like a cold lash'. There was 'bitter hostility' and 'frustration and defeatism in place of hope and constructive ideas'.[80]

The decline in the morale of party activists has already been noted; despite the loyal tone of DLP minute books, many people either left the party or, more commonly, became more grudging about giving

[74] Beatrice Webb diary, 2, 21 Dec. 1929 (Passfield papers); Hankey diary, 26 Sept. 1931, reporting Thomas as saying that over the past six months he had lost £150,000 (Churchill College, Hankey papers, HNKY 1/7); Dalton diary, 29 Sept. 1931, reporting rumours that Thomas was £30,000 to £40,000 in debt (Dalton papers).

[75] Alexander to Albert Ballard (agent), 7 Jan. 1930 (Sheffield Archives Office, Ballard papers, ABC 3/50).

[76] Sankey diary, 15 Oct. 1930 (Bodleian Library, Sankey papers, MSS Eng. hist. e. 284); Citrine, 'The Prime Minister', 29 Jan. 1931 (Citrine papers, 7/8).

[77] Marquand, *MacDonald*, 532.

[78] Lloyd George to Lansbury (replying), 16 Feb. 1931 (British Library of Political and Economic Science, Lansbury papers, vol. 10, ff. 7–9).

[79] MacDonald to Middleton, 25 May 1931 (Ruskin College, Middleton papers, MID 27/27).

[80] E. L. Manning, *A Life for Education: An Autobiography* (London, 1970), 87.

their time to, say, canvassing. This was doubly damaging because Labour was heavily reliant on such voluntary help. There was a tendency, though, to blame not the Government, but capitalism, for the problems faced.[81] And the arguments used by increasingly unhappy Labourites to rationalize their continuing loyalty towards the faltering Government were summarized in a report by North Lambeth DLP on the LCC elections of March 1931:

> The facts are generally well known and relieve the Labour government of any responsibility for the [economic] situation. . . . The shifts and tricks of the Liberal and Tory parliamentarians aided by the foolish and unpractical behaviour of our own extreme left wing are and have been sadly hampering the government in their efforts to deal with this problem. They get much calculated support from the employers and obstruction in the House of Commons is a finer art than ever.[82]

Such loyalty—involving the invocation of what amounted to a conspiracy theory—was testimony to the powerful restraining influences which Labour's being in office exerted on its followers. But DLPs were far from happy with the state of affairs by the early summer of 1931.

The deterioration of relations with the trade unions, the alienation of the left, the increasing debility of the Cabinet, the party's severe organizational and financial problems, and the disastrous string of by-election reverses on top of the party's underlying psephological vulnerability, all suggested defeat at the next general election, with Beatrice's Webb's prediction of almost a year earlier, that the Tories would 'romp back', likely to be fulfilled.[83] However long the election was delayed, this was unlikely to change; it would certainly be the case if it came in 1931. The events of August to October 1931 turned certain loss into a rout, but they did not in themselves cause Labour's defeat.

[81] Houghton-le-Spring DLP, annual report 1930 (Durham County Record Office, Shotton papers, D/Sho 99).

[82] North Lambeth DLP, 'Report on the LCC elections, . . .', 13 Mar. 1931 (North Lambeth Labour Party papers, 1/1).

[83] Beatrice Webb diary, 2 Aug. 1930 (Passfield papers).

2

FROM FAILURE TO THE CERTAINTY OF SUCCESS: THE CONSERVATIVES 1929–1931

THE period 1929 to 1931 was the longest time the Conservatives spent out of office between 1915 and 1945. It was not altogether surprising, therefore, that it saw the Tories in considerable difficulties. What was perhaps more remarkable was the speed of their recovery. In the aftermath of the 1929 election, the party had faced problems of leadership, policy, organization, and political impotence. By July 1931 it had an attractive and secure leadership, a seemingly vote-winning policy promising, if not to cure the slump, then at least to maximize British prosperity within the context of world depression, and also an excellent organization. The other two parties possessed none of these by mid-1931. Only the problem of regaining power remained, but moves were afoot to solve that, too, and anyway, the Conservatives could expect, with reason, that whenever the next election came they would win at least as well as they had in 1924, when they had taken almost half the votes cast and 412 seats, an overall majority of 209, and itself the greatest single-party majority in modern electoral history. Amid great dramas, a quiet revolution had been staged.

Given the scale of its 1924 victory, the Conservative leadership had expected to win the 1929 election, albeit with a reduced majority, so defeat, when it came, caused consternation.[1] The sheer shock of defeat from such a strong position was to be a major factor in the transformation of party policy over the next two years. Refusing to bargain with Lloyd George for Liberal support, Baldwin resigned without meeting Parliament. For Neville Chamberlain, late Minister of Health, defeat was a 'disaster'.[2] This was understandable, but in many ways, the 1929 result was not that bad. The Conservatives had obtained more votes than Labour and could expect that at a

[1] P. Williamson, ' "Safety First": Baldwin, the Conservative Party, and the 1929 General Election', *Historical Journal*, 25 (1982), 385–409.

[2] Headlam diary, 1 June 1929 (Durham County Record Office, Headlam papers, D/He/25); Chamberlain diary, 8 June 1929 (Birmingham University Library, Chamberlain papers, NC 2/22).

subsequent election, given fewer Liberal candidates, they would take many of the 123 seats which Labour held on a minority vote. In addition, many Tories had lost quite narrowly. If in seats where they were second, there was a swing from the leading party to the Conservatives of only 2.5 per cent, they would gain 20 seats from the Liberals and 46 from Labour, giving them 326 seats and a working majority of 37. While some Conservative seats were also vulnerable, the failure of the Labour Government, and the implication of the Liberals therewith, meant that from October 1929 onwards, if not before, the Tories could be reasonably confident of victory at the next general election.

For a party which had become accustomed to power, however, such considerations were secondary in the aftermath of defeat, and the post-mortem was soon in full swing. A number of factors were blamed by Conservatives for their defeat: derating, introduced by 1928–9 as a means of reducing the rate burden on agriculture and industry;[3] Liberal interventions, since many of the 513 Liberal candidates had had no chance of victory but had let in Labour on minority votes;[4] lack of emphasis on safeguarding (a diluted form of protectionism);[5] the enfranchisement of women between 21 and 30 (the 'flapper vote');[6] the hostility of the press, especially the titles controlled by Lords Beaverbrook and Rothermere;[7] and, finally, and ironically in view of events to come, the Government's failure to reduce public expenditure.[8]

Certain of these factors were non-recurrent. Derating would not be an issue at the next election. The flapper voters would have less of an

[3] See e.g. Keighley CA, annual report, 1929 (West Yorkshire Archive Service, Leeds, Keighley CA papers, 4); Chelmsford CA, executive committee, 11 Oct. 1929 (Essex Record Office, Chelmsford CA papers, D/Z/96/6).

[4] Accrington CA, annual meeting, 11 June 1929 (John Rylands Library, Accrington CA papers, A/iii, f. 345).

[5] Ealing CA, executive committee, 13 Sept. 1929 (Greater London Record Office, Ealing CA papers, 1338); Kennington CA, executive committee, 27 Sept. 1929 (British Library of Political and Economic Science, Kennington CA papers, Coll. Misc. 463, vol. 1, ff. 266–9).

[6] Bradford Central CA, central committee, 22 July 1929 (West Yorkshire Archive Service, Bradford CA papers, 36D78/5, f. 412); Steel-Maitland to Mr Swaby (Leeds), 10 July 1929 (Scottish Record Office, Steel-Maitland papers, GD 193/120/3/212).

[7] Kennington CA, executive committee, 27 Sept. 1929 (Kennington CA papers, Coll. Misc. 463, vol. 1, f. 268); Bath CA, executive committee, 17 Sept. 1929 (Bath Record Office, Bath CA papers, minute book 1924–37, f. 208).

[8] Chelmsford CA, executive committee, 11 Oct. 1929 (Chelmsford CA papers, D/Z/96/6); Bath CA, executive committee, 17 Sept. 1929 (Bath CA papers, minute book 1924–37, f. 208).

impact, and could be won over; there was no reason why they should be loyal to Labour. And given the state of the Liberal Party as it emerged from its disappointment in 1929, there would probably be far less to worry about in the way of Liberal interventions next time. However, the questions of protection, press hostility, and public economy would be more persistent, the first two especially.

I

Protection was not a new issue for the Conservative Party; far from it. But since the 1840s it had been seen as highly dubious electorally, and the heavy defeat of 1906 had been widely attributed to Joseph Chamberlain's tariff reform campaign. Therefore in 1922, after the demise of the Lloyd George coalition, the Conservative leader, Andrew Bonar Law, had given a pledge that there would be no fundamental change in this area before the next election. He had won a comfortable majority. A year later, Baldwin, who had succeeded Law as premier, had declared his conviction of the necessity of protection, called an election and been defeated. After the brief interlude of the first Labour Government, the Tories had fought the 1924 campaign with a pledge that, if elected, they would not introduce a general tariff. Baldwin, having won back the former coalitionists in 1923–4, was now aiming to moderate his party's policy in order to win the political middle ground, perceived as being vacated by the declining Liberals. During the 1924–9 Government, certain industries had been 'safeguarded', which meant they were protected from demonstrably unfair foreign competition, but the pledge was kept. The party's manifesto in 1929 advertised the success of safeguarding, but the pledge of 1924, 'that there should be no protective taxation of food and that there should be no general tariff' was renewed.[9]

This negative stance was now thought by many party activists to have cost the party votes at the 1929 election, and protectionist noises were soon being made by Leo Amery (the late Colonial and Dominions Secretary), Chamberlain, and most ominously by the Canadian-born press magnate Lord Beaverbrook, who called for a crusade to promote the fiscal unity of the empire. Initially, there was a backlash. In August 1929 Baldwin repudiated the Conservative candidate at the Twicken-

[9] F. W. S. Craig (ed.), *British General Election Manifestos, 1900–1974*, rev. edn. (London, 1975), 71.

ham by-election for his advocacy of food taxes, and a meeting of the Shadow Cabinet prevailed upon Amery and Chamberlain to ease off a little. The leader was always conscious of the erstwhile unpopularity of protection, and nervous of the democratic franchise which had been introduced since the war. Always afraid that such an electorate might be wooed by easy rhetoric, such as that of the 'big loaf' and 'little loaf' that so characterized free traders, he feared that the new Government, at the height of its prestige that summer, might call a sudden election in the quest for a parliamentary majority. If the Conservatives were caught in a mood of high protectionism, he felt, Labour might succeed in its aim. Also, he wanted to take the whole of the Shadow Cabinet with him when he moved; Churchill and the leader in the Lords, Salisbury, were still free traders and would be difficult. Under pressure, though, Baldwin accepted a vague resolution on empire trade and development proposed by the chairman of the protectionist Empire Industries Association (EIA), Sir Henry Page Croft, at the 1929 party conference, countering Beaverbrook, who had published a manifesto the previous month setting forth his programme of empire free trade.

The next step forward came in March 1930, when the leader met Beaverbrook. Baldwin stated that if he won the next election he would call an imperial conference on tariffs and imperial preference. The decisions of that conference would then be submitted to a second general election. This was scarcely an advance on the 1929 pledge, and Beaverbrook rejected it. They agreed finally that a referendum would replace the second election, and Baldwin agreed not to make statements precluding the imposition of food taxes. The leader unveiled the referendum at a party meeting the following day, but his restatement of the values of *selective* safeguarding hardly suggested future tranquillity.[10]

Baldwin was reasonably satisfied with the referendum, since it allowed him to evade the difficult issue of food taxes, which he believed was especially open to misrepresentation. Others, like Beaverbrook, saw his primarily negative motivation, and were less than delighted, especially as Baldwin's tone regarding food taxes remained dismissive. A dispute over the equivocal protectionism of a Central Office pamphlet in May 1930 gave an increasingly restive Beaverbrook the opportunity to repudiate the March agreement, and on 17 June he

[10] Neville Chamberlain diary, 12 Mar. 1930 (Chamberlain papers, NC 2/22).

appealed to Conservatives to send their party subscriptions to him.[11] This struck a chord with some activists, particularly in southern and agricultural areas, who had shared Beaverbrook's antipathy towards the referendum.[12]

Chamberlain, whose experience of democracy was based in the populist Unionism of Birmingham and who therefore had more faith in the persuadability of the electorate regarding protection, was alarmed and decided that the debate must be advanced, especially when Beaverbrook insisted on running his own candidate in the Bromley by-election in September 1930. In speeches at Midlothian (2 August) and the Crystal Palace (20 September), he called for drastic economy, the introduction of an emergency tariff to protect manufacturing industry, a quota system for wheat, and a free hand to consider permanent tariffs. This reflected the growth of protectionism in a country baffled by the massive impact of the slump. In August 1930 the Associated Chambers of Commerce had come out for extensive safeguarding; and in October the Federation of British Industry was to declare that 96 per cent of its members favoured protection with the widest degree of imperial preference. That month the Shadow Cabinet adopted Chamberlain's policy, and Baldwin's announcement of the new policy to a party meeting was received enthusiastically. Depression had killed off much free-trade sentiment in all parties: Baldwin, although partly forced to move, could also see that protection might now prove popular after all with increasing numbers of electors desperate for any solution. Now the Conservatives could keep their appeal to the middle ground while adopting what had formerly been a highly partisan policy.[13]

The protectionists had won the battle, although Beaverbrook did not come to terms with the party leadership until 30 March 1931. By then, the party was committed formally to the protection of manufactures, imperial preference, and most notably, the use of duties, prohibitions, or quotas on foreign foodstuffs in order to protect British agriculture. More detailed proposals for a three-tier protective tariff (plus free list)

[11] R. K. Middlemas and J. Barnes, *Baldwin: A Biography* (London, 1969), 567–71; A. J. P. Taylor, *Beaverbrook* (London, 1972), 285–6.

[12] Circular from West Fulham CA, 27 June 1930 (Steel-Maitland papers, GD 193/120/3/80); Horncastle CA, finance committee, 1 Aug. 1930 (Lincolnshire Archives Office, Horncastle CA papers, Misc. Dep. 268/1).

[13] L. S. Amery, *My Political Life* (3 vols.; London, 1953–5), iii. 31; S. Ball, *Baldwin and the Conservative Party: The Crisis of 1929–1931* (London, 1988), 154; Middlemas and Barnes, *Baldwin*, 578–9.

and the parliamentary procedure to be followed were worked out by a committee of the Conservative Research Department (CRD), chaired by the former President of the Board of Trade, Sir Philip Cunliffe-Lister. By July 1931 a detailed report was in the hands of the party leadership, and the party had a well-defined policy, and plans to implement it, as soon as it regained office.[14] Hard-line protectionists were jubilant.[15]

The protectionists had gained their victory without inflicting much long-term damage on the party. The few free traders left in the party leadership either acquiesced or stood aside; not much damage was done either way. It said much for the pervasiveness of protectionism within the party that Churchill, though ready to resign from the Shadow Cabinet in October 1930 over food taxes, delayed his formal departure until January 1931, when he could use his opposition to Baldwin's liberal line on India, an issue carrying far more kudos, as his pretext.[16] In June 1931 Salisbury resigned as leader in the Lords, ostensibly because of the party's protectionism; but in fact he had been in poor health for some time and was ready to retire in any case.[17] Other ex-free traders were more adaptable. E. C. Grenfell, the banker and MP for the City of London, told his constituency association that although brought up a free trader and remaining one in theory, he had decided that Britain must retaliate against protectionist competitors.[18] This symbolized the way thousands of minds were moving in all walks of British society. Protectionist Tories continued to do well in by-elections; at the very least, their protectionism was no longer a negative factor, even if its positive appeal must remain, to some extent, a matter of speculation. The slump had suggested to many people formerly lukewarm towards tariffs that they should at least be tried: even some leading Liberals were coming reluctantly to this view. They could hardly make matters worse.

Protection was not the only issue of policy upon which there was

[14] J. A. Cross, *Lord Swinton* (Oxford, 1982), 95–6; Conservative Research Department, 'Tariffs Committee: Final Report and Schedules', 17 July 1931, and Cunliffe-Lister to H. Brooke, 16 June 1931 (Bodleian Library, Conservative Party papers, CRD 1/2/12 and 8).

[15] Brentford to Croft, 1 July 1931 (Churchill College, Croft papers, CRFT 1/15).

[16] Sir Austen Chamberlain to Mary Carnegie, 6 Feb. 1931 (Chamberlain papers, AC 4/1/1306).

[17] Middlemas and Barnes, *Baldwin*, 612; *Dictionary of National Biography, 1941–1950* (London, 1959), 140.

[18] City of London CA, annual meeting, 22 July 1930 (Victoria Library, London, Cities of London and Westminster CA papers, 487/28).

conflict within the party between 1929 and 1931, however. India was as potentially devastating a subject for the Conservatives as Ireland had been. Baldwin's line was to support moves to liberalize British rule, with evolution towards dominion status; this was anathema to die-hard imperialists. Between October 1929 and March 1931 this stance came in for frequent criticism, especially as on occasion he went too far even for moderate Tories, and always too far for the right-wingers among whom Winston Churchill (Chancellor of the Exchequer 1924–9) emerged as the leading figure. However, by the end of March 1931 the position had been squared, partly by the renewed moderation of the nationalists under Gandhi, partly by the ineptitude of Baldwin's die-hard critics, and partly by the concentration of Conservative MPs and activists on more immediate issues. After all, most right-wingers, though not Churchill, were also ardent protectionists: they had much to lose by splitting the party. As Croft wrote, they had 'seen [their] tariff policy thwarted so frequently in the past'.[19] So India took a back seat for the rest of 1931.

II

Despite these contortions over policy, the leader in 1931 was the same man who had led the party to ignominy two years earlier, despite the fact that he had spent most of that time under fierce attack from many directions. There had often been widespread discontent; in September 1930, for example, Chamberlain, by then party chairman, had found 'a general dissatisfaction with the leadership', and Croft informed him that Baldwin had 'so irretrievably lost the confidence of so large a proportion of the Party that [their] chance of success would be gravely imperilled if he continue[d] to lead'.[20] A couple of weeks later, Sir Austen Chamberlain felt that Baldwin was 'too far gone ever to recover his old authority'.[21]

What might well have proved to be the *coup de grâce* was delivered to Neville Chamberlain on 25 February 1931. This document, a memorandum by the party's director general, Robert Topping, suggested Baldwin's prospects were miserable, arguing that he '[could]

[19] Croft to Chamberlain, 14 Nov. 1930 (Croft papers, CRFT 1/7).

[20] Neville to Hilda Chamberlain, 7 Sept. 1930 (Chamberlain papers, NC 18/1/710); Croft to Chamberlain, 28 Oct. 1930 (Croft papers, CRFT 1/7).

[21] Sir Austen Chamberlain to Mary Carnegie, 14 Mar. 1931 (Chamberlain papers, AC 4/1/1307).

not command sufficient support to carry the Party to victory'. 'From practically all quarters,' he went on, 'one hears the view that it would be in the interests of the Party if the Leader should re-consider his position.' If something were not done soon, Churchill might well seize the leadership. This prospect scarcely appealed to the party chairman, and after consulting senior colleagues Chamberlain sent the memorandum to Baldwin on 1 March 1931.[22] Chamberlain felt that the leader had no alternative but to stand down. However, the tide was already running against the leader's critics, especially after the East Islington by-election in February, when a Beaverbrook–Rothermere candidate had split the Conservative vote and so allowed Labour to retain a seat it should have lost. Most Tories saw the continuation in office of the Labour Government as highly dangerous in a worsening national economic situation, and felt that such divisions, and rumblings against a leader who had shown no intention of quitting, were now not only pointless—given that Baldwin had conceded fully their policy demands on protection—but also against the national interest. Baldwin was initially rattled by Topping's report, but decided to stay on and treat the Westminster St George's by-election in March as a vote of confidence. After a bitter campaign, the loyalist Alfred Duff Cooper beat off the insurgent sponsored by Beaverbrook and Rothermere, and Baldwin's position was not only restored—as it had been, in reality, after East Islington—but seen to have been restored, especially as agreement was soon reached with a chastened Beaverbrook. A more vigorous approach to Opposition followed, so that by the early summer of 1931 Baldwin's position was pretty well secure.[23]

A number of factors meant that, apparently against all the odds, Baldwin had beaten off the challenge to his leadership. First, there were his own qualities. Popular, pragmatic, persuadable, he moved just far and just fast enough to retain his position. His concern regarding protection, in any case, was entirely as to its expediency. He had been a solid tariff reformer since the 1890s,[24] but felt that a Conservative Party facing a relatively unknown universal franchise had to mop up sufficient former Liberal (free trade) support to ensure victory against 'socialism'. Since defeat in the election of 1923, when the party had

[22] Chamberlain to Baldwin, enclosing Topping memorandum, 1 Mar. 1931 (Cambridge University Library, Baldwin papers, vol. 166, ff. 47–53); for Chamberlain's account of his behaviour, see Neville to Hilda Chamberlain, 1 Mar. 1931 (Chamberlain papers, NC 18/1/728).

[23] Middlemas and Barnes, *Baldwin*, 589–90.

[24] D. Southgate (ed.), *The Conservative Leadership, 1832–1932* (London, 1974), 203.

lost a healthy majority in a campaign fought on protection, he had been extremely cautious as to its chances of carrying his party to power. The slump changed that; and the disputes of 1929–31 were not, by and large, between protectionists and free traders, but between bold protectionists and cautious protectionists. Baldwin was able to save himself by moving warily towards a fully protectionist policy, which he accepted in October 1930 and which was endorsed by his agreement with Beaverbrook in March 1931. On other matters, too, he was prepared to move when necessary. But he was also prepared to fight, as he showed in March 1931, and he could counter-attack effectively against his critics.

It would be going too far, however, to claim that Baldwin was always master of the situation.[25] A number of other factors also helped him. The main one was the lack of a clear alternative. Churchill was the clear outsider: only disaster for the party could give him the top job. Chamberlain and Lord Hailsham, Attorney-General and Lord Chancellor in the 1920s, were more popular and more plausible; but their positions were complicated, Chamberlain by the fact that he was party chairman, and so compromised and to an extent committed to Baldwin, Hailsham by the fact that he was in the Lords. Neither was a clear alternative; and although on 27 February 1931 each agreed to serve under the other, it was already too late.[26] Baldwin's decision to ignore the Topping memorandum infuriated Chamberlain; and when on 11 March he resigned as party chairman he was, as Baldwin believed, freeing himself to take on the succession.[27] The irony was that by the time a clear alternative—the Chamberlain–Hailsham pairing—had emerged, the need for it had passed.

The nature of the opposition to Baldwin also helped him. Beaverbrook was disliked by much of the party; Rothermere hated. Thus at a crucial party meeting in June 1930, Baldwin was able to secure a triumph by revealing that Rothermere had demanded to know, and by implication control, the policies and personnel of a future Baldwin Government. Lord Bridgeman referred to 'that damned scoundrel, Rothermere'.[28] Very few people hated Baldwin more than they hated Rothermere, and Beaverbrook, though less

[25] Middlemas and Barnes, *Baldwin*, 546, give the wrong impression.

[26] Neville to Hilda Chamberlain, 1 Mar. 1931 (Chamberlain papers, NC 18/1/728).

[27] Neville to Ida Chamberlain, 7 Mar. 1931 (Chamberlain papers, NC 18/1/729); Neville Chamberlain diary, 11 Mar. 1931 (Chamberlain papers, NC 2/22); Middlemas and Barnes, *Baldwin*, 590, 593, 598.

[28] Bridgeman to Croft, 11 Oct. 1930 (Croft papers, CRFT 1/5).

unpopular, was often tarred with the same brush. As Sir Austen Chamberlain wrote, 'if [Baldwin was] saved, it [would] be by hatred of the triumph his fall would give to Rothermere and Beaverbrook', a view reflected by a number of CAs.[29] The stage was set for Baldwin's memorable castigation of the press barons on 17 March 1931, when instead of answering criticisms of his leadership he launched into a formidable attack on them and their newspapers which requires no retelling here.

The loyalty of the wider party was also valuable. True, there was some criticism, for example when in June 1930 Chelmsford CA passed, with one dissentient, a resolution expressing dissatisfaction with the leadership.[30] But a more common response was that of the chairman of the City of London CA, who told a meeting that month that while he had some qualms on policy, 'if we follow our Leader, we shall get something, and if we don't we shall get nothing.'[31] Where criticism was raised, it was often voted down: in early March 1931 Ealing CA passed by 115 votes to 5 a resolution deprecating the 'bitter vendetta' against the leader and assuring him of their continuing support.[32] And all the time, votes of support were being passed unanimously up and down the country.[33]

By the end of March 1931, then, Baldwin was once again the party's undisputed leader. Ironically, Chamberlain had written of him in October 1930 that Baldwin seemed to want 'to hold on until his star

[29] Sir Austen Chamberlain to Mary Carnegie, 9 Oct. 1930 (Chamberlain papers, AC 4/1/1302); York CA, executive committee, 9 Mar. 1931 (York Archives Office, York CA papers, 19).

[30] Chelmsford CA, executive committee, 13 June 1930 (Chelmsford CA papers, D/Z/96/6).

[31] City of London CA, annual meeting, 22 July 1930 (Cities of London and Westminster CA papers, 487/28).

[32] Ealing CA, annual meeting, 13 Mar. 1931 (Greater London Record Office, Ealing CA papers, 1338).

[33] West Dorset CA, annual meeting, 21 March 1930 (Dorset Record Office, West Dorset CA papers, D399/2/1); Warwick and Leamington CA, executive committee, 13 March 1930 (Warwickshire Record Office, Warwick and Leamington CA papers, CR 1392); Middleton and Prestwich CA, finance and general purposes committee, 26 June, 30 Oct. 1930 (Lancashire Record Office, Middleton and Prestwich CA papers, PLC 1/2); North Cornwall CA, executive committee, 14 July 1930 (Cornwall Record Office, North Cornwall CA papers, DDX 381/3); Bath CA, executive committee, 11 Nov. 1930 (Bath CA papers, minute book 1924–37, f. 254); Central and East Bradford CAs, annual meetings, both 11 Mar. 1931 (Bradford CA papers, 36D78/18, 24); West Leeds CA, annual meeting, 28 Apr. 1931 (West Yorkshire Archive Service, Leeds, West Leeds CA papers, 5, ff. 53–4); Waterloo CA, annual meeting, 21 May 1931 (Lancashire Record Office, Crosby CA papers, DDX 806/1/3, f. 161).

rises when he fancies himself handing over the reins to someone else and departing with the regretful affection & respect of his party. Whether things will work out that way', he continued, 'remains to be seen—probably not.'[34] In fact, those were just the conditions under which Baldwin would eventually hand over to Chamberlain—but not until 1937.

III

With the resolution of the problems of leadership and policy, the party required a battle-cry around which to unite. It found it, as Stuart Ball has shown,[35] in the demand for public economy, always a powerful weapon in the Conservative armoury. On 8 January 1931, with CAs increasingly demanding it, Chamberlain told a meeting at Birmingham that when the Conservatives returned to power, 'their first duty' would be 'to reduce national expenditure' and to stop 'extension of social services until the country was in a position to afford it'. Five days later the industrialist, Sir Arthur Balfour, said that another 3d on the income tax would mean 500,000 more unemployed: Britain had reached 'the saturation point in taxation'.[36] A couple of weeks later, the chairman of Lloyd's Bank said that high taxes had 'killed enterprise' and that '[t]rade require[d] some lightening from its vast load of taxation'.[37] In early February, Chamberlain set up a committee of the CRD to investigate ways of reducing public expenditure.[38]

Economy was an excellent rallying cry for the Conservatives, and better than protection at this stage for a number of reasons. This is not to suggest that they saw protectionism as unpopular, or that it needed to be 'covered up'. Far from it. But it did offer complications which controlling public expenditure did not. First, as shown above, economy was, even more than trade policy, the issue of the hour, certainly in business, administrative, and media circles. The Tories were catching a definite mood in favour of retrenchment. Secondly, the various groups demanding economy tended to be less fractious than those demanding protection; in getting the research department to work on proposals for the latter, while directing attention to the former, Chamberlain did the party a great service. There were fewer variables

[34] Neville to Ida Chamberlain, 26 Oct. 1930 (Chamberlain papers, NC 18/1/714).
[35] See Ball, *Baldwin and the Conservative Party*, 159, 216.
[36] *The Times*, 9, 15 Jan. 1931.
[37] *The Times*, 31 Jan. 1931.
[38] J. Ramsden, *The Making of Conservative Party Policy: The Conservative Research Department since 1929* (London, 1980), 54–5.

for Conservatives to quarrel about in spending cuts than there were in tariffs. Partly for that reason, the rhetoric and arguments for economy were easier to use and simpler to understand than the somewhat less concrete notion of trade protection: another advantage. Thirdly, it meant that a point of unity, rather than division, with the Liberals was being stressed; traditional Liberal voters might have lingering free-trade sympathies, but they were also interested in that most Gladstonian of principles, retrenchment. So too, for that matter, were the potential Liberal rebels under Sir John Simon whom Chamberlain was wooing at the time (see below). Fourthly, public expenditure, and unemployment insurance expenditure in particular, were issues on which the Labour Cabinet and the Labour movement generally were known to be divided; thus by stressing this issue the Tories could hope to embarrass and perhaps even destroy the Government. All in all, then, the switch from prioritizing protection to stressing economy in early 1931 meant that the Conservatives were in a very strong position indeed. This did not mean, though, that they dropped protection from their speeches. It remained part of the staple diet, and reading their speeches then and now no one could question that the party intended to turn Britain over to tariffs at the earliest possible opportunity.

IV

The third major problem, organization, had also been overcome by the early summer of 1931. In reality, this had been less difficult. By 1929 J. C. C. Davidson, the party chairman, had made Central Office the most efficient of the three parties' headquarters. At the 1929 election the party fielded 590 candidates, its highest figure between the wars, leaving only 25 seats uncontested, and there was 'an agent and an organisation in almost every constituency'.[39] In addition, at Central Office, Davidson and Joseph Ball—a former MI5 agent who became director of publicity in 1927 and director of the CRD in 1930—maintained an efficient intelligence system, with agents in Labour Party headquarters and at the Odhams Press, whence they received advance notice of all Labour propaganda.[40]

By the spring of 1930, however, Davidson was under fierce attack, for political reasons. He was seen as too lightweight, too negative, and too close to Baldwin. Indeed, many believed that Davidson was to

[39] J. Ramsden, *A History of the Conservative Party, Vol. 3: The Age of Balfour and Baldwin* (London, 1978), iii. 228.

[40] Ibid. 235.

blame for the leader's cautious line on protection, an impression Baldwin, ever the strategist, made little effort to dispel.[41] From April Chamberlain was pressing him to resign; and the failure of Davidson's propagandist 'Home and Empire' campaign in May finally destroyed him.

Davidson's successor was Neville Chamberlain, appointed by Baldwin with a degree of reluctance on both sides.[42] Chamberlain polished up the machinery and brought Central Office to heel. With an able and experienced staff led by Topping, Marjorie Maxse, his deputy, and Sir Patrick Gower, the chief publicity officer, Chamberlain was able to use the position as a political power base, especially in dealing with Beaverbrook. Certain reforms were made: it was, for example, under Chamberlain that the party began to group constituencies in its weakest areas, like Durham, east London, south Yorkshire, and south Wales, in order to maintain a low-cost skeleton organization in those areas.[43] Ironically, though, his greatest achievements derived, not from his short tenure at Central Office, but from his chairmanship of the CRD, which had started in March 1930. A dynamic chief, he ensured that committees were appointed to investigate the major issues of the day, producing a series of reports which, if variable in quality, would be, overall, of great use to the party at the next election, and in Government. It was largely thanks to Chamberlain that the Conservatives were the only British party pursuing serious, systematic policy research in the new, post-Wall Street world.

In March 1931 Chamberlain resigned the party chairmanship, but he remained chairman of the CRD and continued to attend Central Office meetings.[44] Lord Stonehaven, who succeeded him, was a good choice; a Tory MP until 1925, he had then served as Governor-General of Australia until 1930, making him aloof from much recent feuding. He was to prove his worth in the very trying circumstances of the next few months.

In the constituencies, the party was, by mid-1931, in good health and looking forward to the next election with relish. While continued feuding within the party had hindered the improvement in morale

[41] See e.g. Neville to Ida Chamberlain, 25 May 1930 (Chamberlain papers, NC 18/1/696).

[42] Neville to Hilda Chamberlain, 21 June 1930 (Chamberlain papers, NC 18/1/701).

[43] Ramsden, *Age of Balfour and Baldwin*, 228.

[44] *Gleanings and Memoranda*, May 1931.

which should have resulted from the increasing difficulties of the Labour Government, there was some improvement none the less. By mid-1930 Sir Austen Chamberlain was reporting that in his constituency 'all our people are happy' and that there was a very different atmosphere from that of 1929.[45] It was certainly true to say that most CAs were well-run and well-financed at this time, at least relative to the other parties. By the early summer of 1931 the Conservatives had overcome most of their organizational problems and were well ahead of their rivals.

V

They were ahead in electoral popularity, too. Their first by-election went badly, with the near loss of Twickenham in August 1929, when their food-taxing candidate was officially disowned and a collapse in the Liberal vote benefited Labour, reducing the Tory majority from 13.7 to 1.6 per cent. The Conservatives also faced difficulties in certain southern, fairly middle-class seats, where they were opposed by Beaverbrook–Rothermere supporters: in South Paddington, where they lost the seat to an Empire Crusader in October 1930; in East Islington five months later, where an insurgent split the Conservative vote and so allowed Labour to retain a marginal seat; and in Bromley (September 1930) and Westminster St George's (March 1931), where the party held seats against such opposition. What was more noteworthy, however, was the steady improvement of the party's performance at the expense of Labour from February 1930 onwards, gaining four seats from Labour and reducing Labour's majorities severely in many more (see Table 1.1), while generally consolidating their hold on their own seats. The adoption of protectionism during 1930 did not hinder this progress one jot. Clearly, by mid-1931 the Conservatives were well on target for victory. And by July 1931, with 265 candidates adopted to add to their 263 MPs, they were ready for the election whenever it came.[46]

VI

The timing of the election, frustratingly, remained in the hands of

[45] Sir Austen to Lady Ivy Chamberlain, 24 May 1930 (Chamberlain papers, AC 6/1/768).
[46] List of candidates adopted by July 1931 (Conservative Party papers, CRD 1/7/6).

MacDonald and his colleagues, and they clung obstinately to office despite adverse votes and the defeat of important legislation. Some impatient Conservatives decided that the best way to precipitate an election would be to split the Liberal Party, which was helping to keep Labour in office. After all, most Conservatives wanted to see an end to the Liberal Party and the lottery of three-party politics; those like Churchill who favoured co-operation were seen as mavericks.[47] As it became obvious that there was not inconsiderable discontent with Lloyd George's strategy of supporting Labour, the chances of forcing a fatal split improved, and Sir Edward Grigg's return from the Governorship-General of Kenya in 1930 meant that Conservative efforts could begin in earnest. Grigg, a Coalition Liberal turned Conservative, wanted to bring over part of the Liberal Party into firm support for the Tories, on the lines of the Liberal Unionist secession of 1886. This analogy naturally appealed to Grigg's chief prompter, Chamberlain. The two men began to meet regularly in November 1930, and the following month the party chairman met the leading Liberal malcontent, Sir John Simon. Simon was encouraging, stressing that he wanted to oust the Government, and adding that the Conservatives' protectionism need not be an insuperable barrier to close co-operation. (In the coming months, as the Tories increasingly stressed economy over protection, it would become still less of an impediment.) Simon admitted that he could not control many votes in Parliament, but told Chamberlain that many Liberals would be swayed by the offer of a clear run against Labour at the next election. Chamberlain also saw Lord Reading, the former Liberal Cabinet Minister, who was more dubious; but the former remained confident that Simon would soon be forming an independent grouping to work with the Conservatives.[48] To encourage Liberal unrest, he ensured that Central Office continued to produce material critical of Liberal MPs for supporting Labour.[49] However, despite continued promptings, Simon was very slow to move, and it was not until 3 March 1931 that he publicly urged free traders to reconsider their position.[50] Grigg had

[47] Neville to Ida Chamberlain, 9 Feb. 1929 (Chamberlain papers, NC 18/1/642).

[48] Neville Chamberlain diary, 5 Dec. 1929 (Chamberlain papers, NC 2/22); Neville to Hilda Chamberlain, 14 Dec. 1930 (Chamberlain papers, NC 18/1/720).

[49] Neville to Ida Chamberlain, 23 Dec. 1930 (Chamberlain papers, NC 18/1/721); see also Conservative Party pamphlets attacking the Liberals, e.g. 'Going! Going!! Gone!!!' about the decline of the Liberal Party, and 'If you voted Liberal', both 1930.

[50] *The Times*, 4 Mar. 1931.

expected a call for tariffs, but Simon's effort fell far short.[51] Three weeks later, Lloyd George's line in supporting the Government was approved by a vote of 33 to 17 in a meeting of the Liberal parliamentary party (LPP). This had the makings of a serious split, but again Simon failed to give the clear lead the dissentients wanted.[52]

Chamberlain became increasingly frustrated with Simon's immobility. When they met on 30 March 1931, Simon was reticent and stated that only four MPs would follow him, and that as the condition of support in one vote of censure in the House of Commons, they expected a clear run at the next election. Chamberlain dismissed the offer, noting afterwards that they '[could] not found an appeal to local Conservatives to sacrifice their organisation for a single vote and an ineffective one at that'.[53] Simon remained reluctant to make the break; and by the end of May, Chamberlain believed the chances of a Simonite secession were over, and that the next development might well be the entry of a loyalist Liberal into the Cabinet.[54] Finally, however, in late June, Simon and two colleagues resigned the Liberal whip. But they did not take the Conservative whip, and were numerically insignificant anyway. Simon had moved at last, but half-heartedly and with little concrete support. The possibility of splitting the Liberals remained, but Chamberlain was by this time trying to negotiate—through an intermediary and unknown to Baldwin—a deal with Lloyd George whereby the Liberals would help defeat the Government in return for a measure of electoral reform (the alternative vote).[55] These efforts also came to nothing, and it seemed that the Conservatives might have to go on hankering for an election for a while longer.

Short of an election, the Conservatives could regain office by participating in a National Government. The idea was bandied about quite freely from late 1930 onwards, but few took it very seriously. On 5 July, however, Stonehaven told Chamberlain of a conversation a friend had had with MacDonald. The premier had said that the situation was very grave, that he had no love of his present job, and that he wanted to see the formation of a National Government under Baldwin in which he, MacDonald, would serve as Foreign Secretary. Thomas, Snowden, and Greenwood would all come in, continued the report,

[51] Neville to Hilda Chamberlain, 1 Mar. 1931 (Chamberlain papers, NC 18/1/728).
[52] Grigg to Chamberlain, 28 Mar. 1931 (Bodleian Library, Grigg papers, microfilm).
[53] Neville to Ida Chamberlain, 5 Apr. 1931 (Chamberlain papers, NC 18/1/733).
[54] Neville to Hilda Chamberlain, 25 May 1931 (Chamberlain papers, NC 18/1/739).
[55] Neville to Hilda Chamberlain, 4 July 1931 (Chamberlain papers, NC 18/1/746).

because of their hatred of Henderson, their dislike of relying on Liberal votes in Parliament, and their support for the reform of unemployment insurance and the imposition of a tariff. There were, as Chamberlain pointed out, good reasons to doubt the veracity of the story.[56] For example, Snowden was unlikely to be advocating a tariff. However, there was no reason to doubt that a depressed MacDonald, speaking in vague terms, was capable by that stage of making remarks substantially similar to the ones reported. Whether they had any real meaning is more questionable.

Their significance here, though, was that they forced the Conservative leaders to define their attitude towards the idea of a National Government. Stonehaven believed it would be 'impracticable', while Chamberlain and Baldwin agreed that their party 'would not stand it for a minute'; it was 'clearly impossible'.[57] Baldwin said that if the offer was made, he would raise immediately the question of tariffs, and so ward off the danger. Chamberlain was not convinced that it would be so easy. If a heavy potential budget deficit led to panic in the City, a moratorium and increased unemployment, the press might call for a National administration; and if under such circumstances MacDonald, backed by Lloyd George, made the offer, it would be difficult for the Conservatives to refuse.[58] The problem continued to exercise his mind to such an extent that on 29 July he discussed it with his brother, Hailsham, Cunliffe-Lister, and Sir Samuel Hoare. All were opposed to a coalition, and Chamberlain hoped they would be able to avoid it. However, they 'agreed that it might be unavoidable, though only on condition that tariffs were accepted' and so long as Baldwin was Prime Minister.[59]

By the early summer of 1931, then, the Conservatives were in a happy position. Well-organized, united on a policy of public economy, protection, and imperial preference, and under an undisputed leader, they were on course for a victory at least as conclusive as that of 1924, after a run of excellent by-election results. Only their impatience to return to power and, paradoxically, the spectre of a National Government, stood in the way of Conservative jubilation. But by mid-1931, after an often uncomfortable passage, the party was poised for a landslide electoral victory.

56 Neville Chamberlain diary, 6 July 1931 (Chamberlain papers, NC 2/22).
57 Ibid.
58 Ibid. 24 July 1931.
59 Neville to Hilda Chamberlain, 2 Aug. 1931 (Chamberlain papers, NC 18/1/750).

3

FROM BAD TO WORSE: THE LIBERALS 1929–1931

'I TAKE an extremely serious view of the whole situation . . . for the Party,' wrote the Liberal chairman, Ramsay Muir, in May 1930. 'It is a matter of life and death.'[1] Indeed, this period did see a party in its death-throes. Yet only a year earlier, things had seemed quite promising for the Liberals. In October 1926 the party leadership had at last been wrenched from the dead hand of H. H. Asquith, and David Lloyd George elected in his place. While Sir Herbert Samuel set about the revivification of the party in the country, Lloyd George expended huge sums from his political fund on economic enquiries designed to give the party new policies with which to face the problems of post-war Britain, particularly unemployment. The policy which emerged envisaged the use of deficit-financed public works to regenerate the economy and promote employment. In real terms, all this constituted one of the most expensive political campaigns in British history.[2] But the Liberals did not enter the 1929 campaign with only a glamorous if somewhat tarnished leader and an exciting if somewhat untried and unorthodox programme. It also had a degree of unity; even the Liberal Council, set up in 1927 to keep the flame of Asquithianism burning, desisted from parading its hatred for Lloyd George. In private, though, the feuds remained. Walter Runciman, for example, was as opposed to Lloyd George as ever, and had little faith in the new programme.[3] However, Runciman and those who felt like him maintained a low profile, and waited for their leader to dig his own grave.

The Asquithians were not to be disappointed. At the general election the Liberals, with 513 candidates, won over five million votes

[1] Memorandum, Muir to Samuel, 8 May 1930 (House of Lords Record Office, Samuel papers, A/73, f. 3).

[2] M. Pinto-Duschinsky, *British Political Finance, 1830–1980* (Washington, DC, 1981), 91.

[3] Runciman to Vivian Phillips, 28 Feb. 1929 (Newcastle University Library, Runciman papers, WR 215); for attitude on policy, see comments on a circular from Samuel, 15 Mar. 1929 (Runciman papers, WR 221).

(23.6 per cent of the total) but only 59 seats. No leading Liberal had expected the party to win the election, despite their public protestations.[4] Lloyd George had been considering whether he would be better off supporting a Conservative or Labour administration, and was especially keen to reach agreement on electoral reform, while even the more enthusiastic activists were thinking only in terms of 100 to 150 seats.[5] To win only 59 seats, even so, was a 'great disappointment', which forced the chairman of one provincial Liberal federation to admit that he was 'not very hopeful about the future', while even the *Liberal Magazine* noted that the results had 'fallen short of what was expected by even the most sober prophets'.[6]

A deeper look at the implications of the election returns would have suggested cause for something more than disappointment. Twenty-eight seats were held by less than 5 per cent over the second-placed party; in 20 of these, the second party was the Conservatives, for whom 1929 had been a bad year. They could probably expect to do better next time. The Liberals' strength was concentrated disproportionately in the celtic fringe, with 13 of the 71 Scottish seats, 9 of the 35 Welsh, a seat each in the Scottish and Welsh universities plus all 5 in Cornwall. This total of 29 represented half the Liberal parliamentary party (LPP). By contrast, they held only 2 out of 62 London boroughs, and 10 out of 193 English provincial boroughs. And in the counties, it was in agricultural rather than middle-class seats that they did best. Overall, they won 34 of the 150 most agricultural divisions, but only 12 of the 292 most middle class. This was ominous, for in 1929 the Tory Government was widely seen as having a bad record on agriculture, and little to attract the industry in terms of policy, whereas the Liberals had Lloyd George's land policy. If—as indeed had happened by 1931—the Conservatives had a more convincing and appealing policy for agriculture, and the Liberals had been unable to do anything to help, then many Liberal seats might well be vulnerable. By contrast, it was difficult to see many seats which were particularly susceptible to a Liberal challenge. Although in the 100 Conservative seats with a majority of 10 per cent or less, the Liberals were second in 49, 1929

[4] Samuel, memorandum, 2 Feb. 1929 (Samuel papers, A/72); Maclean, memorandum, Feb. 1929 (Bodleian Library, Maclean papers, Dep. c.468, ff. 106–10).

[5] Samuel memorandum, 2 Feb. 1929 (Samuel papers, A/72); Maclean memorandum, Feb. 1929 (Maclean papers, Dept. c.468, ff. 106–10); R. J. Thomas to Henry Haydn Jones MP, 15 Apr. 1929 (National Library of Wales, Haydn Jones papers, letter 216).

[6] Midland LF, executive committee, 20 June 1929 (Birmingham University Library, Midland LF papers, MSS 10/i/5, ff. 333–5); *Liberal Magazine*, June 1929.

had been a bad year for the Tories; a taste of 'socialism' might well, as it had in 1924, turn renegade Conservatives back to their former allegiance. Thus Labour would probably be easier to attack. But of the 107 Labour seats with majorities of 10 per cent or less, the Liberals were second in only eleven. Thus the 1929 result, which left the Liberals vulnerable at the next election, and with few clear avenues available for further advance, presaged disaster in the not-too-distant future.

I

Now that Lloyd George had failed, of course, the Asquithians returned to plague him. On 9 June 1929 Lord Grey indicated privately his hostility by saying that while he had tried to preserve unity at the election, he could not 'under present conditions join in the Headquarters Councils of the Party'.[7] Implacable opposition like this could be marginalized, but to do it, Lloyd George had to seek a strategy that would keep discord to a minimum, and it was in the quest for that strategy that Lloyd George was to be engaged for much of the next two years.

For Lloyd George remained the party leader. Individuals might rail with passion that his leadership was a 'calamity',[8] but the combined prestige, ability, and finance of the former premier made him indispensable. As one (by no means slavish) Liberal MP wrote in January 1930, Lloyd George could not be excluded from the leadership so long as he was alive and in control of his faculties.[9] At a Yorkshire Liberal federation (LF) meeting, only 2 out of 230 delegates supported a motion calling for a change at the top.[10] Against such popularity the Asquithians could not compete, and were wise not seriously to try.

II

In what strategy should Lloyd George lead his party? Before the election he had considered the expediency of supporting each of the

[7] Grey to Reading, 9 June 1929 (India Office Library, Reading papers, MSS Eur. F118/27).

[8] V. Wynn to Haydn Jones, 6 June 1929 (Haydn Jones papers, letter 627).

[9] J. H. Morris-Jones, 'Westminster Diary', 20 Jan. 1930 (Clwyd Record Office, Morris-Jones papers, D/MJ/10).

[10] Yorkshire LF, council meeting, 25 Jan. 1930 (West Yorkshire Archive Service, Leeds, Yorkshire LF papers, 2).

other two parties, but his ideas had not been fixed, other than to hope that he would be in a position to secure a degree of electoral reform, and to wish to avoid another election for as long as possible.[11] He hoped, in short, to get the other parties bidding for his support. This was foiled by Baldwin, however, who tendered his resignation without meeting Parliament and advised the King to send for MacDonald. In such a situation, to oppose Labour might expose the Liberals to the dreaded second election. Therefore Lloyd George was rather compelled to back MacDonald. However, there was no question of a coalition, and at a meeting of the LPP on 13 June 1929 he promised support for bold Government action but warned that '[t]he very hour the Ministry becomes a Socialist administration its career ends.' He also stressed the need for electoral reform and Liberal unity.[12] The LPP backed him; in August MacDonald set up the Ullswater Conference to investigate possible changes in the electoral system. Lloyd George was not averse to keeping his contacts open, however, especially with Churchill.[13] But any faint prospects of a *rapprochement* were scotched by two events in October 1929: the Wall Street crash, presaging the onset of a severe economic depression which seriously dented Labour's electoral prospects against the Conservatives; and Viceroy Irwin's declaration promising dominion status for India, which propelled Churchill into die-hardism and made him an extremely unlikely ally for the Liberals.

The line of general support for Labour went reasonably well until the introduction of the Coal Mines Bill in December 1929. Liberal objections stemmed from dislike of the bill but also from a desire to force concessions on electoral reform. Talks with ministers failed to solve either problem, and Lloyd George led his party into Opposition to the second reading. Two Liberals, however, voted with the Government, and six abstained, leaving the ministry with a majority of eight. But the Liberals continued to move and support amendments, a tactic warmly approved by rank-and-file Liberals as stressing the independence of the party from the Government.[14]

Soon, however, Lloyd George was to have his authority as leader

[11] Maclean memorandum, Feb. 1929 (Maclean papers, Dep. c.468, ff. 106–10).

[12] J. Campbell, *Lloyd George: The Goat in the Wilderness, 1922–1931* (London, 1977), 245.

[13] M. Gilbert, *Winston S. Churchill, Vol. 5: Companion. Part 2* (London, 1981), 103–5.

[14] Muir to Lloyd George, 18 Feb. 1930 (House of Lords Record Office, Lloyd George papers, G/15/6/22).

severely shaken. The Government's continued obduracy on reform meant he was again forced to try to defeat the administration; but Liberals voted in both lobbies, despite the decision of an LPP meeting on 21 February 1930; the Government had a majority of nine. The chief whip, Sir Robert Hutchison, and Lloyd George both threatened to resign. This did not become necessary. On 4 March, at an acrimonious meeting of the LPP, Sir Donald Maclean and Runciman, who had both abstained, were heavily criticized, and a vote of confidence in the leader was passed with one against and four abstaining. Sir John Simon, the long-time opponent of Lloyd George who might have been a focus for discontent, pointed out the 'consternation' of ordinary Liberal supporters, promised not to promote discord, and left in disgust when Maclean and Runciman abstained in the confidence vote.[15]

Strengthened by the vote of confidence, Lloyd George could now move to consolidate the party's position, helped by the Government's announcement on 18 March that it would introduce an electoral reform bill if it remained in office. Two days later, Lloyd George stated that the Liberals would not hinder the Coal Mines Bill further, ostensibly because the fate of the London naval conference was 'hanging in the balance' and it would not do to have the Government embarrassed at such a time. Of course, this was no more than an excuse. Unruffled by accusations of opportunism, Lloyd George also moved to strengthen the party by inviting Maclean and Runciman to join the Shadow Cabinet.[16] Both did so, with misgivings. Simon had declared his loyalty and was, in any case, still immersed in the task of chairing the statutory commission on India. The discussions on electoral reform, plus the Conservatives' move towards protection and food taxes, helped unite the party and to bond it more closely to the free-trade Government.

In May 1930, however, this calm was shattered by the failure of Lloyd George and MacDonald to reach agreement on electoral reform. The former held out for proportional representation, without which the party chairman, Ramsay Muir, believed the party's position to be 'hopeless'; the Cabinet would go no further than the alternative vote.[17] The talks collapsed, but then on 28 May 1930 MacDonald, reeling from Mosley's resignation, appealed for co-operation from the

[15] Morris-Jones, 'Westminster Diary', 28 Feb., 4 Mar. 1930 (Morris-Jones papers, D/MJ/10).
[16] Campbell, *Goat in the Wilderness*, 260.
[17] Muir to Samuel, 8 May 1930 (Samuel papers, A/73, f. 3).

other parties. As expected, Baldwin refused, but Lloyd George accepted, although neither side wanted this to become too close a relationship.[18] The next two months saw a series of friendly though largely fruitless meetings between ministers and leading Liberals.

Closer links came in the autumn, after Lloyd George had brought electoral reform back to the centre of the stage. The Government's delaying tactic, the Ullswater Conference, had died, and Muir had reconsidered: the alternative vote might be worth pursuing after all. He calculated the Liberals would win 70 seats under such a system at the next election, but only 36 under the present set-up.[19] Therefore Lloyd George demanded it as the price of further Liberal support, and on 24 October, four days before the new session began, leaders of the two parties met. No general *entente* appears to have been reached, but in agreeing to include a measure of electoral reform in the King's Speech the Government bound up the Liberals in its own fate: if they wanted the reform to take place they would have to ensure the administration's survival. They remained free, though, to try to amend Government legislation.[20] The party grass roots broadly favoured this line. In November 1930 the Lancashire, Cheshire and North-Western Liberal federation (LCNWLF) urged that while giving general support to the Government and pressing for electoral reform, the party should avoid any long-term pacts, and candidates took the same view.[21] Overwhelmingly, the message was 'thus far—but no further'.

Many Liberals, though, were not so contented, and increasingly during 1930 Sir John Simon emerged as the leading dissident. The Asquithian heir apparent, he had been thwarted by the triumphal accession of Lloyd George to the leadership in October 1926. He had pledged his loyalty to the new leader, but largely in the hope that Lloyd George would prove his own worst enemy. In the spring of 1927 Simon had accepted the chairmanship of the statutory commission on India, which took most of his time. At the 1929 election he had held his seat, largely thanks to Baldwin's persuading the local Conservatives not to oppose him; and increasingly, dislike of Lloyd George and horror at the performance of the second Labour Government propelled him towards the Conservatives. However, he was preoccupied

[18] Muir to Samuel, 8 May 1930 (Samuel papers, A/73, F. 3); *Daily Herald*, 18 June 1930.

[19] Muir, 'Forecast of the Next Election', 6 Nov. 1930 (Samuel papers, A/73).

[20] Snowden, *Autobiography*, ii. 888; cf. J. D. Fair, 'The Second Labour Government and the Politics of Electoral Reform, 1929–1931', *Albion*, 13 (1981), 293–4.

[21] LCNWLF, executive committee, 14 Nov. 1930 (Manchester Central Library, LCNWLF papers, M390/1/7); Campbell, *Goat in the Wilderness*, 279–80.

with the work of the Indian commission until May 1930, and was then concerned mainly with restoring his practice at the Bar.[22] Even so, he had time to make clear that he was more than disgruntled with the state of the Liberal Party. On 4 November five Liberals, including Simon and Hutchison, the chief whip, voted for a Conservative motion attacking the King's Speech, when the official line was to abstain. Hutchison resigned, and worked closely with Simon thereafter. Simon, of course, was not motivated solely by principle. Ambition—no fault in a politician—also played a part; he felt in danger of wasting the rest of his public life.[23] He also felt, fortuitously in the light of his desire to be 'of more general service', that the slump necessitated a reconsideration of all aspects of policy. Four days later, Simon was arranging to meet Neville Chamberlain (the latter having made the first move).[24] So began the series of meetings with leading Tories outlined in Chapter 2.

Discontent grew apace. On 21 January 1931 an acrimonious party meeting discussed the Trade Disputes and Trade Union (Amendment) Bill. Simon led strong opposition to the bill, while Sir Archibald Sinclair, the chief whip, threatened to resign if the party split on the issue. Sinclair also read a letter from Muir, expressing the view that the party was in no position to fight an election, having 'neither the money nor the candidates'. Lloyd George condemned the bill, but stressed that it would be suicidal to defeat the Government now. A motion to abstain on second reading was passed by 33 votes to 10; Simon and other opponents of the leader had left before the vote.[25]

The divisions continued; and on 12 March Sinclair announced that he would resign if there were further instances of cross-voting in Parliament. Lloyd George declared his support for the chief whip, and called for a new spirit of unity: a small united party could do much good, but a 'disorganised rabble' was of no use to him. Those who opposed his line, he added, could go where they pleased.[26] On 16 March, after more splits in the Commons, Sinclair carried out his threat and resigned.[27] (He was eventually prevailed upon, by great

[22] Viscount Simon, *Retrospect: The Memoirs of the Rt. Hon. Viscount Simon* (London, 1952), 144, 156.

[23] Simon to Lord Inchcape, 21 Nov. 1930 (Bodleian Library, Simon papers, 67, f. 23).

[24] See correspondence in Simon papers, 67, ff, 40–57.

[25] Morris-Jones, 'Westminster Diary', 21 Jan. 1931 (Morris-Jones papers, D/MJ/10).

[26] Ibid. 12 Mar. 1931.

[27] Sinclair to Lloyd George, 17 Mar. 1931 (Churchill College, Thurso papers, THRS I 17/4).

pressure from within and without the party, to resume.)[28] Four days after his resignation, he summed up the position cogently, if a little over-optimistically:

> Broadly speaking, the vast majority of the Party are working well together under Mr Lloyd George's leadership. . . . Nevertheless, there are certain Members of the Party—. . . such as Simon and Hutchison—who are definitely bent on turning out the Government and they are in a position to assure those who follow them that they will have no Tory opponent at the next General Election. They constitute a nucleus of disaffection and disloyalty in the Party; their interventions in debate and constant opposition in the division lobby weaken the influence of the Party in the House of Commons, while their criticism of our policy as unprincipled as well as unwise bewilders and discourages our supporters in the country. Runciman is wholly occupied with his business interests and only appears in the House of Commons very occasionally to emphasise by vote or speech some difference with his Liberal colleagues.

Sinclair felt that the Liberals should support Labour on major issues like free trade, India, disarmament, national development, unemployment, and electoral reform, while reserving their right as an independent party to criticize.[29]

Lloyd George had made an offer to MacDonald along those lines on 18 March 1931, and the premier had suggested weekly meetings.[30] At a lengthy LPP meeting six days later, Lloyd George explained his views and threatened to resign if defeated. Simon, Leslie Hore-Belisha, Ernest Brown, and James de Rothschild all spoke against him, but Samuel backed the leader and eventually Lloyd George won by 33 votes to 17.[31] The minority was far too large for comfort, even if it could be divided into those favouring total independence and those favouring closer co-operation with the Conservatives. Morale continued to fall, and by 15 April party meetings were 'the same old farce'.[32] And all the time, Simon and his cohorts were canvassing discreetly among dissident Liberal MPs.[33] In May, at the conference of the national

[28] Sinclair to D. B. Keith, 8 Apr. 1931 (Thurso papers, THRS II 51/1); Morris-Jones to Sinclair, 17 Mar. 1931 (Morris-Jones papers, D/MJ/12).

[29] Sinclair to Fisher, 20 Mar. 1931 (Bodleian Library, Fisher papers, 69, ff. 34–7).

[30] Marquand, *MacDonald*, 593.

[31] Morris-Jones, 'Westminster Diary', 25 Mar. 1931 (Morris-Jones papers, D/MJ/10); *The Times*, 26 Mar. 1931; G. H. Shakespeare, *Let Candles Be Brought In* (London, 1949), 134.

[32] A. England MP to Haydn Jones, 25 Mar. 1931 (Haydn Jones papers, letter 328).

[33] Morris-Jones, 'Westminster Diary', 27 Jan. 1931 (Morris-Jones papers, D/MJ/10).

Liberal federation (NLF), a last try was made to challenge the leader from within the party, when Hore-Belisha, Brown, Rothschild, and Geoffrey Shakespeare moved a critical motion. Its overwhelming defeat suggested to them that drastic action might be necessary.[34] The first to act was Brown, who on 26 June joined Simon and Hutchison in resigning the Liberal whip, on the pretext of the withdrawal of the party's objections to Snowden's plans for land taxes. For Simon, it had been 'a lower depth of humiliation than any into which [the party] had yet been led'.[35] Of course, Simon had been talking to the Conservatives for seven months, and his disaffection with the Liberal Party of Lloyd George covered all aspects of personal and political feeling. The leader's response—a bitter personal attack on Simon in the Commons on 3 July—suggested there was no sorrow in the parting on either side. In many ways, Brown was the most serious loss of the three. He had not been anti-Lloyd George in 1929, and as late as March 1931 had not been seen as at all pro-Conservative. That such a person could be persuaded to resign the whip by the parliamentary tactics of the party leadership was an extremely bad sign.

In many ways, of course, Lloyd George had had little choice but to act as he had. But he had kept other options open. In November 1930 he was telling Grigg that the Conservatives had much to lose by driving the Liberals towards Labour.[36] In October Lloyd George had attended a dinner organized by the former Liberal Cabinet Ministers J. E. B. Seely and Lord Reading, at which a paper strongly advocating a National Government was read out. MacDonald, Churchill, and Sir Robert Horne, the Conservative MP and former Coalition Cabinet Minister, had also been present.[37] Lloyd George's participation in informal talks with Churchill, Mosley, and younger Conservatives is well known.[38] And in the early summer of 1931, he was engaged in negotiations with Chamberlain through an intermediary.[39]

Too much can be read into such contacts, however. They were not, like Simon's talks with Chamberlain and Grigg, aimed at a definite end. Lloyd George loved intrigue, had always derived immense

[34] Shakespeare, *Let Candles*, 134–5.
[35] Simon, *Retrospect*, 165–6; Simon to Sinclair, 26 June 1931 (Simon papers, 68, ff. 92–3).
[36] Neville Chamberlain diary, 21 Nov. 1930 (Chamberlain papers, NC 2/22).
[37] Seely to Reading, 26 Oct. 1930 (Reading papers, MSS Eur. F118/98).
[38] See e.g. O. Mosley, *My Life* (London, 1968), 264.
[39] Neville to Hilda Chamberlain, 4 July 1931 (Chamberlain papers, NC 18/1/746); Neville Chamberlain diary, 24 July 1931 (NC 2/22).

pleasure from frightening Conservatives, and liked nothing better than to gather around himself people who regarded him as a great man of action foiled by the machinations of lesser men. But that was as far as it went: it was simply talk. The reality was a choice between protectionist Conservatives and free trade, alternative vote-bearing Labourites. It would have been impossible for Lloyd George to have persuaded the mass of his party that it was better off with the former than with the latter.

This stark reality has prompted some people to believe that Lloyd George stood on the verge of a coalition with Labour in July 1931.[40] However, there is no concrete documentary evidence for this. The document cited by Frank Owen in his 1954 biography of Lloyd George, to the effect that the latter was to become Foreign Secretary or Chancellor of the Exchequer, has never been found since, while the comment by MacDonald, in a letter to Passfield, that he would have to resort to 'moves which will surprise all of you' to solve the thorny problem of Labour representation in the House of Lords, is susceptible to numerous interpretations, and seems to have been vague because MacDonald himself did not really known what he meant.[41] There is no other reference in the copious papers of either man to suggest a coalition was about to be formed. In addition, the circumstantial evidence is discouraging. In February Lloyd George had told Lansbury that for him to join Labour would antagonize millions of Liberal supporters, a view amply supported by contemporaneous Liberal utterances.[42] Labourites felt a similar antipathy towards closer co-operation with the Liberals, trade unionists especially being incensed by their wrecking of the Trade Disputes Bill in the spring of 1931. In addition, Lloyd George was consistently saying in private that he did not want office again.[43] Similar stories about him joining Labour were to circulate at the time of the 1931 election, and were equally unfounded. The case for arguing that a Lib–Lab coalition was about to be formed in July 1931, therefore, is virtually non-existent.

[40] F. Owen, *Tempestuous Journey: Lloyd George, His Life and Times* (London, 1954), 717; see also Skidelsky, *Politicians and the Slump*, 328–33; Marquand, *MacDonald*, 601–2, is slightly more circumspect.

[41] P. Rowland, *Lloyd George* (London, 1975), 686; Campbell, *Goat in the Wilderness*, 294–6; for various interpretations, see Beatrice Webb diary, 15 July 1931 (Passfield papers); S. Webb, 'What Happened in 1931: A Record', *Political Quarterly*, 3 (1932), 1–5.

[42] Lloyd George to Lansbury, 16 Feb. 1931 (Lansbury papers, 10).

[43] Ibid.; Samuel memorandum, 2 Feb. 1929 (Samuel papers, A/72).

III

Moving back from the world of dreams, it is worth reiterating that for two years Lloyd George's strategy had aimed to avoid an early general election and to secure electoral reform. Both preoccupations stemmed from an awareness of his party's acute financial and organizational weaknesses.

At the centre of the Liberals' financial problems was the Lloyd George political fund. This comprised the profits made by the leader from the sale of honours during his tenure as Prime Minister. This was not as scandalous as has often been pretended, but he had been rather undiscriminating as to who received the honours, and he had retained the money in his own fund, rather than turning it over to the Liberal Party. Between 1926 and 1929, though, he spent lavishly from the fund for party purposes. In particular, constituency associations were revived, agents and organizers appointed, and Liberal candidates enabled to spend large sums of money on their election campaigns in 1929—£786.83 per opposed candidate, compared with £911.77 and £450.44 for the Conservatives and Labour respectively.[44]

After the election it was a different story. The fund's capital was depleted, more so after the crash in share prices later in the year. In September the financial agreement between Lloyd George and the party expired and was not renewed. Samuel had already told the provincial federations that their grants would be cut severely, and it did not augur well for the vigorous proselytization of Liberalism that Samuel told the secretary of the Manchester LF 'to go quietly and conserve . . . resources'.[45] Naturally there were protests, and Lloyd George relented somewhat, the federations being told that they would receive one last payment for the first half of 1930.[46] It was made clear that there was no prospect of an extension, and that the maintenance of the federations now rested entirely in their own hands. But the party in the country had been dependent upon subventions from headquarters since 1905. The known existence of the Lloyd George fund continued

[44] My own calculations, based on PP 114, 1929–30, 'Return of the Expenses of each Candidate at the General Election of May, 1929'.

[45] Manchester LF, executive committee, 25 June 1929 (Manchester Central Library, Manchester LF papers, M283/1/3/5).

[46] C. Cook, *A Short History of the Liberal Party, 1900–1976* (London, 1976), 111; H. F. Oldman (headquarters) to V. Bridgwater (secretary, Midland LF), 10 Jan. 1930 (Midland LF papers, MSS 10/i/5, ff. 389–90); Scottish LF, finance committee, 21 Jan. 1930 (Edinburgh University Library, Scottish LF papers, minute book, ff. 384–5).

to make associations and federations sluggish in raising their own money, and sympathizers reluctant to give it. Attempts to raise more money by subscriptions, bazaars, or appeals to wealthy Liberals were not successful, therefore.[47] Short of scrapping the fund or parting company with Lloyd George, there was no solution to the dilemma. The party was caught in a terrible concatenation of unfortunate circumstances.

Increasingly, therefore, resort had to be made to retrenchment. Cook has suggested that the cessation of central grants in June 1930 resulted in the swift dismissal of all remaining employees.[48] This was not quite so; instead, federations and associations fought long rearguard battles, fending off the final day of judgement. There were redundancies through natural wastage, moves into smaller offices, salary cuts. It all made for low morale and worse organization.[49] Headquarters also suffered from the need to make cuts. At the beginning of 1930 it had only £3,000, plus £12,500 which constituted a final payment from the Lloyd George fund. With this they were expected to pay for all central expenses and by-election campaigns. Previously, £42,000 a year had been provided.[50] By May 1930 Muir was complaining that the staff was so depleted that he was having to do much of the routine work himself, leaving him little time to plan for the future.[51] Meanwhile, by-election after by-election had to be allowed to pass without Liberal intervention; party propaganda suffered similarly, especially as between 1928 and 1931 the Liberal press declined, with the demise of the *Westminster Gazette*, the disappearance of the *Nation* into the *New Statesman*, and the merger of the *Daily News* and the *Daily Chronicle* to form the *News Chronicle*. The Liberal press which remained was often seen as 'rather knock-kneed' by the party faithful.[52]

[47] Muir to Samuel, 8 May 1930 (Samuel papers, A/73, f. 3); Manchester LF, general committee, 4 Sept. 1930; finance committee, 12 Nov. 1930 (Manchester LF papers, M283/1/4/2, M283/1/5/1); Midland LF, executive committee, 19 June 1930, report on meeting with Muir (Midland LF papers, MSS 10/i/6, f. 41); Muir to Sinclair, 30 Oct. 1930, Sinclair to Muir, 31 Oct. 1930 (Thurso papers, THRS II 75/4).

[48] Cook, *Short History*, 112.

[49] LCNWLF, executive committee, 12 July 1929 (LCNWLF papers, M390/1/7); Manchester LF, executive committee, 3, 17 Sept. 1930 (Manchester LF papers, M283/1/3/5); Scottish LF, subcommittee on office staff and finance, 31 Jan. 1930 (Scottish LF papers, minute book, ff. 487–92); Midland LF, executive committee, 4 July 1931 (Midland LF papers, MSS 10/i/6, f. 151).

[50] Muir to Sinclair, 30 Oct. 1930 (Thurso papers, THRS II 75/4).

[51] Muir to Samuel, 8 May 1930 (Samuel papers, A/73, f. 3).

[52] Ibid.

Given all the circumstances, it was not surprising that the prospect of the next election was not one to warm the Liberal heart. In the immediate aftermath of the 1929 election, few if any Liberals felt the party would fight on so broad a front next time. Only two weeks after polling day, the LCNWLF stated privately that, whereas 62 of their area's 83 seats had been contested in 1929, at the next election only 21 should definitely be fought, plus another 22 if resources permitted.[53] In May 1930 Muir argued confidentially that no more than 300 seats were 'seriously worth fighting'. It would cost around £142,000 to contest 350 seats on a sound basis, but '[t]owards this sum nothing [was] available'. Only proportional representation could solve the party's problems, because then they could fight the whole country and poll every Liberal vote with only 200 or 250 candidates.[54] Thus he saw PR not only, perhaps not even mainly, as a means of ensuring fair representation, but also as a way of enabling the impoverished party to continue on a nation-wide basis. In June he told the federation secretaries that the party 'should be unable, unless the finances were augmented, to fight more than 200 seats at the next General Election'.[55] Sinclair wrote reassuringly that putting up 300 candidates in the face of all the party's problems would be a fine achievement, but he must have realized that the party would have been destroying its own credibility in fielding fewer candidates than the number needed to secure a parliamentary majority.[56] It was decided finally, however, to fight on a broader front, with headquarters agreeing to pay all candidates £150 which would, in effect, cover the deposit.[57] In many divisions, therefore, the candidate could not even be sure that he could afford to spend the £150 on his campaign—and that was a derisory sum for an election campaign, anyway.

To spend the money at all, however, the party needed candidates, and these were increasingly difficult to find. In June 1930 the federation secretaries reported serious problems. Eight months later Muir was telling Samuel that even winnable constituencies could not find people to stand; he was 'hard put to it to think of possible people

[53] LCNWLF, executive committee, 14 June 1929 (LCNWLF papers, M390/1/7).
[54] Muir to Samuel, 8 May 1930 (Samuel papers, A/73, f. 3).
[55] Midland LF, executive committee, 19 June 1930 (Midland LF papers, MSS 10/i/6, f. 41).
[56] Sinclair to Muir, 31 Oct. 1930 (Thurso papers, THRS II 75/4).
[57] Midland LF, executive committee, 11 Dec. 1930 (Midland LF papers, MSS 10/i/6, ff. 92–3).

to recommend'.[58] By that time, only 11 candidates had been selected in the Yorkshire LF area, whereas 45 had fought in 1929; by July the figure was only 13.[59] Even before the events of August to October, then, it was clear that the Liberals would be fighting on a much narrower front than they had in 1929.

Where they fought, they could expect to fare badly. The Liberals' electoral position was precarious in the extreme after 1929, and their performance in and regarding by-elections thereafter suggested that that position would be fully exposed when a general election came. Lack of organization, finance, and candidates meant the party often let by-elections pass it by. (No Liberal seat fell vacant.) Out of 33 contested by-elections, the Conservatives and Labour fought 31 each, the Liberals, 14. There was every reason to expect these factors to be repeated at a general election. In May and June 1931 they contested only 2 out of 8 by-elections; and, overall, where they did fight, their record was poor. They lost deposits at Twickenham (August 1929) and Fareham (February 1931) where they had retained them in 1929, and slumped badly in poll share at Central Nottingham (25.1 to 16.9 per cent, May 1930), East Bristol (34.2 to 12.9 per cent, January 1931), East Islington (27.9 to 14.6 per cent, February 1931), Pontypridd (36.8 to 24.2 per cent, March 1931), and Stroud (29.5 to 20.4 per cent, May 1931). It was not all gloom: they increased from 26.6 to 30.2 per cent at Shipley in November 1930, and from 20.8 to 34.1 per cent at Whitechapel the following month. However, the general picture was one of retreat, a fact acknowledged by party headquarters. In November 1930 they had been predicting privately that at the next general election, in 'industrial' seats, the Liberal vote would fall by 10 per cent, and in other seats by 5 per cent, with Labour falling 12 and 5 per cent, and the Conservatives rising 20 and 5 per cent, respectively. The Liberals, the memorandum concluded, would win 36 seats, the Conservatives 343, and Labour 219. Nothing that was to happen between then and August 1931 reduced the Tories' chances or improved those of the Liberals or, for that matter, Labour.

IV

These were not easy years for Liberal ideology, either. The 1929

[58] Muir to Samuel, 9 Feb. 1931 (Samuel papers, A/155(VIII), f. 8).

[59] Yorkshire LF, executive committee, 28 Feb. 1931, annual meeting, 11 July 1931 (Yorkshire LF papers, 2).

platform had been wide-ranging, but by late 1930 free trade and electoral reform were often the only subjects of policy discussion within Liberal federations and associations. Meanwhile, a number of senior Liberals, like Runciman and Simon, were increasingly restive on policy. By March 1931 Simon was talking in terms of a revenue tariff; and he was not alone.[60] In August 1930 the Liberal MP, E. D. Simon, had caused a sensation at the Liberal summer school by proposing a revenue tariff of 10 per cent on all imports except raw materials; early in 1931 the Liberal economist J. M. Keynes confessed a similar conviction.[61] It was largely in response to such challenges, and to the vigorous Conservative propaganda for protection, that a Liberal free-trade campaign was organized for late May and June 1931.

It was not only free trade that was coming into question, however. In May 1930 Lord Lothian wrote to Lloyd George advocating a new programme to include vigorous national development, rigorous economy, anti-dumping measures, the relief of investment capital from taxation, credit facilities to promote rationalization, help for agriculture, imperial development, and international action to reduce tariff barriers.[62] By the following March he was talking of the need for 'a rough Gosplan'.[63] By contrast, the veteran Lord Shuttleworth, who had been a minister under Gladstone, wrote like the avenging ghost of his former master in December 1930:

> In my opinion Liberal leaders should concentrate their efforts on three objects:
> 1. Economy and Retrenchment.
> 2. Reduction of Taxation.
> 3. Defence of Free Trade.
>
> Recent extravagant proposals in Liberal Party publications for a big loan and for vast expenditure on roads, many of which are not needed, have nothing to do with Liberal principles.[64]

[60] *The Times*, 4 Mar. 1931; Simon to Reading, 2 Mar. 1931 (Reading papers, MSS Eur. F118/101).

[61] M. Freeden, *Liberalism Divided: A Study in British Political Thought, 1914–1939* (Oxford, 1986), 121; *Liberal Magazine*, Apr. 1931; Sinclair to R. M. Findlay (secretary of the Free Trade Union), 11 Mar. 1931 (Thurso papers, THRS I 20/5).

[62] Lothian to Lloyd George, 29 May 1930 (Scottish Record Office, Lothian papers, GD 40/17/250/486–7).

[63] Lothian to B. Seebohm Rowntree (unsent draft letter), 13 Mar. 1931 (Lothian papers, GD 40/16/253/747).

[64] Shuttleworth to Lord Allendale, 2 Dec. 1930, enclosed in Shuttleworth to Runciman, 3 Dec. 1930 (Runciman papers, WR 221).

In fact, Shuttleworth's objectives were those of many Liberals by the start of 1931. As early as January 1930, the Yorkshire LF had called for 'drastic reduction of all non-productive expenditure', and demanded the diversion of such cash to productive ends.[65] By early 1931 the latter part of the resolution was often lost in the cry of 'retrenchment'. It was on a Liberal amendment in February 1931 that a committee was appointed under Sir George May of Prudential Insurance to recommend 'forthwith all practicable and legitimate reductions in the national expenditure consistent with the efficiency of the services'.[66] In May the NLF conference called for '[d]rastic economy . . . in every department of State'.[67] By mid-1931 Liberal policy was negative—the reduction of expenditure, the defence of free trade. The Conservatives, on the other hand, while demanding retrenchment, also had a policy with which to combat the Depression—protection. The Liberals' positive policy of 1929 was nowhere to be seen. In its place, *de facto* if not *de jure*, was an unreconstructed and unattractive Gladstonianism.

By mid-1931 the Liberals were in a hopeless state. Their policy was a nonsense, their organization a shambles, their finances almost non-existent, and their right wing on the point of rebellion. In addition, their leader was very possibly on the point of death. On 27 July, Lloyd George was taken seriously ill, and two days later had to have his prostate gland removed. It would be glittering symbolism to be able to write that the party and its leader died on the same day. But of course, they did not. So we are left with a more prosaic conclusion; that, whenever and however it had come, the next general election would have been disastrous for the Liberal Party. The events of August to October 1931 merely snatched catastrophe from the jaws of disaster.

[65] Yorkshire LF, council meeting, 25 Jan. 1930 (Yorkshire LF papers, 2).
[66] *Parl. Deb.*, 5th ser., 248, col. 449, 11 Feb. 1931.
[67] *Liberal Magazine*, May, June 1931; LCNWLF, executive committee, 27 Feb. 1931, discussing resolution from Liverpool Wavertree LA (LCNWLF papers, M390/1/7).

4

A CHANGE OF GOVERNMENT

THE political scene by the early summer of 1931 was by no means straightforward, but a number of things seem clear in retrospect. First, Labour hoped for continued Liberal support, given that the alternative vote legislation was still passing through Parliament. What would happen when, as seemed inevitable, the bill was rejected by the House of Lords was far less clear. Both parties dreaded an election, though; the Conservatives relished the prospect. They hoped to split the Liberal Party to their own advantage, but did not want to participate in a National Government. There was a lot of talk and rumour on the latter subject, but it was, in reality, no more than that, and even enthusiasts like Lord Reading were pessimistic. Thus it was only in the events of August 1931, and particularly of 22 to 24 August, that a real National administration began to emerge. In so far as these events bore more or less directly on the general election of October 1931, they must be studied in some detail here.

I

The roots of the political crisis lay in the financial crisis which engulfed Europe from late 1930 onwards and with especial vigour after the collapse of the leading Austrian bank in May 1931.[1] This led to the freezing of British assets in Austria and Germany; conversely, in trying to preserve financial prestige, the British could not stop foreigners, anxious to cover themselves, withdrawing their deposits from London. These withdrawals were stepped up when a series of events in July began to suggest that Britain's own position was weaker than previously supposed. On 13 July 1931 the Macmillan report on finance and industry highlighted the discrepancies between London's short-term assets and its liabilities, and ten days later bank rate had to be raised 1 per cent to counter a drain of gold. On 26 July the Bank of England borrowed £25,000,000 each from the Federal Reserve Bank

[1] D. Williams, 'London and the 1931 Financial Crisis', *Economic History Review*, 15 (1962–3), 513–28; Aldcroft, *The British Economy*, 49–55; D. B. Kunz, *The Battle for Britain's Gold Standard in 1931* (London, 1987).

(FRB) of New York and the Bank of France. This was announced publicly in the same weekend as an increase in the fiduciary issue and the publication of the report of the May committee on national expenditure, predicting a massive budget deficit. The impression given was that a country already heavily in debt was increasing its liabilities and printing money as a way out—seen as a sure recipe for inflation. The way was opening for a full-blown financial crisis to hit Britain.

The picture painted by the May report was grim. (The minority report, advocating the maintenance of present expenditure, was ignored.) It predicted a budget deficit of £120,000,000 for 1932–3 and urged sweeping public economies totalling £96,578,000, of which £66,500,000 would come from unemployment insurance. To this end, it recommended a 20 per cent cut in unemployment benefit, increased insurance contributions, the extension of the scheme to new classes of workers, and the application of a needs test to applicants who had exhausted their insurance rights. Public salaries should be cut: 20 per cent for teachers, 12½ per cent for the police, and service personnel would all be placed on the lower, 1925 pay-scale. Miscellaneous other savings, including £7,865,000 on the road fund, completed the cuts. New taxation would cover the shortfall. This was a sobering analysis; but as the (Liberal) *Economist* put it, the committee seemed to have set out 'to make the public's flesh creep', and it had 'rather seriously overpaint[ed] the gloom', since it had counted the provision of £50,000,000 for the sinking fund, and £40,000,000 of borrowing for the unemployment insurance fund, as current expenditure, contrary to Treasury practice.[2]

The personnel and terms of reference of the committee had made such a report inevitable, and this was just what Snowden had intended. He believed that the only way out of the economic crisis was to cut expenditure and taxation as far as possible, while maintaining free trade and the gold standard, to encourage enterprise. Then, from this revised capitalism, progress towards socialism could be renewed. There was no alternative; to abandon free trade would damage working-class living standards and lead to profiteering; to abandon gold would lead to hyperinflation, as seen in Germany in 1923. It was a sincerely held, if arguably wrong-headed view, and the Chancellor can at least be credited with having the best interests of Labour voters, as well as the nation, at heart. Snowden hoped to use the report as a tool with which to manipulate the Cabinet into making the 'necessary'

[2] *Economist*, 8 Aug. 1931.

economies. After all, the Government had pursued a mildly expansionist economic policy, for example in liberalizing benefits and increasing the borrowing powers of the unemployment insurance fund from £40,000,000 at the beginning of 1930 to £115,000,000. It had ignored most of the demands for economies made in the interim report (June 1931) of the Holman Gregory commission on unemployment insurance (including a cut of around 12 per cent in standard benefit), agreeing only to legislate on 'anomalies' and thus saving £3,000,000 instead of the report's £32,800,000. Realizing the difficulties, Snowden decided, on the publication of the May report, to let things ride. He was prepared to scare his colleagues into making cuts by giving the appearance of a crisis. Thus his 1931 budget had been a holding operation—he had had no intention of taking half a loaf from the Cabinet in April, when he might be able to force through more substantial económies with the aid of May—and now it was decided to publish the report on the day Parliament rose for the summer, without an accompanying official statement. These were clever tactics, but they ignored the extent to which foreigners were feeling nervous about their deposits in London.[3]

In any case, there was no assurance that the Cabinet would permit itself to be 'bounced' in this way. Although some ministers who wanted the report implemented, notably Bondfield, subsequently lied that they had opposed it from the outset, many in the Cabinet did dislike it intensely. On 6 August Lord Parmoor informed MacDonald that he was 'unable, in any way' to accept 'its reactionary proposals', while Passfield hoped that Henderson would rally the Cabinet against Snowden. High-spending ministers would be still more obdurate. Thus when the Cabinet first considered the report on 30 July it had only a 'preliminary' discussion, leaving details to be worked out by a Cabinet economy committee (CEC) comprising MacDonald, Snowden, Henderson, Thomas, and William Graham, the President of the Board of Trade. All departments were to submit their observations by 18 August, in time for the CEC's first meeting a week later. The financial situation, concluded MacDonald, was now the 'supreme' question before the Cabinet.[4]

[3] *Liberal Yearbook, 1932* (London, 1932), 154; Snowden, *Autobiography*, ii. 904.

[4] Cabinet conclusions, 30 July 1931 (Public Record Office, CAB 23/67/40 (31)); Bondfield, *A Life's Work*, 304; Marquand, *MacDonald*, 588; 'Memorandum by the Minister of Labour', 11 Aug. 1931 (Cabinet papers, NE (31)20); Parmoor to MacDonald, 6 Aug. 1931 (MacDonald papers, PRO 3/69/1314); Beatrice Webb diary, 4 Aug. 1931 (Passfield papers).

The Cabinet was not merely considering the report in the context of insistent demands for economy from business, bankers, and Opposition parties, however. There was also strident opposition to such cuts from within the Labour movement. As early as August 1930, Bevin had been saying that there were strong business and financial pressures to cut wages; it would 'not be very long before there [was] a general attack'. Unemployment benefit, he believed, underpinned wages—if it were cut, wages would follow.[5] (This, of course, was what Snowden and the Treasury intended). In March 1931 the miners called for higher benefits, and two months later the TUC's economic committee was making plans to resist 'large-scale attacks on wages'; if the resistance failed, argued Bevin, working-class living standards would be lower than ever they had been in the nineteenth century.[6] The response to the Holman Gregory report reflected this. The TUC chairman, Arthur Hayday, said he 'did not think any Government would dare to implement' it, while Glasgow Labour Party was one of many to declare that it would 'unflinchingly oppose any proposal to reduce existing payments to the unemployed'.[7] The May report was even more drastic, and so was the response; Hayday condemned it as 'savage and ludicrous . . . a combination of all previous conspiracies against the workers'. Beatrice Webb summed up much Labour feeling when she thundered that '[l]uxury hotels and luxury flats, Bond Street shopping, racing and high living in all its forms [was] to go unchecked; but the babies [were] not to have milk and the very poor [were] not to have homes.'[8]

The odds, therefore, were certainly not stacked in Snowden's favour. But even a united Cabinet would need some Opposition support to get its proposals through Parliament, so the Chancellor sent details of the report to the Conservative and Liberal leaders and asked for their comments over the next two or three weeks: there was 'no great urgency'.[9] If he really believed that, it showed how far the May

[5] General secretary's report, TGWU executive minutes, 19 Aug. 1930 (TGWU papers, MSS 126/T&G/1/1/8).

[6] MFGB, executive committee, 12 Mar. 1931 (South Wales Coalfield Archive, South Wales Miners' Federation papers); TUC, economic committee, 14 May 1931 (TUC papers); general secretary's report, TGWU executive minutes, 19 May 1931 (TGWU papers, MSS 126/T&G/1/1/9).

[7] TUC general council minutes, 12 June 1931 (TUC papers); Glasgow BLP meeting, 17 June 1931 (Glasgow TCBLP papers).

[8] *Daily Herald*, 3 Aug. 1931; Beatrice Webb diary, 4 Aug. 1931 (Passfield papers).

[9] Snowden to Samuel, 5 Aug. 1931 (Samuel papers, A/78).

committee had been allowed to exaggerate the situation for domestic consumption regardless of the European financial crisis. Foreigners were certainly worried; between 4 and 11 August, £21,000,000 was spent by the Bank in supporting sterling against the franc.[10] The Bank's acting governor, Sir Ernest Harvey, and the clearing banks warned Snowden that rapid action must be taken to balance the budget; and he in turn informed MacDonald, holidaying in Scotland, that action must be taken before the first scheduled meeting of the CEC on 25 August. In particular, with unemployment approaching three million and possibly reaching four million in 1932, steps must be taken to reform the unemployment insurance fund. They were 'perilously near' to 'chaos'. MacDonald, alarmed, returned to London, to be told by Harvey, Sir Edward Peacock (a director of the Bank), and Reginald McKenna (chairman of the Midland Bank) that action must be taken in the next few days. Meetings of the CEC were called for 12, 13, and 17 August. Hoping to increase the pressure on the Government to act, the bankers asked—and were granted—permission to see the Opposition leaders.[11]

On 12 August Samuel, acting as Liberal leader in Lloyd George's absence, saw Harvey and confirmed the Liberals' desire for public economy, adding that his party would co-operate in 'any national effort' to restore confidence. The next morning Samuel saw MacDonald, who told him that although the budget would be £170,000,000 rather than £120,000 in deficit, it would be balanced, mainly through economies. Borrowing for the unemployment insurance fund would cease. Doubtless many trade unionists would have been interested to hear the leader of their party add that the fund 'must be put on a self-supporting basis—or very nearly so'. There would be no emergency tariff. MacDonald was committing his Cabinet even before the CEC had completed its deliberations. Samuel, at any rate, was happy, and promised Liberal support for such a programme.[12] The next day Baldwin and Chamberlain did the rounds, seeing City contacts, MacDonald and Snowden, and the bankers. Snowden said

[10] R. S. Sayers, *The Bank of England, 1891–1944* (3 vols.; Cambridge, 1976), ii. 394–5; for the credits being intended as symbolic, see Henderson's comments to Dalton, Dalton diary, 20 Aug. 1931 (Dalton papers); Marquand, *MacDonald*, 612.

[11] Ibid. 612–13.

[12] MacDonald diary, 11 Aug. 1931 (MacDonald papers, PRO 30/69/1753); Chamberlain to Cunliffe-Lister, 15 Aug. 1931 (Churchill College, Swinton papers, SWIN 174/2/1, ff. 11–12); Samuel, memorandum, 13 Aug. 1931 (Samuel papers, A/78, f. 13–16).

he was confident of saving the £96,500,000 proposed by May, a point on which he gave Chamberlain a categorical assurance. Chamberlain, feeling the Conservatives' biggest difficulty would be in approving new taxation, asked for details before their next meeting.[13]

At this stage, then, things looked fairly straightforward. Chamberlain expected big economies and extensive reform of unemployment insurance, with 'equality of sacrifice' demonstrated by a special tax on the investment income of the rentier. The crisis, while certainly not over, seemed to Chamberlain to be under control. He expected the Cabinet to 'face the music', and thus the Conservatives' duty was 'plain'—to 'give the assurance [of support] and hope that [they would] not as a party suffer from it'. Far from hoping for a National Government, Chamberlain was looking forward to the prospect of Labour carrying the cuts and ridding his party of what he considered 'the unpopularity of economy'. At the next election, the Conservatives would be able to 'concentrate on tariffs and Imp[erial] Preference as the restorers of prosperity', which would be more attractive.[14] Chamberlain, then, was in no way trying to obscure his party's protectionism. He saw it as a vote-winner. As for economy, many Tories would not have agreed with him as to its unpopularity with the voters. Had not the party been fighting a vigorous retrenchment campaign for most of the year? Baldwin returned to holiday in France, expecting Labour to get 'a lot of the dirt cleared up', and Chamberlain and Hoare were left as the chief Conservative negotiators.[15] This also meant that Baldwin would be able to avoid committing himself to anything for a while.

II

The CEC met on 12, 13, 17, and 18 August.[16] No official record was kept, but the outline can be reconstructed. At its first meeting

[13] Neville to Sir Austen Chamberlain, 14 Aug. 1931 (Chamberlain papers, AC 39/3/26).

[14] Neville to Hilda Chamberlain, 16 Aug. 1931 (Chamberlain papers, NC 18/1/752).

[15] Baldwin to Chamberlain, 15 Aug. 1931, quoted in Middlemas and Barnes, *Baldwin*, 621.

[16] This paragraph is based largely on 'Summary of the Proceedings of the Cabinet Sub-committee on Economy' (also known as the 'Graham memorandum'), enclosed with Greenwood to Morrison, 25 Sept. 1931 (Nuffield College, Morrison papers, E/16). Although doubt has been cast previously on the veracity of this report, there is no inconsistency in matters of fact with the only other firsthand account, MacDonald's

Snowden tried to increase the pressure by revealing that the deficit would be nearer £180,000,000 than May's £120,000,000. He and MacDonald added, to the surprise of Henderson and Graham, that they had already consulted the Opposition leaders. The Chancellor pressed for the full May cuts of £96,500,000, but was defeated when the benefit cut was deleted. In addition, there were no details decided on how £23,000,000 was to be saved on transitional benefit, a problem which was to chase the Government to its grave. Then on 17 August Henderson questioned the committee's whole approach, arguing that they should have talked about revenue first, to reduce the economies to a minimum. But apart from a few general comments, Snowden would say little about new taxation, partly because he wanted to concentrate on economy, but also because he feared Thomas would use the information for speculation—a situation which did Thomas, Snowden, and especially MacDonald little credit.[17] At the final meeting on 18 August, Thomas proposed a 10 per cent revenue tariff which, on the value of imports in 1930 (£1,043,975,261) would have produced a considerable amount. At first only he supported it, but when presented as an alternative to a benefit cut, only Snowden opposed it. Loath to force his resignation, and believing it might be possible to get by without either option, the majority left a final decision to the full Cabinet. Snowden also discouraged ideas of an early debt conversion operation—clearly, he was keeping the pressure on.

The report of the CEC, as presented to the full Cabinet on 19 August, anticipated a budget deficit of £170,000,000, to offset which revenue would be increased by £88,500,000 and expenditure reduced by £78,500,000. Of the revenue, £62,000,000 would come from direct, and £26,500,000 from indirect, taxation. The economies were very much in line with the May report, except for education (£11,400,000 instead of £13,600,000) and unemployment insurance (£48,500,000 instead of £66,500,000, the effect of deleting the 20 per cent cut in benefit). The £48,500,000 saved on unemployment insurance comprised £20,000,000 from transitional benefit; savings under the 'anomalies' act of £3,000,000; the reduction of entitlement to 26 weeks, yielding £8,000,000; the increase of contributions, yielding £15,000,000; and Henderson's pet scheme of the 'premium',

diary. See R. Bassett, *Nineteen-Thirty-One: Political Crisis* (London, 1958), 65–6, 69, and H. Berkeley, *The Myth That Will Not Die* (London, 1978), 41–2. For import figures, see *Statistical Abstract for the United Kingdom*, 82 (Cmd. 5903; London, 1939), 372.

[17] Dalton diary, 29 Sept. 1931 (Dalton papers).

whereby unemployed workers would lose a shilling a week of their benefit as their contribution to the fund.[18]

After the fall of the Government, there was controversy over this report, Graham and Henderson claiming it had not comprised recommendations, merely suggestions.[19] This argument has been criticized; yet they could not record their dissent in the non-existent committee minutes, and would hardly have added to their reputations by spiking the Cabinet's discussions of the report at the outset. Despite misgivings, they seem to have decided to let the full Cabinet have a free run.[20]

On 19 August the Cabinet discussed the report from 11 a.m. until 10.30 p.m., (with two short breaks), and made, ultimately, a number of decisions.[21] On the revenue side, it approved additional taxation. Fifteen ministers supported the revenue tariff in preference to a benefit cut: five, including Henderson, were even prepared to impose a tariff on food. However, six—Snowden and Alexander, who would have been serious losses, had they resigned, and Passfield, Parmoor, William Wedgwood Benn (India), and H. B. Lees-Smith (Education), who would not—opposed any interference with free trade.[22] The Chancellor was especially obdurate, demanding later that the vote be rescinded, and adding that he could not stay in a Cabinet where fifteen were in favour of a tariff. He was especially bitter about Graham, his long-time acolyte: the accusations surrounding this vote were to help to haunt Graham into an early grave within six months.[23] Given that opposition, the tariff issue was allowed again to lapse. On economies, the Cabinet endorsed rejection of a cut in the standard rate of benefit, accepted the £28,500,000 savings on unemployment insurance, but refused to transfer responsibility for transitional benefit to over-burdened local authorities. Therefore a Cabinet committee to find an alternative way of saving £20,000,000 under this head was set up, comprising Graham, Bondfield, Arthur Greenwood (Minister of

[18] 'Report of the Cabinet Committee on the Report of the Committee on National Expenditure' (CAB 27/454, CP 203(31)).

[19] Graham memorandum (Morrison papers, E/16).

[20] See e.g. Bassett, *Nineteen Thirty-One*, 70–1; Berkeley, *Myth*, 47–8; Skidelsky, *Politicians and the Slump*, 360–2, 375.

[21] Cabinet conclusions, 19 Aug. 1931 (CAB 23/67/41(31)).

[22] For 15 in favour, and 5 in favour of tariffs on all imports, see MacDonald diary, 19 Aug. 1931 (MacDonald papers, PRO 30/69/1753); for Henderson, see Sankey diary, 19 Aug. 1931 (Sankey papers, MSS Eng. hist. e. 285); for the names of the free traders, see Beatrice Webb diary, 22 Aug. 1931, 4 a.m. entry (Passfield papers).

[23] Dalton diary, 27 Aug. 1931 (Dalton papers).

Health), and Thomas Johnston (Lord Privy Seal), to report to MacDonald at noon the following day. There was stickiness from Greenwood, Johnston, and Lansbury about the cuts.[24] But Lees-Smith and the Scottish Secretary, William Adamson, who raised difficulties regarding the proposed cut in teachers' pay, were told that no concession could be made. The remainder of the economies were approved without recorded dissent. But it had not been an easy meeting, and it was difficult to see how the Cabinet committee could secure quickly a scheme to save £20,000,000 on transitional benefit. Yet without it, the economies would total less than £60,000,000, or just over half of what the Conservatives were demanding.

III

On the morning of 20 August, MacDonald and Snowden met Chamberlain, Hoare, Samuel, and Maclean.[25] The Chancellor put forward the £78,000,000 of economies proposed by the CEC, rather than the £56,000,000 agreed by the Cabinet the previous day. He has been criticized for this,[26] but in theory the Cabinet still aimed at the higher figure, having appointed the committee on transitional benefit. But Snowden advanced even the £78,000,000 without conviction. To stiffen the Opposition leaders' resolve, he mentioned that the budget deficit would be £170,000,000, and Chamberlain was not slow to rise to the bait, condemning the £78,000,000 scheme as inadequate, stressing that it would be 'wrong' to produce a lower total than May, and arguing that the benefit cut was the key to the whole scheme. Samuel concurred. MacDonald and Snowden appeared to agree, the latter adding that benefits had risen in real terms by 36 per cent since 1924. Again, he was goading the Opposition in order to increase his own leverage in Cabinet, and also—in ruling out Samuel's suggestion of borrowing to meet the sinking fund obligation—keeping their eyes firmly on economy. Ironically, the Tories felt that armed services cuts had gone too far, while the Liberals wanted a cut of 15 instead of 20 per cent in teachers' salaries.

Attempts were being made, meanwhile, to square the Labour

[24] Ibid.

[25] Samuel, 'The Course of Events August 20th–23rd, 1931' 23 Aug. 1931 (Samuel papers, A/78, ff. 20–7); Viscount Templewood [Hoare], *Nine Troubled Years* (London, 1954), 17; Neville Chamberlain diary, 22 Aug. 1931 (Chamberlain papers, NC 2/22).

[26] See e.g. C. L. Mowat, *Britain between the Wars, 1918–1940* (London, 1955), 388.

movement. That morning the consultative committee of the PLP was briefed by Henderson, Graham, Thomas, and MacDonald. Henderson thought the committee's attitude 'very reasonable' and expected no problems, which suggested he felt the PLP as a whole could be talked round, provided the economies were not too severe. Also, at this stage the Cabinet decision was that there would be no cut in the standard rate of unemployment benefit.[27]

More troublesome at this stage was the attitude of the trade unions. That afternoon the party's NEC and the TUC general council, at the Government's behest (and after much pressure from Henderson) met to hear a statement from MacDonald. The meeting was a disaster for the Government. The trade unionists' pleasure at being consulted soon turned to anger as they were treated with little short of contempt by MacDonald, whom Henderson had hoped would make a 'frank' statement.[28] It was far from that; his main point seemed to be that he could divulge no figures because of the danger of leaks. Not only was the integrity of the general council and the NEC insulted; so was their intelligence, as MacDonald spoke with the utmost vacuity, saying, in one memorable passage, that '[i]f the banking situation was allowed to go on it was going to become a matter for the working classes unless they could stop the movements that were going on'. Any stock of goodwill upon which the Government might have been able to draw was now exhausted. Why, asked Citrine, had they been invited to the meeting to be told 'no more than had already appeared in the leading articles of many papers'? Without more specific information, the general council would have to reserve its judgement. This forced a reluctant Snowden—who believed the unions had no right to be consulted—to speak. First, he said that no final decisions had been reached, but they had decided on increased unemployment insurance contributions and the restriction of benefit to 26 weeks. They had not cut benefit, though. He then detailed the other cuts, adding a few words about new taxation—though refusing to be specific—and the need for equality of sacrifice. Confused questioning followed: A. J. Cook, secretary of the MFGB, shouted that they were being 'stampeded'; Susan Lawrence, an NEC member, asked whether the unemployed were to be 'thrown onto the Poor Law'. This was ominous, coming from a junior health minister; equally ominously,

[27] Cabinet conclusions, 20 Aug. 1931 (CAB 23/67/42(31)).

[28] Lord Citrine, *Men and Work: An Autobiography* (London, 1964), 281; Henderson to J. S. Middleton, 14 Aug. 1931 (Labour Party papers, LP/PRO/31/2).

there was no reply. Then, to cap a dismal afternoon, Bevin, who even before the meeting had been predicting the Government's early demise, attacked MacDonald and the Cabinet generally for dramatizing the situation. The two committees then went their separate ways.[29]

After a short meeting, at which Henderson—who confessed to feeling 'a double loyalty . . . loyalty to my Cabinet colleagues & loyalty to the Movement outside'—and Clynes made statements, the NEC agreed to leave matters to its representatives in the Cabinet.[30] The general council, however, was angry, and in 'an animated discussion', no one spoke in favour of the Cabinet's proposals.[31] They ruled out 'any new burdens on the unemployed' at all. The reductions in the pay of government employees, and in provision for the road fund and unemployment grants committee, were also rejected. The council did not simply throw out the Government's proposals, however. It suggested the taxation of fixed interest-bearing securities, reduction of the war debt burden, and suspension of the sinking fund.[32] There was a lengthy discussion of a revenue tariff, but although Citrine pushed hard for its inclusion, Bevin for one was more cautious, and it was referred to congress, due to meet in eighteen days' time.[33] With only three dissentients, in a meeting of twenty-six, it was decided to put these views before the CEC.

Meanwhile, the Cabinet had also been meeting. Snowden suffered another set-back when the transitional benefit committee revealed its findings. Aiming now at economies of £28,000,000 it had dismissed the 'premium' as 'impracticable', a view endorsed by the Cabinet despite Henderson's 'vigorous' objections. It suggested the introduction of a 'needs test' for transitional benefit, to save £5,000,000 a year, and an additional insurance contribution of 2d per week from the worker, making his or her contribution a shilling a week in all. This would bring in a further £4,000,000. But this left a shortfall of over

[29] Dalton diary, 20 Aug. 1931 (Dalton papers); minutes of joint meeting of NEC and TUC general council, 20 Aug. 1931 (Labour Party papers, LP/PRO/31/3–4); Snowden, *Autobiography*, ii. 940–1; general secretary's report, TGWU executive minutes, 17 Aug. 1931 (TGWU papers, MSS 126/T&G/1/1/9).

[30] Dalton diary, 20 Aug. 1931 (Dalton papers).

[31] Citrine, *Men and Work*, 284.

[32] TUC general council minutes, 20 Aug. 1931 (TUC papers).

[33] Ibid.; Citrine, *Men and Work*, 284; Citrine, 'Note on "Ernest Bevin" by Francis Williams', 7 Nov. 1952, and 'Bevin's Note to me on Revenue Tariff at Meeting with Lab. Gov. Aug. 1931' (Citrine papers, 7/4).

£19,000,000. Snowden made a strong plea for sterner action, saying benefits were over 30 per cent higher than in 1924, when the first Labour administration, at a time of handsome budget surpluses, had accepted them as adequate. No decision was reached before the CEC met a deputation of five from the general council, including Bevin, Citrine, and Hayday.[34]

That meeting was the final disaster in a disastrous day for the Government. Citrine put forward the council's views; and Bevin added a more general point which showed that he, at any rate, was irreconcilable, saying the council was opposed to further deflation. Snowden replied that their attitude was 'quite comprehensible', but this was an emergency, and he summed up his own attitude by saying that 'if sterling went the whole industrial financial structure would collapse, and there would be no comparison between the present depression and the chaos and ruin that would face us in that event. There would be', he went on, 'millions more unemployed, and complete industrial collapse.' This view was not going to be affected by Citrine's concluding comment that 'the Council were not convinced that the situation was quite so desperate as was alleged,' there being 'enormous resources in the country', and MacDonald noted subsequently that the unions' attitude was 'practically a declaration of war'.[35] The TUC had not been squared; for Snowden, its views were based on 'a pre-crisis mentality'.[36]

IV

'A pre-crisis mentality'—only economies would do. As Harvey told MacDonald the next day, '[i]n no other way could foreign confidence be restored'.[37] But in fact, certain of the alternative proposals floated were rather more respectable than has sometimes been realized. At the most fundamental level, few questioned that the gold standard should be maintained. Even the Macmillan report on finance and industry (July 1931), which saw the return to gold at par in 1925 as a mistake,

[34] Cabinet conclusions, 20 Aug. 1931 (CAB 23/67/42(31)); for Henderson and the 'premium', see 'Note by the Deputy Secretary', 26 Aug. 1931, in Cabinet conclusions, 21 Aug. 1931 (CAB 23/67/43(31)).

[35] Minutes of meeting of general council subcommittees and Cabinet subcommittee, 20 Aug. 1931 (Churchill College, Bevin papers, BEVN II 7/8); MacDonald diary, 21 Aug. 1931 (MacDonald papers, PRO 30/69/1753).

[36] Cabinet conclusions, 21 Aug. 1931 (CAB 23/67/43(31)); cf. Snowden, *Autobiography*, ii. 42–3.

[37] Cabinet conclusions, 21 Aug. 1931 (CAB 23/67/43(31)).

felt the error could not be rectified by leaving gold now. Keynes wrote on 5 August that Britain should leave before it was forced off, but he was very much a maverick figure.[38] That it would be 'a dangerous leap in the dark' was a view held by members of all major parties.[39] And to orthodox economists, it would almost certainly lead, given the unbalanced budget, to unprecedented economic difficulties and distress, even to the extent of Britain being unable to pay for vital food imports. In a way, the policy was mistaken, as the stability of sterling after the departure from gold in September was to demonstrate. But the point was that, in August, and under a Labour Government deeply distrusted by the international financial community, hardly anyone could see how leaving gold, the symbol of stability, could help Britain, whereas many believed they could see how it could be seriously damaging. At its most basic, it was a risk no one in authority thought worth taking.

Leaving aside the somewhat vague demands of Labourites for higher taxation of the rich, and the calls of ultra-protectionist Tories like Amery for the immediate imposition of protective tariffs, five specific expedients emerged during the crisis as alternatives to or alleviations of the drastic economies proposed by Snowden *et al.* First, there was the proposal to suspend the sinking fund. This was advocated by Keynes as well as Samuel; Harvey, when discussing the possibilities of a loan for the Government on 22 August, had no compunction about telling the governor of the FRB that this course would be followed.[40] Secondly, taxation of fixed interest-bearing securities was somewhat less depraved than was generally admitted in polite society. It had been favoured by an EAC economists' report of October 1930 to compensate for wage cuts; Walter Layton, the Liberal editor of the *Economist*, favoured it; while on 14 August Neville Chamberlain expected it with equanimity. But it was dismissed by the Treasury as impracticable, and so excluded from Snowden's *Weltanschauung*, on 17 August.[41] Thirdly, the 'mobilization' of foreign

[38] *Economist*, 18 July 1931; Keynes to MacDonald, 5 Aug. 1931, quoted in S. Howson and D. Winch, *The Economic Advisory Council, 1930–1939: A Study in Economic Advice during Depression and Recovery* (London, 1979), 89.

[39] F. W. Pethick-Lawrence, *Fate Has Been Kind* (London, n.d. [1943]), 164.

[40] B. C. Malament, 'Philip Snowden and the Cabinet Deliberations of August 1931', *Bulletin of the Society for the Study of Labour History*, 41 (1980), 33.

[41] Howson and Winch, *Economic Advisory Council*, 195; Layton to Snowden, 11 Aug. 1931 (Trinity College, Cambridge, Layton papers, Box 87); Neville to Sir Austen Chamberlain, 14 Aug. 1931 (Chamberlain papers, AC 39/3/26); memorandum, 17 Aug. 1931 (Treasury papers, T 171/288).

investments held by British nationals (not part of the TUC proposals of 20 August, though included in the Labour joint manifesto a week later) was favoured by Layton (as a last resort) and by Snowden's number two at the Treasury, F. W. Pethick-Lawrence. The controller of finance and supply services at the Treasury, Sir Richard Hopkins, also saw 'nothing impracticable about it', and even offered to explain its merits to Snowden.[42] Fourthly, war debt conversion had been favoured widely for some time. To continue paying interest at 5 per cent when bank rate had been below that figure since February 1930, and at a time of falling prices, was extravagant; and Snowden had been keen to push through a conversion scheme. But he felt that a forced conversion at a time when Britain's budgetary practices were already under close scrutiny would adversely affect confidence, and he ignored advice to attempt a voluntary conversion.[43] Finally, the idea of a revenue tariff was neither new nor, to anyone except staunch free traders like Snowden and Alexander, disreputable. Even many Liberals were coming to view it favourably. Snowden was the rock against which the proposal broke; in the crisis he could not be forced out without adverse effects on confidence, but the resultant loss in potential revenue was massive. The proposals might not have been able to pass through Parliament, though, given free-trade opposition and the probable hostility of Conservatives who wanted a protective, rather than a revenue, tariff.

There was no shortage, then, of ideas as to alternative expedients with which to balance the budget, and the general council did a service in advancing a few of them. However, where the council broke ranks with almost everyone outside the Labour movement—except Keynes, Amery, and Beaverbrook—was in its refusal to accept any economies.[44] Hopkins, for example, would have viewed with horror the use of

[42] Layton to Snowden, 11 Aug. 1931 (Layton papers, Box 87); Pethick-Lawrence, *Fate Has Been Kind*, 164; cf. Pethick-Lawrence to Wedgwood Benn, 4 Feb. 1935 (House of Lords Record Office, Stansgate papers, ST 95, ff. 6–7); Pethick-Lawrence to Snowden, undated draft copy (Trinity College, Cambridge, Pethick-Lawrence papers, P-L 5/41).

[43] Snowden, *Autobiography*, ii. 927–8; Layton to Snowden, 11 Aug. 1931 (Layton papers, Box 87); Pethick-Lawrence to Snowden, undated draft copy (Pethick-Lawrence papers, P-L 5/41).

[44] Keynes in *New Statesman*, 15 Aug. 1931, favoured suspension of the sinking fund, imposition of a revenue tariff, and continuation of borrowing for unemployment insurance; for Beaverbrook and Amery, see Beaverbrook to Amery, 11 Sept. 1931, and Amery to Beaverbrook, 26 Aug., 4 Sept. 1931 (House of Lords Record Office, Beaverbrook papers, C/6).

foreign investments in order to maintain current levels of public expenditure, rather than to bolster sterling pending budgetary readjustments. It has also to be doubted whether, given the panic induced by the economy campaign and the May report, measures on any lines other than those of drastic economy could have restored confidence. But MacDonald and Snowden were probably too eager to stick to the line of maximum economies plus marginal increases in existing forms of taxation. They were, of course, in the midst of a serious crisis, and feared touching off a catastrophe. Even so, when after the meeting with the general council deputation Henderson proposed balancing the budget on the basis of the £56,000,000 economies already agreed, plus suspension of the sinking fund and the imposition of a revenue tariff, it hardly merited MacDonald's scorn: it was worth up to £200,000,000 a year.[45] The premier may well have been correct, though, in believing that by this stage only heavy cuts, including a reduction in unemployment benefit, could satisfy the Opposition parties and the bankers, and restore confidence in sterling. For confidence, like all human emotions, is produced less by convincing intellectual arguments than by the satisfaction of perceived needs, however irrational. The perceived need in financial circles was a cut in public expenditure, and especially spending on unemployment insurance; and that made things difficult for MacDonald, who still hoped to be able to save his Government.

V

On the morning of Friday 21 August the Prime Minister saw Harvey, who told him that cuts of £56,000,000 were insufficient. At least half the deficit must be met by economies, especially in unemployment insurance; action must be taken immediately.[46] At the five-hour Cabinet meeting which followed, MacDonald tried to use these views to prise more economies out of his colleagues. Cutting the standard rate of unemployment benefit was discussed. Eleven ministers were ready to accept a 10 per cent cut, and seven a 5 per cent reduction, while three—Greenwood, Johnston, and Lansbury—refused to vote.[47]

[45] MacDonald diary, 21 Aug. 1931 (MacDonald papers, PRO 30/69/1753). The £200,000,000 would have comprised £50,000,000 from the sinking fund; £56,000,000 of economies; and around £100,000,000 by a 10 per cent revenue on all imports (1930 figure).

[46] Cabinet conclusions, 21 Aug. 1931 (CAB 23/67/43(31)).

[47] Ibid.; Sankey diary, 20 Aug. 1931 (from internal evidence, relates to Cabinet meeting of 21 Aug.) (Sankey papers, MSS Eng. hist. e. 285).

The 5 per cent proposal was seen as inadequate to meet the demands for economy, and its proponents preferred no cut at all to the 10 per cent; the matter lapsed. The Cabinet then endorsed the introduction of a needs test for transitional benefit and the extra increase of 2d per week in the employee's insurance contribution, and reiterated its support for the £56,000,000 package agreed two days earlier. MacDonald agreed to put suspension of the sinking fund to the Opposition leaders, although Snowden argued that this (and further borrowing) would be impracticable without a larger economy package. Henderson and others then tried to pressurize the Chancellor by saying they would only accept the withdrawal of the revenue tariff proposal if he would rule out further economies on unemployment insurance, but after an outburst from Snowden, MacDonald was able to thwart the manœuvre. Finally, it was agreed that MacDonald should put the £56,000,000 package, and the proposal to suspend the sinking fund, to the Opposition leaders.[48] The majority of the Cabinet seems to have felt that it had succeeded in formulating a reasonably satisfactory programme, and that its work was now complete. They probably believed that the Opposition leaders had been bluffing them into proposing larger economies; their bluff had been called. The arrangements for passing the necessary legislation were discussed: most ministers, including Henderson, expected to place the £56,000,000 programme before Parliament when it met.[49]

MacDonald and Snowden were a good deal less sanguine, especially after the bankers told them that the £56,000,000 programme would probably make matters worse, especially because of the lack of drastic action on unemployment insurance. This was vitally important, because the Bank could only hold out for four more days, and needed a short-term credit almost immediately. Even so, MacDonald urged Harvey to approach the FRB on the basis of the £56,000,000 package.[50] With the deputy governor's warnings ringing in their ears, MacDonald and Snowden met the Opposition leaders: Chamberlain, who wanted economies of around £100,000,000, and Samuel, who was ready to accept cuts of £78,000,000. When MacDonald and Snowden

[48] Cabinet conclusions, 21 Aug. 1931 (CAB 23/67/43(31)); Dalton diary, 27 Aug. 1931 (Dalton papers).

[49] Memorandum of conversation between Lords Reading and Tyrell, the latter reporting Henderson's views, 7 Oct. 1931 (Reading papers, MSS Eur. F118/131).

[50] Cabinet conclusions, 22 Aug. 1931, 9.30 a.m. meeting (CAB 23/67/44(31)); P. Williamson, 'A "Bankers' Ramp"? Financiers and the British Political Crisis of August 1931', *English Historical Review*, 99 (1984), 799.

put forward the £56,000,000 package (with little conviction), therefore, the Opposition leaders were, to say the least, disgruntled. When asked what would happen if it failed to restore confidence, the Chancellor replied 'the deluge'; when Hoare protested, MacDonald retorted 'Well, are you prepared to join the Board of Directors?' a throwaway put-down rather than an invitation to join a National Government. Embarrassed, Hoare gave an evasive reply, and the Opposition leaders then withdrew to consult their colleagues.[51] When they returned, MacDonald was alone. They felt confident that they could prise further economies out of the Government, given their knowledge of the real views of premier and Chancellor. Thus they told him that they would defeat the £56,000,000 package in Parliament; that the crash would have come before then; and that it was his duty to find a solution. Chamberlain added that the Conservatives were 'ready to give him any support in [their] power for that purpose either with his present or in a reconstructed Government': they would serve under MacDonald if necessary. No one mentioned a National administration specifically, though Chamberlain felt that 'it was fairly clear that we were not excluding such an eventuality'. Much as he disliked the idea, Chamberlain was so impressed with the gravity of the crisis, and its potential to wreck his party's chances of victory at the next election, that if Labour could not be forced to pass the necessary legislation he was ready to accept a National Government. But MacDonald was still hoping to preserve the Labour Government, and called a Cabinet for the following morning, at which he planned to 'assert his own views, invite his colleagues to support him and tell those who would not [to] "go where they liked" '.[52] His final bolt-hole was closed when Samuel refused to support the £56,000,000 package independently of the Conservatives.[53] (Samuel was soon to have cause to regret that decision.) Now MacDonald was forced to try to assert a leadership over the Cabinet which he had shown all too rarely over the past two years.

It was not a particularly receptive Cabinet which greeted MacDonald and Snowden the following day: no one likes having their holidays

[51] Ida to Neville Chamberlain, 21 Aug. 1931 (Chamberlain papers, NC 18/2/745); Samuel memorandum, 23 Aug. 1931 (Samuel papers, A/78, ff. 23–5); Neville Chamberlain diary, 22 Aug. 1931 (Chamberlain papers, NC 2/22).

[52] Samuel memorandum, 23 Aug. 1931 (Samuel papers, A/78, ff. 23–5); Neville Chamberlain diary, 22 Aug. 1931 (Chamberlain papers, NC 2/22).

[53] MacDonald diary, 22 Aug. 1931 (MacDonald papers, PRO 30/69/1753).

interrupted, still less their return to them delayed. Still, the two men battled hard to secure further concessions from their somewhat bemused colleagues.[54] The premier opened by explaining the views of the bankers and Opposition leaders, especially with regard to the need for 'adequate' savings on unemployment insurance. He added that it was intended to give the Cabinet's 'final decision' to the Opposition leaders at noon. He then left Snowden to do the bulk of the fighting, along familiar lines. Alternative policies, like suspension of the sinking fund or the curtailment of block grants to local authorities, were derided: the budget must be balanced 'in an honest fashion'. The root of the problem 'from the international financial point of view would only be rectified by drastic treatment of the Unemployment Insurance figures'. The economy proposals had been whittled down, 'by decisions with which he personally was not in agreement', to an unacceptably low figure, and so 'the first question . . . was whether the cabinet would now review their findings . . . and add a further £25–30 millions of economies to the present figure of £56 millions gross'. In particular, only substantial savings in unemployment insurance could restore confidence. Snowden also bullied his colleagues: when the lone voice of Addison suggested that it might be better to leave the gold standard, 'Snowden was more insulting to him than anyone had ever been in his life before';[55] and he pointed out that the position of ministers would be 'very difficult' if they tried to oppose a succeeding Government which introduced the £56,000,000 package plus cuts in unemployment benefit, a statement which events were soon to justify. And again he stressed his genuinely held view of the issue at stake:

> So far as he was concerned, he had no doubt whatever, if he was compelled to choose between retaining the Labour Movement in its present form and reducing the standard of living of the workmen [*sic*] by 50%, which would be the effect of departing from the gold standard, where his duty would lie; and he felt confident that his views would be shared by every responsible Leader of the Party. . . . [T]he Chancellor outlined the appalling consequences to trade and industry and to all engaged therein of a collapse of sterling. The position could only be rectified by resolute facing of this Unemployment Insurance question.

Impressive, but ineffective: his colleagues had heard it before. Therefore only he and Thomas supported MacDonald's suggestion

[54] Cabinet conclusions, 22 Aug. 1931, 9.30 a.m. meeting (CAB 23/67/44(31)).
[55] Dalton diary, 3 Nov. 1931 (Dalton papers).

that the Opposition leaders be offered additional economies of £20,000,000 comprising a 10 per cent benefit cut and further unspecified savings of £7,750,000 on unemployment insurance. A stronger appeal from the Prime Minister, defining the alternatives as a benefit cut or a moratorium by Wednesday, gained agreement to ask the Opposition parties whether they would support such a proposal, on the understanding that the (uncommitted) Cabinet was only seeking information. Although the question of a National Government was raised, probably by Thomas, there was 'a general feeling' against the idea, Henderson and others 'hotly' rejecting it and Snowden stating firmly that 'the Cabinet as a whole would be unanimous against the formation of such a Government'.[56]

The prospects of getting the extra £20,000,000 of economies through the Cabinet were very slim, however. Henderson's mind had been made up by the Opposition leaders' insistence on heavier and what he saw as open-ended cuts; to him, the Conservatives were only trying to inflict the maximum damage on Labour before bringing the Government down, and in a very real sense putting party before country. Although he had been prepared, despite the general council, to put forward the £56,000,000 package, he realized that it would be 'impossible' to keep the unions in line on a package including the benefit cut.[57] How would the national interest be served by the resulting fragmentation of the Labour Party and the consequent unleashing of extremism, possibly led by the far left, 'class against class' Communist Party? That lunch-time, Henderson first attended a meeting of oppositional ministers in Lansbury's room.[58] Meanwhile Graham thought the City was 'bluffing' the Government, while Passfield felt tempted to let the Conservatives take over and 'stand the racket'.[59] The uneasy consensus which had existed after the previous day's meeting had been shattered by the attempt of MacDonald and Snowden, at the behest of the Opposition leaders and bankers, to bludgeon a Cabinet unused to strong leadership. To the unease felt by many at the prospect of making cuts at all, especially in the face of TUC opposition, had been added the real prospect of having to cut

[56] Ibid.; Beatrice Webb diary, 23 Aug. 1931 (Passfield papers).

[57] Henderson at TUC, 10 Sept. 1931, *Manchester Guardian*, 11 Sept. 1931; Beatrice Webb diary, 23 Aug. 1931 (Passfield papers); memorandum of conversation between Reading and Tyrell, 7 Oct. 1931 (Reading papers, MSS Eur. F118/131).

[58] MacDonald diary, 23 Aug. 1931 (MacDonald papers, PRO 3/69/1753); Blaxland, *Thomas*, 247–8.

[59] Beatrice Webb diary, 23 Aug. 1931 (Passfield papers).

benefits, which repelled them on humanitarian as well as political grounds.

MacDonald and Snowden, however, proceeded to meet the Opposition leaders. The premier told them that it was 'just possible' that he might carry a 10 per cent benefit cut by a majority, although resignations would probably follow. The Opposition leaders said that they privately favoured far larger economies, but that the situation was now so urgent that they would accept the proposals if the Government's financial advisers would.[60] The relieved Prime Minister then blundered. Chamberlain asked to what extent the Tories would be committed to supporting any figure of economies accepted by the bankers. MacDonald, hoping to keep him sweet, replied that 'agreement' only meant that the Conservatives would allow the Government to present its proposals to Parliament; they would be free to call for higher cuts by putting amendments. Some amendments might be fatal to the Government, but Labour would have to take the chance. No attempt was made to bind the Conservatives; they were given *carte blanche* to play politics against the proposals to their hearts' content. Henderson's fears were justified, as Chamberlain confirmed gleefully:

> I saw at once that [MacDonald] had played straight into our hands. For if the Govt. announced that it had resolved on cuts which included a reduction in Unempt. benefit (which was R. M.'s proposition) then the Labour Party was inevitably split and their sting would be drawn. While we, under his definition, would still be free to claim that the Economies were wholly inadequate and fight his proposed taxation to our hearts' content.[61]

That afternoon MacDonald reported the Oppositions' views to the Cabinet and said he felt sure the bankers would accept the proposals as adequate. Harvey was coming to Downing Street in less than half an hour, he added: could he submit the same proposals to the deputy governor, who would then submit them to New York? This attempt to bounce the Cabinet into accepting the £20,000,000 package failed, however, and it was merely agreed that MacDonald and Snowden should see Harvey on the same uncommitted basis as the Opposition leaders, and that Harvey should be permitted to discuss the matter with the FRB authorities.[62] Harvey and Peacock, however, doubted

[60] Samuel memorandum, 23 Aug. 1931 (Samuel papers, A/78, ff. 25–6).

[61] Neville to Annie Chamberlain, 23 Aug. 1931 (Chamberlain papers, NC 1/26/447).

[62] Cabinet conclusions, 22 Aug. 1931, 2.30 p.m. meeting (CAB 23/67/45(31)).

whether the programme would be sufficient to restore confidence; and Harrison, governor of the FRB, was not confident of being able to raise a loan among private financiers on such a basis (the FRB itself could not lend money to foreign governments). J. P. Morgan & Co. of New York, however, had agreed to convene a meeting for the following day to await an official request.[63] The Cabinet then agreed, by a majority, to approve an approach to New York, to meet next day at 7 p.m. to receive a report from MacDonald on their reply, and to decide finally on the 10 per cent benefit cut and the other economies totalling £20,000,000 in all. As MacDonald said, they must reach a final conclusion by the time trading opened on Monday morning.

Lansbury wrote later, with good reason, that regardless of the American bankers' reply, the Cabinet would have split up. Seven ministers—including, it may be surmised, Henderson, Greenwood, Johnston, and Lansbury himself—had voted against putting the question to New York, and were now almost certain to resign. Only if the bankers' reply was so unfavourable as to drive even MacDonald and Snowden into Opposition, could the ministers be held together. So Henderson—though not, perhaps, all his cohorts—wanted an unfavourable reply. Labour could then resign *en bloc* and regroup in Opposition, rather discredited but reasonably united.[64] The view that, if Labour left office, the unemployed would be left totally at the mercy of Conservatives and Liberals keen on swingeing economies, played little part in ministers' thinking. Tired, confused, uncomfortable, and not on top of the situation, they realized only that they could do little more than discredit themselves if they dabbled with further cuts, particularly in the dole, and especially without guarantees that the larger cuts would not ultimately be carried in any case. And there was also a feeling that if they refused to cut the dole, then it would not be cut. This was sheer folly.

Signs that the crisis was coming to a head were mounting outside the Cabinet room, too. That morning (22 August) King George V was called back from Balmoral, grumbling that 'there was no use shilly-shallying at a time like this'.[65] Meanwhile, on 20 August Chamberlain had summoned Baldwin to return, and the following day the leader

[63] Ibid.; Williamson, 'A "Bankers' Ramp"?', 800; Marquand, *MacDonald*, 631–2.

[64] Lansbury, 'The Cabinet Crisis of 1931', Sept./Oct. 1931 (Lansbury papers, 25/III/n); Dalton diary, 27 Aug. 1931; Cabinet conclusions, 22 Aug. 1931, 2.30 p.m. meeting (CAB 23/67/45(31)); Henderson at TUC, 10 Sept. 1931, *Manchester Guardian*, 11 Sept. 1931.

[65] H. Nicolson, *King George the Fifth: His Life and Reign* (London, 1952), 460.

was met in Paris by Davidson, who was under orders from Chamberlain to persuade Baldwin of the merits of a National Government. This proved only that Chamberlain wanted Baldwin—whose antipathy towards coalitions was a by-word—to rule out nothing in advance. Davidson met with only limited success, and on his return the leader repeatedly said that having destroyed one coalition (something of an exaggeration in itself), he did not wish to form another.[66] The whole position was very confused, Baldwin conjecturing whether he might be asked to form a Government or not; like everyone else, though, he realized that the gravity of the situation precluded a general election.[67] However reluctantly, he was keeping all other options open.

VI

The next morning, Sunday 23 August, the King arrived in London. At 10 a.m. he saw MacDonald, who said he might soon be forced to resign. The King was 'relieved' when told he would not be advised to send for Henderson; instead, MacDonald wanted him to see Baldwin and Samuel. George encouraged MacDonald, saying he would advise the Opposition leaders to support him and that he was 'the only person who could carry the country through'. The premier emerged from the meeting believing that the King wanted a National Government.[68] Sir Clive Wigram, the King's private secretary, then tried to contact Baldwin, but the latter was—possibly deliberately, given his continuing desire to avoid committing himself—incommunicado, talking with the editor of *The Times*, Geoffrey Dawson. Therefore the King saw Samuel, who in an amicable meeting offered Liberal support to anyone proposing the 'necessary' measures; preferably the Labour Government but, failing that, a National administration under MacDonald. The two things he did not want were a general election or—though he did not say this—a Conservative Government likely to interfere with free trade. The King was impressed with Samuel's views, but the

[66] Middlemas and Barnes, *Baldwin*, 622–5; J. C. C. Davidson, *Memoirs of a Conservative: J. C. C. Davidson's Memoirs and Papers, 1910–37*, ed. R. Rhodes James (London, 1969), 367; Templewood, *Nine Troubled Years*, 18.

[67] Baldwin to his wife, quoted in Middlemas and Barnes, *Baldwin*, 624.

[68] MacDonald diary, 23 Aug. 1931 (MacDonald papers, PRO 30/69/1753); Marquand, *MacDonald*, 630–1.

meeting, contrary to Samuel's belief, was not decisive; the idea of a National Government was not new to George, and he had already intended to press Samuel and Baldwin to support MacDonald. But the Liberal had at least said what George had wanted to hear.[69] Baldwin visited the palace that afternoon, to be told that after the expected fall of the Labour Government, the King would send for him. Both men thought this the most likely outcome, although the Conservative leader agreed, to the monarch's delight, to serve under MacDonald if requested. It had been a good day's work for George.[70]

That morning, MacDonald had communicated the Government's proposals to Morgan's New York partners with a promise that there would be no more borrowing for the unemployment insurance fund, and that in future the budget would be balanced. On this basis, he asked for a long-term loan, a short-term credit, or both, of £50,000,000; a similar sum was to be raised in Paris. Harvey would give the Americans no definite guidance as to whether the economies proposed would restore confidence, and this placed them in a dilemma. As Harrison put it, it was 'impossible' at such a distance to assess whether the proposals would suffice.[71]

By the time the cabinet met at 7 p.m. (2 p.m. New York time), therefore, no reply had been received. MacDonald, though, told his colleagues that he expected a favourable response, in which event the Opposition parties would support the Government's proposals. Discussion of 'the precise position regarding the Parliamentary situation' followed: it may be surmised that MacDonald's view was challenged, Henderson and others arguing that the Tories were simply allowing Labour to humiliate itself before turning it out and imposing even harsher terms on the unemployed. The premier was unable convincingly to counter this argument, and on this unpromising note, the meeting adjourned to await the reply from New York. When the meeting resumed at 9.10 p.m., MacDonald read out Harrison's reply. The latter stressed his response was provisional, but he assured MacDonald that the New York bankers would do their 'utmost' to meet the Government's wishes. A long-term loan was impossible, at least until Parliament had met, but a short-term credit would be 'far

[69] Samuel memorandum, 23 Aug. 1931 (Samuel papers, A/78); Beatrice Webb diary, 23 Aug. 1931 (Passfield papers).

[70] Neville to Annie Chamberlain, 23 Aug. 1931, reporting Baldwin (Chamberlain papers, NC 1/26/447); Nicolson, *King George the Fifth*, 461–2.

[71] Williamson, 'A "Bankers' Ramp"?', 801.

less difficult', and a definite answer could be given at the close of business the next day. He continued:

> Are we right in assuming that the programme under consideration will have the sincere approval of the Bank of England and the City generally and thus go a long way towards restoring internal confidence in Great Britain. Of course our ability to do anything depends on the response of public opinion in Great Britain to the Government's announcement of the programme.

This later gave rise to stories of a 'bankers' ramp', but it was not so discouraging as to prevent MacDonald trying to carry on. Therefore he made an impassioned plea for a united acceptance of the 10 per cent benefit cut. The conditions stipulated by Harrison were, he said, fulfilled: the Bank of England and Opposition parties both supported the revised package of economies. He 'most sincerely hoped' the Cabinet would accept the proposals, but as the loan was essential to alleviate the crisis, they must resign if they could not agree to take the necessary steps. He was 'strongly in favour' of the economy programme, he added, although it 'represented the extreme limit to which he was prepared to go'. If confidence was not restored, there would be a flight from the pound resulting in a fall of at least 20 per cent in all real incomes. The proposals would involve 'very great political difficulties' for Labour, but when the immediate crisis was over there would be the chance 'to give the Labour Party that full explanation of the circumstances which . . . could not be given at the moment'. Given the fact that earlier that day Snowden's own DLP had condemned all economies, such an attempt at elucidation might well have had a rough ride. For MacDonald the proposals were 'the negation of everything that the Labour Party stood for', but the only alternative was national ruin. He concluded by saying that any 'important' resignations must mean the Government's own departure from office.[72] Though it has often been said, it is worth reiterating for the record that MacDonald was not trying to destroy his own administration here.[73] His—understandable—fault had been, not in forcing the premature fall of the Government, but in continuing to prop up the body after 22 August when it had, in effect, died. He had already said that a decision must be made by the opening of business

[72] Cabinet conclusions, 23 Aug. 1931 (CAB 23/67/46(31)); Colne Valley DLP, executive committee 23 Aug. 1931 (Colne Valley DLP papers, on microfilm at West Yorkshire Archive Service, Kirklees).

[73] L. M. Weir, *The Tragedy of Ramsay MacDonald* (London, n.d. [1938]), 382; Mowat, *Britain between the Wars*, 392; Snowden, *Autobiography*, ii. 953.

on Monday, 24 August. It was late; the time for decision had come. The only course open was to ask each minister in turn whether he or she would accept the additional economies. A large minority of nine refused; and since it included Henderson, Graham, and, barring Morrison, the pick of the middle-ranking ministers, it was obvious that the Government must resign.[74] Ministers agreed to MacDonald's proposal that he should meet Baldwin and Samuel the next day, and placed their resignations in his hands. They expected MacDonald to resign with them.[75]

VII

The Labour Government had collapsed, and the remaining point at issue was the form its successor would take. It is worth pausing, though, to dispose of any lingering myths. The first is that Labour ministers were excessively partisan or personally ambitious, compared with the 'patriotic' Conservatives and Liberals. Certainly, party political considerations were not absent from ministers' calculations. But if they had been their sole preoccupations, they could have resigned far earlier and fought against the May report without having compromised themselves. They had all, often with misgivings, agreed to cuts of £56,000,000; they had dispersed on the evening of 21 August expecting to face Parliament with that package. The final straws were the unhelpful attitude of the Opposition parties and the proposal to cut the standard rate of benefit, especially as they had already ruled out the latter twice, on 19 and 21 August. For all sorts of reasons, ranging from the belief that it was the key to wage rates to basic humanitarianism, benefit was probably the most emotive issue for many Labourites. It would be excessive to condemn all this merely as manœuvring for party advantage. Also, the Conservatives and Liberals took party considerations into account. Chamberlain hoped to saddle Labour with what he saw as the unpopularity of economy;

[74] Despite conflicting reports, it seems the vote was 10:9 in favour of the cut, with MacDonald also favouring it and Parmoor, who would very possibly have opposed it, absent, probably through ill-health. As well as MacDonald, those in favour were: Snowden, Thomas, Sankey, Amulree (who all joined the National Government), Bondfield, Passfield, Morrison, Shaw, Lees-Smith, and Wedgwood Benn. Those against were: Henderson, Graham, Clynes, Lansbury, Alexander, Greenwood, Johnston, Addison, and Adamson.

[75] Cabinet conclusions, 23 Aug. 1931 (CA 23/67/46(31)); Webb, 'What Happened in 1931', 8; Snowden, *Autobiography*, ii. 950.

Samuel wanted to avoid a Tory Government for fear that it might interfere with free trade. In addition, the charge of personal ambition lacks hard evidence, and in some cases is patently absurd. For example Henderson had wanted the Government to remain in office because he believed it was the best hope for the success of the world disarmament conference, due to start in February 1932, and over which he was to preside. He had no desire to take the party leadership from MacDonald. Exhaustion, rather than ambition, accounts for the relief with which some ministers left office.[76]

Similarly, it was unreasonable to attribute the Government's fall to outside agencies. This was the explanation of many people at the time, but no historian would support such a view today. Doubtless there were bankers and trade-union leaders who rejoiced in Labour's departure from office, albeit for different reasons, but there was, as many historians have shown, no substance in charges of 'trade union dictation' or a 'bankers' ramp'.[77] The Government had asked the TUC and the bankers for advice. Both had given it, honestly and to the best of their ability. Some trade-union leaders did not mind obstructing MacDonald, given his failure to deliver so many of their demands over the past two years; but it is clear that the wider Labour movement would not have accepted the economies even if the general council had. There might have been a growth of grass-roots militancy, of shop stewards' movements outside the control of the unions' official leadership. The general council was not, therefore, being as bloody-minded as was believed by people who forgot that trade-union leaders were not merely 'actors' in the 'drama' of high politics. Similarly, Morgans were asked for a loan; were they expected to hand over the money regardless of the creditworthiness of their client, which was, after all, the issue at the root of the whole crisis of confidence? There was nothing unreasonable in asking for assurances that the proposals

[76] For Henderson's wanting a peerage, for reasons which suggested he had no desire for the leadership, see Dalton diary, 16 Apr. 1931 (Dalton papers); see also A. J. Thorpe, 'Arthur Henderson and the British Political Crisis of 1931', *Historical Journal*, 31 (1988), 117–39.

[77] For TUC dictation, see e.g. Hoare's letter to his constituents, *The Times*, 17 Sept. 1931; Snowden, 'Labour's Little Lenins', *Daily Mail*, 20 Oct. 1931; *Morning Post*, 9 Sept. 1931; *Parl. Deb.*, 5th ser., 256, col. 42, Churchill, 8 Sept. 1931. For the bankers' ramp, see Webb, 'What Happened in 1931', 8; *Daily Herald*, 25 Aug. 1931; Lansbury, 'The Cabinet Crisis of 1931' (Lansbury papers, 25/III/n, f. 16); speech by Addison to Swindon DLP, 26 Aug. 1931 (Bodleian Library, Addison papers, 99/55/11); A. V. Alexander, 'Resignation was Right: Choice of Governing or Accepting Outside Dictation', *Reynolds's Illustrated News*, 30 Aug. 1931.

advanced would, in fact, be enacted. The fault was with the Government, in putting itself in such a position. For Henderson, at any rate, the decisive moment had come, not at the joint meeting on 20 August, but with his realization of the Tories' splitting tactics, and the renewal of the proposal to cut unemployment benefit, two days later. Until then he and his colleagues had been willing, however reluctantly, to push the £56,000,000 package regardless of the general council. As for the bankers, two more points should be made. First, as Lansbury wrote, the Cabinet would have resigned regardless of the reply from New York; and secondly, some Labour ex-ministers and MPs, including Henderson and Johnston, either at the time or subsequently, dismissed the whole idea of a 'bankers' ramp', a view since confirmed by Philip Williamson, among others.[78]

VIII

After the Cabinet meeting, an agitated MacDonald went to Buckingham Palace. He told the King he had no alternative but to resign; however, George tried once again to steel his premier's resolve, telling him that 'he was the only man to lead the country through this crisis'. He hoped MacDonald would reconsider, for the Opposition parties would back him. MacDonald then requested a three-party conference, as he had been authorized to do by the Cabinet. He then returned to Downing Street, told his colleagues what he had done, arranged a Cabinet for noon the next day, and invited Baldwin, Chamberlain, Samuel, and Maclean round to be informed of the situation.[79]

That afternoon, MacDonald had decided that if the Government fell, he ought to sit as an independent MP giving general backing to a Conservative–Liberal administration.[80] This was the line he took with the Opposition leaders. There would be, he said, no point in his joining the new Government; he would be 'a ridiculous figure unable to command support' and would 'bring odium' on the administration as well as himself. Snowden agreed. Chamberlain then set out to change the premier's mind. He had been keen to see Labour implement the economies, both to demonstrate to those affected that

[78] Lansbury, 'The Cabinet Crisis of 1931' (Lansbury papers, 25/III/n, f. 16); *Parl. Deb.*, 5th ser., 256, col. 37, Henderson, 8 Sept. 1931; T. Johnston, *The Financiers and the Nation* (London, 1934), 193, and *Memories* (London, 1952), 108; Kenworthy, *Sailors*, 232–3.

[79] Sir Clive Wigram, quoted in Nicolson, *King George the Fifth*, 464.

[80] Marquand, *MacDonald*, 631.

they were not motivated by the Tories' class prejudices, and also to minimize 'irresponsible' Labour Opposition, which might further impair confidence. There would now be a Labour Opposition. But it would be defused to some extent if MacDonald was in the new Cabinet. Accordingly, Chamberlain wooed the premier, stressing how important it was that he should serve; Samuel spoke in similar terms. But it was unclear whether they had any effect. Snowden, present throughout, went to bed expecting a Baldwin-led Conservative or Conservative–Liberal Government to be formed. Baldwin himself said he approved of Chamberlain's comments, but felt there was no prospect of MacDonald's adherence; and the Tory leaders discussed with Samuel the position if MacDonald stayed out. Samuel showed that, like Chamberlain, he was not averse to seeking to further his party's interests during the national crisis. He pledged Liberal support for economies, but warned against introducing tariffs, tried to ascertain what offices Liberals could expect, and suggested that they should press on with the electoral reform bill. The general view, then, was that MacDonald would resign as premier, and would be very unlikely to serve under Baldwin, who expected to have to form a Government.[81]

Yet by noon the following day, MacDonald had agreed, not only to serve in, but to head, a National Government. This was, ostensibly, such a breathtaking turn-around that it has fuelled fallacious speculation that he had had a 'grand design' for such an outcome. This view was finally exploded some years ago by David Marquand, whose life of MacDonald was the first to be based on the latter's personal papers. Still less plausibly, Chamberlain has been seen as plotting for the formation of a National Government.[82] In fact, it was the attitude of the King which was decisive. George V was, in 1931, an old sixty-six, and had had an unhappy year punctuated by bereavements. In April he had been especially upset to hear of the revolution in Spain, and sympathized with the deposed king, Alfonso XIII. In July he had been advised by Wigram that a financial crisis might well necessitate the formation of a National Government.[83] Now, in the middle of his annual vacation, he was faced with a first-class political crisis. Like

[81] Neville Chamberlain diary, 23 Aug. 1931 (Chamberlain papers, NC 2/22): Snowden, *Autobiography*, ii. 950–1; Baldwin to his wife, 24 Aug. 1931, quoted in Middlemas and Barnes, *Baldwin*, 628.

[82] J. D. Fair, 'The Conservative Basis for the Formation of the National Government of 1931', *Journal of British Studies*, 19 (1980), 142–64.

[83] Nicolson, *King George the Fifth*, 452, 449.

most Conservatives, he was keen to see Labour, or at least some Labour ministers (and especially MacDonald, whom he liked personally), remain in office to prevent any serious polarization of society. Accordingly, when it became apparent that the Labour Government was likely to come to grief, he was eager to retain the premier. Twice on 23 August George had buoyed him up; at the palace conference the next morning, he set out to do so again.

Opening the meeting, the King told MacDonald, Baldwin, and Samuel that there must be no more delay. This was common property: already the deadline of that day's start of business had been missed. However, George also set the context of the discussion after MacDonald had said that he had the Cabinet's resignation 'in his pocket':

> [T]he King replied that he trusted there was no question of the Prime Minister's resignation: the leaders of the three Parties must get together and come to some arrangement. His Majesty hoped that the Prime Minister, with the colleagues who remained faithful to him, would help in the formation of a National Government, which the King was sure would be supported by the Conservatives and Liberals. The King assured the Prime Minister that, remaining at his post, his position and reputation would be much more enhanced than if he surrendered the government of the country at such a crisis.[84]

The King then withdrew, leaving the party politicians to draw up a statement. MacDonald's doubts were subdued; after an hour the communiqué (released that afternoon) was ready:

> The specific object for which the new Government is being formed is to deal with the national emergency that now exists. It will not be a Coalition Government in the usual sense of the term, but a Government of Cooperation for this one purpose. When that purpose is achieved the political parties will resume their respective positions.

Parliament, it concluded, would meet on 8 September to approve a supplementary budget and to enact economy legislation.[85]

MacDonald then reported back to the Labour Cabinet, stating that with a reluctance only overcome by the gravity of the financial situation he had agreed to form an emergency National Government. There would be no party political legislation, and at the general election 'which would follow the end of the emergency period', there would be

[84] Memorandum by Wigram, quoted in Nicolson, *King George the Fifth*, 465–6.
[85] *The Times*, 25 Aug. 1931.

'no "coupons", pacts or other arrangements'. The economy programme would not exceed the £56,000,000 plus the £20,000,000 from unemployment insurance, including the 10 per cent benefit cut. When pressed, MacDonald could give no more information about election dates. With a vote of thanks to the Prime Minister, the meeting broke up.[86] The second Labour Government was dead; there would not be a third until 1945.

It is unclear whether MacDonald asked for support, and seems more likely that sympathizers stayed behind to offer their backing. Ultimately, four members of the Cabinet followed him, rumours about Morrison, Shaw, and Wedgwood Benn notwithstanding.[87] Snowden did so unenthusiastically, motivated by political considerations which were stronger than his considerable antipathy towards MacDonald. Thomas also stayed on, motivated by political conviction, loyalty to MacDonald and to the King, and the fact that he could ill afford to lose Cabinet rank on financial grounds.[88] Sankey stayed on, partly out of loyalty to MacDonald and partly because of his involvement in the Indian round table conference.[89] Lord Amulree, Air Secretary, also remained in his post, although he was excluded from the new Cabinet.

At 4 p.m. MacDonald resigned as Labour Prime Minister, whereupon the King asked him to form a National Government; by the following day he had done so. The Cabinet was restricted to ten: MacDonald, Snowden, Thomas, and Sankey remained in their old jobs; Baldwin (Lord President of the Council), Chamberlain (Minister of Health), Hoare (Secretary of State for India), and Cunliffe-Lister (President of the Board of Trade) represented the Conservatives; and Samuel (Home Secretary) and Lord Reading (Foreign Secretary and leader of the Lords) represented the Liberals. There were some hiccups; for example, Sir Austen Chamberlain felt insulted at only getting the Admiralty, while Samuel's abortive offer of the War Office to Runciman was so inept that it worsened their relations even further.[90]

[86] Cabinet conclusions, 24 Aug. 1931 (CAB 23/67/47 (31)).

[87] For Wedgwood Benn, *Daily Mail*; for Shaw, *Manchester Guardian*; for Morrison, *Morning Post*, all 25 Aug. 1931. Morrison in fact came close to joining: see Marquand, *MacDonald*, 645, and B. Donoughue and G. W. Jones, *Herbert Morrison: Portrait of a Politician* (London, 1973), 164, 166–7.

[88] Dalton diary, 29 Sept. 1931 (Dalton papers); see also A. J. Thorpe, ' "I am in the Cabinet": J. H. Thomas's Decision to Join the National Government in 1931', *Historical Research* (forthcoming).

[89] Sankey diary, 24 Aug. 1931 (Sankey papers, MSS Eng. hist. e. 285).

[90] Telegrams and correspondence between Samuel and Runciman, 25 Aug., 3 Sept. 1931 (Runciman papers, WR 215).

Ultimately, however, the seeming chimera of a National Government attained reality.

Many difficulties awaited the new administration. The financial situation was grave. Parliament had still to be faced. It remained to be seen how well the much-vaunted experiment of a National Government would work in practice under crisis conditions. And would it be possible to determine when 'the immediate crisis' was over, and party politics could be resumed? On the other hand, Labour also had problems. The Cabinet had split on a very narrow issue, after two years of disappointment and failure. Would it be able to revitalize itself by opposing the new administration, or would it be discredited completely? The next six weeks were to answer these questions.

5

THE NATIONAL GOVERNMENT AND THE CALLING OF THE ELECTION

The specific object for which the new government is being formed is to deal with the national emergency that now exists. It will not be a Coalition Government in the usual accepted sense of the term, but a Government of co-operation for this one purpose. When that purpose is achieved the political parties will resume their respective positions.[1]

AN unequivocal statement—or so it seemed, when issued by MacDonald, Baldwin, and Samuel on 24 August 1931. Within six weeks, however, the Cabinet had decided to fight a general election under MacDonald, and was to win the most sweeping victory in modern British electoral history. The events of the weeks after 24 August were to determine the nature and scale, if not the fact, of that triumph.

I

The new Government, formed to save sterling by balancing the budget, was soon at work on its economy proposals, which, as incorporated in the National Economy Bill, stuck, more or less, to the Labour Government's £56,000,000 package and added the proceeds of a 10 per cent cut in unemployment benefit. Not only was this convenient; it also had a valuable political side-effect in that the entire Labour Cabinet had accepted the £56,000,000, and a majority the larger, package. Indeed, at £70,000,000 the economies totalled less than the £78,500,000 brought forward from the CEC, of which Henderson and Graham, now leading the Labour Opposition, had been members. Snowden's budget, introduced on 10 September, increased taxation by £82,000,000, and with provision for the sinking fund cut by £20,000,000, the Government could claim that it was balancing the national finances, especially as the measures were certain to obtain parliamentary approval. In a crucial vote of confidence on 8 September, it had a majority of 60, as shown in Table 5.1. This majority held for the rest of the session; but whether it would

[1] *The Times*, 25 Aug. 1931.

Table 5.1. *The Commons vote on 8 September 1931 (including tellers)*

	Government	Opposition	Paired	Absent Unpaired
Conservatives	243	–	14	3
Labour	12	242	14	12[a]
Liberal	53	–	–	5
New Party	–	4	–	–
Irish Nat.	–	2	–	–
Independent	3	3	–	–
TOTAL	311	251	28	20

[a] Of whom 5 definitely abstained.

Source: Bassett, *Nineteen Thirty-One*, 221. The twelve National Labour MPs were: MacDonald, Snowden, Thomas, Malcolm MacDonald, Sir William Jowitt, C. M. Aitchison, Sir Ernest Bennett, A. G. Church, G. M. Gillett, H. Knight, J. A. Lovat Fraser, and D. S. T. Rosbotham. R. D. Denman, S. F. Marham, and D. Hall Caine joined later. The five known abstainers were Denman, N. Angell, E. Picton-Turbervill, G. R. Strauss, and J. C. Wedgwood.

have done on, say, tariff proposals was extremely doubtful. Since trade policy was generally seen as needing attention, it was unlikely that the administration could last for very long.

Most Conservatives were pleased that the life of the new Government seemed strictly circumscribed. Cunliffe-Lister felt that it would be 'very unpleasant',[2] while William Ormsby-Gore, soon to become Postmaster-General, believed they could 'carry protection in the country at an early general election, if the position [were] not seriously compromised by coalition with Liberal Free Traders'.[3] Right-wingers were 'much disgruntled [to] have been jockeyed out of their certain victory'; the EIA, while supporting the new Government, also demanded its early demise and the introduction of protection, matters on which Croft, its chairman, was relieved to receive reassurances from Baldwin.[4] Party activists took a similar line: they would support the Government so long as its purpose was clear and its life short. The overwhelming Conservative feeling was an almost masochistic sense of

[2] Cunliffe-Lister to his wife, 24 Aug. 1931 (Swinton papers, SWIN III 313/1/5).
[3] Ormsby-Gore to Baldwin, 24 Aug. 1931 (Baldwin papers, vol. 44 (ii), f. 50).
[4] Lord Croft, *My Life of Strife* (London, n.d. [1948]), 192; Croft to Baldwin, 25 Aug. 1931, Baldwin to Croft, 26 Aug. 1931 (Croft papers, CRFT 1/3, ff. 9–10).

self-sacrifice in the national interest—in contrast to Labour's supposedly 'party first' attitude. Bath CA praised Baldwin's 'unselfish Statesmanship', 'courage and patriotic action', in, as Waterloo (Lancashire) CA put it, 'putting country before party'. There was little if any sense of delight that the party was back in office, but rather a feeling that party interests had been subordinated for a limited period, after which 'the discredited Socialists' would be roundly beaten and a Conservative administration installed.[5]

It was only a matter of time, then, before pressure for an early election began to mount. Although a party meeting on 28 August gave Baldwin a great ovation and a unanimous vote of confidence after he had promised an early election against Labour and for tariffs, Conservative MPs soon became impatient. They had been itching for an election, and confident of victory before the financial crisis; now they had the power to force events in that direction. When Parliament met on 8 September, both Amery and Churchill demanded an early election on party lines, the latter making, ironically, a strong plea for protective tariffs. Basically, he was signalling the end of his divisive stance on trade policy because he now saw party unity as vital in the fight against 'socialism'; also, he might have been trying to maximize his own support within the party should Baldwin come to grief. Next day, the EIA decided that pacts with the Liberals must depend on the Liberal candidate's acceptance of protection. The aim here was still to draw off the followers of Sir John Simon from the rest. But as September wore on, and it became increasingly obvious that Labour dreaded an election, more moderate Tories also came to like the idea. They, however, were ready to accept an appeal by the National Government, and some were even prepared to allow MacDonald to remain Prime Minister. Thus a *Times* editorial along those lines on 16 September resulted in 'a Conservative rally to the same view' at Westminster.[6] However, the presumption behind keeping MacDonald and Thomas was that they would accept tariffs, and Lord Stanhope wrote on 21 September that '[w]hatever the next Govt. call[ed] itself the key positions must be held by Tories'.[7]

[5] Bath CA, executive committee, 8 Sept. 1931 (Bath CA papers, minute book 1924–37, f. 208); Waterloo CA, council meeting, 4 Sept. 1931 (Crosby CA papers, DDX 806/1/3); Birmingham CA, management committee, 11 Sept. 1931 (Birmingham Reference Library, Birmingham CA papers, minute book 1931–2, ff. 119–20).

[6] Dawson diary, 16 Sept. 1931 (Bodleian Library, Dawson papers, 35).

[7] J. R. Remer MP to Beaverbrook, 18 Sept. 1931 (Beaverbrook papers, B/203); Lord Stanhope to Bridgeman, 21 Sept. 1931 (Shropshire Record Office, Bridgeman papers).

The Conservative leadership had to be careful here because the coalition nature of the new Government meant more than the usual number of disappointed office-seekers. There was some resentment, for example, that Baldwin had not battled harder with Samuel for non-Cabinet posts, especially given Tory opinions of the quality of some of the Liberal appointments.[8] Three Conservatives posed special difficulties: Hailsham, Amery, and Sir Edward Hilton Young (Churchill, out of the Shadow Cabinet, defeated for the time being over India, and equivocating wildly on trade policy, was widely seen as disqualified for the foreseeable future). On 24 August Chamberlain pressed hard for Hailsham's inclusion in the Cabinet, but MacDonald vetoed him as 'particularly obnoxious to the Labour Party' and hence a potential source of embarrassment. Baldwin, against whom Hailsham had plotted earlier in the year, did not push the matter; and Sankey's refusal to take the India Office meant he could not even be made Lord Chancellor outside the Cabinet. Hailsham refused more minor office, and remained a potential source of trouble until mid-September when, by going on holiday at a time of national crisis, he dented his image.[9] Another irritant was Amery, who thought the new Government 'disastrous'. Wanting tariffs and imperial preference rather than expenditure cuts, he felt that the earlier the election, the bigger the Tory majority would be.[10] Finally, Hilton Young (eventually to gain very minor office on 3 September) was disgruntled, and in so far as Baldwin had promised him a seat in the next Conservative Cabinet, had a stake in the demise of the present 'artificial, and laughable' Government.[11] This is not to say that the National administration was about to be brought down by a clique of frustrated office-seekers, but it does show the dangers to the Baldwin–Chamberlain leadership in going any further towards 'national unity', especially in trade policy, than they already had.

This message, among others, was coming from Conservative Central Office by mid-September. First, there should be an early election, most agents reporting that delay for six months would leave

[8] See e.g. Walter Elliot to Miss Tennant, 28 Aug. 1931, quoted in C. Coote, *A Companion of Honour: The Story of Walter Elliot* (London, 1965), 124.

[9] Neville Chamberlain diary, 24 Aug. 1931; Neville to Annie Chamberlain, 26 Aug., 1 Sept. 1931; Sir Austen to Ida Chamberlain, 26 Sept. 1931 (Chamberlain papers, NC 2/22, NC 1/26/450, NC 1/26/454, AC 5/1/555).

[10] Amery to Beaverbrook, 26 Aug., 14 Sept. 1931 (Beaverbrook papers, C/6).

[11] Young to Sir Austen Chamberlain, 4 Sept. 1931; Neville Chamberlain diary, 25 Aug. 1931 (Chamberlain papers, AC 39/3/29, NC 2/22).

Tory prospects 'dismal in the extreme'. Secondly, while a National appeal might be acceptable, there should be clear limits, with pacts only where Liberals fully accepted tariffs, and even then only when the alternative would be a Labour MP. Finally, MacDonald could not remain as premier of such a Government: ordinary Conservatives would 'bitterly resent' tariffs being introduced by a lifelong free trader.[12] Joseph Ball of the CRD gave such statements a more calculated edge on 16 September by estimating that an electoral pact with tariffist Liberals would give 94 Conservative and 15 Liberal gains from Labour, thus securing a protectionist government, which would prove so popular that it would win the next election as well, forcing 'socialism . . . to take a back seat for the best part of a generation'.[13]

The greatest problem of the Tory ministers had always been finding a way to break up the National Government; and by mid-September they were coming round to views similar to those of Ball. Hoare, as India Secretary, generally favoured an early election, but was dominated by departmental concerns. Cunliffe-Lister had more time to cogitate. Initially he hoped for a party election in November, but by 8 September he felt the present administration, shorn of its free traders and led by Baldwin, could do the job.[14] Similarly, Chamberlain's ideas changed. On 3 September he favoured the swift passage of the economy legislation, followed by a party election, and rejected Beaverbrook's suggestion of a reconstructed National Government. Within nine days, however, he had come round, hoping to keep MacDonald and to prise the Liberals apart at last by replacing the Samuelite free traders with Simon and his followers; and by 19 September he was hoping that MacDonald would force an early appeal by such a ministry through the Cabinet.[15] But of course, Baldwin remained the Conservatives' leader. He had been reluctant to enter the new Government, and was appalled at any hint of a repetition of the 1918 'coupon' election. His views changed, however. This was partly because he liked MacDonald and found life as deputy premier

[12] Gower to Baldwin, 16 Sept. 1931; memorandum by Gower, Topping, and Maxse, enclosed with Stonehaven to Baldwin, 18 Sept. 1931; Stonehaven to Baldwin, 18 Sept. 1931 (Baldwin papers, vol. 44 (iii), ff. 141–2, 150–2, 148–9).

[13] Ball to Chamberlain, 16 Sept. 1931 (Conservative Party papers, CRD 1/7/15).

[14] Cunliffe-Lister to his wife, 24 Aug., 1, 8, 15 Sept. 1931 (Swinton papers, SWIN III 313/1/5).

[15] Neville Chamberlain diary, 3, 19 Sept. 1931; Neville to Hilda Chamberlain, 12 Sept. 1931; Neville to Ida Chamberlain, 19 Sept. 1931 (Chamberlain papers, NC 2/22, NC 18/1/754, NC 18/1/755).

easier than being Prime Minister. But it was due also to his belief that the need of the moment was to inflict a severe defeat on the Labour Party. As he saw it, the Labour ex-ministers had deserted at a time of national crisis, and then tried to make party capital out of the fact, thus offending against every canon of political behaviour he held dear. Baldwin was also rather nervous of the universal adult franchise introduced between 1918 and 1928; it was still an unknown quantity, with the only election so far under it having produced the only Labour victory. A National appeal would reduce the number of imponderables in a murky situation. Thus on 7 September he seemed 'a little reluctant' to end the National Government; and talks with Geoffrey Dawson and MacDonald further developed his thoughts. He remained alive to the potential difficulties, especially over tariffs and the premiership, but by the weekend of 19–20 September he, like his party, had moved a long way towards the idea of some form of National appeal.[16]

II

The same could certainly not be said of the Liberals, who were hostile to an election on any basis. At least, that was the line of Lloyd George, Samuel, most MPs, and the party organization; but there were, predictably, many conflicting voices.

Lloyd George had been a spectator of the events leading to the formation of the National Government. His initial reaction seemed favourable; and in correspondence, while warning against an early election, he praised MacDonald's 'truly heroic' performance.[17] In private, he was much less supportive, disliking the emphasis of Samuel and Maclean on retrenchment; and on 24 August he told his secretary that he was 'keeping outside' the new administration. He was glad he was ill because he 'would not have taken office under MacDonald and yet it would have been impossible to have refused'.[18] When his son,

[16] Amery diary, 7 Sept. 1931, quoted in Amery, *My Political Life*, iii. 62; Dawson diary, 10 Sept. 1931 (Dawson papers, 35); MacDonald diary, 14 Sept. 1931 (MacDonald papers, PRO 30/69/1753); Runciman to his wife, 17 Sept. 1931 (Runciman papers, WR 303).

[17] MacDonald to Lloyd George, 26 Aug. 1931 (Lloyd George papers, G/13/2/15); Lloyd George to MacDonald, 30 Sept. 1931 (MacDonald papers, PRO 30/69/1314).

[18] A. J. Sylvester, *Life with Lloyd George: The Diary of A.J. Sylvester, 1931–1945*, ed. C. Cross (London, 1975), 37, entries for 23, 24 Aug. 1931.

Gwilym, took a post, Lloyd George 'offered no opinion'.[19] Some of his admirers, certainly, were pleased he remained in reserve. His role was limited to urging the Liberal ministers to ward off an early election, to which anti-dumping legislation—a clear breach of free trade—would be preferable, and ensuring that the Liberal ministerial appointments suited his palate.[20] The Liberal ministers seemed equally opposed to an election, seeing the Government's task as being the long-term stabilization of the country's finances. On 18 September, the Shadow Cabinet declared emphatically against an election or any electoral pact with the Conservatives.[21] However, some ministers were wavering, notably Lord Reading, who in proposing to MacDonald a barter scheme for Canadian wheat and British manufactures seemed to confirm Tory beliefs that he would not resign over free trade even if Samuel did so.[22] Sinclair (now Secretary of State for Scotland) felt an election in late October was 'extremely likely'.[23]

The mood of the parliamentary party appeared harmonious: on 28 August, with one dissentient, the formation of the National Government was approved by the LPP; on 17 September, again with one dissentient, an early election was opposed.[24] But in fact, it was on the verge of a disastrous split. The main concern of Samuel, as acting leader, throughout the crisis was the maintenance of free trade. Many Liberal MPs, however, were at least as concerned with keeping their seats, and in many cases saw free trade as an increasingly out-worn shibboleth: if the price of Conservative withdrawal in their constituencies was an early tariff election, they were happy to pay it. The circumstances were now favourable for that fissure for which Simon and Chamberlain had been working, intermittently, for over a year.

Widespread discontent over Liberal ministerial appointments helped fan the flames. As one incipient Simonite put it, Lloyd George, who had manipulated the process, had vetoed 'all those patriotic Liberals

[19] Lloyd George to his wife 'Wednesday' [26 Aug. 1931] (National Library of Wales, Lloyd George family papers, NLW MS 20440C/1872).

[20] Reading, memorandum, 11 Sept. 1931 (Reading papers, MSS Eur. F118/131).

[21] Maclean to Runciman, 19 Sept. 1931 (Runciman papers, WR 245).

[22] Reading to MacDonald, 11 Sept. 1931 (Public Record Office, PREM 1/97, f. 91). The idea was blocked by Snowden; see Cabinet committee on the financial situation, first meeting, 14 Sept. 1931 (CAB 27/462, f. 8).

[23] Miss Mackenzie (Sinclair's secretary) to D. B. Keith, Sept. 1931 (Thurso papers, THRS 51/1).

[24] R. Douglas, *The History of the Liberal Party, 1895–1970* (London, 1971); Maclean to Runciman, 19 Sept. 1931 (Runciman papers, WR 245).

who foresaw the coming crises'.[25] Chamberlain wanted Brown to be his deputy at the Ministry of Health, but Lloyd George vetoed the move despite the urgings of Samuel, Reading, and Sinclair.[26] Runciman's already considerable discontents were fuelled by the War Office fiasco; on 10 September, in the budget debate, he delighted Conservatives by demanding a ban on luxury imports; and he was soon favouring an early, National, election. Meanwhile, within the LPP, the old catchcry was being discarded, many '[s]taunch free traders now [being] in favour of a tariff' which seemed to the back-bencher J. H. Morris-Jones 'certain to come'.[27] In the budget debate on 15 September, Simon gave a lead to this movement, calling for the imposition of tariffs during the emergency period. The real danger now was not protection, but Labour. The former would not damage, and might help, the situation; a Labour Government, which he saw as the only alternative, would, he felt, lead to catastrophe. Seen in this light, Samuel was indulging in fractious party politicking at a time of grave national crisis. Thus it was a far more serious split that now rent the Liberal Party than any mere clash of personalities. Before Britain left the gold standard, Hore-Belisha was telling MacDonald that he had ten Liberal MPs ready to come into a new, Simonite party which he was planning, with the prospect of at least as many to come,[28] and such Liberals began to ape their leader by making pro-tariff speeches.[29]

All this uncertainty damaged the work of Liberal Party headquarters, which became increasingly obsessed with free trade to the detriment of all else. This was unlikely to reunite the party. A meeting of the elections committee (comprising Lord Stanmore and Goronwy Owen, the respective chief whips, Thomas Tweed, party organizer and Lloyd George's chief of staff, and Lord Mersey) showed this barrenness, as Tweed reported:

It was impossible to fasten them down to discussing candidates, finance, and other mundane matters of detail because the discussion took the form of considering what would be the fate of the party at the next General Election on a policy of Economy and negative Free Trade, and pictures were drawn of a

[25] Collins to Runciman, 28 Aug. 1931 (Runciman papers, WR 215); Morris-Jones papers, 'Westminster Diary', 7–11 Sept. 1931 (Morris-Jones papers, D/MJ/10).

[26] Reading, memorandum, 11 Sept. 1931 (Reading papers, MSS Eur. F118/131).

[27] Morris-Jones diary, 14 Sept. 1931 (Morris-Jones papers, D/MJ/12).

[28] R. Rosenberg (reporting Hore-Belisha) to MacDonald, 18, 19 Sept. 1931 (MacDonald papers, PRO 30/69/1314).

[29] See e.g. Morris-Jones at Llangollen, 17 Sept. 1931, *The Times*, 18 Sept. 1931.

rather grim future with about twenty Members in the House, no money at Headquarters, and possibly no front bench ... Stanmore and Mersey expressed themselves as being just as keen Free Traders as ever, but, if sacrificing Free Trade would delay the election and arrangements [be] made subsequently for electoral pacts with the Tories, they were all for it.

'Leadership is urgently needed', he concluded, 'or shortly it will be too late and good-bye to the Liberal Party'.[30] But there was no conciliatory Campbell-Bannerman waiting in the wings.

Party activists welcomed the formation of the new Government. The LCNWLF, for example, endorsed it and suggested to divisional associations that they should 'devote their meetings to explanations of the crisis and defence of the Government and ... suppress controversial matters for the time being'.[31] In addition, many Liberals hoped to gain breathing space. On 4 September W. D. Hackney, secretary of Manchester LF, wrote that there was 'strong feeling' there that the Government should not call an early election, but should remain in office for some time to deal with the crisis.[32] Ironically, he was soon to become chief organizer for the Liberal National Party in that very election.

III

MacDonald aside, National Labour attitudes tended to be far less equivocal. Snowden had entered the new Government without enthusiasm and retaining his intense personal dislike of MacDonald. But he had accepted that he had no choice, given that he believed the alternative was the collapse of the currency, runaway inflation, and 'the certain loss of all I have fought for—the destruction of the social services and the reduction of the standard of life for a generation'.[33] In poor health, he had already notified his constituency chairman of his intention to stand down at the next election; and originally, he was not averse to an early poll on party lines. The repudiation of all economies

[30] Tweed to Sinclair, 15 Sept. 1931 (Thurso papers, THRS III 3/5).
[31] LCNWLF, executive committee, 11 Sept. 1931 (LCNWLF papers, M390/1/7); see also e.g. Scottish LF, executive committee, 9 Sept. 1931 (SLF papers, minute book 1930–8, f. 83); Midland LF, executive committee, 10 Sept. 1931 (Midland LF papers, MSS 10/i/6, f. 160); A. C. Curry to Reading, 8 Sept. 1931, conveying resolution of the Northern Counties LF (Reading papers, MSS Eur. F118/131).
[32] Hackney to Reading, 4 Sept. 1931 (Reading papers, MSS Eur. F118/131).
[33] Snowden to E. J. Heywood (chairman of Colne Valley DLP), 22 Aug. 1931, in Snowden, *Autobiography*, ii. 961.

by the ex-ministers on 27 August antagonized him, however, making him doubt that he could ever work with them again; and, so long as tariffs were off the agenda—a concession he gained at the outset—he got on well with his new colleagues.[34] In Parliament, irritated by Labour MPs' 'irresponsibility', he began to taunt them by quoting patriotic verse and predicting their imminent electoral demise. Thomas, meanwhile, had been far keener from the outset, and any doubts were allayed by the NUR's demand that he should resign from the Government and its withdrawal of his pension rights. On 11 September he attacked Labour with gusto; he was a known protectionist. By 17 September, therefore, Runciman could write that no one desired an early election 'more keenly than Snowden and Jim Thomas'.[35]

MacDonald was more doubtful. Although believing that he had done the right thing, and feeling bitterly let down by Labour, his moods changed frequently. However, the repudiation of all economies by the ex-ministers, and Labour MPs' attitudes after Parliament met, led him to doubt that he could ever rejoin the party.[36] Meanwhile, he felt as early as 29 August that the Government's life would have to be extended, and was soon telling Baldwin he would accept tariffs: on 13 September, Dawson understood him to be 'quite prepared for a National Government appeal' and to believe a tariff 'essential'.[37] But he saw considerable difficulties: how could he serve under Baldwin, while not becoming a Conservative; what if the only result of co-operation was to install a right-wing Government with a huge majority; and so on. Trade policy and the vulnerability of sterling were additional problems. On the other hand, an early election would catch Labour at its most vulnerable, and a National victory would stabilize the whole situation.[38] In short, MacDonald had not decided. Tired, disheartened, locked in unpleasant correspondence with his DLP at Seaham, and heading for a minor breakdown, he gave no real lead; anyway, no serious lead needed to be given as yet. And other, more pressing, matters were shortly to intrude.

Opinions among National Labour MPs varied. His son Malcolm was

[34] Ibid. ii. 957, 962–4.

[35] Runciman to his wife, 17 Sept. 1931 (Runciman papers, WR 303).

[36] MacDonald diary, 26 Aug., 8 Sept. 1931 (MacDonald papers, PRO 30/69/1753).

[37] MacDonald to Middleton, 29 Aug. 1931 (Middleton papers, MID 27/29); MacDonald to Baldwin, 5 Sept. 1931 (MacDonald Papers, PRO 30/69/1176); Dawson diary, 13 Sept. 1931 (Dawson papers, 35).

[38] MacDonald diary, 18, 16 Sept. 1931 (MacDonald papers, PRO 30/69/1753).

not alone in continuing to believe that the Government would dissolve after a short tenure.[39] For those who had been effectively 'deselected' as Labour candidates, though, National Labour was as much of a lifeline as the Social Democratic Party was to be for others half a century later.[40] Such people would follow their leader since he was now their political meal-ticket. By 19 September, preparations were being made for the formation of an organization to run National Labour candidates at the general election.[41]

IV

The bankers, however, were anxious to avoid any such conflagration. While the formation of the new Government had steadied the financial position, withdrawals had continued. Political stability was needed. On 17 September, Harvey reported to the Cabinet finance committee (MacDonald, Snowden, Chamberlain, and Reading) that certain financial centres 'were apprehensive about the prospects of an early General Election . . . and were removing their money pending the result'. It would be 'disastrous' for the pound to crash in mid-campaign, and '[m]uch would turn on whether the Election resulted from an appeal by the National Government to the country . . . [F]rom the point of view of raising further credits abroad it would be fatal for the three Parties to enter on an Election independently on the old lines.' Peacock was even more forthright, arguing that 'the ideal course would be for the present Government to announce whatever steps were necessary to restore the trade balance and to go to the country after and not before they had taken them'. In that event investors who 'were in doubt where to put their money might . . . decide to keep it [in Britain]'. However, Peacock was overruled, Snowden and Chamberlain both pointing out that balancing the trade account would be no short job.[42] In truth, both men were hankering after an early election; neither wanted to delay it at Peacock's behest.

[39] M. MacDonald, *People and Power: Random Reminiscences* (London, 1969), 21, and private information; for a pro-MacDonald Labour candidate taking the same view, see Lord Elton, *Among Others* (London, 1938), 269.

[40] See e.g. the cases of Holford Knight: South Nottingham DLP, quarterly meeting, 6 July 1930, and *passim* thereafter (South Nottingham DLP papers, DDPP 7/1, ff. 169–70), and A. G. Church: Labour Party NEC minutes, 20 Aug. 1931 (Labour Party papers).

[41] Rosenberg to MacDonald, 19 Sept. 1931 (MacDonald papers, PRO 30/69/1314).

[42] Cabinet committee on the financial situation, second meeting, 17 Sept. 1931 (CAB 27/462, ff. 15–28).

V

Nor, by the third week in September, would most Conservative newspapers have taken Peacock's words kindly. The new Government had been welcomed by all non-Labour/Communist titles on 25 August, with Dawson's *Times* being especially fulsome. The relative reticence of the *Daily Express*, owned by Beaverbrook, and the right-wing *Morning Post*, edited by H. A. Gwynne, was not too discouraging, given that both men had private reservations.[43] This early unity soon cracked, however, as editorial columns began to divide, generally along party lines, on the question of an election. On 9 September the *Daily Express* called for an appeal led by MacDonald on the programme of empire free trade. More realistically, and more influentially, *The Times* on 16 September advised 'a National Appeal' as soon as possible, by the present or a reconstructed National Government under MacDonald fighting on a policy of tariffs. This lead was followed on 17 September by the *Morning Post*, on 18 by the *Daily Telegraph*, and on 19 by the pictorial *Daily Sketch*. The only Conservative papers to oppose an election were the Rothermere titles, the *Daily Mail* and the *Daily Mirror*; they were joined by the two Liberal dailies, *News Chronicle* and the *Manchester Guardian*. With the provincial and Sunday presses forming similar alignments, there was a general split by Saturday 19 September (see Table 5.2).

VI

The whole situation was then transformed, at least temporarily, by a renewed sterling crisis. Withdrawals had continued despite the new Government; from 2 to 12 September, between £1,450,000 and £3,600,000 were withdrawn every working day, and the general trend was upwards, possibly reflecting foreign disquiet at the perceivedly vociferous Labour Opposition in Parliament, which had opened on 8 September. The trend continued on Monday 14 (£3,340,000) and Tuesday 15 (£2,800,000) as worry about the security of the Government's position, allied to a banking crisis in Amsterdam, urged depositors to withdraw.[44] Then, on 16 September, *The Times*, seen

[43] Neville Chamberlain diary, 3 Sept. 1931 (Chamberlain papers, NC 2/22); Beaverbrook to Amery, 11 Sept. 1931 (Beaverbrook papers, C/6); Neville to Annie Chamberlain, 25 Aug. 1931 (Chamberlain papers, NC 1/26/449).

[44] Figures from 'Total Withdrawals of Sterling 13 July–19 Sept. 1931' (PRO, Prime Minister's Office papers, PREM 1/97).

Table 5.2. *Press editorials and an election*

Date	Pro-election O					Anti-election X			
	Tim	*DTe*	*MPo*	*DEx*	*DSk*	*NCh*	*MGd*	*DMa*	*DMi*
27 Aug.						X			
4 Sept.								X	
5						X			
7						X		X	X
8						X		X	
9				O					X
10									
11								X	
16	O							X	
17			O			X			
18		O	O			X	X		
19				O	O	X			X
21									
22				O			X	X	
23	O	O	O	O		X	X	X	
24						X			
25	O	O			O	X	X	X	
26	O		O	O		X			
28	O	O	O			X	X	X	X
29	O					X	X	X	
30	O		O					X	
1 Oct.		O		O		X			
2			O			X	X		X
3	O	O	O			X	X		
5		O		O		X	X		X

Key:			
Tim	*The Times*	*NCh*	*News Chronicle*
DTe	*Daily Telegraph*	*MGd*	*Manchester Guardian*
MPo	*Morning Post*	*DMa*	*Daily Mail*
DEx	*Daily Express*	*DMi*	*Daily Mirror*
DSk	*Daily Sketch*		

abroad as Britain's most influential newspaper, called for an election which, as foreigners saw it, would give the 'irresponsible' Labour Party, pledged to reversing the ministry's stabilizing measures, a chance of gaining power. And that morning's newspapers also contained the news that ratings of the Atlantic Fleet, stationed at

Invergordon on the Cromarty Firth, and refused to put to sea when ordered.

This gave rise to mythology; so it is worth summing up the fruits of recent research on the subject. The 'Invergordon Mutiny' was not an unnecessary aberration caused solely by misunderstandings and poor communications; there were real grievances involved, and the men had good reason to be concerned.[45] Nor was British press coverage of the unrest unduly sensational. All the morning papers carried the story on 16 September, but it was not even the lead story in most, and except for the *Mirror*, with its headline 'Navy Sensation: Unrest among Men', such reports as appeared were reassuring. Significantly, Harvey criticized the French but not the British press for sensationalism;[46] and, given the mild civil unrest which had occurred in Bristol on 7 September, Whitehall on the following day, and in Glasgow sporadically throughout the month, a less scrupulous press might well have felt compelled to 'play up' the incident. Perhaps as much as the naval unrest—suspended on 16 September after an Admiralty announcement that cases of hardship would be investigated—these events worried foreign depositors.

Whatever the precise balance of factors, withdrawals continued apace. On 16 September £5,000,000 drained away, the highest figure of the month so far, and Harvey warned that the credits would soon be exhausted; £10,000,000 were lost next day, and on the evening of Friday 18 September, after further withdrawals of £18,000,000, Harvey admitted defeat; it would now be 'merely a waste of money' to attempt to stay on gold. Peacock's valedictory statement that 'by having balanced the Budget, whatever happened, this country had at least demonstrated her will to play the game at all costs', must have left a bitter taste in his mouth.[47] The half day's trading on Saturday saw a further £10,000,000 disappear, and that afternoon MacDonald, Baldwin, and Samuel formally agreed to suspension of the gold

[45] D. Divine, *Mutiny at Invergordon* (London, 1970), 123–30; A. Carew, 'The Invergordon Mutiny, 1931: Long-Term Causes, Organization and Leadership', *International Review of Social History*, 24 (1979), 157–89.

[46] Cabinet committee on the financial situation, second meeting, 17 Sept. 1931 (CAB 27/462, ff. 15–28).

[47] Cabinet committee on the financial situation, second meeting, 17 Sept. 1931 (CAB 27/462, ff. 15–28); third meeting, 19 Sept. 1931 (ff. 30–1); 'Note of a Meeting at 9.45 pm on Friday, September 18th between the Prime Minister, the Deputy Governor of the Bank, and Mr Peacock' (PREM 1/97, ff. 84–9).

standard, which was endorsed by Cabinet the following day.[48] The attempt to remain on gold had proved futile: in a sense, the Government had failed in what it had set out to do. Given world conditions, and in retrospect, it is difficult to see how it could have succeeded. In that sense it was a mistaken policy. On Monday 21 September the Gold Standard (Amendment) Bill was rushed through Parliament, bank rate was raised from 4½ to 6 per cent, and a reassuring message was issued by the Government. The last blamed foreigners' nervousness regarding their own position, and stressed that 'the internal position of the country [was] sound':

> It is one thing to go off the gold standard with an unbalanced budget and uncontrolled inflation; it is quite another thing to take this measure, not because of internal financial difficulties, but because of excessive withdrawals of borrowed capital. The ultimate resources of this country are enormous, and there is no doubt that the present exchange difficulties will prove only temporary.[49]

This was a face-saving exercise and many who had heard pundits talking of the terrible consequences which would follow a departure from gold could have been forgiven for having a wry smile—if nothing more—at the Government's expense. But at least the attempt had been made, and that had bolstered confidence by showing that the Government actually meant budgetary business. In the narrow sense, then, the Government had failed to do what it had been formed to do—retain the gold standard—but more broadly it had 'succeeded'—as much, perhaps, by luck as by judgement—in the sense that sterling did not crash. For it fell from $4.86 to around $3.90; fluctuating slightly, it remained generally above $3.80 until the beginning of November. By then, the election had taken place.

VII

Indeed, the departure from gold and the resultant devaluation of sterling, though forced on the National Government, freed its hands to grab the opportunity of an early election. At first, some people felt a dissolution must now be out of the question for some time to come. Perhaps it was to be expected that Sir Maurice Hankey, as Cabinet

[48] Cabinet committee on the financial situation, third meeting, 17 Sept. 1931 (CAB 27/462, ff. 29–35); Cabinet conclusions, 20 Sept. 1931 (Cab 23/68/60(31)).
[49] Sayers, *The Bank of England*, iii. 264–5.

secretary, would see the question disappearing 'in the overwhelming need for national unity', but this was also the reaction of some Conservatives. One northern candidate felt it must be abandoned as a short-term possibility, since the inevitable devaluation of sterling would lead to an increase in the cost of living which, with higher taxes, and wage and benefit cuts, would be unlikely to increase Government popularity. And on 20 September, MacDonald wrote to Samuel that 'there [was] not even a theoretical justification for an election now.'[50]

But on the whole, Conservative pressure for an election hardly abated. On the evening Britain went off gold, in the midst of press rumours that Henderson was about to lead Labour into a reconstructed National administration, the 1922 Committee of Tory back-benchers called for an early dissolution. The executive of the EIA followed suit.[51] An obstacle was removed that evening when, having heard that a recurrence of the naval unrest was imminent, MacDonald, his hands freed by the departure from gold, announced that, due to the rising prices expected to follow devaluation, none of the Government's cuts would exceed 10 per cent.[52] Two days later, a deputation from the EIA saw Baldwin, who said that he favoured an early election, much to their surprise and delight.[53] He realized that his party's mood would permit him to take no other stance. As Hoare said, rank-and-file pressure was 'so overwhelming' that the Tory ministers 'would be left, high and dry' if Parliament were not dissolved soon. Baldwin also felt an election 'absolutely essential' because the Government had no mandate and an insufficient majority (to introduce tariffs).[54] On 24 September Baldwin set out his views to leading Tory colleagues, saying the election should be held as soon as possible, and fought by the National Government appealing for a free hand. MacDonald should lead the appeal, although he was unsure as to whether the Scot should remain Prime Minister thereafter. (Here Baldwin was probably seeking to avoid criticism of deferring too readily to MacDonald.) With the possible exception of Amery, they agreed with the leader's line, 'provided the

[50] Hankey diary, 20 Sept. 1931 (Hankey papers, HNKY 1/7); Headlam diary, 21 Sept. 1931 (Headlam papers, D/He/27); MacDonald to Samuel, 20 Sept. 1931, in Viscount Samuel, *Memoirs* (London, 1945), 209.

[51] P. Goodhart and U. Branson, *The 1922: The Story of the Conservative Backbenchers' Parliamentary Committee* (London, 1973), 45; Croft, *My Life of Strife*, 194.

[52] 'Most Secret' proceeding at the Cabinet meeting of 21 Sept. 1931 (CAB 23/90B, ff. 31–78); see also Hankey diary, 26 Sept. 1931 (Hankey papers, HNKY 1/7).

[53] Croft, *My Life of Strife*, 194.

[54] Hankey diary, 26 Sept. 1931 (Hankey papers, HNKY 1/7).

programme embodied the full tariff'; and they added that if MacDonald were premier during the campaign, he must be afterwards.[55] Now the Conservatives had a clearly defined strategy.

This plan of campaign reflected the mood of the party faithful. Spirits were high; Lady Astor's agent, for example, reported that she would get 'the biggest majority recorded for many years' in Plymouth.[56] Associations were keen to have an early National appeal, so long as their Conservative colours were not too heavily tinged. Few went as far as West Dorset CA, which wanted the election 'fought as a National Party, avoiding as far as possible the use of the word Conservative so as to make it easier for members of other Parties to support the national cause'; more common was the view of Middleton and Prestwich CA that 'an early General Election [was] desirable provided it [was] fought on broad National lines and that the . . . Conservative Party with its programme of tariffs [was] fully supported by Messrs Ramsey McDonald [*sic*], J. H. Thomas, and Sir John Simon, as representing the National viewpoint'. Far from seeing the free-trade Liberals as an asset, Conservatives were eager to be rid of them, especially in seats with a Liberal MP, such as North Cornwall, where the CA was unwilling to support Maclean because he was 'an unmitigated Free Trader' who 'had voted consistently with the Socialist Party in the late Government'. Therefore they were 'doubtful . . . whether they could trust him to wholeheartedly support a National Party with a programme of Tariffs'.[57] They did well to doubt, and ultimately they opposed him at the election. In addition, the party was in a state of readiness, as it had been even before the fall of Labour. No time was lost in making final preparations.

The Conservatives' attitude made the position of the Liberal Party almost impossible. Should Reading and Samuel be able to decide to act together—no foregone conclusion—and threaten to resign, their Tory colleagues would let them. Indeed, many Conservatives wanted this, the Shadow Cabinet agreeing 'as to the great importance of

[55] Neville Chamberlain diary, 24 Sept. 1931 (Chamberlain papers, NC 2/22); for the possibility that Amery dissented, see Amery, *My Political Life*, iii. 67–8.

[56] G. E. Rogers (agent) to Lady Astor, 24 Sept. 1931 (Reading University Library, Astor papers, 1416/1/1059).

[57] West Dorset CA, executive committee, 25 Sept. 1931 (West Dorset CA papers, D399/3/1); Middleton and Prestwich CA, finance and general purposes committee, 24 Sept. 1931 (Middleton and Prestwich CA papers, PLC 1/2, f. 57); North Cornwall CA, executive committee, 29 Sept. 1931 (North Cornwall CA papers, DDX 381/3).

pitching [its] tariff demands high enough to make sure of getting rid of Samuel and, if possible, Reading'.[58] Chamberlain was 'determined' that Samuel should 'swallow the whole programme or go out'.[59]

It was in many ways unfortunate that Samuel should have been leading the Liberals at this juncture. A shrewd party manager, he was not a politician of great ability, had an unfortunate knack of making enemies, and was widely seen as having more pro-Labour than pro-Conservative sympathies. Dislike of him soon surfaced, and even Baldwin became intensely irritated with him within a month of the Government's formation.[60] Some of this can be put down to anti-semitism; much, to what Tories saw as his irrational adherence to the discredited policy of free trade. But he was not being perverse for the sake of it, since his opposition to an election and tariffs was shared by most Liberals, especially at the grass roots. On 22 September the mouthpiece of ordinary Liberals, the NLF, reaffirmed its faith in free trade and stressed the need to give 'steady support' to the *present* Government.[61] Of course it was not just a matter of principle; when Yorkshire LF took a similar line, it was not being entirely disinterested, for by the start of October it had still only adopted 12 candidates for 54 seats.[62] Even where the machinery was healthy, associations and federations were still having difficulty in obtaining candidates, while in Scotland, the federation's continued financial difficulties made the serious consideration of further candidatures impossible.[63] Where, as in Lincoln, an association accepted an early election on a free hand including tariffs and suggested the joint selection of a candidate with the Conservatives, it was a sign of a weak party not wanting totally to be sidelined.[64] Meanwhile, Lloyd George remained implacably opposed to an election. The situation was still 'grave' and a dissolution would be

[58] Amery, *My Political Life*, iii. 68, quoting his diary for 24 Sept. 1931.

[59] Neville to Hilda Chamberlain, 26 Sept. 1931 (Chamberlain papers, NC 18/1/756).

[60] Bridgeman journal, 'October 1931' (Bridgeman papers); Hankey diary, 20 Sept. 1931 (Hankey papers, HNKY 1/7); MacDonald diary, 25 Sept. 1931 (MacDonald papers, PRO 30/69/1753).

[61] 'The NLF and Free Trade', 22 Sept. 1931 (Thurso papers, THRS III 3/5).

[62] Leeds LF, executive committee, 21 Sept. 1931 (West Yorkshire Archive Service, Leeds, Leeds LF papers, 7); Yorkshire LF, executive committee, 2 Oct. 1931 (Yorkshire LF papers, 2).

[63] See e.g. Manchester LF, executive committee, 22 Sept. 1931 (Manchester LF papers, M283/1/3/5); Scottish LF, eastern organising committee, 30 Sept. 1931 (Scottish LF papers, minute book 1930–38, f. 86).

[64] Lincoln LA, executive committee, 1 Oct. 1931 (Lincolnshire Archives Office, Lincoln LA papers, Misc. Dept. 96/1, f. 331).

'mad' given the continuing uncertainty over sterling; the present Government should carry on.[65] This line was taken by the LPP meeting on 23 September, and Samuel expressed its views in a Cabinet paper which was submitted the next day and discussed by the Cabinet four days thereafter.

In his paper, Samuel argued that the Government had failed to maintain the gold standard for two reasons: Labour's formation of a strong and hostile Opposition, and the press campaign for an early election during the week ending 19 September. The announcement of a dissolution now, he continued, would renew the flight from sterling, because it was well known that such an election could not be fought unitedly by the National Government. This was the fault of the Conservatives, who would accept nothing less than 'the full protectionist programme', involving 'tariffs of unspecified rate and food taxes'. This would lead to controversy between Government supporters and 'would not conduce to the defeat of the opposition at the polls'. Samuel went on to sketch conditions as they might be a month thence, the time when an election would be taking place if the Tories had their way. Due to devaluation, prices would be rising; the unemployed would be on lower benefits; the pound might again be under strong pressure; prices would be rising, and profiteering taking place; and there would be civil unrest, with demonstrating unemployed in 'frequent' clashes with police, possibly resulting in 'rioting with loss of life'. All in all, '[c]onditions more unpropitious for a general election could hardly be imagined'. At the same time, Labour would be mounting 'a most formidable campaign', condemning the Government's economies, attacking its failure to save the pound and peg prices, and denouncing its plans further to increase the cost of living by tariffs and food taxes:

> Calculations, made a few weeks ago on the basis that the nation would be rallied to the saving of British credit, to the support of a successful Government and the defeat of a wholly discredited and reckless opposition, might be wholly disappointed. Instead of the easy victory that was anticipated, the result might be precisely the opposite. It is a gamble on which we have no right to embark while the country is in the grave financial difficulties in which it now finds itself.

It could hardly be worse, he argued, to wait for a few months: and this, he claimed, was the view of Liberals, 'of every school of thought' from

[65] Reading, memorandum, 25 Sept. 1931 (Reading papers, MSS Eur. F118/131).

Lloyd George to Grey, and including most Liberal MPs. The Government should announce its intention of carrying on, consider any measures to restore the trade balance, and deal with the international gold problem as a matter of urgency. The adjournment of Parliament at the beginning of October would give time to tackle the Indian round table conference and other pressing matters, such as the approach of the disarmament conference. 'After that breathing space,' he concluded, 'the question of a general election might again be considered.'[66]

This *tour de force* was flawed in many ways. First, it was more of a polemic than a reasoned argument. Samuel dragged in anything he could to help his case, without really dismissing the alternatives. For example, would it not have been better if a new Government with a fresh mandate were to take responsibility for the great issues being discussed at the round-table conference, rather than a makeshift administration without a popular mandate, of indeterminate life-span and which had admitted to itself—if it followed Samuel's reasoning—that it dare not face the electorate? Secondly, he never addressed properly the point that the Government's chances of re-election might have deteriorated seriously by early 1932. Nothing was said or implied to indicate any reason why Labour, having spent the winter mounting 'a most formidable campaign', should be in a weaker position by then. But of course, Samuel overstated greatly the strength of Labour in September 1931. The very week in which Samuel was writing, Henderson was widely known to be in great difficulties with his party; indeed, MacDonald and Thomas were aware of Labour feelers for admission into an enlarged National Government.[67] Furthermore, Samuel's assumptions about the electoral unpopularity of protection were grounded in 1906 and 1923, not 1931, and none of his Conservative colleagues would have shared them. The Conservatives, in fact, might have been forgiven for cynicism: after all, delay could hardly harm the Liberal Party. Theoretically at least, it still held the balance of power in the House of Commons. That situation was unlikely to be maintained by an early election. Liberal organization and finances might be helped by the delay and, of course, Lloyd George would be fully fit again, on an optimistic prognosis, by February 1932. None of these factors was likely to impress men of the stripe of

[66] 'The Present Situation. Memorandum by the Home Secretary', 24 Sept. 1931 (Cp 243 (31)).

[67] See e.g. MacDonald diary, 28 Sept. 1931 (MacDonald papers, PRO 30/69/1753).

Chamberlain and Cunliffe-Lister as compelling reasons to postpone an election. Finally, Samuel grossly overstated the extent to which his views were backed by the LPP and even by Reading.

In fact, the meeting of the LPP on 23 September had been nowhere near as unanimous as Samuel pretended. Many MPs were not at all irreconcilable to an election, and the meeting was anything but amicable. The danger of delay was stressed by Runciman's statement that there might be five or six million unemployed by Christmas.[68] More ominously still, on the night of 21 September twenty-two Liberal MPs had presented a memorial to MacDonald assuring him of their support 'in any steps which [he] may consider it necessary to take in the interests of the finance and trade of the country'; six more had signed the following day. (Twenty-four of these stood as Liberal Nationals at the general election.)[69] In other words, almost half the LPP was now taking its lead neither from Samuel nor Lloyd George, but from MacDonald. A number of senior Liberals like Simon, Brown, Runciman, Hutchison, Hore-Belisha, Shakespeare, and George Lambert were included, and a Simonite organization was soon being set up. By 24 September, Conservative Central Office was using its influence to prevent local associations from nominating Tory candidates against sitting Simonites, and money soon began to pour in in response to appeals from Simon—including £10,000 from the motor manufacturer William Morris and £1,000 from the shipping magnate Lord Inchcape. By early October, the Liberal Nationals had set up as a separate party with paid organizers, and blown wide apart Samuel's claim to speak for almost all Liberal MPs.[70]

Nor were Lords Reading—thoroughly enjoying his work at the Foreign Office—and Grey wholehearted supporters of Samuel's line. Reading disliked protectionism, but he disliked the prospect of a Labour victory more, and by 27 September, assured by MacDonald

[68] Morris-Jones diary, 23, 24 Sept. 1931 (Morris-Jones papers, D/MJ/12).

[69] Rosenberg to MacDonald, undated, enclosing three lists of signatures (MacDonald papers, PRO 30/69/1317). The 24 who stood as Liberal Nationals were: J. Blindell, E. Brown, L. Burgin, Sir G. Collins, E. C. Davies, Sir W. Edge, Viscount Elmley, A. E. Glassey, A. Harbord, L. Hore-Belisha, Sir R. Hutchison, F. Llewellyn Jones, R. M. Kedward, G. Lambert, M. MacDonald, I. Macpherson, J. H. Morris-Jones, S. Peters, P. J. Pybus, T. Ramsay, W. Runciman, R. J. Russell, G. H. Shakespeare, and Sir. J. Simon. One, A. England, did not stand. Three signatories stood as Samuelites: N. Birkett, F. K. Griffith, and R. Morris.

[70] Simon to Lord Inchcape, 24 Sept.; Morris to Simon, 3 Oct.; Inchcape to Simon, 7 Oct. 1931 (Simon papers, 68, ff. 127, 156, 172); Manchester LF, executive committee, 7 Oct. 1931 (Manchester LF papers, M283/1/3/5).

that any election would be fought on a formula of a free hand to examine tariffs on their merits, he was firmly committed to a National appeal.[71] Grey, meanwhile, felt that an election could not be postponed; the risk had to be taken. The alternative would be mounting uncertainty; a new mandate was needed, and they could 'hardly exclude all consideration of tariffs'.[72] On 3 October, Grey made these views public in a letter to *The Times*, calling for an appeal based on anti-socialism, public economy, and a free hand.

Samuel could not have hoped, seriously, to swing the Conservatives over to his viewpoint. He was trying instead to gain the support of the undecided MacDonald. The latter had time to reflect on the situation during a short rest at Sandwich Bay following a breakdown on the night of 21 September. There he veered towards an election, writing to Baldwin:

> My city friends are unanimously opposed. . . . If one thinks of the problems in action which it will raise . . . it seems to be but a new entanglement & trouble. On the other hand, we must protect the country from an election fought at a time when influences which will make for unsettlement & harum-scarum will be at their maximum power.[73]

In short, he was ready for an early election if a suitable programme could be arranged. However, his mind was by no means made up, and when he returned to London on 25 September he was surprised to find the election agitation intensified. Although he refused to become a 'Tory tool',[74] he doubted whether an election could be avoided; even so, his support remained to be won, not least as feelers continued to come from Labour.[75] On 28 September, however, the Prime Minister was expelled from the Labour Party; by then he had, it seems, already decided to lead the National Government in its appeal to the electorate, for on 26 September he had presented a Cabinet paper very much to that effect.

MacDonald opened by saying that he would have preferred to have avoided an election, because 'with no achievement except cuts and extra taxation, [they would] be open to a serious attack'. But events had

[71] Reading, memorandum, 26 Sept. 1931 (Reading papers, MSS Eur. F118/131).
[72] Grey to Samuel, 29, 30 Sept. 1931 (Samuel papers, A/72, ff. 34–8).
[73] MacDonald to Baldwin, 23 Sept. 1931 (Baldwin papers, vol. 44 (iii), ff. 166–9).
[74] MacDonald diary, 25 Sept. 1931 (MacDonald papers, PRO 30/69/1753).
[75] Rosenberg to MacDonald, 22, 23, 26 Sept. 1931; MacDonald diary, 25 Sept. 1931 (MacDonald papers, PRO 30/69/1314, 1753).

taken over, and he was now 'assured . . . that the unsettlement of the public mind ha[d] gone so far on account of propaganda in favour of an Election that it ha[d] become politically impossible for [the] Government to continue in office for any length of time and that it must venture now'. Continuing pressure from the press, Opposition propaganda, and the possible deterioration of law and order would be far more damaging than a dissolution of Parliament. However, he rejected the idea that a body comprising Conservatives, a few dissident Liberals, and 'something like a score' of National Labourites could call itself a National Government. It was, therefore, imperative that '*[a] national appeal must be made by those who ha[d] formed the National Government*'. However, they must ask for a free hand to use any powers to rectify the position, including 'specifically' a tariff, should it be found necessary. The alternatives, he concluded, were clear: either the rejection of his formula and the break-up of the Government, or a National appeal, with the administration breaking up much later in 'a businesslike finish to the co-operation, and an orderly return to the essential conflicts which arise in the government of a State'.[76]

Even before he knew of his expulsion from the Labour Party, therefore, MacDonald was trying to find a way for an appeal by the National Government, and stating his price: Conservative acceptance of the free-trade Liberals, and free-trade Liberal acceptance of the possible use of tariffs. So long as he stuck to this line, and the Liberals were ready to co-operate, the Conservatives' preferred solution of a reconstructed Government with the Simonites replacing the free traders, but with MacDonald remaining premier, was excluded. Anyway, he believed that to fight on an explicitly protectionist programme would 'enable all sections of the Opposition to unite . . . in a most formidable array'.[77] He specifically refused to lead in the implementation of 'the partisan plans of any Party', while complaining to Baldwin of Tory boasts that they had the premier in their pocket.[78] It did not really merit Samuel's comment that MacDonald had surrendered unconditionally to Conservative pressure.[79]

Meanwhile, National Labour forces for the coming battle were being mobilized, spurred especially by their expulsion from the Labour

[76] 'Notes by the Prime Minister on a General Election', 26 Sept. 1931 (CP 247(31)).

[77] MacDonald to Sir Thomas Inskip, 29 Sept. 1931 (MacDonald papers, PRO 30/69/1314).

[78] MacDonald to Grey, 28 Sept. 1931; MacDonald to Baldwin, 27 Sept. 1931 (MacDonald papers, PRO 30/69/1320).

[79] Samuel, *Memoirs*, 210.

Party on 28 September. MacDonald was adamant that they should not become a mere adjunct of Conservative Central Office. By early October, the nascent organization had listed 34 seats it wanted to fight; already 14 out of 15 MPs, plus 10 candidates were ready to stand, and 9 or 10 candidates could be secured 'in a very short time'.[80] Financially, Beaverbrook's offer of £100,000 seems not to have been accepted; instead, MacDonald's Conservative parliamentary private secretary collected money from non-Conservative sources for the use of National Labour at the election. A board of trustees was appointed to administer the cash to ensure that there was no repetition of the Lloyd George fund. Money was not slow to come, notably £250 from Sir Alexander Grant, on whose relations with MacDonald allegations of corruption had centred in 1924, and £2,000 from the Duke of Westminster via the erstwhile honours tout, Maundy Gregory.[81] Meanwhile, Conservative headquarters offered its support and every co-operation in the constituencies.

This support, of course, was given on the understanding that MacDonald would not long delay an election. The Tory right was nervous, and the EIA executive met daily to monitor events. Chamberlain, however, continued to believe that as long as the Conservatives held their own and prodded him at the critical moments, he would be forced into action without an ultimatum.[82]

On Monday, 28 September the Cabinet had its first discussion specifically relating to an election, on the basis of the papers submitted by MacDonald and Samuel. Predictably, it boiled down to tariffs; Samuel was intransigent, and no conclusion was reached.[83] The next day's meeting was rather less inconclusive, thanks largely to Chamberlain, who produced a draft formula as the basis for a National appeal. The statement asked the electors to 'trust' the Government to do all it could to set matters to rights, 'without hampering them by pledges which would tie their hands', since any expedient might be

[80] 'Labour Supporters of the National Government', 25 Sept. 1931 (MacDonald papers, PRO 30/69/1320); Rhodes James, *Memoirs of a Conservative*, 375.

[81] Amulree to MacDonald, 3 Oct. 1931; Grant to MacDonald, 2 Oct. 1931; H. B. Usher to Gregory, 7 Oct. 1931 (MacDonald papers, PRO 30/69/1535, 1320, 1535).

[82] Croft, *My Life of Strife*, 195; Amery, *My Political Life*, iii. 68, quoting his diary for 29 Sept. 1931.

[83] Cabinet conclusions, 28 Sept. 1931 (CAB 23/68/65(31)); MacDonald diary, 28 Sept. 1931 (MacDonald papers, PRO 30/69/1753).

needed: it was too soon after the departure from the gold standard to be more precise. No expedient would be excluded from consideration, but, '[i]n particular', imports would have to be dealt with, 'whether by prohibition, tariffs, or other measures'. (It was to this section that Samuel objected.) The formula ended with a nod in the direction of imperial preference. MacDonald, now regarding 27 October as a likely date for polling, and Reading urged Samuel to discuss the formula, but he refused, arguing that the contentious clause would provide a mandate for protection. Of course it would—that was why Chamberlain had included it, and to omit it would allow Liberal candidates to make anti-tariff pledges. Samuel was simply looking for an excuse to block the election, and the fairly harmless passage in Chamberlain's formula provided it. Even Snowden was prepared to accept the draft. The rest of the Cabinet saw Samuel's tactics, however, and told him that a decision must be taken at the latest by the end of the week.[84] Thomas, for one, was ready to tell him to 'go to hell' if he would not come to heel, while the Conservative ministers hoped he would go, if not there, then at least to the back benches.[85] That evening Samuel and his leading Liberal colleagues agreed to consult Lloyd George.

The Cabinet met on 30 September before Samuel had a chance to meet the invalid. Knowing Lloyd George's general antipathy towards an election, however, he remained obstructive, while reducing Conservative leverage to saying that he would bow, ultimately, to MacDonald's judgement. But while he acknowledged the Tories' right to press their policy, he refused to advance an alternative formula, much to their irritation. By this stage there was serious unrest in the Conservative ranks, and a general feeling that Samuel was trying to trick them out of obtaining a mandate for protection. The Conservative press was increasingly restive, and alternative leaders like Hailsham, Amery, and Churchill were hovering threateningly. Hence Baldwin and Chamberlain were worried that Samuel was exposing them to ridicule—and worse.

After the Cabinet meeting, Samuel departed for Churt, Lloyd George's Surrey home. Lloyd George was now firmly set against an election (which surprised Reading, who had—mistakenly—thought

[84] Cabinet conclusions, 29 Sept. 1931 (CAB 23/68/66(31)); 'Note of Events during the Week Ended Saturday, October 3rd, 1931' (Hankey papers, HNKY 1/8); Hankey to MacDonald, undated, re. possible polling dates (CAB 21/350, f. 94).

[85] 'Note of Events . . .' (Hankey papers, HNKY 1/8); Neville Chamberlain diary, 29 Sept. 1931 (Chamberlain papers, NC 2/22).

him favourable),[86] and he gave Samuel a violently worded memorandum damning the very idea of a dissolution. The paper was littered with strong phrases. An election would be 'an incredible act of reckless folly', 'a gamble', 'a dog-fight', 'a month of national civil war', with 'incalculably bad' effects on sterling. The agitation for a dissolution was a 'conspiracy . . . engineered merely with the object of enthroning the Conservative Party in power'. To accept the formula would be to accept tariffs; to accept tariffs would 'sign the death warrant of the Liberal Party as a separate Party', and after the election the Liberal ministers would be 'a miserable row of plucked boobies'. Instead, he argued, the Liberals should stick by Samuel's Cabinet paper.[87] Doubtless Lloyd George realized that delay would give him a better chance of being fit for the election when it did come. But whatever Lloyd George's intentions, the memorandum was a useful tool for Samuel. Now he could pose more moderately in Cabinet, while pointing mock-regretfully at his leader's attitude to show how limited was his freedom of action.

Samuel could point also to more widespread Liberal hostility. On 30 September he received a memorial from eleven prominent Liberals deprecating an election and stating that many MPs and candidates would accept no compromise on free trade nor any arrangement by which Conservatives would be elected 'under a so-called "free hand" '.[88] From Liverpool, a Liberal businessman reported that he could not find 'a single commercial man of whatever politics' in favour of an election, and similar reports came from Glasgow.[89] But the most striking example of Liberal opposition came from Asquith's widow, who 'implore[d]' Reading 'to stand with Lloyd George' against an election fought on protection.[90] Misery does indeed acquaint a man with strange bedfellows.

In Cabinet on 1 October, therefore, Samuel was able to pose as a man of moderation and reason at the side of the intransigent Lloyd George. Even so, he said Lloyd George's was not the last word: if the Liberals were not forced to commit themselves to tariffs 'here and

[86] Rosenberg, memorandum, 26 Sept. 1931 (MacDonald papers, PRO 30/69/1320).

[87] 'Memorandum from Mr Lloyd George (Churt. Sept. 30th 1931)' (Samuel papers, A/81).

[88] Memorial from eleven Liberals, 30 Sept. 1931 (Samuel papers, A/73, f. 49).

[89] H. R. Rathbone to Simon, 1 Oct. 1931 (Simon papers, 68, f. 143); Sir D. M. Stevenson to Lloyd George, 5 Oct. 1931 (Lloyd George papers, G/33/1/30).

[90] Margot, Lady Oxford to Reading (telegram), 2 Oct. 1931 (Reading papers, MSS Eur. F118/131).

now', some agreement should be possible. Accordingly, the Cabinet appointed a committee of MacDonald, Chamberlain, and Samuel to draw up a formula. When the drafting committee met that evening, the acting Liberal leader maintained his moderate pose. Chamberlain, hoping to retain MacDonald and oust Samuel, was dismayed when 'after a rather feeble protest Samuel accepted everything except some limiting words of no importance'.[91] In 'the depths of gloom', senior Conservatives agreed with Chamberlain that they 'could not keep [the Liberals] out if they swallowed everything [the Conservatives] put before them'.[92] However, Samuel's approval was subject to the other Liberal ministers' confirmation; and after a very short meeting they rejected it, ostensibly on the grounds that it made no reference to the desirability of lowering international tariff barriers. Samuel then reported their views back to the Cabinet.

The conduct of Samuel in accepting a formula he had previously rejected, and then accepting its summary rejection by his Liberal colleagues, appears strange, but there was a plausible explanation. He was attempting to show his moderation, and that he could not go too far for fear of alienating the Liberal Party from the Government. He knew he had no chance of winning over the Conservatives, but wanted to impress and woo MacDonald, who knew all about having difficult followers. Hence the pose. But, of course, he had agreed to the barely revised formula knowing his colleagues would reject it. It was all a manœuvre to win the sympathy of the premier and to gain more time. The Cabinet was prepared to concede little to him in the latter respect, however, telling him that a final decision would have to be reached at the following day's meeting. The Conservatives, delighted by Samuel's apparent discomfiture, had no intention of letting him off the hook.[93] Still, Samuel had gained a few more hours in which to try to manœuvre the Conservatives out of the Government. For this was now his aim. But he would need to persuade the King.

Immediately after the formation of the National Government, King George V had returned to Balmoral, whence he had written a most effusive letter to MacDonald, commenting with admiration on the

[91] 'Note of Events . . .' (Hankey papers, HNKY 1/8); Neville Chamberlain diary, 1 Oct. 1931 (Chamberlain papers, NC 2/22).

[92] Amery, *My Political Life*, iii. 69, quoting his diary for 1 Oct 1931; Neville Chamberlain diary, 1 Oct. 1931 (Chamberlain papers, NC 2/22).

[93] 'Note of Events . . .' (Hankey papers, HNKY 1/8); Cabinet conclusions, 1 Oct. 1931 (CAB 23/68/68(31)); Amery, *My Political Life*, iii. 69, quoting his diary for 1 Oct. 1931.

premier's 'strength of character', 'courage', and 'devotion to duty', by which his name would 'always hold an honoured place among British Statesmen'.[94] At first, George had been somewhat upset by talk of an early election; the salient question was—'Is it certain that the Conservatives will get in?'[95] By the time of his return from Scotland on 29 September, however, the answer seemed certain, and George was firmly in the pro-election lobby. Two days later Baldwin assured him of his desire to co-operate with MacDonald and to restrain his own party's more ardent spirits, which further encouraged him.[96]

Samuel's idea of a Liberal–Labour coalition under MacDonald, therefore, had not the slightest chance of success. He did not realize this: after all, his last meeting with the King, on 23 August, had been very amicable, and Samuel was to believe to the end of his life that his advice had been decisive in persuading George of the merits of a National Government. However, Samuel's latest suggestion left the King unimpressed, to put it mildly, and the interview became 'rather heated', as the monarch reported to his Prime Minister the next day.[97] George must have controlled his rage quite well, though, because Samuel remained hopeful that the new alignment might be brought about, as he told Hankey later in the day.[98] The Liberal leader had kept this option open by deadlocking the Cabinet meeting earlier on 2 October, when the Liberals' insistence on a reference to efforts to reduce international tariff barriers was used both by him and the Conservatives as a means of avoiding agreement. Thus the Cabinet log-jam remained over the weekend, it being decided to hold no meeting then in order to give MacDonald a rest.[99]

The premier, back on 3 October from Seaham, where the DLP had finally repudiated him, was dismayed that a solution was as remote as

[94] King George V to MacDonald, 27 Aug. 1931 (MacDonald papers, PRO 30/69/1314).

[95] Sir Clive Wigram to MacDonald, 16 Sept. 1931 (MacDonald papers, PRO 30/69/1314).

[96] Middlemas and Barnes, *Baldwin*, 646, quoting the King's own account.

[97] See Hankey diary, 3 Oct. 1931 (Hankey papers, HNKY 1/7) referring to 2 Oct., where Hankey is unsure whether Samuel put the idea to George or to an equerry; cf. Reading memorandum, 4 Oct. 1931 (Reading papers, MSS Eur. F118/131), where MacDonald is reported reporting the King's comments, making it clear that Samuel did put the idea to the monarch. For Samuel's rather unconvincing efforts to explain away his remarks, see Samuel to Wigram, 5 Oct. 1931 (Samuel papers, A/73, ff. 83–4).

[98] Nicolson, *King George the Fifth*, 492–3, quoting the King's diary for 2 Oct. 1931; Hankey diary, 3 Oct. 1931 (Hankey papers, HNKY 1/7).

[99] Cabinet conclusions, 2 Oct. 1931 (CAB 23/68/69(31)).

ever. He felt 'convinced' that an election was needed to end uncertainty; and delay would mean having to fight on less propitious territory at a less propitious time.[100] That morning Thomas and Baldwin steeled his resolve, and he began to accept the former's view that Samuelites should be replaced by Simonites, given the disloyalty implicit in Samuel's suggestion of a Lib–Lab coalition. Depressed, MacDonald told the King that he was 'beginning to feel that he had failed and had better clear out'. Once more, though, George boosted his Prime Minister's confidence, telling him to 'brace himself up to realise that he was the only person to tackle the present chaotic state of affairs'; it was his duty to find a solution. He added that even if MacDonald tendered his resignation, he 'would refuse to accept it'. So all the premier's other options were closing. He must remain Prime Minister; he, like the King, ruled out an alternative coalition; and he was now ready to bring in the Simonites. Only one doubt remained, apparently: would the Conservatives 'cart' him as soon as the election was over? Baldwin reassured him, and, however morosely, he moved towards the Conservative/Thomas line.[101] With the Conservative Party and the bulk of the Conservative press now screaming for an election (see Table 5.2), it seemed that a final decision would be reached at the next Cabinet meeting. However, MacDonald was not only indecisive, but also irresolute in decisions reached.

VIII

MacDonald's misgivings about the Conservatives were revived by Lloyd George in a meeting at Churt on Monday, 5 October, and it was only with some difficulty that Baldwin and Chamberlain persuaded him to call a Cabinet meeting that evening.[102] At that meeting, the premier outlined the alternative courses available: the Government could break up, carry on without an election, or go to the country on a platform of economy, anti-Labour, and a free hand to rectify the trade balance. The first option was dismissed by all present as impossible, given sterling's vulnerability. It was on the second option that controversy arose. Hankey, taking the minutes, believed MacDonald

[100] MacDonald to Lord Lothian, 3 Oct. 1931 (MacDonald papers, PRO 30/69/1320).

[101] Hankey diary, 3 Oct. 1931 (Hankey papers, HNKY 1/7); Nicolson, *King George the Fifth*, 493, quoting Wigram's account; for MacDonald's fears, see MacDonald to Baldwin, 2 Oct. 1931 (MacDonald papers, PRO 30/69/1320).

[102] Neville Chamberlain diary, 5 Oct. 1931 (Chamberlain papers, NC 2/22).

only advanced it to show its impossibility, and the premier himself took this line after the meeting. However, Thomas, Chamberlain, and Samuel all believed he had actually favoured the proposal. Thus if only a masquerade, it was a very convincing one. The attitude of the Cabinet majority, though, made it clear that this was an impossible course. Therefore the third option had to be taken up; and when MacDonald stated that there must be an election, Samuel, his own alternative options now closed, concurred.[103] It was agreed that MacDonald should issue a manifesto 'setting forth the general policy of the National Government . . . asking for a free hand, nothing excluded'. Only a general mention of import restrictions should be made, and 'no attempt should be made to embody an agreed formula'. The three party leaders would be free to deal with measures to right the trade deficit in their own manifestos, but ruling out nothing in advance. The writs would be issued on 7 October, nomination day would be 16 October, and polling day Tuesday, 27 October.[104]

The Liberal climb-down in accepting an immediate election, rather than resigning, has long been a source of debate. Lloyd George spluttered that Samuel had 'sold every pass that [the Liberals] held!', while others felt they were relieved simply to remain in office and reduce the prospect of Conservative opposition in their constituencies.[105] Yet what, in reality, was Samuel's alternative? Blocking the Conservative pressure for an election had been a sensible tactic, so long as it gave him a chance to advance his alternative plan of a Lib–Lab coalition, but was pointless once that alternative had been ruled out on 3 October. By 5 October further obstruction was impossible. The Conservatives and Thomas now saw the departure even of MacDonald as being preferable to further delay. Samuel had either to agree to a dissolution or resign. Little would have been gained from the latter course. The only other firm free trader in the Cabinet, Snowden, was adamantly for an election; the other Liberal, Reading, was not passionately opposed.[106]

[103] Cabinet conclusions, 5 Oct. 1931 (CAB 23/68/70(31)); Hankey diary, 5 Oct. 1931 (Hankey papers, HNKY 1/7); Neville Chamberlain diary, 5 Oct. 1931, and Neville to Hilda Chamberlain, 10 Oct. 1931 (Chamberlain papers, NC 2/22 and 18/1/758); Samuel to Lloyd George, 6 Oct. 1931 (Samuel papers, A/73, ff. 86–7).

[104] Cabinet conclusions, 5 Oct. 1931 (CAB 23/68/70(31)).

[105] Douglas, *Liberal Party*, 219; Morris-Jones diary, 2 Oct. 1931 (Morris-Jones papers, D/MJ/12).

[106] Samuel, 'Action of the Liberal Party, Sept.–Oct. 1931', Dec. 1932 (Samuel papers, A/73, ff. 95–6).

Furthermore, even if all the ministerial Liberals had resigned, other Liberals would have been ready to take their places. On 5 October, it was widely known that, concurrently with the Cabinet, twenty-two Simonite MPs were reaffirming their 'firm support in any steps [MacDonald] decided were necessary'.[107] It was with great discomfiture that they learned of Samuel's non-resignation. In addition, Samuel felt that to resign would be to allow the Simonites to gain the support of middle Liberal opinion, represented by such people as Grey. The official party might have been pushed to the periphery of British politics. For the position of the Liberal Party, had it withdrawn from the National Government, would have been untenable. As Lord Lothian put it, '[h]ow can you, in a grave emergency, resign on a "free hand"?'[108] And unlike Lloyd George, Samuel did not doubt that there was a national emergency. Thus it would be impossible for the Liberals to fight outside the Government on free trade alone; as he wrote subsequently, they would have been 'heavily defeated'. As it was, they could still produce their own manifesto and were not forced to advocate tariffs, merely restrained from attacking them. They could also try for constituency pacts with the Conservatives, which led Lothian to hope that they could 'secure the return of a considerable body of Liberals . . . as a moderating force or as the nucleus of a second opposition'.[109] They could also defend free trade from the inside as, indeed, most Conservatives had feared they would. By remaining in the Government the Samuelites were acknowledging their profoundly weak position.

Conservative displeasure might have been expected, but relief at getting an election overcame it. On 6 October, Baldwin told an 'enthusiastic' parliamentary party to go all out for tariffs, though he also warned against splitting the anti-Labour vote and ruled that Conservative ministers must not speak against Liberal ministers in the latters' constituencies. He expected to inflict a crushing defeat on Labour, as indeed did many Conservative MPs.[110]

A number of formalities remained. On the morning of 6 October the King cheerfully granted a dissolution to MacDonald who then, with Snowden, Samuel, and Chamberlain, met Harvey and Peacock. The

[107] Simon to MacDonald, 5 Oct. 1931 (Simon papers, 68, f. 163).
[108] Lothian to Lloyd George, 7 Oct 1931 (Lothian papers, GD 40/17/257/282–4).
[109] Ibid.
[110] Croft, *My Life of Strife*, 197–8; Geoffrey Lloyd to Bridgeman, 7 Oct. 1931; Geoffrey Dawson to Bridgeman, 6 Oct. 1931 (Bridgeman papers).

bankers had become reconciled to the idea of an election, especially after the return from convalescence of the governor of the Bank of England, Montagu Norman, who favoured an early poll.[111] Harvey and Peacock assured ministers that the pound could be held during the campaign. MacDonald then discussed his election manifesto with Baldwin and Samuel, and the Cabinet set up a committee to deal with Cabinet business, including candidates' questions, during the campaign.[112] Meanwhile, Parliament had passed the Foodstuffs (Prevention of Exploitation) Act, a brief measure allowing action to be taken against anyone profiteering 'in food or drink of general consumption' in case of inflation. To apply for six months only, it was designed 'purely for election purposes', as Labour put it.[113] Next day the election campaign began.

The election had come about because of Conservative pressure, but also because, with varying degrees of reluctance, the Conservatives' allies had felt that it was either imperative and or the least among evils. It is difficult to see in the actions of the Conservatives dishonesty, or an attempt to mask their protectionism, when their most 'unscrupulous' move—the attempt to force out the free-trade Liberals—would have allowed the Government to appeal on a more avowedly protectionist platform. In particular, the abandonment of any notion of an agreed formula save for MacDonald's fairly vacuous 'doctor's mandate' was a defeat for the Conservatives, not a victory for their duplicity. They were, as Baldwin said, to go all out for tariffs. The only qualifications to this would be the need to maintain at least a semblance of National unity, and, in the case of a small minority of candidates, their own lack of enthusiasm for protection. The fact that the Samuelites decided to remain in the Government was a defeat for the Conservatives, and would cause difficulties over trade policy both during and after the election campaign. But was it not tempting fate to anticipate the result: was there not a strong possibility that Labour might win the election?

At the meeting with the bankers on 6 October, MacDonald had pointed out that 'there could be no doubt as to what the result of the election would be' and that 'he had no shadow of a doubt as to the

[111] Thomas Jones diary, 29 Sept. 1931 (National Library of Wales, Jones papers, Z/1931, 50).

[112] Cabinet committee on the financial situation, fourth meeting, 6 Oct. 1931 (CAB 27/462, ff. 36–41); MacDonald diary, 6 Oct. 1931 (MacDonald papers, PRO 30/69/1753); Cabinet conclusions, 6 Oct. 1931 (CAB 23/68/71(31)).

[113] *Parl. Deb.*, 5th ser., 257, col. 1036, Alexander, 6 Oct. 1931.

response of the country'. Snowden added that '[i]t might be taken for granted that the appeal . . . would be answered by the country with no uncertain voice'. For the election had not been called to see whether the electors might prefer a Labour Government. Rather, as MacDonald said, its purpose was 'to convert a temporary and somewhat precarious majority in the House of Commons into a permanent, stable and strong majority, upon which a truly national administration could be based'.[114] Even at the outset, then, the leaders of the National Government expected a large majority. Certainly little that had happened in their opponents' camp in the previous six weeks suggested they would be disappointed.

[114] Cabinet committee on the financial situation, fourth meeting, 6 Oct. 1931 (CAB 27/462, ff. 36–41).

6

LABOUR TRIES TO READJUST

'THE first result of JRM's defection may be the consolidation of the Labour Movement, political and industrial, under Henderson's leadership—with a sterner outlook, a more disciplined behaviour and a more scientific programme,' wrote Beatrice Webb on the formation of the National Government.[1] She was not alone in thinking MacDonald and Snowden had been obstacles to progress towards these goals, and that Labour's aims could now be achieved. Yet within six weeks, the party was to be faced with the prospect of a general election for which it was organizationally unprepared, lacking firm or decisive leadership, and without credible policies, in the expectation of certain defeat. In seeking to explain Labour's dismal showing in the general election of 1931, therefore, it is essential first to understand why Mrs Webb's hopes came so speedily to naught.

It is useful to see the events of these six weeks, and indeed of the whole 1931 crisis, in terms of a struggle within the Labour movement for control of the Labour Party. Henry Pelling's view, that the general council of the TUC took over, is instructive for the period after 27 October 1931, but oversimplifies the situation before then.[2] A number of contemporary views of the party's position can be discerned. First, the general council—especially Bevin and Citrine—wanted to complete their turn towards a more corporatist approach, started after the General Strike, in order to make a future Labour Government more responsive to union demands, and also to foster better relations with non-Labour ministries. Ultimately they were, very largely, to succeed. Secondly, the Labour left, represented mainly by the ILP, wanted the party to become more openly militant, resisting the new Government outside Parliament and adopting socialist policies. Their defeat was to lead to the disaffiliation of the ILP in 1932. Thirdly, right-wingers like Henderson argued that the second Labour Government had been a success in many ways, that the 1928 programme *Labour and the Nation* was the right one, and that the party should now wait for a majority at

[1] Beatrice Webb diary, 24 Aug. 1931 (Passfield papers).
[2] H. Pelling, *A Short History of the Labour Party*, 4th edn. (London, 1972), 71–4.

a future election. They too were to be defeated, Henderson to such an extent that he had virtually abandoned domestic politics by the end of 1932. Finally, the mass of the party was confused, sometimes frightened, by the defection of MacDonald, and clung increasingly to the fundamentals of 'socialism'.

I

The rank-and-file organizations of the Labour movement were not slow to praise the ex-ministers and the general council for resisting demands for economies. Such votes were usually passed unanimously, or with, at the most a couple of dissentients.[3] Even MacDonald's own divisional party at Seaham repudiated him, though only after a struggle.[4] Activists tended not to support unconstitutional action against the Government, however.[5] Trade-union attitudes towards the National administration showed how little room for manœuvre the general council would have had, had it wanted it. The MFGB instructed its sponsored MPs to oppose the Government; the dying A. J. Cook feared it might develop into fascism.[6] The Builders and General and Municipal Workers were also quick to oppose the Government.[7] Among the railway unions, ASLEF and the NUR were very hostile, but the Railway Clerks' Association (RCA), whose members were not part of the unemployment insurance scheme, was far less so, criticizing those of its members who were attacking MacDonald, whom it believed to be acting bravely and sincerely, if wrongly.[8] Then again, the ASW was critical even of the Labour ex-ministers, who, its journal said, had been 'committed to the major

[3] Penistone DLP, ordinary general meeting, 19 Sept. 1931 (Penistone DLP papers, on microfilm at Birmingham Reference Library); Leeds City LP, general committee, 16 Sept. 1931 (West Yorkshire Archive Service, Leeds, Leeds City Labour Party papers, 4/7, f. 482); Doncaster DLP, special executive committee, 2 Sept. 1931 (Doncaster Labour Party papers, DS 7/1/5, f. 32).

[4] Marquand, *MacDonald*, 651–3, 664.

[5] See e.g. Newburn local Labour Party, special members' conference, 22 Sept. 1931 (Wansbeck DLP papers, NRO 527/B/2).

[6] MFGB, executive committee, 27 Aug. 1931 (South Wales Miners' Federation papers); see also e.g. Ayrshire Miners' Union, monthly meeting of delegates, 29 Aug. 1931 (National Library of Scotland, Ayrshire Miners' Union papers, dep. 258(2)): J. E. Williams, *The Derbyshire Miners: A Study in Industrial and Social History* (London, 1962), 833; Cook to Sankey, 30 Aug. 1931 (Sankey papers, MSS Eng. hist. c. 508).

[7] George Hicks to Henderson, 25 Aug. 1931 (Modern Records Centre, AUBTW papers, MSS 78/AU/1/1/12); E. A. and G. H. Radice, *Will Thorne, Constructive Militant: A Study in New Unionism and New Politics* (London, 1974), 113.

[8] *Railway Service Journal*, Sept., Oct. 1931.

portion of the economy policy' and who had 'only [shrunk] from the precipice when they found that the representatives of organised labour . . . were uncompromisingly opposed to any economy at the expense of the working classes.'[9]

Union leaders were not radicalized. Citrine was happy to meet Sir Edward Peacock at the home of a leading Conservative on the day the National Government was formed.[10] Bevin, though, was angered by the conduct of MacDonald, whom he felt had acquiesced in the demands of bankers and employers for reductions in working-class living standards. Thus he was glad that the premier and his cohorts had taken 'their feet of clay elsewhere'.[11] Since Bevin, as chairman of the *Daily Herald* board, and leader of one of the largest unions (with twelve sponsored MPs and nearly 10 per cent of the total party block vote), was, arguably, the most powerful individual in the Labour movement, these views would be difficult to ignore.

More easily disregarded were the militant views of the ILP and the CPGB. The former was not surprised by the formation of the National Government, and now expected 'the sharpest possible expression of the class struggle', and a situation in which moderation on Labour's part would be nonsensical. In particular, public expenditure cuts would intensify the Depression by reducing purchasing power further.[12] Meanwhile the Communists—sunk since 1929 in the depths of the 'class against class' line, by which all other parties were seen as effectively fascist—were quick to attack, not just the new Government, but also Labourites from Henderson to the ILP leader, James Maxton, for the second Labour Government's 'record of starvation, wage-cuts and oppression'. The Communists proposed repudiation of the war debt, a graduated income tax, confiscation of all income over £5,000 a year and fortunes exceeding £1,000, and the abolition of expenditure on armaments.[13] This made sobering reading for men like Henderson, who believed that unless Labour opposed the new Government and its programme, the working-class movement would fall increasingly under the spell of the far left.

[9] ASW, *Monthly Journal*, Oct. 1931.

[10] Steel-Maitland, 'Diary of Events during Crisis of 1931', and Steel-Maitland to Peacock, and vice versa, 25 Aug. 1931 (Steel-Maitland papers, GD 193/120/3/444–7x, 111–12).

[11] Bevin, 'First Draft' of undated circular to 'The Permanent Officials, Branch Officials and Members' (Bevin papers, MSS 126/EB/TG/10/10).

[12] *New Leader*, 28 Aug. 1931; A. F. Brockway, *Socialism over Sixty Years: The Life of Jowett of Bradford, 1864–1944* (London, 1946), 293.

[13] *Daily Worker*, 25, 26 Aug. 1931.

The attitude of Labour back-benchers and erstwhile junior ministers had also to be taken into account. It is clear that hostility towards MacDonald and his followers was not universal. Press estimates of a substantial National Labour contingent were belied by events, and many were glad to be rid of him, for example, Clement Attlee, Susan Lawrence, and Hugh Dalton.[14] Cripps and Shinwell firmly rejected offers of posts from MacDonald. But others, like Cecil Malone and Herbert Dunnico, were much more reluctant to refuse; and many MPs, though clear in opposing the Government, wished the premier well, Sir Ben Turner hoping that he would return soon and G. R. Strauss writing that his 'respect and affection' for MacDonald 'so far from diminishing [had] been immeasurably increased by [his] action during the crisis'.[15] Thus there were more cross-currents within the PLP than anti-MacDonald observers like Dalton and Beatrice Webb were prepared to admit; and the fact that the ranks of the ex-ministers contained similar cross-currents reduced the chances of their fighting a successful rearguard action against the TUC.

Among the nine resisters, especially, there was bitterness. Addison, for example, was relieved to be rid of MacDonald, and on 26 August became the first of the late Cabinet to declaim the theory of the bankers' ramp. Lansbury condemned the financiers, while Alexander spoke of the need to resist 'dictation'. Johnston stated that the Cabinet had refused to see 'humanity crucified on a cross of gold'.[16] Greenwood, however, expressed concern that his progressive policies at the Ministry of Health would be undone.[17] On the other hand, the six ministers who had supported the 10 per cent benefit cut yet not followed MacDonald—Bondfield, Lees-Smith, Morrison, Passfield, Shaw, and Wedgwood Benn—were in a very tight spot indeed. In three cases—Morrison, Shaw, and Wedgwood Benn—there was press speculation that they would join the Government: Morrison almost did.[18] On 24 August, the *Daily Herald* printed the names of eight

[14] Dalton diary, 24, 25 Aug. 1931 (Dalton papers).

[15] E. Estorick, *Stafford Cripps: A Biography* (London, 1949), 88–9; Shinwell, *Conflict Without Malice*, 110; Dalton diary, 27 Aug. 1931 (Dalton papers); Dunnico to MacDonald, 8 Sept. 1931; Tillett to MacDonald, 9 Sept. 1931; Turner to MacDonald, 29 Aug. 1931; Strauss to MacDonald, 11 Sept. 1931 (MacDonald papers, PRO 30/69/1314, 383, 1315, 383).

[16] *Reynolds's Illustrated News*, 30 Aug. 1931; *The Co-operative Review*, Sept. 1931; *Forward*, 29 Aug. 1931.

[17] *News Chronicle*, 26 Aug. 1931.

[18] For Morrison, see *Morning Post*, 25 Aug. 1931, and Donoughue and Jones, *Morrison*, 164–7; for Shaw, see *Manchester Guardian*, 25 Aug. 1931; for Wedgwood Benn, see *Daily Herald* and *Daily Mail*, 25 Aug. 1931.

ministers who had opposed the dole cut (excluding Clynes, who was however included the next day), which hardly delighted those not on the list. It seems likely that Bevin, who was taking a close editorial interest in the *Herald* at this time, ordered its publication, to divide and discredit the ex-ministers, and so impair their ability to resist the general council.

Arthur Henderson, now seen as Labour's *de facto* leader, had similarly mixed feelings. His recent relations with MacDonald had been poor, but he was to continue to see the premier's return to the party leadership as most desirable. Furthermore, while opposing the benefit cut, Henderson had been ready to meet Parliament with the £56,000,000 programme of economies. Thirdly, far from being radicalized by the fall of the Labour Government, he felt even more strongly the need to moderate Labour's Opposition, not least in order to reduce the chances of a permanent political realignment unfavourable to Labour or the total alienation of MacDonald. This would be difficult, given the attitudes not just of Bevin, but also of many of his former Cabinet colleagues. The next six weeks were to be, arguably, the most disastrous of Henderson's long and varied career.

II

After the Cabinet meeting on 24 August, Henderson, Lansbury, and seven other ex-ministers lunched together and tried to assess the situation. Since 'bitter attacks & controversy were not expected', it was agreed to make no statement unless one became unavoidable, and to announce no policy before Parliament met.[19] This suggested a fairly relaxed approach to Opposition which events were soon to prove was, in fact, far too leisurely. That afternoon saw two such events. First, MacDonald saw the Labour junior ministers and, while urging them not to jeopardize their careers by following him, he also gave hints that he wanted some of them to do precisely that—an impression confirmed by his actions over the next few days. In ruling out a 'coupon' election, he also seemed to be clearing the way for potential Labour followers.[20] This was worrying for the Labour leadership. Unless there was some clear indication of Labour's attitude towards the new Government, the party, especially the PLP, might start to

[19] Beatrice Webb diary, 25 Aug. 1931 (Passfield papers); Passfield to Beatrice Webb, 24 Aug. 1931 (Passfield papers, II 3 (1)27, f. 89).
[20] Dalton diary, 24 Aug. 1931 (Dalton papers).

fragment in confusion. Secondly, a meeting of Henderson, Dalton, Lansbury, Middleton, Bevin, Citrine, and Stanley Hirst (a TGWU official and that year's party chairman) gave Bevin the chance to lay down the law. The union leader's offer of financial help was very welcome to the party leadership; less so was Bevin's bellicose statement that the situation was 'like the General Strike'—for then the unions had, basically, ridden roughshod over the parliamentary party.[21] Although Henderson continued to hope—as he indicated to MacDonald's principal private secretary the following day—that he would be able to give the party 'responsible guidance' along moderate lines, and that the premier would be able to return, such hopes were beginning to look somewhat forlorn.[22]

The events of the next three days showed this to be the case. On 26 August, the *Daily Herald* trumpeted—tendentiously, and doubtless at Bevin's behest—that there was 'little doubt' that the joint meeting of the general council, NEC, and PLP executive, planned for later that day, would decide on 'complete dissociation from the Government and repudiation of those ex-Ministers associated with it'; that Morrison, Shinwell, and Wedgwood Benn had all denied, *when asked*, that they were to join the Government; and that that Friday the PLP was 'bound' to elect Henderson as its new leader. The joint meeting itself was acrimonious. The general council was suspicious and Hayday's opening statement, attacking the very notion of 'equality of sacrifice', set the tone. After statements by Henderson, Clynes, Lansbury, and Morrison—the last probably provocatively favourable to MacDonald—there were questions, during which Henderson was 'rattled' by Cook and Bromley. Then, instead of coming to a decision, the three committees parted for further consultations. The likeliest explanation for this seems to be that the general council, faced with the ex-ministers' equivocation, adopted brinkmanship tactics, threatening to 'go it alone'. Ultimately a compromise was reached; that the reconvened joint meeting should pass unanimously a motion opposing vigorously the new Government, approving *en bloc* the actions of the ex-ministers, and taking Labour into Opposition.[23] Threatened with further disintegration, the ex-ministers felt they had no alternative,

21 Dalton diary, 24 Aug. 1931 (Dalton papers).

22 Memorandum by C. P. Duff, 25 Aug. 1931 (MacDonald papers, PRO 30/69/1316).

23 Dalton diary, 26 Aug. 1931 (Dalton papers); Labour Party NEC minutes, joint meeting, 26 Aug. 1931 (Labour Party papers); Donoughue and Jones, *Morrison*, 167; A. Bullock, *The Life and Times of Ernest Bevin* (3 vols.; London, 1960–83), i. 493.

despite the danger of permanently alienating the National Labourites. So unity was achieved; but it was a cosmetic sham, hiding manifold and deepening difficulties and divisions.

The joint meeting also appointed a committee, comprising three members each of the NEC and the consultative committee, plus the general council's ten-strong economic committee, to draft a manifesto. The predominance of union representatives meant that the terms of that document were assured in advance, and on 27 August the resumed joint meeting approved it with a few minor changes.[24]

The 27 August manifesto was not half-hearted. It condemned the new Government as a tool by which financiers aimed to reverse recent trends in social policy. All the cuts were condemned, but especially that in unemployment benefit. Britain was not on the verge of bankruptcy; the press had deliberately exaggerated the problems in order to help force through an economy package. On the positive side, the manifesto advocated the mobilization of foreign investments (a notable advance on the general council's 20 August programme), the temporary suspension of the sinking fund, taxation of fixed interest-bearing securities and other unearned income, and measures to reduce the burden of war debts. As in the rest of the document, the voice of Bevin boomed loud in the statement that economies would only boost unemployment, and that attempts to enforce wage cuts could only mean 'embittered conflict and industrial chaos'.[25] Significantly, a revenue tariff was not among the measures proposed. While it still had its advocates, notably Citrine, it was viewed with suspicion by Bevin; and the very fact that it had been discussed by Labour ministers showed how grave they had believed the crisis to be; now, free from office, lifelong free traders reverted to type.

The manifesto had a mixed reception. In fact, it was neither 'very good' (Dalton) nor 'a crude appeal to ignorance' (*Daily Telegraph*).[26] It had some economic merits, and in refusing to consider deficit financing or a revenue tariff, has even been criticized for erring on the side of orthodoxy. But its rejection of all economies discredited the programme utterly in the eyes of most intelligent observers. And of course, the adhesion of the ex-ministers to such a programme seemed the height of dishonesty and opportunism, since they had all, whatever

[24] Labour Party NEC minutes, joint meeting, 27 Aug. 1931 (Labour Party papers).
[25] Labour Party, *Annual Report, 1931* (London, 1931), 5–6.
[26] *Daily Telegraph*, 28 Aug. 1931; Dalton diary, 27 Aug. 1931 (Dalton papers).

they said subsequently, been committed on the evening of 21 August to an economy package of £56,000,000; some of them had been associated with even larger sums. The general public, and most politicians, did not know this as yet; they did know, however, that the Cabinet had met almost endlessly to discuss economies, and it took little to realize that some commitments must have been made. Snowden in particular saw their attitude as thoroughly dishonest.[27]

While there was an air of desperate rallying around this programme on the grounds that at least it was better than nothing, alternatives had been mooted, such as Henderson's £56,000,000 cuts plus revenue tariff plus suspension of the sinking fund, or the proposals put by Pethick-Lawrence to his constituents. The latter comprised measures not dissimilar to the 27 August programme, but accepted that there must also be 'substantial economies'. This was a programme at least as convincing as that adopted, and it would also have made the ex-ministers seem less unscrupulous.[28] But in reality, such considerations were secondary. A programme was needed; Bevin was being difficult; the drafting committee was dominated by trade unionists. The general council could not be beaten, and the ex-ministers decided to accept their proposals as the lesser evil. Henderson, for one, thought it better to be accused of dishonesty than further to split the party; and in fact, he put his name to the 27 August manifesto and proceeded to ignore it in his speeches, as did his late colleagues. They were more concerned to justify their role in the crisis, attack the National Government, and in some cases, propagate the theory of the 'bankers' ramp'. At their point of greatest weakness, the ex-ministers had been unable to resist having the programme of the general council rampant forced upon them. The question now was whether this balance of forces would continue, or whether the party leadership would be able to restore its position.

The election of a new leader was the first step along this road. At a meeting of ex-ministers on 27 August Henderson agreed to take the job, though with considerable reluctance given his age, his other commitments (party secretary and treasurer, and president of the forthcoming world disarmament conference), his involvement with economies as a member of the CEC, and the fact that his election

[27] Snowden, *Autobiography*, ii. 956–7.

[28] Pethick-Lawrence to his constituents, 26 Aug. 1931 (Churchill College, Philip Noel-Baker papers, NBKR 3/62); Keynes 'sympathise[d] entirely' with it: Keynes to Pethick-Lawrence, 28 Aug. 1931 (Pethick-Lawrence papers, P-L 2/208).

would be seen by MacDonald as a provocation.[29] The problem was that there was no alternative. The star of Clynes, the deputy leader, had fallen steadily since 1922; and despite Henderson's urgings that he was a better orator and less open to charges of dishonesty because not a member of the CEC, he refused the leadership with a show of magnanimity and, probably, not a little relief.[30] In his absence there was no choice but for Henderson to take the job, none of the promising younger men, like Alexander, Morrison, Dalton, Graham, Greenwood, or Johnston, being ready yet, although Graham became joint deputy leader with Clynes.

The PLP meeting on 28 August was attended by the general council and the NEC, at Henderson's insistence. This was partly to 'mark unity' (Dalton) and to intimidate the waverers (Pelling), but also to force the general council to respond to any misgivings regarding the new policy.[31] The mood of the meeting was mixed: Dalton thought people were 'very cheerful', but Pethick-Lawrence found 'both ex-Ministers and rank and file bewildered and distressed'.[32] Both MacDonald and Snowden had sent their apologies for absence, MacDonald claiming that he had been notified too late to cancel plans to take a break in Scotland, Snowden that, as the party had already decided on its new financial policy, no good purpose would be served by his attendance. Sankey and Malcolm MacDonald, the premier's son, did attend, however. The former explained his own views, and concluded that they were not leaving the party; 'nothing would ever drive them out'. Dalton's contribution, that the first Labour Government 'had been destroyed by a Red Letter, the second by a Bankers' Order', though nonsensical, was loudly applauded, suggesting that Sankey was being somewhat optimistic. Dalton added, more sensibly, that 'slogans were not enough'; they must 'hammer out a concrete, detailed policy of socialist reconstruction in industry & finance'. A resolution approving the move into Opposition was passed. The only ostensible note of division came when five or six ILPers opposed the election of the arch-disciplinarian, Henderson, to the leadership. However, there were also latent misgivings on the right, where strong

[29] Dalton diary, 27 Aug. 1931 (Dalton papers); E. A. Kaiser to Thomas, 27 Aug. 1931 (Thomas papers, U 1625/O14); Dalton diary, 24 Aug. 1931 (Dalton papers).

[30] *News Chronicle*, 28 Aug. 1931; Dalton diary, 28 Aug. 1931 (Dalton papers); J. R. Clynes, *Memoirs* (2 vols.; London, 1937–8), ii. 198.

[31] Dalton diary, 28 Aug. 1931 (Dalton papers); Pelling, *Short History*, 71.

[32] Dalton diary, 28 Aug. 1931 (Dalton papers); Pethick-Lawrence, *Fate Has Been Kind*, 166.

feelings for MacDonald remained, as the MP R. D. Denman reported to Sankey:

> I talked to a few of our men, Oldfield, Strauss, & Malone, & found they held the view that while the Party should go into Opposition, its opposition should be discriminating & that we ought to maintain friendly contact with the P.M. . . . I hope that when the House meets we shall have a slight influence in mitigating Party hostility.[33]

Elected to the leadership, Henderson made one of the scarcely euphoric statements which were to characterize his tenure of the position, saying he would 'give it a trial, in spite of his other work as secretary & treasurer of the Party'.[34] His aim was to moderate Labour's opposition and keep the way open for MacDonald's return.[35] As he told the editor of the *Observer*, J. L. Garvin, he realized the gravity of the national situation and would try not to aggravate it.[36] But this line was unlikely to succeed in an increasingly bellicose party. As Garvin put it in the *Observer*, '[b]y the usual irony of politics, his triumph in his party is the beginning of his ordeal'.[37]

III

The PLP meeting on 28 August ended the first flush of high-profile Labour activity, and there was an apparent hiatus pending the meeting of the Trades Union Congress in Bristol on 7 September and the beginning of the emergency session of Parliament the following day. In fact, however, these days saw a number of important shifts and developments within the party which presaged the victory of 'socialism' over pragmatic corporatism which was to take place by the time of the general election.

First, the 27 August programme soon fell into disuse. The ex-ministers had never particularly liked it, and it failed spectacularly to win any extra-party support, even Layton, who had urged many of its component parts on Snowden, believing it 'fallacious and a threat to confidence'.[38] Party spokesmen refused to be bound by it, especially in

[33] R. D. Denman to Sankey, 28 Aug. 1931 (Sankey papers, MSS Eng. hist. c. 508). Since both Malone and Sankey, at least, are known to have been Freemasons, 'our men' probably refers to a Masonic group within the PLP.

[34] Dalton diary, 28 Aug. 1931 (Dalton papers).

[35] See his comments to the subsequent press conference.

[36] Garvin to Lothian, 26 Aug. 1931, reporting Henderson to Garvin, 25 Aug. 1931 (Lothian papers, GD 40/17/257/263).

[37] *Observer*, 30 Aug. 1931.

[38] *Economist*, 5 Sept. 1931.

its total repudiation of public economy. Thus, on 3 September, Graham regaled *Daily Herald* readers with 'My Way to Balance the Budget'. As if oblivious to party policy, he not only supplemented the 27 August package with, for example, withdrawal of derating relief from industry, but also contradicted it—as for example in advocating rigidly rationing the expenditure of Government departments and making 'innumerable other savings' without too much difficulty. This implied a blissful amnesia regarding the travails the late Cabinet had had in finding such fat to trim; and his proposals of increased indirect taxation and a widening of the income tax net would have hit working-class voters hard. This plan might or might not have balanced the budget in theory; it is impossible to tell. What it did do was expose the fundamental divisions and confusion which existed within the Labour leadership on policy. This confusion, not surprisingly, spread throughout the party, one MP writing that 'the right sort of economy' was 'urgent', a flat contradiction of the 27 August line.[39]

In general, there was a swing to the left, as many people stopped discussing expedients to balance the budget and concrete policies in general, and started instead to talk about 'socialism', however defined. The apocalyptic strain in Labour rhetoric became stronger and stronger. Naturally, the ILP was in the van of this tendency, calling for new revolutionary tactics rather than budgetary gymnastics, and making attempts to work with the Communist-led National Unemployed Workers' Movement.[40] But others were moving in the same direction, notably Sir Stafford Cripps, late Solicitor-General. MacDonald, eager to keep his legal team together, had asked him to stay on, but he refused and was soon surprising people by talking of the need to abandon reformism, 'to throw off once and for all the attitude of compromise . . . and to come out boldly with a slap-up Socialist policy for dealing with the whole industrial and financial situation'. Graham replied on 3 September, surprisingly in view of his pedantic article published the same day, that he agreed with 'practically everything' Cripps had written and that they must 'build up a constructive Socialist case'. By 12 September Cripps felt that there had been 'a strong swing to the Left in the Party'.[41]

Fundamentals ousted the pragmatism of the 27 August manifesto in

[39] R. J. Wilson, MP, in *New Dawn*, 12 Sept. 1931.

[40] *New Leader*, 4 Sept. 1931; R. K. Middlemas, *The Clydesiders: A Left-Wing Struggle for Parliamentary Power* (London, 1965), 261.

[41] Estorick, *Stafford Cripps*, 88–9, 92–3, 96.

another area: trade policy. While that programme had ignored the question, it was well known that a revenue tariff had been under consideration by general council and Cabinet. Now the free traders began to fight back. On 2 September Lees-Smith said a tariff would hit the unemployed hardest of all, and four days later the Co-operative newspaper, *Reynolds's Illustrated News*, put pressure on the TUC over the issue, anticipating 'with confidence' that delegates to congress would douse any protectionist sparks.[42] Already a free trade virtually indistinguishable, in itself, from classic Cobdenism was threatening to re-rivet itself to the party.

The lull before the opening of Parliament, and the preoccupation of the union leaders with preparations for the Bristol congress, allowed the ex-ministers to begin to regain control. Heavily criticized on all sides, they had initially been shell-shocked, but now they began to fight back, if in some cases rather tentatively. Firstly, they explained their actions in speeches, often with heavy emphasis on the 'bankers' ramp' theory. On occasions, though, these expositions could prove embarrassing, as on 6 September when Greenwood told a meeting that it was 'true' that Labour, by coming out of office, had 'let the unemployed down', but that 'under no circumstances would he help to impoverish the unemployed.'[43] But by resigning and leaving the unemployed to the tender mercies of Neville Chamberlain at the Ministry of Health Greenwood could be said to have done just that. Secondly, they agreed memoranda regarding the events leading up to the Government's fall. Subsequently christened the 'Graham' and 'Greenwood' memoranda, they were reasonably accurate accounts of events in the CEC and Cabinet respectively, except in so far as they underplayed ministers' commitment to cuts. In particular, as is clear from the Cabinet minutes and Henderson's speech in Parliament, the Greenwood memorandum played down to the point of falsehood the fact that Cabinet had been agreed on the £56,000,000 package until the morning of 22 August, a fault pointed out by Morrison.[44]

This last point suggests, correctly, that it would be wrong to see the ex-ministers as a monolith. The nine oppositionist ministers made most of the running. All but one were elected to the PLP executive, while only one of the others even stood (see Table 6.1). Similarly, in Parliament Bondfield (diplomatically ill) and Wedgwood Benn were

[42] *News Chronicle*, 3 Sept. 1931; *Reynolds's Illustrated News*, 6 Sept. 1931.
[43] *Manchester Guardian*, 7 Sept. 1931.
[44] Morrison to Greenwood, 10 Sept. 1931 (Morrison papers, E/12).

Table 6.1. *PLP executive committee, September 1931*

1. T. Johnston	151 votes
2. G. Lansbury	140
3. H. Dalton	137
4. A. Greenwood	131
5. J. Barr	125
6. C. Addison	109
7. A. Alexander	108
8. E. Edwards	95
9. F. Pethick-Lawrence	87
10. E. Shinwell	81
11. H. Lees-Smith	79
12. D. Grenfell	68
13. M. Hamilton	68

Ex-officio: A. Henderson (leader); J. Clynes and W. Graham (joint deputy leaders)

Source: Dalton diary, 28 Aug. 1931 (Dalton papers).

silent in the pre-election session; Shaw spoke just once; and only Morrison, eager to regain kudos within the party, made much of a contribution. The balance had shifted away from the more pro-MacDonald members of the party leadership.

Even so, many Labourites continued to think well of MacDonald, and some links remained. On 27 August Middleton wrote to ask him when the election might be, though the premier's offhand reply seemed to belie his supposed wish to return to Labour,[45] as did his refusal to give Henderson advance notice of parliamentary business, despite the latter's assurance that he wanted 'to do everything in the proper way'.[46] The premier did keep up links with the *Daily Herald*, though his attempts to gain its support were blocked by Bevin.[47] And the prospective candidate for Gloucester was not alone in believing that the premier would always remain a socialist.[48] However, others

[45] Dalton diary, 7 Sept. 1931 (Dalton paper.

[46] Middleton to MacDonald, 27 Aug. 1931; M...Donald to Middleton (replying), 27 Aug. 1931; undated note reporting a telephone conversation with MacDonald's secretary reporting the premier's views (Labour Party papers, LP/PRO/31/5–7); *Parl. Deb.*, 5th ser, 256, col. 10, Henderson, 8 Sept. 1931.

[47] Dalton to Noel-Baker, 4 Sept. 1931 (Noel-Baker papers, NBKR 3/62).

[48] R. B. Carrow to Gloucester TCLP, special general council, 15 Sept. 1931 (Gloucester TCLP papers, on microfilm at Birmingham Reference Library).

were less sympathetic, Dalton seeing his belief that he could return as a 'delusion', and the chairman of Glasgow BLP being one of many who believed MacDonald had, in forming his new Government, ceased automatically to be a party member.[49] The tide of opinion was running away from the premier in the wider party too.

This made a more permanent political realignment and a general election more likely, but at this stage many Labourites welcomed the fact. This buoyant morale was nowhere more apparent than in Graham's astonishing *Daily Express* article of 31 August. After referring to 'a financial crisis, in the reality of which only a fraction of the Labour movement believes', and assuming that the new Government would remain in office until after the 1932 budget, he wrote that the Liberals and Conservatives would be discredited by passing unpopular economies, while Labour, reunited in Opposition, would gain credit as the record of the 1929–31 Government was forgotten by an electorate in which 'the trained students of politics and economics and the long view [were] in a hopeless minority'. The erstwhile Snowden acolyte continued:

> The next election will be fought, not by a Labour Government on an admittedly difficult defensive, but by a Labour movement united and eager. . . . At one stroke, without an election, and with time to prepare for an election on unusually favourable ground, [Labourites] have been relieved of their anxieties. Yesterday they dreaded a contest; to-day they are almost within sight of their clear majority in the British House of Commons.

When the *Observer* noted that a 'more cynical article was never written by a politician', it might have added, 'a more stupid article'.[50] It should never have been written, certainly not for a Conservative newspaper. Labour complained at the time and has complained since of press and Government 'misrepresentations' in 1931, but it took no misrepresentation to show this article's utter cynicism. As Sir Robert Horne put it, in Graham's mind 'the only things that now matter are the personal and political prospects of Mr William Graham':

> The anxieties of the business man, the apprehensions of the investor, the fears of the multitude with regard to their savings and their wages—all sink into insignificance in comparison with the portentous issue of the fate of the Labour Party and the place in it of Mr Willy Graham. . . . The ignorance of the populace is to be deliberately exploited in order to inflame the propaganda of

[49] Dalton diary, 5 Sept. 1931 (Dalton papers); Glasgow BLP, executive committee, 8 Sept. 1931 (Glasgow TCBLP papers).

[50] *Observer*, 6 Sept. 1931.

the Labour opposition. . . . Was ever a campaign of deceit so carefully planned and so blatantly acknowledged?[51]

It was small wonder that a directorship kept open for Graham since 1929 was now closed.[52] But Graham was not the only Labourite to feel confident. Reports from the constituencies suggested an 'admirable' feeling among activists, while Dalton felt Labour would do well whenever the election was held—and especially if it was delayed.[53] By 7 September, however, Adamson, Alexander, Lansbury, Lees-Smith, and Wedgwood Benn were anticipating an early poll. It seems unlikely that they were pessimistic yet.[54] Given time, they would be.

IV

The TUC, which opened at Bristol the same day, seemed to mark no great departures. The left was defeated repeatedly, and attempts to move the unions away from 'Mondist' corporatism failed, despite the argument that such 'industrial gradualism' should be discarded with the political gradualism of MacDonald and Snowden. In fact, political gradualism had not been jettisoned, but the clash between rhetoric and reality implied in the argument ran deeply through the week's proceedings. As Bevin said, 'let us have our head in the clouds if we like, but for God's sake let us keep our feet on the ground'.[55] Thus while one miners' delegate called for devaluation, not as a means towards socialism but merely to provide 'a little more work', another argued that the last three weeks had exploded 'the whole idea of the peaceful transition from capitalism into socialism'.[56] Similarly, Arthur Pugh's proposals for a steel cartel with price-fixing and import-restricting powers hardly met the specification of a Labour Party increasingly talking as though it were within spitting distance of the socialist millenium.

These contradictions aside, congress saw two further developments. First, anti-tariff sentiment hardened. It was well known that the general council had discussed a revenue tariff on 20 August, but left a decision to congress. In fact, the proposal was never debated, and if it had been it might well have been defeated. It was largely due to the

[51] *Daily Express*, 2 Sept. 1931.
[52] Dalton diary, 30 Sept. 1931 (Dalton papers).
[53] Dalton to Noel-Baker, 4 Sept. 1931 (Noel-Baker papers, NBKR 3/62); Johnston, interviewed 26 Aug. for *Forward*, 29 Aug. 1931.
[54] Passfield to Beatrice Webb, 7 Sept. 1931 (Passfield papers, II 3(1)27, f. 92).
[55] TUC, *Report, 1931*, 364.
[56] Ibid. 419, 432.

provision for protection that Pugh's steel cartel proposal almost fell, Ebby Edwards of the MFGB admitting that his union was 'afraid of the implication of being committed to tariffs'.[57] And when Henderson, in his fraternal address, admitted that the Cabinet had discussed a tariff, it was, as the *Manchester Guardian* put it, very much 'an historical reference'.[58] The fight for the revenue tariff, which with all its faults might have been a useful tool in convincing the electorate that Labour possessed immediate expedients as well as grandiose but vague plans, had been abandoned.

Secondly, the general council's hold over the party was weakened. On 10 September Henderson received a great ovation, suggesting that the perceived heroism of the ex-ministers had gone a long way towards softening ordinary trade unionists' memories of the second Labour Government. In addition, the reassertion of industrial gradualism separated the unions somewhat from the apocalyptic strains within the party, while the hostility evinced towards the revenue tariff showed Bevin and Citrine could not depart too far from the minds of their followers. Still, TUC leaders could be pleased that the ill-will shown towards MacDonald, Snowden, and Thomas and their programme of cuts further limited the prospects of future reconciliation.

A number of other factors also served to weaken the unions' hold. The meeting of Parliament moved the centre of gravity to Westminster, where union power was more difficult to wield, and the increasing preoccupation of both party and union leaders made the administration of the party by unwieldy joint meetings impossible. In addition, press and Government attacks on 'trade union dictation' made union leaders less keen to take a high profile. A more convenient means of exercising control would have to be found. But if it had been a disappointing week for Bevin and the general council, it had been little short of disastrous for Henderson and the party leadership.

Henderson's eve of Parliament message to Labour MPs, issued on 7 September, provided hints of his continuing moderation. He made little of Labour's move into Opposition, stressed the need to stand by the 1929 manifesto—a long way from the 27 August programme—and was most emphatic when demanding the avoidance of 'personal recrimination against old colleagues, who doubtless were actuated by deep convictions'.[59] But few noticed Henderson's equivocation at the

[57] TUC, *Report, 1931*, 451.
[58] *Manchester Guardian*, 11 Sept. 1931.
[59] *Daily Herald*, 7 Sept. 1931.

time, and the next morning's PLP meeting was a high-spirited affair at which the ex-ministers faced no problems.[60]

That afternoon, however, Labourites were somewhat disappointed as Henderson's speech opposing the Government's vote of confidence said nothing much about alternative policies, but dwelt instead on the great loss involved in the departure, 'be [it] long or short' of MacDonald and his cohorts; admitted to accepting, albeit 'provisionally', economies of £56,000,000; stated that he objected not to the formation of the Government, but to the manner of its formation; and, at a time when Labourites everywhere were telling the tale of the 'bankers' ramp', dismissed the idea, saying he had no complaint. By the time he sat down it seemed that his only objections to the Government were the manner of its nativity and the cut in unemployment benefit: a narrow basis upon which to lead the Opposition.[61] It was left to Alexander to make a more fighting speech from the front bench, attacking the economies as the prelude to a wage-cutting campaign, arguing that the Labour Cabinet had made no final decisions, and defending free trade. He was also rather more critical of the bankers.[62] The Government, even so, won its vote of confidence, and Labourites began to realize that their mere resignation and Opposition could not prevent the economies being implemented.

As the week wore on, there were further blows to Labour morale. On 10 September the budget included economies of only £70,000,000, comprising the £56,000,000 to which all the ex-ministers had agreed, however reluctantly, plus the 10 per cent unemployment benefit cut which many of them had accepted. The next day Thomas, in a series of revelations regarding the extent of the Labour Cabinet's commitment to cuts, 'discomfited the opposition to an extent such as [Hankey had] never before witnessed in parliament'.[63] Since even National back-benchers were unaware of the extent of these commitments, it

[60] Passfield to Beatrice Webb, 8 Sept. 1931 (Passfield papers, II 3(1)27, f. 93).

[61] *Parl. Deb.*, 5th ser., 256, cols. 25–40, Henderson, 8 Sept. 1931; cols. 86–7, J. C. Wedgwood, 8 Sept. 1931; Maclean, memorandum, 14 Sept. 1931, Runciman to his wife, 9 Sept. 1931 (Runciman papers, WR 245, 303).

[62] *Parl. Deb.*, 5th ser., 256, cols. 113–23, Alexander, 8 Sept. 1931. It was the best speech of the night, according to the assembled journalists: see F. Sulley of the press gallery to Alexander, 8 Sept. 1931 (Churchill College, Alexander papers, AVAR 5/2, f. 143).

[63] H. L. Nathan to Lloyd George, 13 Sept. 1931 (Lloyd George papers, G/15/7/21); Hankey diary, 13 Sept. 1931 (Hankey papers, HNKY 1/7).

was not surprising that Labour MPs were 'rattled'.[64] The continuing trickle of defections, though slight, also began to affect morale. Thus by the weekend of 12–13 September, spirits had taken a definite dip. A delayed election might (it was thought) see Labour doing well, but Conservative pressure for an early dissolution was growing, and Henderson was predicting a poll in mid-November.[65] Small wonder, then that he for one was 'very depressed and upset' that weekend.[66]

The events of the following week did little to restore his, or anyone else's, morale. A spirit of bravado, variously evinced by Dalton, Maxton, and the *Daily Herald*, often masked private doubts. Snowden's comment that many Labour MPs would soon be MPs no more had a ring of truth. And revelations about the ex-ministers' commitments continued. As one critic put it, '[t]heir followers watched with growing consternation' as '[o]ne after another' ex-ministers 'got up to try to wriggle out of their responsibility' and as '[o]ne after another they went down—"like nine-pins", as a laughing Ministerialist put it'.[67] Meanwhile, the party in the country, alarmed by developments, began to express disquiet at the PLP's 'negative policy'.[68] This was a very unhappy situation. Henderson's PPS, Philip Noel-Baker, felt that at an early election Labour would 'do badly' because time was needed to get across Labour's 'real case'.[69]

But what was Labour's 'real case'? The truth was that, with the influence of the general council decreasing, party policy was reverting very much to type. On 27 August the party had adopted a bold, specific (if arguably wrong-headed) policy; as September wore on it began to readopt vaguely defined pseudo-panaceas instead. The Conservatives had researched extensively on policy since 1929, whereas Labour, borne down by the cares of office, had done very little. Now, analysis of the failings of the second Labour Government, and research on new

[64] For National ignorance, see Neville to Hilda Chamberlain, 12 Sept. 1931 (Chamberlain papers, NC 18/1/754); for Labour, see Dalton diary, 7 Sept. 1931, referring to the following days (Dalton papers).

[65] Estorick, *Cripps*, 96; D. Graham Pole MP to Shaw, 9 Sept. 1931 (Borthwick Institute of Historical Research, Graham Pole papers, UL 5/8/1, unpublished memoir, f. 184).

[66] Sankey diary, 12 and 13 Sept. 1931 (Sankey papers, MSS Eng. hist. e. 285).

[67] *News Chronicle*, 15 Sept. 1931.

[68] Leeds City LP, general committee, 16 Sept. 1931 (Leeds City LP papers, 4/7, f. 482).

[69] Noel-Baker to Harold Butler, 14 Sept. 1931; Noel-Baker to Stephen King Hall, 18 Sept. 1931 (Noel-Baker papers, NBKR 3/62, 2/3).

policies, were required. But little was done. A policy committee under Graham confined itself largely to finance, and despite efforts to tap City personnel for information did not function particularly well.[70] As well as lack of time, there was also a lack of will, Labourites becoming increasingly reluctant to 'tinker' with a perceivedly decaying capitalism. The failure of the second Labour Government could be blamed on MacDonald and Snowden; its fall on the bankers. In a sense, what policy research took place was largely negative in intent, to stop the financiers behaving in future as they were believed to have behaved in August. And while the leadership consulted Keynes, the name of the latter was derided by back-bench Labourites.[71]

In addition, the reassertion of free trade continued at all levels of the party. York DLP, for example, saw tariffs as an attack upon the workers' standard of living.[72] Labour speakers, seeking to move onto the offensive on other than the boggy ground of economies, stressed the Conservatives' protectionism in the hope that the slump would have caused no rethinking on the subject, and that it would therefore prove as unpopular as in 1906 and 1923. The *Daily Herald* argued desperately that Labour was 'not Cobdenite' and would not 'oppose the proposals of the High Protectionists with the sterile negations of orthodox Free Trade', but closer to Labour hearts by this time was *Reynolds's* comment that 'to play with the tariff issue is to court political disaster'.[73] The end result of all this, of course, was that the utterances of Labour's leaders did little to convince people of their grasp of the problems which faced the country. Bad luck stories, conspiracy theories, and special pleading about the last days of the late Cabinet were not enough. All in all, Labour's 'real case' was becoming, not more, but less well-defined.

V

The lack of firm leadership did nothing to help matters. Henderson, depressed because he now expected an early election, and overworked, still hoped some reconciliation with the National Labourites would be possible. However, his acquiescence in moves to bring this about, plus,

[70] Dalton diary, 7, 11 Sept. 1931 (Dalton papers).

[71] Ibid. 1 Oct. 1931; for derision, see e.g. *Parl. Deb.*, 5th ser., 256, col. 81, A. Maclaren, 8 Sept. 1931.

[72] York DLP, delegate meeting, 9 Sept. 1931 (York DLP papers, 1/5, f. 90).

[73] *Daily Herald*, 14 Sept. 1931; *Reynolds's Illustrated News*, 13 Sept. 1931.

more broadly, reactions to his fairly pacific approach, were soon to force him and the party into rather more vigorous opposition.

On 16 September, *The Times*'s influential editorial calling for a National appeal was published; significantly, the next few days saw rumours that Henderson wanted to bring Labour into the Government: on 19 September the *Manchester Guardian* called explicitly for such a move. Henderson, meanwhile, trailed his coat to the former Liberal Cabinet Minister J. E. B. Seely, who had been plotting the formation of a genuinely all-party Government since autumn 1930. The Labour leader said he 'hated the position into which he had been forced against his will', that he wanted 'to put the country first', and that he would help in negotiations regarding the implementation of the cuts. He would also be glad to see MacDonald, if Seely could arrange it.[74] He was obviously, as he put it, 'keep[ing] an open mind'.[75]

The weekend of 19–20 September saw further developments. Staying with the Webbs in Hampshire, Henderson received a telephone call asking him to see MacDonald. In fact it was to be briefed about the decision to leave the gold standard, but the Webbs and their guest expected a request to bring Labour into the National Government. He said he would take no action without consulting the executive committees of the Labour movement, but the idea clearly appealed.[76] However, the rather strained meeting with MacDonald seems to have passed off without any mention of reconstruction, although it did give rise to much speculation.[77]

Such speculation was not dampened by Henderson's performance in the following day's debate on the Gold Standard (Amendment) Bill. In a conciliatory speech, he reminded Snowden that the lack of national unity was not the fault of Labour alone; urged reconsideration, but not necessarily full repeal, of the economies; and promised full Labour co-operation in passing the bill. This was certainly not what Labour MPs wanted to hear. After two weeks of parliamentary setbacks, defeats, and humiliations, here was a chance to ridicule the spectacle of a Government formed to preserve the gold standard abandoning it. Back-bench criticism was bad enough, but then

[74] Seely to Reading, 18 Sept. 1931 (Reading papers, MSS Eur. F118/131).
[75] Beatrice Webb diary, 20 Sept. 1931 (Passfield papers).
[76] Ibid. 21 Sept. 1931.
[77] MacDonald diary, 20 Sept. 1931 (MacDonald papers, PRO 30/69/1753); for speculation, see e. g. Amery to Beaverbrook, 22 Sept. 1931 (Beaverbrook papers, C/6); *News Chronicle*, 22 Sept. 1931.

Addison, winding up from the front bench, launched a spirited assault on the Government. These splits were carried into the division lobbies; against Henderson's advice to abstain, 112 Labour MPs opposed the second reading, and 193, including a number of former Cabinet and junior ministers, supported an amendment to give the Bank more power over British owned balances.

It is possible that Henderson's conduct simply reflected a patriotic desire to make the departure from gold as painless as possible. Clearly that was part of it; but it is not unlikely that he also wanted to see how far a conciliatory approach would take him, given his realization that an early election would be disastrous for Labour. Earlier that day MacDonald had limited all the cuts to a maximum of 10 per cent, which could be interpreted as an olive branch, because the real reason—that a revival of the naval unrest was feared—could not be given.[78] As press speculation mounted, two Labour MPs who had been loath to part from MacDonald, Malone and Dunnico, told MacDonald's secretary, Rose Rosenberg, that they were working to see what support the premier had within the party, and also that Henderson might be prepared to enter the Government.[79] He, however, spent the morning of 22 September under fierce attack from a PLP meeting for his weak leadership. He was forced to deny the existence of any 'plot', and finally—having complained about the lack of support he was receiving—demanded a meeting of the PLP executive that afternoon.[80] There he offered his resignation, and although he was cajoled into staying on, he remained on poor terms with some leading colleagues. Meanwhile, rumours began to spread that many Labour MPs would prefer Lloyd George as their leader.[81]

Malone and Dunnico, meanwhile, continued their moves to effect a reconciliation with MacDonald. Malone told Rosenberg that Henderson and many other Labourites would be ready to come to terms and would enter the National Government in order to prevent an election. This anxiety was prompted, he went on, by Labour's expectation of up to a hundred losses in an early poll. He felt that a gesture of leniency towards the unemployed would 'immediately' bring over 'the best

[78] Hankey diary, 26 Sept. 1931 (Hankey papers, HNKY 1/7).
[79] Rosenberg to MacDonald, 22 Sept. 1931 (MacDonald papers, PRO 30/69/1314).
[80] Ibid.; Beatrice Webb diary, 16 Sept. 1931 (Passfield papers); *Daily Telegraph*, 23 Sept. 1931.
[81] Rosenberg to MacDonald, 23 Sept. 1931 (MacDonald papers, PRO 30/69/1314).

element' of the party, leaving the ILP and sundry left-wingers in Opposition.[82] Such confidence, however, was probably superficial; certainly by 25 September the press was talking merely of a possible secession by twenty MPs including two ex-ministers, and that, correctly, with great caution.[83] Malone and Dunnico, however, did not give up, arranging to see MacDonald on 28 September. That meeting was a sad anticlimax, however. Having seen Henderson first, and got, if no more, his acquiescence, they urged the Prime Minister to return or to make some concessions and ask Henderson to join the Government. MacDonald, whose main priority now was to find a basis upon which the National Government could fight against Labour, lectured them on the state of the Labour Party, said he intended soon to retire from politics, and went to bed.[84] The plot was now well and truly dead, although some forlorn efforts to reunite MacDonald with the party still lay in the future.

In reality, of course, it could never have succeeded. First, MacDonald had no desire to work again with Henderson, and little longing to return to the Labour Party. Secondly, the proposed entry of Labour would have provoked a revolt among the bulk of the Government's supporters, Conservative MPs, who wanted an early election to obtain a mandate for protection. The adhesion of free-trade Labour, at the expense of an unemployment benefit cut which they favoured, had no appeal at all. The evening Britain left gold, the 1922 Committee called for an early National appeal. Finally, Labour feeling had hardened to such an extent that even had they seen it in terms of entry into the Government or certain electoral defeat, most Labour MPs would have preferred the latter. A mere 'gesture' towards the unemployed would not now suffice. As the MP J. J. McShane said, 'I despise the proposals in [the Economy] Bill, and I despise anyone who has the hardihood to vote for them.'[85] And while the general council's potential for positive action was weaker than it had been a month earlier, union leaders still possessed an effective veto over so important a question. Henderson's acquiescence in the Malone–Dunnico plot shows, however, his sheer desperation by mid-September.

[82] Rosenberg to MacDonald, 23 Sept. 1931 (MacDonald) papers, PRO 30/69/1314).
[83] *Daily Telegraph*, *Manchester Guardian*, *News Chronicle*, 25 Sept. 1931.
[84] MacDonald diary, 28 Sept. 1931 (MacDonald papers, PRO 30/69/1753).
[85] *Parl. Deb.*, 5th ser., 257, col. 104, McShane, 28 Sept. 1931.

VI

The patent failure of this line, and the obvious impatience of the PLP, led to two significant departures. First, at Burnley on 25 September, Henderson made a keynote speech which was to form the basis of Labour's election programme. He opened by criticizing the Government and saying its policies would increase unemployment, and he attacked the Conservatives for putting party before country by forcing a general election at such a critical time. Labour, he said, was committed to a balanced budget, and he advanced a basket of short-term measures to stabilize the situation, such as the possible mobilization of foreign securities, public control of banking, and machinery to prevent profiteering following devaluation. Tariffs would not help, he added, condemning them in classic free-trade terms as increasing living costs, enriching private interests at the expense of the public, and promoting industrial inefficiency. In the longer term, he advocated public control of the 'main' industries as public corporations or co-operatives; marketing schemes for agriculture; and, especially, international action to reduce tariff barriers, encourage economic co-operation, restore the basis of world credit, and promote peace.[86]

Ostensibly impressive, this speech begged many questions. For example, which industries were classed as 'main', and which of them would become public corporations, and which co-operatives? Where were Labour's detailed plans for such bodies? What if—as had happened repeatedly in recent years—the hopes for international action came to naught? No Labourite could have given an authoritative answer. In short, Henderson neither showed how the third Labour Government would differ appreciably from the second, nor advanced a realistic alternative to tariffs as a short-term means of maximizing British prosperity within the context of world depression.

While many Labourites liked the speech, the general council, which had not been consulted despite the clear breach of the 27 August programme, was less than delighted, and was reported as considering it 'thoroughly unconvincing'.[87] Although a front of unity was kept up, even to the extent of Bevin agreeing to fight Gateshead at the general election, it is difficult to avoid the view that the union leaders had more or less given up hope of retaining full control over the party, for the present. Citrine, for one, certainly seemed bored with Labour

[86] *Manchester Guardian*, 26 Sept. 1931. [87] *Observer*, 4 Oct. 1931.

politics.[88] Instead, knowing that Labour would be defeated at the election, they hung back, realizing that they would be able to move in for the kill on the morrow of defeat—as in fact happened. On 30 September, the general council decided that the joint meetings with the party executives had been 'more or less ineffective' and that therefore the national joint council (comprising representatives of the NEC, the PLP, and the unions), on which the TUC had a formalized preponderance, should be revived. The ground for the take-over was being prepared.[89]

The second result of the failure of Henderson's ultra-moderate policy was the explusion from the party of MacDonald and his followers by the NEC on 28 September. Too much should not, perhaps, be made of this; it was the first meeting of the committee since late August, and the subject might have been discussed anyway. However, the rumours regarding a reconciliation with MacDonald undoubtedly encouraged a pre-emptive strike, and a resolution was passed to the effect that all Labour supporters of the Government had expelled themselves. The only dissentient was Henderson, who refused to sign the letters of expulsion, thus necessitating the use of the 'rubber stamp' which gave MacDonald such grounds for self-pity in future years.[90] There can be no doubt that the NEC was reflecting the views of the wider party in taking this action: on 3 October, for example, one back-bencher called MacDonald 'the biggest and blackest traitor ever known in this country'; when an article sympathetic to MacDonald appeared in *Reynolds's*, it excited a flood of angry remonstrances; and while 69 NUR branches voted confidence in Thomas, 213 endorsed the union leadership's actions against him.[91] Given this mood, it was understandable that, at the NEC and PLP meetings of 28 and 29 September, Henderson took trouble to deny the existence of approaches to and negotiations with MacDonald.[92]

[88] Beatrice Webb diary, 23 Sept. 1931 (Passfield papers).

[89] Bevin to F. J. Cook (Odham's Press Ltd.), 15 Sept. 1931 (Bevin papers, MSS 126/EB/MC/2/75); TUC general council minutes, 30 Sept. 1931 (TUC papers).

[90] Labour Party NEC minutes, 28 Sept. 1931 (Labour Party papers); Hamilton, *Henderson*, 399; Lord Citrine, *Two Careers* (London, 1967), 357.

[91] *Parl. Deb.*, 5th ser., 257, col. 55, Gordon Macdonald, 28 Sept. 1931; *Daily Herald*, 5 Oct. 1931; *Reynolds's Illustrated News*, 27 Sept., 4 Oct. 1931; NUR, executive committee, 14–19, 21–5 Sept. 1931 (Modern Records Centre, NUR papers, MSS 127/1/1/19, f. 176).

[92] Labour Party NEC minutes, 28 Sept. 1931 (Labour Party papers); *Daily Herald*, 30 Sept. 1931.

The NEC on 28 September also agreed resolutions which, subject to approval by the following week's party conference, would form the election manifesto. Only after the meeting were Graham and Dalton deputed to secure the approval of Bevin and Citrine. The trade unionists were not happy, and obtained some concessions, but for the most part they kept their reservations to themselves.[93] The next day the PLP endorsed the programme, and Harold Laski set about drafting the manifesto. Meanwhile, preparations for the campaign continued, not helped by the fact that the bulk of the stock literature—much of it only recently produced—was now obsolete, carrying pictures of MacDonald and dealing with the situation prior to the fall of the Labour Government. To sort out the chaos, Henderson's son, William, head of the press and publicity department, was forced to announce that he would not be defending his seat at Enfield. This left Enfield DLP in a very difficult position. It also suggested considerable pessimism about Labour's prospects.[94]

Enfield was not the only divisional party with problems. In some, like Cambridgeshire, where the MacDonaldite candidate had withdrawn his financial support, the party almost collapsed.[95] Some divisional parties had been quick to make preparations—in the case of, for example, Doncaster, East Bristol, Woolwich, and York, within a fortnight of the demise of the Labour Government—but others had allowed matters to drift, either through financial or organizational problems, or through a mixture of confusion and apathy.[96] Now, agents were primed, and *Labour Organiser* urged DLPs to be ready, with yet more helpings of false optimism.[97]

[93] Dalton diary, 28 and 29 Sept. 1931 (Dalton papers).

[94] Labour Party, *Annual Report, 1932* (London, 1932), 63; Labour Party NEC minutes, 2 Oct. 1931 (Labour Party papers).

[95] Cambridgeshire TCLP, special executive committees, 12, 26 Sept. 1931 (Cambridgeshire TCLP papers, 416/0.4).

[96] Doncaster DLP, special executive committee, 2 Sept. 1931 (Doncaster DLP papers, DS 7/1/5, ff. 32–3); H. E. Rogers (agent) to G. R. Shepherd, 18 Sept. 1931 (East Bristol DLP papers, Acc. 39035/60); Woolwich BLP, executive committee, 8 Sept. 1931 (Woolwich BLP papers, minutes 1924–31, f. 1070, on microfilm at Birmingham Reference Library); York DLP, delegate meeting, 9 Sept. 1931 (York DLP papers, 1/5, f. 91). For more tardy parties, see e.g. Canterbury DLP, which held its first meeting after the fall of the Labour government on 29 Sept. (Kent Archive Office, Canterbury DLP papers, U1760/A1/1); Batley and Morley DLP, which held its first on 26 Sept. (West Yorkshire Archive Service, Bradford, Batley and Morley DLP papers, 13D84/11).

[97] Marion Phillips to George Ford, 28 Sept. 1931 (Phillips papers, MP 1/330); *Labour Organiser*, Sept. 1931.

The start of the party conference at Scarborough on 5 October did little to help these preparations. The conference, held in the shadow of the dissolution, was a rather grim affair. The NEC resolutions were passed comfortably, but despite the great reception accorded to Henderson, and the fairly easy ride given to the ex-ministers, there were deep divisions.[98] There was an obvious clash between the apocalyptic strains of people like Cripps—'[t]he one thing that is not inevitable now is gradualness'—on the one hand, and those pragmatists like the prospective candidate who called for anti-dumping legislation.[99] While some erstwhile moderate leaders were making apparently radical speeches—Morrison saying Labour should make socialism 'the fundamental and the most acute issue' and Pethick-Lawrence saying capitalism was 'breaking to pieces before [their] eyes'—others, like Graham, were stressing Labour's commitment to free trade and the balanced budget.[100] Meanwhile, Henderson professed his unwillingness to serve in another minority Government but quashed a proposal that Labour should never again take office without a majority.[101] Therein lay the paradox. Labour talked as though it were on the threshold of the millenium, yet its leaders acted as though about to resume office in the second Labour Government.

Other sores remained. First, the trade unions were less enthusiastic than their financial generosity would suggest. They did agree to an increase in affiliation fees from 3d to 4d per member per year, and some unions did make large donations—£5,000 from the NUGMW, £2,500 from the TGWU, £2,000 from the NUR, and £500 each from the RCA and the NUDAW.[102] However, leading trade unionists were still very wary of the parliamentary leadership, and this financial generosity has to be seen in a wider context. It would, after all, add strongly to the unions' post-election claims to take over if they could show that they had done everything possible to help Henderson and his colleagues during the election. And, secondly, the clash with the ILP was not resolved, the new, tighter standing orders of the PLP being endorsed by 2,117,000 votes to 193,000. Maxton argued that this expelled him, effectively, from the Labour Party, and the ILP was now set firmly on the road to disaffiliation and oblivion. Two days

[98] Dalton diary, 2–8 Oct. 1931 (Dalton papers); Beatrice Webb diary, 10 Oct. 1931 (Passfield papers).

[99] Labour Party, *Annual Report, 1931*, 171, 205, 188, 199.

[100] Ibid. 172, 177, 188; *Manchester Guardian*, 8 Oct. 1931.

[101] Labour Party, *Annual Report, 1931*, 236.

[102] Ibid. 209, 222.

later, the NEC decided that, to be officially endorsed, candidates must sign an undertaking to abide by standing orders. Where they refused, the DLP would be permitted to run a second candidate in that constituency.[103] On the eve of the election, then, Labour's divisions were getting wider.

And how would Labour fare at that election? To listen to some conference delegates, very well indeed. C. T. Cramp (NUR) argued that the party would 'win well', while George Hicks (Builders) could not 'conceive of any set of circumstances more favourable for [their] propaganda'.[104] The *Daily Herald* commented on 6 October that, given unity, Labour's prospects were 'definitely good'. There can be little doubt, however, that much of this was merely a combination of partisan over-confidence and sheer bravado. No one was going to come out publicly and predict defeat on the eve of an election campaign, least of all the *Daily Herald*. Yet defeat looked increasingly likely to be the outcome, and Transport House was widely rumoured to expect the loss of anything up to 100 seats.[105] Many of Labour's seats were held tenuously. Labour had had its most successful year to date in 1929; some reverses were almost inevitable, given the record of the second Labour Government and the fact that in most constituencies Labour would be fighting a single opponent. The continuing attraction of MacDonald, Snowden, and Thomas to many erstwhile Labour voters would also be a factor, and the failure of Labour in Opposition since August to devise a credible alternative policy was unlikely to help. The chances of securing the extra seats necessary to achieve a Labour majority Government were nil; a serious reverse was very likely. The events of the next three weeks were to bring about the latter on an unimagined scale, and also allow Labour to become after the election what it had not been before it: the general council's party.

[103] Ibid. 179; Labour Party NEC minutes, 7 Oct. 1931 (Labour Party papers).
[104] Labour Party, *Annual Report, 1931*, 201, 208.
[105] See e.g. *Daily Telegraph*, 22 Sept. 1931. For confirmation of Transport House pessimism, see G. R. Shepherd to H. E. Rogers, 17 Nov. 1931 (East Bristol DLP papers, Acc. 39035/60).

7

THE PARTIES' ELECTION PROGRAMMES

THE parties' election manifestos in 1931 did not attain a mass readership. However, in so far as they informed the policy basis of each party's campaign, and of each candidate's election address—mailed free to every household in a constituency—they were of great significance.

I

The Cabinet had agreed that each National party should issue its own manifesto, and that these were to be linked by a general statement from MacDonald. His was the first manifesto to be issued, on 6 October, in time for inclusion in the newspapers on the morning of the dissolution. It was noteworthy in a number of ways. First, it was, as prescribed, vague on specific policies, beyond the need to balance the budget and to re-establish confidence in sterling. MacDonald only mentioned two specific further aims: the possible cancellation of war debts and reparations, and the need to reduce unemployment. The central point was the 'free hand' or 'doctor's mandate':

> These are times of exceptional urgency and exceptional conditions, which demand exceptional treatment. As it is impossible to foresee in the changing circumstances of to-day what may arise, no one can set out a programme of detail on which specific pledges can be given. The Government must therefore be free to consider every proposal likely to help, such as tariffs, expansion of exports, and contraction of imports, commercial treaties, and mutual economic arrangements with the Dominions. It must also watch how the devaluation of money and the economies which had to be made . . . affect the lives of our people, and take every step which can be made effective to protect them against exploitation.

This was drafted well enough to permit protectionists and free traders to act together, so long as they ruled out nothing in advance. It also held out the hope—but no more—that the economies might be revised if prices rose. The third outstanding feature of the document was its insistence on the need for 'a comprehensively national' Government to restore confidence. No mention was made of the Labour Opposition; one could almost imagine that Labour had followed its erstwhile leader into the administration, an impression not marred by his insistence that 'the immediate tasks are temporary, and, when finished, [would] be followed by normal political activities'. This seemed to suggest that he was expecting the Government to dissolve itself quite soon, but in fact reflected MacDonald's dread of being seen as a prisoner of the Conservatives. Finally, he stressed the vital link between the Government's re-election, the national credit, and the well-being of the British people. Credit must be 'unassailable' because it was 'the basis of every security which our people have'. Upon it depended 'how the tables and cupboards of working-class families are to be stocked, as well as whether we are to have sound national Budgets or Budgets which are the prelude to bankruptcy'.[1]

With the ground rules thus set, the Conservatives and Liberals could set about producing their own manifestos. The former, published on 8 October, was drafted by Baldwin and toughened up by Chamberlain.[2] This was significant in itself. Baldwin was always somewhat nervous of democracy, especially after his election defeat of 1923 when he had appealed for a mandate for protection, and after the success of the Liberals in 1929 in taking a number of Conservative votes with what he saw as empty and flashy promises to reduce unemployment and assist agriculture. Thus, particularly on protection, he was reluctant to be too specific and tended to hide behind formulae such as the 'doctor's mandate'. But Baldwin was not—as the events of March 1931 had shown all too well—the Conservative Party. Neville Chamberlain was far more self-assured in many ways: the populist, protectionist Unionism of Birmingham, allied to a far less neurotic temperament, made him more ready to advance protectionism without the nuances and qualifications which Baldwin felt compelled to use. There was to be, indeed, something of a dichotomy running through the Conservative campaign in 1931, between Baldwin on the one hand and his more confident colleagues and candidates on the other; the former more cautious in advancing protectionist arguments, and less willing to place tariffs at the centre of his campaign, than the latter. But the starching of the manifesto by Chamberlain meant that it was based

[1] 'An Appeal to the Nation by the Rt. Hon. J. Ramsay MacDonald, Prime Minister', in Craig, *Election Manifestos*, 91–3.

[2] Neville to Hilda Chamberlain, 10 Oct. 1931 (Chamberlain papers, NC 18/1/758).

squarely on party policy as evolved before the crisis: economy, protection, imperial preference, and help for agriculture. For the moment, it argued, 'heavy' and, hopefully 'temporary' sacrifices by 'every class of the community' had been necessary to balance the budget. However, the country still faced 'ultimate bankruptcy' unless the trade deficit could be rectified. It was essential, therefore, that the Government won a large majority and that Labour's programme, which would turn the 'grave' situation into 'one of chaos and catastrophe' was totally rejected. After a nod in the direction of the possibility of international action to solve some of Britain's problems, and stressing the party's willingness 'to examine any method which can effect what is required', the manifesto moved into a straight exposition of party policy. First, a 'carefully designed and adjusted tariff' was 'the quickest and most effective' way of protecting the home market and promoting the reduction of existing tariffs against British goods. Secondly, agriculture must be helped by the prohibition of dumping and 'a free hand . . . to use prohibitions, quotas or duties as may seem most effective'. Thirdly, imperial economic unity must be secured when the imperial conference resumed at Ottawa. In short, the manifesto did not hide the Conservative Party's light under the National bushel. Rather, it advanced party policy as clearly as Baldwin's misgivings would allow. At the same time, nothing they said was inconsistent with MacDonald's definition of the 'free hand', which only prohibited the elimination of options in advance.[3]

The Liberal Party had rather more difficulty with its manifesto. On the evening of 7 October, a draft was much amended by senior Liberals. They wanted the approval of the party's leader, Lloyd George, and its other Cabinet Minister, Reading, though; so next day, Samuel sent the chief whip, Goronwy Owen, to Churt with a copy of the document and a letter pleading for the leader's signature, which would be 'of great importance to the preservation of the Party'. Samuel also offered to visit the invalid, having decided to change his plans and return to London on 9 October after speaking in Bradford, instead of going straight on to his marginal Lancashire constituency. Perhaps this rearrangement was supposed to flatter Lloyd George and soften his hostility, but he had already declared his position, and his son had resigned from the Government. Accordingly, he was unreceptive when he saw Owen: there was too much criticism of Labour, but none of the

[3] 'The Nation's Duty: Mr Stanley Baldwin's General Election Message', in Craig, *Election Manifestos*, 90–1.

Conservatives who, he believed, had behaved far worse in forcing an election. In addition, he would accept no compromise on trade policy. Therefore he refused to sign and Samuel, under pressure to get the manifesto out, had to accept this as his leader's final word. Thus the last attempt to reconcile Lloyd George had failed; the publication of the manifesto had been held up for nothing, despite the urgent need to clear up the confusion of Liberal activists who, only three days before, had been expecting to fight the election against the National Government. Next day, further disaster seemed likely as Reading objected to the manifesto's blatant opposition to food taxes, which he saw as contrary to the 'free hand'. Eventually, he agreed with reluctance to a diluted version to the effect that '[t]axation on the staple foods of the people has always been opposed by the Liberal Party and would lay fresh burdens on those least able to bear them'. On the evening of 9 October the Liberal manifesto, after much travail, was finally issued. It was an inauspicious start to the party's campaign.[4]

The Samuelite Liberal manifesto itself was a profoundly unhappy document which, while professing its commitment to the Government, betrayed with every syllable the party's longing to be free from the Conservative embrace. Thus it opened with a complaint against holding an election, although adding that it was now their duty to co-operate in securing 'a strong and stable Government composed of men of all parties'. After stressing the overriding need to avoid inflation leading to 'financial disaster', which it argued would be the result of a Labour victory, the manifesto demanded international action to stabilize currency and deal with war debts and reparations. It also urged the importance of the forthcoming world disarmament conference, the League of Nations, and the Indian round table conference. While regretting the check on social reform and national development necessitated by the demand of sound finance—the one link with the bold proposals of 1929—it condemned Labour's plans to restore the recent economies. However, the manifesto only became really spirited when it discussed means of restoring the balance of trade. While accepting the free hand, it attacked existing tariffs as 'one of the principal causes' of depression and unemployment. Britain should produce more food, to cut imports, and increase its exports, although

[4] Samuel to Lloyd George, 8 Oct. 1931 (misdated 9 Oct.) (Lloyd George papers, G/17/9/17); Owen to Samuel, 8 Oct. 1931, and Sinclair to Samuel, 9 Oct. 1931 (Samuel papers, A/81, ff. 90–1, 93–4); Reading, memorandum, 10 Oct. 1931 (Reading papers, MSS Eur. F118/131).

how was not made clear. Their faith in free trade as the only ultimate basis for prosperity was reaffirmed: high tariffs had not saved the USA and Germany from heavier unemployment than free-trade Britain was suffering. The argument that it was the move to protectionism, rather than protection itself, which would boost British industry and agriculture was not addressed. Next came the criticism of food taxes, followed by a statement which stretched the free hand to, if not, beyond, breaking-point. 'The abandonment by Great Britain of her free trade policy', it said, 'would aggravate the divisions between nations and would check the growing realisation throughout the world of the disasters towards which they have been leading mankind.' These noble sentiments might not have been appreciated by the workers in numerous industries, such as steel, woollen textiles, hosiery, and lace, which were buckling under the pressure of competition from dumped foreign goods. Finally, the manifesto stressed the independence of the Liberal Party, 'a barrier against both reaction on the one hand and rash and injurious changes on the other', and asked voters 'to ensure that Liberal ideas [should] have a powerful expression and an effective influence both in the Government and in the coming Parliament'. The implication that the Conservatives were reactionary, and the stress on the coming *Parliament*, suggested that Liberal participation in the administration might not be a particularly long drawn-out affair; and on the whole, the Liberal manifesto in 1931 was a profoundly unhappy and fairly unsuccessful attempt to be all things to all Liberals.[5]

Naturally, it was not acceptable to the Liberal Nationals. Simon's election address to his constituents in Spen Valley formed their manifesto. It was fulsome in its praise of MacDonald, Snowden, and Thomas, for their courage, and Baldwin, for his magnanimity. The electors should be similarly motivated against 'the common danger', the TUC-dominated Labour Party, whose election would be a 'calamity'. In addition to this main issue, Simon felt that 'some application of tariffs [would] be found necessary'. In short, Simon asked, like MacDonald, for the voters' trust, although, unlike the premier, he was quite ready to accept Conservative domination and was happy to announce that the Government's work would take 'some years' to carry out. After all, many of the Simonites had been trying to be taken prisoner by the Tories for long enough.[6]

[5] 'Liberal Address to the Nation', in Craig, *Election Manifestos*, 99–100.

[6] 'A National Call to Liberals: Sir John Simon on the Need for National Unity', ibid. 93–4.

Two major points of dispute stood out in these manifestos. First, trade policy: all four parties accepted the free hand, involving an enquiry into future policy immediately after the election. If, as expected, this recommended the imposition of an emergency tariff, all parties—even the Liberals—indicated that they would be ready to accept it. However, there was no common ground on permanent policy. The Conservatives wanted permanent protection with imperial preference; the Liberal Nationals and National Labour implied that they would accept this. The official Liberals, however, went no further than a temporary tariff. Thus Samuelites could only be reconciled so long as there was no final decision, so long as the 'temporary' period lasted. The second point of dispute stemmed from this. The Conservative and Liberal National manifestos both envisaged a long tenure for the National Government after the election, as did MacDonald, in reality. However, the Liberals seemed to yearn for an end to a not unembarrassing situation. In short, the Parliament elected in 1931 was likely to outlive the existing Government. Almost everyone at high political level seems to have realized this, as did many active Conservatives and Liberals on the ground. Therefore some fierce fights between the two parties in the constituencies were inevitable, and perhaps the surprising thing was the amount of co-operation obtained at local level.

II

Labour's manifesto, drafted by Harold Laski, was approved by the NEC on 5 October and published four days later. The longest of the manifestos, it was forceful if not terribly convincing, except to the dedicated partisan. The capitalist system, it declared, had 'broken down'. The theory of the bankers' ramp was proclaimed, despite Henderson's earlier denial. The manifesto went on to argue that the 'so-called "National" Government' had failed in its sole object of preserving the gold standard:

> Having failed completely in its original object, it now seeks from the electorate a mandate for the impossible task of rebuilding Capitalism. . . . [T]his ill-assorted association of life-long antagonists seeks a blank cheque from the people for purposes it is unable to define. Acutely divided within itself; headed by men who are now acting in direct contradiction to their own previous convictions, certain, in the near future, to split into fragments, it makes the shameless pretence of being the instrument of national unity.

This was followed by a somewhat less sure-footed commentary on the record of the second Labour Government, defending its domestic policies and claiming that in foreign affairs its record had been 'pre-eminent'. It had been unable to do more because of its minority position and House of Lords obstruction; the latter would be overcome next time by the use of emergency powers. Labour's positive proposals were then outlined. 'We must plan our civilisation or perish', it argued. It might have been better had the party planned some of its policies in greater detail, because there existed complete plans for few of the proposals advanced. First, the manifesto dealt with finance. Under this head, banking and credit would be nationalized, a national investment board set up, prices stabilized, and international conferences called to deal with monetary problems and to cancel war debts and reparations. Secondly, trade policy was discussed. Tariffs were denounced in classical terms: they would enrich private interests at the expense of the community, increase artificially the cost of living, and damage international relations. They had not prevented high unemployment in the USA and Germany—although, like the Samuelites, Labour did not answer the argument that the *change* to protection would be the invigorating factor. Instead of tariffs, Labour favoured the nationalization of power, transport, and iron and steel, price regulation, and the setting up of import and export boards to regulate international commerce. Coal would also be taken into public ownership 'at the first opportunity'. Promises made in 1929 and not fulfilled were repeated—repeal of the 1927 Act for the TUC, and unemployment insurance and a national wages board for agricultural workers, for example. In the international field, Labour recorded its commitment to the League, the disarmament conference, and the round-table conference. Next, the manifesto pledged Labour to reverse the cuts in unemployment benefit 'immediately' and public servants' salaries as soon as possible thereafter. They could not all be restored at once, for Labour remained fully committed to a balanced budget. Finally, the alternatives were set out: a finance- and business-dominated National Government whose victory 'would perpetuate the degradation and misery of unemployment', or a Labour majority administration pledged to make 'unsparing efforts to remove the spectres of want and insecurity from the homes of the people, that this and succeeding generations may be assured of a fuller and richer life'.

These were noble sentiments. However, if Labour had won the

election it would have had little for which to thank its manifesto. First, in trying to offer something to practically everyone, it gave a significant number of hostages to fortune: the ex-ministers had agreed to a tariff and economies. Furthermore, the boosting of the record of the second Labour Government was somewhat unfortunate, given that many workers' experience of its policies had been unemployment, longer hours, and lower wages. The liberalization of unemployment benefits had been reversed partly by the Labour Government itself, and to boast now of Labour's education policy could only further alienate much-needed Catholic votes. Secondly, it was the height of disingenuousness for Labour to make a great show of promising to fulfil its broken promises. And finally, the manifesto was very vague on specific policies, reflecting the party's weakness in policy research. Lack of precision was not, of course, the monopoly of Labour; but the National parties had far less to prove. Their policies were more familiar to the electors. Labour, on the other hand, had to convince people. To suggest the public ownership and control of finance, land, power, coal, transport, and iron and steel was very ambitious. To advance them without even a clearly agreed view of the form each nationalized industry would take was plainly ludicrous, and open to much warranted criticism as well as misrepresentation. For example, the nature of public corporations was still the subject of fierce debate within the Labour movement, especially over the question of whether trade unions should be represented on the boards. Furthermore, nationalization and the expansion of bureaucracy which it would entail meant, at least in the short term, greatly increased public expenditure. Yet the manifesto and party leadership remained firmly committed to fiscal orthodoxy including the balanced budget. And on the nationalization proposals rested Labour's claim to be able to reduce unemployment; if they proved impossible to implement, there remained little in the Labour manifesto to offer much hope to the unemployed beyond the restoration of the cut in benefits. All in all, then, the Labour manifesto was a deeply self-contradictory and rather irrelevant document in the conditions of 1931; and it seems to have been adopted more as an article of faith for the future, and to keep what remained of the party together, than as a programme for immediate government, in the firm expectation of a National victory.[7]

[7] 'Labour's Call to Action: The Nation's Opportunity', ibid. 94–8.

III

Before turning away from the party manifestos, it is worth looking at the proposals of the more important of the smaller parties—the Independent Labour Party, the Communist Party, and the New Party.

The essentials of the ILP programme were summed up in James Maxton's election address in Glasgow, Bridgeton. For him, the crisis in Britain represented the collapse of capitalism, and the only real way out was 'the speedy replacement of the Anarchy of Capitalism by a Socialist Commonwealth'. He urged increases in benefits and pensions, the reduction of rents, abolition of the means test, and the establishment of a 'National Living Wage' supplemented by child allowances. He also urged the nationalization of banking and all major industries, conversion of war debt to a lower rate of interest, and the establishment of import and export boards. Abroad he, like Labour and the Liberals, had high hopes of the disarmament conference; unlike them, he also favoured the 'liberation' of the colonies. Despite similarities, it was well to the left of the official Labour programme. At least it was internally consistent, unlike the Labour proposals; but, of course, it had even less prospect of being implemented.[8]

To the left of Maxton and the ILP stood the CPGB, whose line could be seen in the address of Shapurji Saklatvala in North Battersea. He argued that the election was 'a cunning effort to prevent the mass action of the workers', and to impose tariffs, which would further impoverish the working class. Labour, he argued, was as committed as anyone to protection, and indeed, Saklatvala's main fire was reserved for Labour, a reflection of the 'class against class' line by which all other parties were seen as effectively fascist. The workers 'must drive from their ranks all open *and disguised* [my italics] agents of the starvation government'; to vote Labour was to vote for 'a vicious capitalist offensive'. The record of the second Labour administration had been one of wage cuts, starvation, and oppression at home and 'naked militarist imperialism' abroad, while the cuts were as much Labour's as the Nationals' doing. The worker's only friend was the CPGB. There should be immediate restoration of the cuts; a seven-hour working day; rent reductions; the defence of free trade; drastic cuts in armaments; independence for the colonies; and the provision of unemployment benefit from taxation. Finally, Saklatvala stressed that

[8] 'Socialism in our Time', Maxton's election address (Conservative Party papers).

the cause must be advanced by 'demonstrations and mass action' as well as through Parliament, the latter being only one (and implicitly not the most important) arena of the revolutionary struggle. It was a somewhat eclectic programme; but, since the main aim was not to espouse a policy for government but to arouse interest in and support for the CPGB, it served.[9]

At the other extreme—as most people now saw it—stood the New Party, which ran 24 candidates, rather than the 400 of which Mosley had once bragged. Formed earlier in 1931 after the secession of Mosley, his wife, three other Labour MPs, and one Conservative, and later joined by a Liberal, the party had had a difficult time since, as a press boycott and internecine squabblings—culminating in the resignations of John Strachey and Allan Young in July—prevented it from making any serious attempt to gain a wide following. Thus Mosley's election address in Stoke-on-Trent (Stoke) is mainly interesting as a demonstration of how close Mosley already was to fascist ideas (the British Union of Fascists was to be formed in late 1932).

First, Mosley condemned the 'old gang' who had misruled Britain since the war, and who had now come together in the National Government. But he reserved much of his vitriol for Labour, which had been weak in office and just as responsible for the cuts as the National Government it now condemned. The New Party, on the other hand, opposed the cuts because the solution was 'to "build up" not to "cut down" '. Mosley said he wanted to establish a parliamentary bridgehead for a 'great advance' at the next election. He then outlined his party's policy. In fact, it was less original than has often been claimed. Certainly, high-wage Tory protectionists like Amery and Beaverbrook would have agreed with the need to obtain well-paid jobs rather than implement benefit cuts; like them, he also favoured imperial preference, and they would have agreed that this would bring cheap food and stable agricultural prices. Of course, where Mosley scored over people like them was in marrying protectionism with the kind of planning being advocated by people like Lord Lothian and the recently formed Political and Economic Planning (PEP) and adopted somewhat unthinkingly in the Labour election manifesto. A national planning council would reorganize key industries: 'We organised the country in the War,' he argued, 'why not do it again for the greater

[9] 'Saklatvala's Message to You!', his election address (Conservative Party papers).

purposes of peace?' Finally, he added the two features which did distinguish the New Party from the political mainstream. The first was his impatience with parliamentary democracy. Parliament must become 'a workshop instead of a talkshop' with far greater executive control. Although it would keep a right of veto, it would spend far less time discussing legislation; inevitably, despite his protestations, this looked like a charter for dictatorship, for Mussolini had used and Hitler would use similar arguments to suppress parliamentary democracy in Italy and Germany. The second distinctive feature of his address was the call to youth and ex-servicemen:

> We appeal to our own generation, to those who fought in the War and to the young who came to maturity after the War. Like me, they have trusted the old leaders and the old parties and have been let down. . . . But we appeal [also] . . . to all the 'young in heart' of whatever time and circumstance.

Mosley's policy, then, was more eclectic than original, although the synthesis was unique and showed direct antecedents of British Union of Fascists (BUF) policies. It was hardly surprising that left-wingers labelled him a fascist and began to break up his meetings.[10]

The respective parties' programmes both reflected and projected the political and economic realities of Britain in 1931. Of the Opposition parties, the Communists and the ILP were firmly on the left. Labour, on the other hand, was on the verge of a great transition, and its manifesto reflected the fact. It was not an unimpressive programme, superficially, but, based on the rather vague gradualist proposals of the 1928 party programme, *Labour and the Nation*, and suffering from the acute lack of detailed policy work undertaken by the party, it was too unspecific to be convincing. In a sense it was a transitional document; when many of its proposals were repeated fourteen years later, better researched and better presented to a more receptive audience, the party was ready to implement them and the country was ready to give it the opportunity. In 1931 the manifesto was little more than an article of faith from an already doomed and pessimistic party. Above all, Labour could not really show that a third Labour Government would be appreciably different from the second, or escape its image as the party of depression and failure. On the right, Mosley's proposals clearly presaged his move to fascism. On the Government side, the

[10] 'Sir Oswald E. Mosley, the New Party Candidate', his election address (Conservative Party papers).

Liberal Nationals and, to a slightly lesser extent, National Labour signalled their intention to stick with the Conservatives; the Liberals, on the other hand, did little to conceal their embarrassment at the position in which they found themselves. And what of the Conservatives? Here, surely, was a party with a programme whose time had come. The country, buffeted by economic ill-winds of varying intensity since the end of the First World War, was now ready to look at the Tories' innovatory protectionist programme as a way, if not of ending the slump overnight, then at least of maximizing British prosperity within the context of world depression. Policies alone did not win the general election of 1931; but it was no coincidence that the party which did best also had the set of policies which seemed the best worked-out and the most easily implemented. Put simply, one does not need to be a Conservative or a protectionist to see why many more people favoured such a programme in 1931, after two years of slump and Labour government, than had favoured an ostensibly similar policy eight years earlier. All other concrete constitutional solutions seemed to have been tried, and found wanting.

8

HOLDING THE LINE: THE NATIONAL PARTIES DURING THE CAMPAIGN

THE National Government entered the general election campaign in the full expectation of victory, and the more aware—or candid—Labourites shared their assurance. The Government's leaders felt that Labour had to be dealt a crushing blow; and the only way that the impact of such a blow might be mitigated was if Labour was allowed to benefit from three-cornered contests. It had won 123 of its 287 seats with less than 50 per cent of the votes in such contests in 1929. The most straightforward means of ensuring that each Labourite had only a single National opponent would have been to issue official letters to approved candidates. However, this method of 'coupons' had been discredited by the use made of them by Lloyd George and Bonar Law in 1918, and MacDonald and Baldwin—both of whom continued to see the post-war Coalition as all that was bad in politics—were repelled by the idea.[1] But this made it more difficult to avoid serious clashes in the constituencies and to whittle down the number of National candidates before nomination day on 16 October. Given the poor relations which often prevailed, the wonder is perhaps not the number of constituencies in which National candidates ultimately stood against each other as the number of straight fights achieved.

I

There were early signs that co-operation would be difficult. A proposed all-party committee to deal with National candidates' policy enquiries was aborted by Ball who, as head of the CRD, regarded the idea as 'ludicrous', given that Tories and Samuelites would probably be fighting each other in a number of seats. He ensured that Conservative candidates were dealt with by a party committee under Hailsham instead.[2]

[1] K. O. Morgan, *Consensus and Disunity: The Lloyd George Coalition Government, 1918–1922* (Oxford, 1979), 2.

[2] Ball, memoranda, 8, 14, Oct. 1931 (Conservative Party papers, CRD 1/7/10/2).

This showed considerable distrust of the Samuelites, with reason: many official Liberals were having difficulty in defining their position to a confused rank and file. Samuel, contrary to expectations, had remained in the Government; the Liberal Nationals had defected; Lloyd George was about to follow suit; and the publication of the election manifesto had been delayed. Therefore on 6 October Muir, as chairman of the NLF, issued a statement to the effect that while Labour must be defeated, it was important to elect as many Liberal free traders as possible and to avoid making 'a present of the Free Trade case to the Labour Party by paltering with it ourselves'.[3] This created as much confusion as it solved, so when on 8 October Samuel made the first major speech of the campaign, his words were eagerly awaited. He stressed that the country was in grave danger, and that a Government victory was imperative. But he devoted most of his speech to scarcely veiled criticism of the Conservatives, saying the election had been unnecessary, denying the need for tariffs especially in view of the devaluation of sterling, and condemning 'quack' remedies (implying protection). While accepting an enquiry into the balance of trade, he set his face firmly against food taxes. As a whole, his speech suggested that the greater danger came, in fact, from the Tories. Given his recent preference for a Lib–Lab coalition, this seems hardly surprising.[4]

These impressions were confirmed by the supposedly private letter Muir sent to Liberal candidates and associations the following day. How he expected it to remain private is difficult to say, and he probably meant it to be leaked in order to put pressure on the Conservatives. Like Samuel, he criticized the Tories' forcing of the election as a 'wild gamble' to secure 'party advantage'. The worst conceivable outcome was a Labour Government; this was more likely to come about if the Liberals abandoned free trade. Above all, they should feel free to fight all seats except where such intervention would let Labour in.[5] In short, Muir envisaged a fairly minimal level of co-operation. Thus if it helped to clear the air for some Liberals—though not all, some seeing it as excessively partisan—it also helped to create a first-class row with the Conservatives. Sir Austen Chamberlain, for example, wrote privately that Muir and Samuel had 'done everything possible to cloud the

[3] *Manchester Guardian*, 7 Oct. 1931.
[4] Samuel at Bradford, 8 Oct., *Manchester Guardian*, 9 Oct. 1931.
[5] *Manchester Guardian*, 10 Oct. 1931.

issue, weaken confidence and save the Socialists from ruin'.[6] In so far as the last thing Samuel wanted was a huge Tory majority which could afford to do without the votes of Liberal MPs, this was by no means an inaccurate assessment.

In his own constituency, Darwen in Lancashire, Samuel's attitude caused him problems as the local Conservatives refused to withdraw their candidate. In all, eleven sitting Liberals faced such opposition. Samuel and his supporters, including *The Times*, condemned the Conservatives for being fractious at a time of grave national crisis, but supporters of the Tory, Alan Graham, rejected this, arguing that Samuel had been a consistent supporter of the second Labour Government in Parliament; had urged increased spending when retrenchment had been necessary; and remained a staunch free trader. Similarly, North Cornwall CA felt justified in opposing Maclean, the Samuelite President of the Board of Education. In both cases the hopelessness of the Labour candidate's position greatly eased any Tory misgivings.

The problem, of course, was that almost every case could be seen as special in some way or other; there seemed an outside danger of the National appeal falling apart within days of its launch, and a more probable one of seriously denting the image of National unity. With this in mind, Baldwin, opening his campaign on 9 October, said he regretted the opposition to Samuel as 'not . . . quite what I should call playing the game'. However, to reassure his own activists he also asked Samuel to repudiate Muir's letter. It is difficult to see how Baldwin could have done more to help the Samuelites without rearousing vigorous criticism of his leadership; even in going as far as he did he irritated many Tories, who disliked Samuel intensely. In fact the only action taken by Central Office with regard to Baldwin's statement was to circulate it to all CAs, and no more was done for Samuelites of whatever rank.[7]

This is not to say that there was no co-operation in the constituencies; far from it. By nomination day the *Manchester Guardian*

[6] Sir Austen to Lady Ivy Chamberlain, 11 Oct. 1931 (Chamberlain papers, AC 6/1/831).

[7] Baldwin at Birmingham, 9 Oct., *The Times*, 10 Oct. 1931; for Central Office not intervening, and Baldwin's refusal to send messages of support to Samuelites, see papers relating to Maclean and North Cornwall: North Cornwall CA, executive committee, 8 Oct. 1931 (North Cornwall CA papers, DDX 381/3); A. M. Williams to Baldwin, 13 Oct. 1931 (Baldwin papers, vol. 45 (v), ff. 40–1); H. B. Usher to MacDonald, 24 Oct. 1931 (MacDonald papers, PRO 30/69/388).

estimated that 44 Conservatives had withdrawn, 18 of them in favour of Samuelite Liberals (16 having withdrawn for Simonites, and 10 for National Labourites), while 25 official Liberals had stood down in favour of Tories.[8] In other seats, possible last-minute candidates were not adopted, and in many constituencies there was no lack of co-operation and good feeling. In Maidstone, the Conservative dropped party colours so that others would feel more free to support him.[9] Somewhat more concretely, Sheffield was only one of many cities—another example was Bristol—where a tradition of Conservative–Liberal co-operation against Labour at muncipal level led local Liberal leaders to urge their followers to vote Conservative, or *vice versa*.[10] In other areas, like Ayr Burghs, the Tory candidate's satisfactory replies to Liberal questions earned him the support of the LA, while the Samuelite MP in Cardiganshire similarly pleased local Conservatives and was allowed a free run.[11]

But there were also many examples of ill-feeling and obduracy. Kingston LA, for example, did not run a candidate, but urged its activists to campaign for Liberals in nearby seats and offered no advice on how to vote. Hythe LA advised Liberals to abstain; Manchester LF did nothing to prevent Liberals being nominated against sitting Conservatives in the city.[12] But when Liberal co-operation was offered, Conservative associations were sometimes chary about accepting it, not wanting the Liberals to be able to claim any share in the triumph. The same could apply in the opposite direction: Wrexham CA's offer of assistance to the Liberal candidate was refused.[13] On the whole, Conservative associations tended to be more supportive towards Liberal candidates than vice versa.

The efforts of Lloyd George, who continued to oppose the election as a protectionist ramp, did not help Conservative–Liberal relations. On 10 October he met Henderson and found there was nothing so objectionable about Labour as to prevent him launching a fierce attack on the Government. On 12 October it was announced that some

[8] *Manchester Guardian*, 16 Oct. 1931.

[9] Maidstone CA, general council, 9 Oct. 1931 (Kent Archives Office, Maidstone CA papers, U1634/A3/1/1A).

[10] *The Times*, 20 Oct. 1931.

[11] *The Times*, 24 Oct. 1931.

[12] Statement by Kingston LA, n.d. (Thurso papers, THRS I 20/2); *The Times*, 26 Oct. 1931; Manchester LF, executive committee, 7 Oct. 1931 (Manchester LF papers, M283/1/3/5).

[13] See e.g. Middleton and Prestwich CA, finance and general purposes committee, 5 Oct. 1931 (Middleton and Prestwich CA papers, PLC 1/2, f. 59); *The Times*, 17 Oct. 1931.

money from his fund would be available to Liberal candidates, so long as they stood for free trade 'without quibble or reservations'.[14] Of course, this ruled out most Liberal candidates, who were fighting officially on the 'free hand'. Only two Liberals outside the four-strong 'family group' stood as Lloyd Georgeites: Frank Owen, at Hereford, and the crime novelist Edgar Wallace, at Blackpool. On 15 October, Lloyd George finally signalled his departure from Samuel when he broadcast that whereas socialism was as bad as protectionism, there was no danger of the former since Labour had no chance of gaining a majority, whereas the Conservatives might very well dominate the new House of Commons. Accordingly, electors should vote Labour where no Liberal was standing, and he maintained this line throughout the campaign, much to the discomfiture of the Liberal leadership.[15] Some Liberal activists took his advice. Morrison's Liberal opponent in South Hackney in 1929 spoke for him, as did the former adversary of C. W. Bowerman in Deptford, while a number of prominent local Liberals also backed the Labour candidate in Llandaff and Barry, North Islington, Watford, Central Edinburgh, and South Bristol.[16] However, when the Labour candidate in Lincoln asked to be allowed to address the LA he was refused, and generally Liberal assistance to Labour was fairly exceptional.[17] In any case the attraction of Labour as a free-trade party was diminished by Snowden's revelations the day after Lloyd George's broadcast about the extent of the Labour Cabinet's commitments regarding tariffs. Lloyd George alone could not break up the National front; indeed, his opposition probably made old Asquithians like Grey still more determined to support it. However, he was another irritant in an already delicate situation.

Disputes between the Conservatives and the Liberals continued. Samuel never repudiated Muir's letter publicly, though privately he assured MacDonald that he would work to minimize its effects.[18] This added grist to the mill of Central Office party managers who, sick of the Samuelites, began to encourage people like Beaverbrook and Croft

[14] *Manchester Guardian*, 12 Oct. 1931.

[15] Lloyd George, broadcast, 15 Oct., *The Times*, 16 Oct. 1931. See also interview in *Daily Herald*, 24 Oct. 1931; Samuel to MacDonald, 16 Oct. 1931 (MacDonald papers, PRO 30/69/1176).

[16] *Daily Herald*, 13, 20, 17 Oct. 1931.

[17] Lincoln LA, executive committee, 7 Dec. 1931 (Lincoln LA papers, Misc. Dep. 96/1, f. 337).

[18] Samuel to Baldwin, 11 Oct. 1931; memorandum [Geoffrey Fry?] to Baldwin, 13 Oct. 1931 (Baldwin papers, vol. 45 (v), ff. 30–1, 34).

in attacking and trying to unseat the free traders. This was the more remarkable in so far as Croft's speeches were virulent in the extreme, one referring to Samuel as 'Slippery Sam . . . this political acrobat . . . this human eel . . . who will wriggle in any direction for his own or his party's advantage'.[19] Paradoxically, however, these disputes became more public and more acrimonious between nominations and polling. An agreement between Samuel and Baldwin on which of their candidates should receive their respective letters of support was scuppered by Central Office, which issued Baldwin's best wishes to practically all Conservative candidates.[20]

Then, on 19 October, relations took another nosedive with the publication of a questionnaire for candidates in the Liberal *News Chronicle*. The idea behind the seven questions was that candidates' responses would help Liberals decide who to support where no Liberal candidate was standing; associations should send replies to the local press and to Liberal headquarters. Obviously this initiative had official party backing, and the Tory chairman, Stonehaven, was quick to respond, demanding a retraction. The Liberal chairman, Stanmore, replied that the questionnaire merely sought information, and he also intimated that he saw the 'free hand' formula as ruling out any system of general protection or imperial preference before a second election. Stonehaven, not surprisingly, took this as a misreading of MacDonald's manifesto and an attempt to commit candidates in advance.[21]

Both men had a point. Stanmore could claim Conservatives elected with the help of Liberal free-trade votes should refuse to change the fiscal system without a further, party, election. After all, five million people had voted Liberal in 1929. However, this was not a particularly convincing argument, and not only because it fell foul of the 'free hand'. Stanmore's argument was based on the premiss that the only reason why the Liberals had not run 500 candidates who would obtain five million votes was that they did not want to shatter the image of National unity. But this was nonsense. In a party election, the Liberals

[19] Sir George Bowyer to Croft, 12 Oct. 1931 (Croft papers, CRFT 1/10, f. 3); Gower to Beaverbrook, 15, 21, 23 Oct. 1931; Topping to Beaverbrook, 9 Oct. 1931 (Beaverbrook papers, B/197, B/205).

[20] Samuel to Baldwin (copy), 17 Oct. 1931, Samuel to MacDonald, 26 Oct. 1931 (MacDonald papers, PRO 30/69/388); telegram, Baldwin to Samuel, n.d. (probably 17 or 18 Oct. 1931) (Baldwin papers, vol. 45 (v)).

[21] Stonehaven to Stanmore, 19 Oct., *The Times*, 20 Oct. 1931; Stanmore to Stonehaven, 19 Oct., *News Chronicle*, 20 Oct. 1931; Stonehaven to Stanmore, 20 Oct., *The Times*, 21 Oct. 1931.

would not have been able to run 300 candidates. Thus in more than half the seats, there would have been no 'Liberal vote' as such in any case. Furthermore, all the evidence of the past two years suggested that the Liberals would do far worse in terms of votes per candidate than in 1929. Many of the five million were now probably ready to vote for the Conservatives anyway, even if offered the alternative of a Liberal candidate, and many had died. Finally, it was surely the height of arrogance for the Liberals, who could only run 111 candidates not because of their great magnanimity but because their party was dying on its feet, due to lack of support, and splitting in all directions, to presume to have a veto over the actions of a Government the vast majority of whose members had made and were making no secret of the fact that they would rather the official Liberals were on the Opposition benches. Further disputes, for example over official Liberal speakers' notes attacking protection, broke out sporadically until the eve of polling.[22]

It is difficult to assess the impact of these disputes. Most electors would have taken little notice, especially as in most constituencies Conservatives and Liberals were not fighting each other. It is worth noting, though, that relations came to be generally seen to be bad only after nomination day and when it was already clear that Labour was going to be well beaten. Thus as well as showing the strong underlying antipathy between Conservative and Liberal headquarters, these disputes also signified the start of a process of jockeying for power in the post-election Government and a definite attempt by the Samuelites, notwithstanding the 'free hand', to circumscribe its powers in advance. They also showed the desire of Conservative Central Office to be seen to be doing something. Hard-line Tory activists were demanding more support for people like Graham, fighting against Samuel in Darwen. Central Office was prevented by the party leadership from complying with those demands, and had to appease activists by quarrelling with the Samuelites at every reasonable opportunity.

II

There were also problems between the Conservatives and National Labour. Before the campaign, Central Office had been eager to persuade MacDonald that there would be no difficulties.[23]

[22] Stonehaven to Baldwin, 23 Oct. 1931 (Baldwin papers, vol. 45 (v), ff. 102–4).
[23] Rosenberg, memorandum, 29 Sept. 1931 (MacDonald papers, PRO 30/69/388).

S. F. Markham, secretary of the National Labour electoral organization, left a meeting with Conservative officials confident that this would be so, and drafted a list of 35 constituencies in which he hoped the Conservatives would allow them a clear run.[24] Things then took a turn for the worse; by 7 October negotiations were going so badly that MacDonald had to write to Baldwin protesting about the attitude of Central Office. However, Tory officials and activists alike might have asked what right MacDonald had to claim Birmingham, Erdington, or North Kensington, both of which had fallen to Labour for the first time in 1929 (the former by only 133 votes) after years of being Conservative-held.[25]

There were also problems with some sitting National Labour MPs, however, and here MacDonald's complaints were more justified. In some places, of course, there was full co-operation: in Seaham and Derby, the Tories were delighted to be associated with MacDonald and Thomas respectively, while in Kilmarnock the Lord Advocate, Craigie Aitchison, found the entire Conservative machine at his disposal.[26] And where there were difficulties, they could be overcome, as in Central Leeds where, with some pressure from MacDonald and Baldwin, Grigg, the prospective Conservative candidate, withdrew, leaving Denman a straight fight against Labour. A similar outcome was reached at Lichfield, albeit only after the National Labour candidate, J. A. Lovat Fraser, had undergone fierce questioning from local Conservatives, eschewed Labour colours, and omitted all references to himself as a Labour man.[27]

Some National Labourites found even greater difficulties. Sir William Jowitt and A. G. Church withdrew from their own seats because of general local hostility, fought university seats opposed by other National candidates, and were defeated. Derwent Hall Caine, on the other hand, was determined to defend his seat, Liverpool Everton, but local Conservatives refused to withdraw their candidate. This was not incomprehensible; Hall Caine had only gained the seat from the Tories in 1929 by a narrow majority. Central Office pressed the CA to withdraw, but it refused. Even moderates who were sympathetic to

[24] Markham, memoranda, n.d., 25 Sept. 1931 (MacDonald papers, PRO 30/69/1778, 1320).

[25] MacDonald to Baldwin, 7 Oct. 1931 (MacDonald papers, PRO 30/69/1320).

[26] *Daily Herald*, 14 Oct. 1931.

[27] Denman to MacDonald, 10, 16 Oct. 1931; Lovat Fraser to MacDonald, 10, 14 Oct. 1931 (MacDonald papers, PRO 30/69/1320, 1321).

Hall Caine believed that if they withdrew, the orangemen of the Liverpool Protestant Party would nominate a candidate who would stop Hall Caine and let Labour in; and the experience of nearby Kirkdale, where the Liverpool Protestant Party candidate took a quarter of the vote against Tory and ILP opposition, suggested this was so.[28] Meanwhile, Markham himself, at Chatham, was forced to withdraw, faced with a Conservative opponent determined to go to the polls.[29]

All this led National Labour headquarters to feel bitterly let down by the Conservatives. In published correspondence with Stonehaven, Earl De La Warr, the National Labour chairman, pointed out that their original agreement had specified 35 candidates; yet by 14 October there were only 25 left, of whom 10 were still facing Tory opposition.[30] Ultimately, only 20 National Labour candidates were nominated, of whom 2 withdrew before polling day because the Conservatives' refusal to do so threatened to split the National vote (Central Newcastle and Colne Valley) and one who faced similar difficulties with the Liberal Nationals (Gateshead). In 4 of the remaining 17 seats, they faced Conservative opposition and were defeated. Therefore Central Office's promise of a clear run in 35 seats emerges as over-optimistic, if not downright deceitful: basically, it seems that they had made these promises to make the idea of an election more palatable to MacDonald. After all, the prospect of a phalanx of 25 to 35 National Labour MPs must have attracted him. There were faults on both sides, though—National Labour made idiosyncratic choices of constituencies to fight. In addition, local Conservative feeling often ran strong, especially against MPs like Church, who seemed to be acting with as much opportunism as patriotism. And the character of other National Labour candidates—'unknown candidates introduced at the last moment', as Stonehaven put it—did not help, either.[31] Even so, men like Hall Caine must have wondered whether their sacrifices had been worthwhile; and public relations between the Conservative and National Labour organizations ended the campaign in a poor state.

[28] Sir John Sandeman Allen to MacDonald, 14 Oct. 1931 (MacDonald papers, PRO 30/69/1176).

[29] Earl De La Warr to MacDonald, 13 Oct. 1931 (MacDonald papers, PRO 30/69/1176).

[30] De La Warr to Stonehaven, 14 Oct., *The Times*, 15 Oct. 1931.

[31] Stonehaven to MacDonald, 23 Oct. 1931 (MacDonald papers, PRO, 30/69/388).

III

Generally, the Conservatives got on best with the Liberal Nationals. After all, they had been promoting a split within the Liberal Party for the past year, and the Simonite revolt was its fruition; they liked and respected many of Simon's followers; and, of course, the political views of the latter tended to be congenial. In addition, the fact that most Liberal National candidates were either sitting MPs or fighting Labour in areas like Durham, where the Liberal tradition was stronger than the Conservative, also helped matters. Negotiations between the two parties regarding seats were not easy, but they were productive, and by 11 October Sir Robert Hutchison could predict that no more than 2 of their MPs (out of the 27 who were standing) would face Conservative opposition. In the event he was almost right; T. B. W. Ramsay in the Western Isles would be added to the two he identified, R. M. Kedward in Ashford (Kent) and A. E. Glassey in East Dorset.[32] Of the three, only Ramsay was to keep his seat.

Central Office pressure was unable to secure the withdrawal of the Conservative candidate in the face of especially strong local feeling in both Ashford and East Dorset. In the former case, the CA had an especial animus against Kedward, who had campaigned against tithe collection and voted frequently with the Labour Government. Since no Labour candidate was nominated, they felt there were no arguments against fighting, and went ahead, despite headquarters pressure.[33] In East Dorset there was a similarly fierce fight, the CA nominating the hard-line protectionist Geoffrey Hall Caine (brother of the National Labour MP), who had represented the constituency for seven years until 1929, when he had lost narrowly. The fact that Labour had no chance of victory steeled their resolve, despite the resignation in protest of their association president. Glassey, trying to keep his Liberal support, prevaricated on food taxes during the campaign, and Hall Caine, receiving avid support from Croft and Beaverbrook, won the seat.[34] These exceptions aside, however, Conservative–Liberal National relations remained good, and, in places like Southampton, excellent.[35]

[32] Sir Robert Hutchison to Simon, 'Sunday Evening' [11 Oct. 1931] (Simon papers, 69, ff. 36–7).

[33] Sir Auckland Geddes, *The Times*, 17 Oct. 1931.

[34] Stonehaven to Croft, 20 Oct. 1931 (Croft papers, CRFT 1/19, f. 12); Croft, *My Life of Strife*, 201.

[35] *The Times*, 14, 16, 23 Oct. 1931.

Indeed, the problem facing some Liberal National candidates came from the other flank: Liberal activists. In north Wales, the MP for Denbigh, J. H. Morris-Jones, had come out in favour of tariffs in mid-September; thus when he faced his constituency association at his adoption meeting on 8 October he only obtained a vote of confidence by 46 to 22, and many of his supporters were 'very perplexed'. After the meeting, Morris-Jones felt that 'had there been then & there a strong Liberal free trader available, he might have been adopted'.[36] Ultimately, though, he was returned unopposed. In nearby Flintshire, the Liberal National MP Frederick Llewellyn-Jones faced similar difficulties. On 8 October, the 'utterly bewildered' Liberal executive met. The member stressed that he was still a Liberal, and in full agreement with MacDonald and the free hand. He believed, he said, in 'the ultimate triumph of Free Trade', but felt a temporary departure might be necessary. After a lengthy discussion, it was agreed with only two dissentients that the LA should take no part in the election, and a subsequent, desperate promise that he would resist food taxes 'with all the means in his power' could not reverse this decision. Central Office prompting ensured more co-operation from the local Conservatives; and, in fact, Llewellyn-Jones was elected with full Tory, but no official Liberal, support.[37] Under such circumstances, a degree of scepticism about the political honesty of the candidate and his backers might be justified. The LA should, perhaps, have become involved in the campaign, if only to be able to claim that it had been partly responsible for his re-election. But feelings ran high in an area where Labour was weak. As so often in 1931, the real fault lay in trying to reconcile the irreconcilable.

These problems did not apply solely to MPs. In Barnsley and Huddersfield the Liberal National candidates, having been adopted by staunchly free-trade LAs, tried to distance themselves from Simon despite the fact that it was their association with him which had helped them to secure straight fights against Labour.[38] Overall, however,

[36] Morris-Jones diary, 8 Oct. 1931 (Morris-Jones papers, D/MJ/12).

[37] Flint LA, executive committee, 8 Oct.; general meeting, 10 Oct. 1931 (Clwyd Record Office, Flint LA papers, D/DM/350, ff. 186–90); Flint CA, special general meeting, 12 Oct. 1931; Llewellyn-Jones to Spencer Summers (chairman), 19 Nov. 1931 (2 letters) (Clwyd Record Office, Flint CA papers, D/DM/307/3).

[38] Simon to Mabane, 10 Oct. 1931; W. D. Hackney to Mabane, 21 Oct. 1931; Simon to Hore-Belisha, 22 Oct. 1931 (Simon papers, 68, f. 176; 69, ff. 13, 9–10); Ashley Mitchell (Huddersfield LA) to Samuel, 25 Oct. 1931 (Samuel papers A/84, f. 1); T. S. Hickman (agent, Huddersfield LA) to Mabane, 4 Nov. 1931 (West Yorkshire Archives Service, Kirklees, Mabane papers, DD/WM/C/C/O/2).

relations between the Conservatives and the Liberal Nationals were as good as those between the former and the official Liberals were poor.

'[I]t is remarkable how largely the troubles which were inevitable have been overcome,' wrote Samuel to Baldwin on the eve of the poll, and this was a fair assessment.[39] Table 8.1 shows how few clashes there were between National candidates in the constituencies. This can be contrasted with the number of unopposed returns secured—Conservative 49, Liberal 5, and Liberal National 7, as opposed to only 5 Labour and 1 unendorsed Labour—and with the number of straight fights against Labour, ILP, or independent Labour candidates (see Table 8.2). And in other seats where there was a three-cornered fight, the basic fight was between a National and a Labour candidate with the addition of a minor party candidate who was not supporting the Government (see Table 8.3). There were also 9 constituencies where 4 candidates but only 1 National supporter stood.

Table 8.1. *Contests between national candidates*

	Con	Lib	LibN	NLab
Con	–	79	4	4
Lib	79	–	–	–
LibN	4	–	–	1
NLab	4	–	1	–
TOTAL = 88				

Table 8.2. *Straight fights against Labour*

	Lab	ILP	IndLab	Total
Con	302	8	3	313
Lib	21	–	–	21
LibN	25	–	–	25
NLab	10	1	–	11
Nat	1	–	–	1
TOTAL = 371				

[39] Samuel to Baldwin, 26 Oct. 1931 (Baldwin papers, vol. 45 (v), ff. 123–4).

TABLE 8.3. *Three-cornered contests involving minor parties*

	Lab/Ind & CPGB	Lab & NP	Lab & Ind	Lab & SNP	Lab & CWLP	ILP & LPP
Con	15	12	1	2	1	1
Lib	1	–	–	1	–	–
LibN	1	–	–	1	–	–
NLab	1	–	–	–	–	–
Nat	1	–	–	–	–	–
TOTAL = 38						

Key CPGB Communist Party of Great Britain
CWLP Common Wealth Land Party
ILP Independent Labour Party
LPP Liverpool Protestant Party
SNP Scottish National Party

The National line held very well indeed during the campaign, considering the pressures to which it was repeatedly subjected. Disputes remained to be settled after the election. But for Labour, one of whose best hopes was that the Government would fall apart during the campaign, it was a sorry situation. For whatever else divided them, the National parties all agreed that a Labour victory would be disastrous. Their commitment to that view ensured still further that Labour had no chance whatever of winning the 1931 general election.

9

ELECTIONEERING AND THE MEDIA

HOW did the politicians' messages reach the voters? This chapter was out to answer this question, first by reference to the parties' own electioneering, and secondly, by analysis of the news media during the election. It is worth noting in parentheses that the campaign was not exceptionally short; on the contrary, at twenty days it was of identical duration to that in every general election between 1922 and October 1974, with the single exception of 1966.

I

For many Labour supporters, the campaign opened with great enthusiasm. Transport House declared that 500 seats would be contested, while activists even in difficult constituencies were 'splendid and full of enthusiasm'.[1] Their opponents were rather sceptical of this mood. After all, Graham had predicted a 'savage' fight, while Henderson had spoken privately to the Conservative junior minister, Kingsley Wood, in very gloomy terms, and predicted publicly that it would be 'the most bitter election' of his career. Transport House was anticipating the loss of anything up to a hundred seats.[2] This pessimism eventually percolated through to the wider party. Initially, Transport House was receiving enthusiastic reports from all over the country which seemed to point to a Labour victory. But, as the national agent wrote subsequently, '[t]he information was too good to be true', so they 'invited Agents during the contest to give [them] a detailed report on their campaigns with a special reference to canvassing. The receipt of these documents', he went on, 'certainly discounted some of the reports [they] had received up to that time.'[3] Thus it was sheer bravado when on 25 October Henderson told a Sunday newspaper that the reports which were reaching him were 'amazingly good'.[4]

[1] Kate Spurrell to Sir Charles Trevelyan, 11 Oct. 1931 (Newcastle University Library, Trevelyan papers, CPT 98).

[2] *Daily Herald*, 8 Oct. 1931; Sir Austen to Lady Ivy Chamberlain, 10 Oct. 1931 (Chamberlain papers, AC 6/1/828).

[3] G. R. Shepherd to H. E. Rogers, 17 Nov. 1931 (East Bristol DLP papers, Acc. 39035/60).

[4] *Reynold's Illustrated News*, 25 Oct. 1931.

At the start of the campaign, though, there had appeared to be real reasons for good cheer. Relations with the trade unions seemed much improved; and if in some cases this was something of a veneer, there was concrete union backing. Unions sponsored 131 of the 491 Labour candidates (see Table 9.1). Secondly, cash poured into central party funds. By 15 October the Labour Majority Fund had raised £12,000 from unions as well as £4,000 from individuals. A TUC manifesto was issued and sent in bulk to union members; individual unions, like NUDAW, also issued their own pro-Labour programmes. In addition, DLP-sponsored candidates were often sent donations: the RCA, for example, gave £50 to seven candidates as well as fully sponsoring seven others. In some places, like Hamilton, union offices and staff were placed at the full disposal of the divisional party.[5]

There were some problems, however. Many unions were in financial difficulties; the Foundry Workers could afford nothing more than the sponsorship of one candidate, Henderson, while the Derbyshire Miners' Association announced that its precarious finances precluded it from making any contributions to candidates.[6] In Scotland the MFGB almost refused to sponsor its seven candidates because the Scottish unions were almost two years in arrears with the payment of their political levy.[7] In short, union money could be elusive, and its coverage was, at best, patchy. Occasionally, wealthy candidates financed themselves, at least partly; in Nuneaton, the MP paid £250 out of £360 expenses, while at Broxtowe the MP paid £200 out of £333.[8] Other constituencies were not so fortunate, however, and rural divisions like West Derbyshire and Roxburgh and Selkirk, with little trade unionism, less money, and no appreciable help from Transport House, had to forgo a contest.[9]

[5] *The Times*, 15 Oct. 1931; RCA, executive committee, 15 Nov. 1931 (RCA papers, MSS 55B/RCA/1/EC/15, ff. 70–1); Hamilton DLP, special general committee, 11 Oct. 1931 (Hamilton DLP papers, on microfilm at Birmingham Reference Library).

[6] Williams, *The Derbyshire Miners*, 833.

[7] MFGB, executive committee, 9 Oct. 1931 (South Wales Miners' Federation papers); Lanark Miners' County Union, council, 7 Oct. 1931 (National Library of Scotland, Lanark Miners' County Union papers, Dep. 227/45A).

[8] Frank Smith (ex-MP) to Walter Lewis (agent, Nuneaton DLP) n.d. [Nov. 1931] (Warwickshire Record Office, Walter Lewis papers, CR 2000/1); Broxtowe DLP, special executive committee, 'Saturday' [10 Oct. 1931] (Nottinghamshire Record Office, Broxtowe DLP papers, DDPP 6/6, f. 57).

[9] Roxburgh and Selkirk DLP, quarterly meeting, 10 Oct. 1931 (National Library of Scotland, Roxburgh and Selkirk DLP papers, Acc. 4145(1)); West Derbyshire DLP, special general meeting, 10 Oct. 1931 (Derbyshire Record Office, West Derbyshire DLP papers, D1650 G/M1).

Table 9.1. *Sponsorship of Labour candidates, 1931*

Divisional Labour parties	322
Miners' Federation of Great Britain	42
Independent Labour Party	23
Co-operative Party	15
National Union of Railwaymen	10
National Union of General and Municipal Workers	9
United Textile Factory Workers' Association	8
Railway Clerks' Association	7
Amalgamated Society of Woodworkers	5
National Union of Boot and Shoe Operatives	5
Boilermakers	4
British Iron, Steel and Kindred Trades Association	4
National Union of Distributive and Allied Workers	4
London Society of Compositors	2

Fourteen unions sponsored one candidate: Amalgamated Engineering Union; Amalgamated Union of Building Trade Workers; Chainmakers; NATSOPA (Printers); National Society of Print Workers; National Union of Foundry Workers; National Union of Life Assurance Workers; National Union of Textile Workers; National Union of Vehicle Builders; Operative Bleachers' Association; Patternmakers' Association; Shop Assistants' Union; Typographical Association; NASOHSPD (Painters).

Source: Labour Party, *Annual Report, 1932*, 11–27.

Candidates were something of a problem for Labour in 1931, and although it is possible to make too much of this as a factor in the party's defeat—the difficulties were often in rather hopeless seats, and even where candidatures were arranged well in advance Labour did badly—it did not help matters. In the end Labour nominated 491 official candidates, but many were adopted at the last minute. In West Woolwich, the prospective candidate, Commander Reginald Fletcher, withdrew at the last moment; his replacement, however worthy, had little hope of making much impact in the short time left to him.[10] The difficulties caused in Enfield by Will Henderson's resignation have already been noted. But the greatest problems came where the MP or

[10] Woolwich BLP, special executive committee, 9 Oct. 1931; annual report for 1931 (to annual meeting, 12 Apr. 1932) (Woolwich BLP papers); Labour Party, *Annual Report, 1932*, 10. It is intriguing to speculate as to whether the future Lord Winster's withdrawal had anything to do with his commitments to the intelligence services: see A. Boyle, *The Climate of Treason*, rev. edn. (London, 1980), 137, 237.

candidate had followed MacDonald. The DLPs concerned were often slow to make replacements, South Nottingham and Central Leeds only doing so on 11 October.[11] In Cambridgeshire, the divisional party was forced to ask its candidate in 1929, G. T. Garratt, to stand. Garratt was by then resident in India, but was fortuitously in London for the round-table conference, and agreed, as the party's annual report subsequently put it, to 'step into the breach'.[12] This hardly suggested any real expectation of victory; yet in 1929 Garratt had come within 5.9 per cent of defeating the Conservative, and Cambridgeshire was, on the basis of 1929, the twenty-ninth most marginal Conservative seat where Labour had come second. As such, it was a seat Labour must win to have any chance of an overall majority. The general belief that Garratt had no chance speaks volumes for the true attitude of many Labour activists in 1931. To talk of split DLPs, though, would certainly be to overdraw the picture: doubtless many activists still felt affection or respect for the premier, but people like the former Labour mayor of Newport, who defected, were the exceptions.[13]

The dispute with the ILP also caused difficulties, because candidates who refused to sign a pledge agreeing to obey the PLP's new standing orders were not endorsed. Thus 23 candidates (11 of them MPs) who had been selected by their DLP were refused endorsement; 17 ran as ILP candidates, and 6 as Independent Labour. Among them were 3 former Cabinet Ministers (Sir Charles Trevelyan, F. W. Jowett, and Josiah Wedgwood) and men like Maxton and Fenner Brockway. In addition, two MPs were not nominated by their DLP, but ran anyway as ILPers. In some places, non-endorsement caused few problems. For example, the ILP and Labour candidates in the two-member seat of Norwich advised their supporters to give their second vote to the other; but in Stockport, also a double seat, the divisional party spurned the ILP's suggestion of a similar arrangement.[14] In Glasgow, Shettleston, John McGovern had been selected as Labour candidate in 1930 by suspect, if not downright fraudulent,

[11] South Nottingham DLP, quarterly meeting, 11 Oct. 1931 (South Nottingham DLP papers, DDPP 7/1, f. 213); Central Leeds DLP, executive committee, 7, 11 Oct. 1931 (Central Leeds DLP papers, 63/3).

[12] Cambridgeshire TCLP, annual report 1931–2 (Cambridgeshire TCLP papers, 416/0.20).

[13] Newport DLP, general committee, 13 Nov. 1931 (Newport DLP papers, A/6, f. 136).

[14] *Daily Herald*, 13 Oct. 1931; Stockport TCLP, executive committee, 8 Oct. 1931 (Stockport TCLP papers, on microfilm at Birmingham Reference Library).

means. The party conference at Scarborough had condemned him as being unfit to act as a Labour candidate, and Glasgow BLP decided to nominate an official candidate against him. However, the latter lost his deposit and McGovern kept the seat.[15] At Peckham, longstanding difficulties within the DLP culminated in the nomination of an official Labour candidate against the ILP MP, John Beckett, and there was also a National Labour candidate. Unremarkably, the Conservative romped home. Difficulties with the ILP were confined to a small number of constituencies, but where they existed they often exacerbated an already unfavourable situation for Labour.

The Conservatives were in a far happier position at local, as well as national, level. The days of Beaverbrook–Rothermere insurgents had long passed; in South Paddington the Empire Crusader, E. A. Taylor, who had defeated a Conservative in October 1930, was now the official party candidate. Beaverbrook ran no separate candidates at the election, although he made special efforts to unseat Liberal free traders. The overall picture was one of harmony and high spirits. Morale among activists was high. In West Birmingham, Sir Austen Chamberlain, who had won by only 43 votes in 1929, was very confident of success, having more voluntary helpers than ever before. By 24 October he was cautiously anticipating a majority of 2,000; his aides were much more confident, and were justified by the final margin of nearly 12,000.[16] In Northwich the secretary had 'the most willing band of helpers [she had] ever had'; in Chelmsford voluntary assistance and transport came as never before.[17] With a great ground swell of popular support, the whole-hearted backing of practically the entire national press, the obvious discomfiture of Labour, and the practical assurance of a Conservative majority, it would, perhaps, have been surprising had rank-and-file Tory spirits been anything less than effervescent.

Candidates and finance posed few problems. By July 1931 the Tories had adopted 265 candidates, in addition to their 263 MPs, or 528 in all. No candidates resigned as a result of the formation of the National Government, and although the dissolution brought the usual

[15] Glasgow BLP, executive committee, 6, 13 Oct. 1931 (Glasgow TCBLP papers).

[16] Sir Austen to Lady Ivy Chamberlain, 12, 16 Oct. 1931; to Ida Chamberlain, 24 Oct. 1931 (Chamberlain papers, AC 6/1/833, 837; 5/1/561).

[17] Northwich CA, women's finance and general purposes committee, 18 Nov. 1931 (Cheshire Record Office, Northwich CA papers, LOP 1/2/3); Chelmsford CA, executive committee, 11 Dec. 1931 (Chelmsford CA papers, D/Z/96/6).

retirements, in most cases these had long been anticipated and replacements already found. Financially the party was in a healthy state; and where there were shortages—as, for example, in the Conservative Film Association—it could soon be rectified by an appeal to wealthy supporters.[18] Candidates like R. A. Butler in Saffron Walden paid all their own election expenses,[19] while extra voluntary help made the campaign far cheaper than in 1929 (see Table 9.2). A Central Office appeal on 19 October secured a 'gratifying' response, including a generous donation from William Morris, and ended any immediate financial worries.[20]

The Liberals were in a far less comfortable position. The withdrawal of financial support from the Lloyd George fund on 8 October was a blow, though too much can be made of its impact. Even assuming Lloyd George's full co-operation, the alternatives presented by Muir had been either to fight 300 seats with around £400 being given to each for expenses, or else to fight on a broader front with 500 candidates who would receive only £150, to guarantee their deposit. In the latter case, it was highly debatable whether enough people would come forward. At one stage, in June 1930, a mere 200 seats had seemed possible. Thus the withdrawal of support from Lloyd George's seriously depleted fund was not decisive. At most, it prevented the adoption of, say, 50 last-minute no-hopers who would have further embittered relations with the Conservatives. A Liberal or Liberal National stood in 137 of the 250 seats where the Liberals had gained over 25 per cent of the vote in 1929. Of the remaining 113, 87 were divisions in which they had come second to the Conservatives: even had all 87 been contested, given the respective fortunes of the two parties since 1929, it is difficult to see how the Liberals could have won a single one. Only in the 18 seats where they had come second to Labour in 1929 and no Liberal stood, could it be argued realistically that they might have won. Thus the withdrawal of Lloyd George's money should not be overstressed, especially as the *News Chronicle* stressed on 13 October that the NLF had raised 'sufficient funds' to make it possible for candidates to stand anywhere there was a reasonable prospect of success. In fact, the Liberals could not find the

[18] T. J. Hollins, 'The Presentation of Politics: The Place of Party Publicity, Broadcasting and Film in British Politics, 1918–1939', Ph.D. thesis (Leeds, 1981), 70.

[19] P. A. Hunt (secretary, Saffron Walden CA) to Butler, 14 Dec. 1931 (Trinity College, Cambridge, Butler papers, J. 21).

[20] *The Times*, 19, 21 Oct. 1931; Jones diary, 29 Oct. 1931 (Jones papers, Z/1931/59).

Table 9.2. *Candidates' election expenses, 1931 (£)*

Totals			
Government		Opposition	
Conservative	347,071	Labour	179,265
Liberal	58,712	ILP/Ind Lab	4,947
Liberal National	23,544	CPGB	2,555
National Labour	12,512	New Party	11,423
National	2,432	Ind Liberal	5,211
		Others	6,422
TOTALS	444,271		209,823
GRAND TOTAL = 654,104			

Averages per opposed candidate	1929	1931
Conservative	911.77	727.94
Liberal	786.83	538.06
Liberal National	–	671.47
National Labour	–	625.60
National	–	608.00
Labour	450.44	386.62
ILP/Ind Lab[a]	–	206.13
CPGB	235.52	98.27
New Party	–	475.96
Ind Liberal	–	744.43
Others	429.70	267.58
OVERALL AVERAGE	704.02	528.17

[a] included in 'others'.

Source: Return of the Expenses of each Candidate at the General Election of October, 1931 (PP 109; London, 1931–2).

candidates; they lacked the organization; they lacked sufficient electoral support. The plight of the Liberals in 1931 was the logical outcome of the developments of the past two years, perhaps the past two decades; and Liberal candidates still had far more money, on average, to spend than Labour candidates. Few Liberals had many illusions regarding the outcome of the election. Low morale, though sometimes masked by bravado, was inevitable; yoked to the Conservatives and with only 111 candidates, theirs was a miserable position.

As far as finances went, both the Liberal Nationals and National Labour did very well during the campaign. It seems highly unlikely, although firm evidence is lacking, that the Conservative Party supported them financially. MacDonald was obsessive about such charges, and responded swiftly when they were made by the *Daily Herald*. During the campaign, National Labour headquarters received £2,400 in donations of £100 or more, in addition to several large contributions already made, while, ironically, Clynes's son acted as an intermediary with various other potential subscribers.[21] On average, opposed National Labour candidates spent well. The Liberal Nationals, meanwhile, continued to rake in money, as well as getting their premises rent-free.[22] On one day, 13 October, over £3,000 in cash and cheques poured in, and when the flow began to dry up, an appeal brought a gratifying response.[23]

So much for the means and morale behind electioneering; what of electioneering itself? The best-organized associations and parties made very full provisions. Stockton CA's finance committee met every morning to monitor events, and Keighley CA set up groups to deal with all aspects of the work.[24] Labour Parties, often composed mainly of industrial workers, found difficulty in meeting during the daytime; nevertheless, Batley and Morley DLP planned an ambitious campaign to comprise public meetings, large gatherings of the unemployed, lunch-time meetings at mill and factory gates, circulars opposing teachers' salary cuts, distribution by hand of the party manifesto and the candidate's election address, and use of the free postage nearer to polling day to send out a polling card reminding people to vote Labour.[25] In hopeless seats, however, with more limited resources, campaigning might start as late as 17 October and, with fewer members, be far less comprehensive.

Electioneering itself comprised mainly canvassing, the distribution

[21] Undated memorandum (MacDonald papers, PRO 30/69/1535).

[22] Ernest Benn to Simon, 5 Oct. 1931; G. H. Shakespeare to Simon, 14 Oct. 1931 (Simon papers, 68, ff. 164, 185).

[23] W. D. Hackney to Simon, 13 Oct. 1931 (Simon papers, 68, f. 180); *The Times*, 21 Oct. 1931.

[24] Stockton CA, finance committee, 7 Oct. 1931 (Durham County Record Office, Stockton CA papers, D/X 322/5); Keighley CA, finance and general purposes committee, 7 Oct. 1931 (Keighley CA papers, 4).

[25] Batley and Morley DLP, executive committee, 8 Oct. 1931 ((Batley and Morley papers, 13D84/11).

of printed propaganda, and public meetings. The Conservatives had always envied Labour's surfeit of voluntary help at elections, but now it was they and their allies who benefited, especially in canvassing, where women often worked all day long.[26] It is difficult to give an overall view of Labour's efforts. Some DLPs, such as Wansbeck, made a full canvass, and exceptionally efficient ones like East Bristol canvassed the entire division twice.[27] But the marked antipathy to canvassing noted since mid-1930 remained, *Labour Organiser* noting that less canvassing took place than at any election since 1918.[28] Under the circumstances, it was hardly surprising.

The distribution of printed propaganda was also important. Labour had great difficulties in this direction, too. Most of its stock literature had had to be scrapped, and the replacement material was poor quality and often arrived too late to be of much use.[29] The party did issue a series of notes for activists and candidates suggesting awkward questions to put to their National opponents, quoting MacDonald's past free-trade utterances and Snowden's commitments to the nationalization of banking, and offering formulae for dealing with questions on church schools, disarmament, and the means test. What such material could not do, of course, was wash away the extent of the ex-ministers' commitment to economies, or suggest how, specifically, a Labour Government would begin to restore prosperity to Britain. If *Labour Organiser* wanted such material it was asking for history to be changed. Efforts at local level helped to fill the gaps. As well as distributing headquarters propaganda, DLPs produced their own: for example, 17,000 copies of Cripps's speech in Parliament against the cuts were distributed in East Bristol.[30] Many parties issued four-page election news sheets once or twice during the campaign, although they varied greatly in quality. One notably disastrous effort was that of the Labour candidate in North Portsmouth, Rear-Admiral K. G. B. Dewar. The caption to a picture of the fleet stated that the British Navy had defeated the Kaiser at Jutland in 1916 and that it had

[26] See e.g. Sir Austen to Lady Ivy Chamberlain, 24 Oct. 1931 (Chamberlain papers, AC 6/1/843); Sheffield City CA, women's advisory committee, annual report 1931–2 (Sheffield Archives Office, Sheffield City CA papers, LD 2108).

[27] Wansbeck DLP, 'Agent's Report for Six Months Ending 31/12/31' (Wansbeck DLP papers, NRO 527/A/2); H. E. Rogers to Cripps, 15 Nov. 1931 (Nuffield College, Cripps papers, 603).

[28] *Labour Organiser*, Nov. 1931.

[29] Ibid.; Cambridgeshire TCLP, annual report, 1931–2 (Cambridgeshire TCLP papers, 416/0.20).

[30] H. E. Rogers to Cripps, 15 Nov. 1931 (Cripps papers, 603).

defeated Montagu Norman at Invergordon in 1931. As such, it aroused the ire of the national press, and caused a minor sensation on the eve of polling in which Labour was presented in a very unfavourable light.[31]

The Conservatives did not reach the peak of printed propaganda they had attained in 1929, but still produced a respectable amount. Much of their stock literature was revamped by the simple expedient of superimposing 'vote for the National Government' over 'vote Conservative'. At local level, methods were much the same as Labour's, although the Tories and their National allies made more use of advertising hoardings, and of publicity boards in supporters' gardens.[32]

The Conservatives also possessed their own unique means of electioneering—22 cinema vans. These vans projected film onto a screen and could be used anywhere and at any time, exciting great interest, particularly in rural areas. During the campaign, they visited 79 towns, holding a total of 543 meetings. In addition, 9 loudspeaker vans went to 48 towns and held 404 meetings. Some of the party's films, such as a 1930 cartoon satire of MacDonald and Snowden, could not be used, but the vans were successful in adding to the party's and the Government's electoral impetus. Before the August crisis, Labour had been making tentative moves towards the production of film propaganda, but these were thwarted by the onset of the crisis.[33]

The public meeting remained the most prominent feature of campaigning, however. It could take one of four basic forms: the mass meeting in a large hall, often with an invited audience, addressed by a national politician; the schoolroom meetings which were the staple fare of most candidates; outdoor meetings in market-places and public squares; and meetings at factories, usually held at lunch-time either on the premises (a privilege usually reserved for National candidates) or at the gates.

For the party leaders, schedules were heavy, although less travelling was involved than in more recent election campaigns (MacDonald, however, did use air transport to travel from his north-eastern seat to the Midlands). Some politicians were more mobile than others, especially Baldwin who, being unopposed at Bewdley, was free to

[31] *Morning Post*, 26 Oct. 1931.

[32] West Dorset CA, finance committee, 5 Feb. 1932; (West Dorset CA papers, D399/4/1); Houghton-le-Spring DLP, annual report, 1931, to annual meeting, 12 Mar. 1932 (Shotton papers, D/Sho 99).

[33] Hollins, 'Presentation', 69–70, 191.

make a major tour of the North and Scotland, areas he had always believed crucial to the success of protectionism at the polls. But even though Chamberlain was opposed, he felt secure enough to speak widely in the North and Midlands. Their counterparts were less favourably placed, Samuel, Simon, MacDonald, Henderson, Clynes, and Graham all being largely confined to their own constituencies and their immediate hinterlands. It was not especially helpful for a Labour Party trying to play down charges of TUC dictation that much of the travelling campaigning fell on trade unionists, especially Citrine and Cramp.

Individual candidates often faced even more gruelling schedules. A typical example was Sir Arthur Steel-Maitland, who addressed two or three meetings every day in the two weeks up to polling. In Wansbeck, 82 Labour meetings were held between 10 and 27 October, the majority being addressed by the candidate; in Cambridgeshire the figure was 94. This kind of timetable was especially punishing in large rural divisions. National candidates tended to take Sunday off; many Labour candidates, perhaps through desperation, carried on campaigning. The eve of the poll saw everywhere a crescendo of public meetings; in Bishop Auckland, Dalton addressed more than twenty such gatherings in the day.[34]

Reports from National meetings were generally very good. In Birmingham there were 'exceptional attendances' and overflow meetings had to be held regularly. Sir Austen Chamberlain found his audiences not only large, but also keenly attentive. His half-brother, travelling round the north of England, had similar experiences. All his meetings were 'packed out'; for example, at Wakefield his speech at one rally was relayed by loudspeaker to another meeting and out into the street. Lord Bridgeman, who spoke in St Helens, Ashton, Brighouse, Wolverhampton, Burslem, Burnley, and Blackburn, had similar experiences. Only at Swadlincote (South Derbyshire) did he experience any barracking. Reports from, for example, York, Durham, and Hampshire confirmed the pattern.[35]

Many Labourites also reported good meetings, however. Some of

[34] Undated memorandum (Steel-Maitland papers, GD 193/282/2/193–5); Wansbeck DLP, 'Agent's Report for Six Months Ending 31/12/31' (Wansbeck DLP papers, NRO 527/A/2); Cambridgeshire TCLP, annual report, 1931–2 (Cambridgeshire TCLP papers, 416/0.20); Headlam diary, Oct. 1931, *passim* (Headlam papers, D/He 27); Dalton diary, 26 Oct. 1931 (Dalton papers).

[35] Birmingham CA, chief agent's report to management committee, 13 Nov. 1931 (Birmingham CA papers, minute book 1931–2, ff. 128–32); Sir Austen to Lady Ivy

these reports, made publicly, were efforts to 'talk up' the Labour vote, as some candidates who tried to stress the positive side of the party's programme experienced 'a certain difficulty in getting the case over'.[36] But, privately, many Labour politicians felt meetings had gone well, and after the election *Labour Organiser* commented that meetings had been very enthusiastic 'almost everywhere'.[37] In fact there is no need to doubt that many Labour meetings did go well. After all, it was not hard, especially at the start of the campaign, to fill schoolrooms or even larger halls with Labour supporters who rejoiced in the action of the ex-ministers in refusing to impose the dole cut. This did not mean that Labour was winning the election, however.

The point about the 1931 election was that it did see greater public interest than, say, 1929. Although the turn-out was not appreciably higher overall than in the latter year, there was a qualitative difference. All the evidence suggests that people who voted in both elections were more willing to attend meetings, more curious about the issues, in 1931. Thus attendances at meetings generally increased. What was significant was the differential rate at which meetings became larger and more enthusiastic. For example, at Bolton Drill Hall Henderson commanded an excellent audience of 2,000, which would certainly justify his being encouraged. But a few days later, Chamberlain packed the hall and an overflow, addressing in all 8,000 to 10,000 people.[38] Obviously, Labour candidates did not attend their opponents' meetings, and thus were justified in thinking they were doing well. The fact was, of course, that however well they were doing, their opponents were doing better. The fallacious argument that the Post Office savings scare had caused massive last-minute defections was the best way of rationalizing this state of affairs that many Labour candidates could manage.

Another myth which gained credence was that the election saw uniformly 'grim, silent audiences' (according to Mowat, who seems to have believed that electors could only be cheerful if intending to vote

Chamberlain, 24 Oct. 1931; Neville to Ida Chamberlain, 18 Oct. 1931 (Chamberlain papers, AC 6/1/843; NC 18/1/758); Bridgeman to Baldwin, 25 Oct. 1931 (Baldwin papers, vol. 45 (v), ff. 121–2); York CA, annual report, 1931 (York CA papers, 53); Headlam diary, 10–21 Oct. 1931, *passim* (Headlam papers, D/He 27); Hilda to Neville Chamberlain, 21 Oct. 1931 (Chamberlain papers, NC 18/2/755); Croft, *My Life of Strife*, 201.

[36] Dalton diary, 12 Oct. 1931 (Dalton papers).

[37] *Labour Organiser*, Nov. 1931.

[38] Neville to Hilda Chamberlain, 24 Oct. 1931 (Chamberlain papers, NC 18/1/759).

Labour) and that there was very little violence and disorder at meetings.[39] In fact there was no lack of disorder, mostly at National, and especially National Labour, meetings. On 15 October, MacDonald was refused a hearing in his constituency, and the same thing happened three days later to Thomas at Liverpool.[40] In Finsbury, G. M. Gillett announced on 23 October that disruption was compelling him to abandon his remaining indoor meetings of the campaign.[41] Conservatives and Liberals also faced disruption; in Portsmouth, the Conservative, Sir Bertram Falle, cancelled all his meetings due to rowdyism, and on 22 October two Tory meetings at Preston turned into 'pandemonium', with speakers unable to make themselves heard, fist fights breaking out, and the police being called to restore order. Fighting carried on in the streets.[42] In Stockton, Harold Macmillan experienced what he described later as his most violent campaign, finding it 'impossible to speak at all' at most of his meetings.[43] The most serious disturbances attended the campaign of Sir Oswald Mosley, already seen on the left as a fascist; on 17 October, a crowd estimated at 15,000 rioted to prevent him speaking in Birmingham. Mosley's response was to organize stewards to deal with the disruptive elements, an expedient also adopted by Sir Austen Chamberlain.[44]

Who was responsible for such outbreaks? It was a great piece of propaganda for Gillett to be able to blame Labour for the unrest at his meetings. However, it seems more likely that much of the disruption came from the far left, especially the Communists. A number of factors point to this conclusion. Disrupters of meetings in Battersea, Petersfield (Hampshire), and Middlesex were identified as CPGB members, while George Lansbury, no lifelong ardent anti-Communist, blamed the NUWM for trouble at his meetings.[45] Then there is more circumstantial evidence. The CPGB and its more sizeable agent, the NUWM, were at this time expanding (the party from 2,724 members

[39] Mowat, *Britain between the Wars*, 411; Stevenson and Cook, *Slump*, 102.

[40] *The Times*, 16, 19 Oct. 1931.

[41] R. D. Denman, *Political Sketches* (Carlisle, 1949), 14; *Gleanings and Memoranda*, Nov. 1931.

[42] *The Times*, 23 Oct. 1931; A. McClure to Beaverbrook, 19 Oct. 1931 (Beaverbrook papers, B/201); *Manchester Guardian*, 23 Oct. 1931.

[43] H. Macmillan, *Winds of Change, 1914–1939* (London, 1966), 279.

[44] Skidelsky, *Mosley*, 274–5; *Daily Herald*, 19 Oct. 1931; Sir Austen to Lady Ivy Chamberlain, 15 Oct. 1931 (Chamberlain papers, AC 6/1/836).

[45] *Daily Herald*, 5, 22 Oct. 1931; *Morning Post*, 24 Oct. 1931; Lansbury to Graham Pole, 14 Oct. 1931 (Graham Pole papers, UL 5/2).

in June to 6,279 in November) and leading a vigorous fight against the cuts and also, due to the 'class against class' line, against Labour. The *Daily Worker*'s celebration of civil disorder in London, Manchester, and Glasgow suggested that similar unrest at political meetings was not to be discouraged. The decision to run 'demonstration candidates' in seats where the party could not afford the £150 deposit suggested a similar intention to disrupt.[46] Finally, the behaviour of individual Communist candidates suggested that they welcomed such disruption of their opponents' meetings. However, Labour activists' feelings were also running high, and there was a tradition of disturbances at British elections which long pre-dated the foundation of the CPGB.

II

Newspapers were still the means by which electors kept abreast of the progress of the campaign; and while there had been more titles during an election, there had never been so wide a circulation of papers. In 1910, year of two elections, there had been seventeen London morning and evening newspapers with a combined circulation of 4,230,000.[47] In 1931 the three leading morning titles alone accounted for sales of 4,878,000, and the total circulation of the nine main London morning titles was 8,536,000, which, with sales of 1,700,000 for the three evening titles, made a total of 10,236,000, The inter-war assuredly saw the extension of the habit of newspaper reading to the working class. It was a moot point, of course, whether readers were particularly interested in the press's political coverage. Contemporary surveys suggested politics was only one, and not the major, subject of interest to the average reader; news of accidents, the weather, crime and divorce, and local news, was far more popular. Therefore we must be cautious about generalizations regarding the impact of the press on public opinion. However, elections are times of heightened political awareness, as the surveys pointed out, and so it seems reasonable to attribute to the press a degree of influence on the electorate.[48]

It was a press increasingly under the control of large groupings (for ownership, circulation, etc., see Tables 9.3 and 9.4). Five combines

[46] *Daily Worker*, 7, 8, 10, 12 Oct. 1931.

[47] N. Blewett, *The Peers, the Parties and the People: The General Elections of 1910* (London, 1972), 301.

[48] PEP, *Report on the British Press: A Survey of its Current Operations and Problems with Special Reference to National Newspapers and their Part in Public Affairs* (London, 1938), 248.

Table 9.3. *National daily papers and the 1931 election*

Title	Type	Proprietor	Approx. Circulation	Alignment
The Times	Q	J.J. Astor/J. Walter	186,000	National
Daily Telegraph	Q	Berry	200,000	National
Morning Post	Q	Duke of Northumberland	145,000	National
Daily Express	P	Beaverbrook	1,685,000	National
Daily Herald	P	Odhams Press/TUC	1,130,000	Labour
Daily Mail	P	Rothermere	1,793,000	National
Daily Mirror	P	Rothermere	1,071,000	National
Daily Sketch	P	Berry	926,000	National
News Chronicle	P	Cadbury	1,400,000	National
Daily Worker	Pty	Communist Party	15,000	Communist

Key: Q Quality, P Popular, Pty Party

Note: All cost 1d except *The Times* (2d).

Table 9.4. *National Sunday papers and the 1931 election*

Title	Type	Proprietor	Approx. Circulation	Alignment
Observer	Q	Lord Waldorf Astor	200,000	National
Sunday Times	Q	Berry	153,000	National
News of the World	P	Lord Riddell	3,411,000	National
People	P	Odhams Press	2,499,000	National
Reynolds's Ill. News	P	Co-op. Society	400,000	Labour
Sunday Chronicle	P	Berry	930,000	National
Sunday Dispatch	P	Rothermere	1,197,000	National
Sunday Express	P	Beaverbrook	995,376	National
Sunday Graphic	P	Berry	940,000	National
Sunday Pictorial	P	Rothermere	2,100,000	National
Sunday Referee	P	Ostrer	73,000	National

Key: Q Quality, P Popular

Note: All cost 2d.

controlled most of the national press. The Berry group (*Daily Telegraph*, *Daily Sketch*, Manchester *Daily Dispatch*; *Sunday Times*, *Sunday Graphic*, Manchester *Empire News*; around twenty provincial titles) was the largest, and firmly pro-Conservative. Second came the Rothermere chain (*Daily Mail*, *Daily Mirror*, *Sunday Dispatch*, *Sunday Pictorial*; London *Evening News*; around a dozen provincial titles) which followed its proprietor's own characteristically right-wing brand of Conservatism. After Rothermere were another idiosyncratic Tory, Beaverbrook (*Daily Express*; *Sunday Express*; London *Evening Standard*), the Liberal Cadburys (*News Chronicle*; London evening *Star*), and the Odhams Press (*Daily Herald*, co-owned with and under the editorial control of the TUC; the more neutral Sunday *People*). Outside the large chains were: the Baldwinite *Times*, owned by J. J. Astor; the die-hard *Morning Post* and the Communist *Daily Worker*, as well as four Sundays. These were: the heavyweight, pro-Conservative *Observer*, the *News of the World* (a popular paper of limited political content, whose 'banality, sentimentality and lubricity'[49] helped it to the highest circulation in the world); *Reynolds's Illustrated News* (owned by the Co-operative Society, and pro-Labour); and finally, the *Sunday Referee* (owned by the head of Gaumont British Pictures).

As well as the national press, there were numerous provincial and local daily and weekly newspapers.[50] Most of the main provincial titles tended to favour the Conservatives, the most notable exception being the Liberal *Manchester Guardian*. Among the local papers, a declining number favoured the Liberals, but most were Conservative. None normally favoured Labour in this manner.

In addition, it should be remembered that Scotland stood somewhat aloof from England and Wales. Only the *Daily Express*, which alone of the national dailies had a Scottish edition printed in Scotland, the *Daily Mail*, and the *Daily Herald* of the English papers achieved a significant share of the market north of the border. There were five morning titles vying for the rest: the *Scotsman* (Edinburgh), the *Glasgow Herald*, the *Daily Record and Mail* (Glasgow), the *Aberdeen Press and Journal*, and the *Courier and Advertiser* (Dundee). All were to back the National Government in the general election of 1931.

In doing so, they proved that in some respects at least there was no difference in substance between the northern kingdom and the rest of

[49] K. von Stutterheim, *The Press in England* (London, 1934), 121.

[50] *Report of the Royal Commission on the Press, 1947–1949* (Cmd. 7700; London, 1949), 188.

Table 9.5. *Types of newspapers in 1931*

		Morning	Evening	Sunday
National		10	–	10
London		1 (suburban)	3	–
Provincial:	England	24	68	5
	Wales	1	2	–
	Scotland	6	9	2
TOTALS		42	82	17

the country. Out of twenty national titles (excluding the *Daily Worker*), Labour had the support of only two—the *Daily Herald* and *Reynold's Illustrated News*—against the Government's eighteen (the *Manchester Guardian* also supported Labour). There was an all-pervading and bitter partisanship which left few newspapers, of whatever status, and on whatever side, untouched.

> The most objectionable feature of election coverage in most of the tabloids was not the partisanship of the leader columns but the pervasive impact of these political preferences on election news coverage. In many cases, this amounted to a rejection of any professional standards of journalism.[51]

Those words were written of the 1983 election campaign, but might just as well be applied to practically the entire press in 1931. (Tables 9.6 and 9.7 show national papers' lead stories during the campaign.)

Of the daily newspapers, *The Times* had the strongest tradition of fair reporting. Like the other quality dailies, it certainly gave extensive coverage to the campaign, with lengthy reports of speeches, reports on the campaign in the regions, and news of and editorial comments on the progress of the election. Its editor, Dawson, was very much in favour of the National appeal, and the paper's editorial line reflected the fact. Labour's leaders were accused of running away, its manifesto was described as destructive, and if the party won the election it would be the downfall of the nation. Given that the defeat of Labour was *The Times*'s main objective, it was inevitable that clashes between Government supporters in the constituencies were condemned. This line dominated news coverage, with little reporting of Labour

[51] M. Harrop, 'Press', in D. E. Butler and D. Kavanagh, *British General Election of 1983* (London, 1984), 197–8.

Table 9.6. *National press headline stories, 8–27 Oct. 1931*

Date	*The Times*	*Daily Telegraph*	*Morning Post*
8	MacDonald's manifesto	MacDonald's manifesto	MacDonald's manifesto
9	Conservative manifesto	Conservative manifesto	Conservative manifesto
10	National party pacts	Baldwin at Birmingham	Baldwin at Birmingham
12	National candidates withdraw	Difficulties of Con–Lib co-operation	Danger of apathy
13	MacDonald at Seaham	MacDonald at Seaham	Unemployment falling
14	MacDonald denies funds for N.Lab	More pacts	More pacts
15	More candidates to withdraw	More pacts	More pacts
16	Nomination day	Nomination day	Lloyd George's broadcast
17	Nominations	Snowden's letter to N.Lab candidates	Nominations
19	Grey, Baldwin speeches, Snowden's broadcast	Grey, Snowden & Samuel reassure free traders	Snowden's broadcast
20	MacDonald's election address	Snowden defends his broadcast	Henderson in the Midlands
20	Baldwin at Leeds	Heavy Labour losses likely	Danger of over-confidence
22	MacDonald's reply to Graham's broadcast	Government victory probable	Snowden's reply to Graham
23	Baldwin's broadcast	Good prospects for 3-figure majority	Baldwin's broadcast

24	Confusion among working-class voters	Need to keep working to secure victory	Even Cobden opposed dumping
26	MacDonald's broadcast	MacDonald's message to *Telegraph* readers	Eve-of-poll messages
27	Duty of voting	Duty of voting	Duty of voting

Date	*Daily Express*	*Daily Mail*	*News Chronicle*
8	MacDonald's manifesto	MacDonald's manifesto	MacDonald's manifesto
9	National party pacts	Conservative manifesto	Conservative manifesto
10	Cons to oppose free traders	Liberal & Labour manifestos	Liberal manifesto
12	Tory revolts against election pacts	More pacts	[Five die in car crash]
13	Unemployment falling	MacDonald at Seaham	Funds available for Lib cands
14	Beaverbrook at Limehouse	MacDonald at Seaham	More pacts
15	Australian senators want empire free trade	N.Lab complaints to Cons over seats	[Motor Show contest]
16	Lloyd George's broadcast	Dangers of split National vote	[Policeman dies in accident]
17	Snowden's letter to N.Lab candidates	Snowden's letter to N.Lab candidates	Nominations
19	[Death of Edison]	Interview with MacDonald	Questionnaire to candidates
20	105 seats Labour will lose	Snowden's article 'Labour's Little Lenins'	Cons reaction to questionnaire

Table 9.6. *Continued*

Date	*Daily Express*	*Daily Mail*	*News Chronicle*
21	Unemployment down	Industry recovering	Reactions to questionnaire
22	Beaverbrook at Birmingham	Snowden's reply to Graham's broadcast	MacDonald at Tamworth
23	Prosperity returning	Danger of apathy & over-confidence	[Cypriot revolt]
24	Dewar's propaganda in Portsmouth	Big Government victory expected	Questionnaire
26	'People' newspaper wants National Govt.	Post Office savings bank scare	Predictions of National victory
27	Vote to bring back prosperity	Duty of voting	'Truth' re. Post Office scare
Date	*Daily Mirror*	*Daily Sketch*	*Daily Worker*
8	[New head of Metropolitan police named]	[Kingsford Smith's flight to Australia]	Demonstrate against cuts
9	Dissolution of Parliament	Baldwin's manifesto	March in Manchester today
10	Baldwin at Birmingham	Ishbel MacDonald campaigning for father	150,000 march in Glasgow
12	[Five die in car crash]	[Society wedding]	100,000 march in Hyde Park
13	MacDonald at Seaham	MacDonald's campaign	Resist wage and dole cuts
14	[Factory explosion in Leeds]	[Aga Khan's double win at Newmarket]	CPGB manifesto

15	Darwen: Conservative 'wrecker'	[Thames flooded]	Dole cuts today
16	[Policeman killed in road accident]	[Policeman killed in road accident]	Resistance to cuts
17	[Earl engaged to debutante]	Simon's broadcast	Communist candidates
19	Snowden's broadcast	[Death of Edison]	Snowden's letter to N.Lab cands
20	Labour's banking policy	[Suicide pact in Sussex]	Resistance to dole cuts
21	MacDonald in Bassetlaw	MacDonald in Bassetlaw	Wage-cutting campaign
22	Mid-Bedfords: Conservative 'wrecker'	[Prince of Wales in Colchester]	Unemployment & inflation up
23	[Duke's son to wed actress]	[Cypriot revolt against Britain]	Baldwin's firm's profits
24	Mrs Snowden speaking for Samuel at Darwen	[Society wedding]	Need for revolution
26	'Bolshevism Run Mad'	[Society wedding]	Resistance to means test
27	Duty of voting	Duty of voting	Vote Communist

Table 9.6. *Continued*

Date	*Manchester Guardian*	*Daily Herald*
8	MacDonald's manifesto	MacDonald's manifesto
9	National problems on tariffs	Henderson at party conference
10	Tweed's resignation from Lib organization	Labour manifesto
12	Henderson meets Lloyd George	John Burns to stand in North Battersea?
13	MacDonald at Seaham	Cons help to N.Lab candidates
14	Nat argument over free hand	Henderson at Burnley
15	N.Lab disputes with Cons over seats	Benefit cuts take effect tomorrow
16	Nomination day	Lloyd George's broadcast
17	Nominations	RAF ferrying MacDonald's supporters
19	Snowden's broadcast	Ex-ministers reply to Snowden's broadcast
20	Chamberlain, Snowden clash on free hand	Free traders rallying to Labour
21	Baldwin at Leeds	Conservatives' detailed plans for protection
22	Snowden's reply to Graham's broadcast	Labour expects to do well
23	Con–Lib–N.Lab clash in Colne Valley	Snowden's commitment to 'Labour and the Nation'
24	Grey at Dewsbury	Interview with Lloyd George
26	Maclean appeals for Baldwin's help	Henderson warns against National scares
27	MacDonald in Seaham	Vote early & turn govt. out

Table 9.7. *Sunday press headline stories, 11–25 Oct. 1931*

	11	18	25
Observer	Henderson meets Lloyd George	Baldwin at Finsbury Park	MacDonald's broadcast
Sunday Times	Henderson meets Lloyd George	Baldwin at Finsbury Park	MacDonald's broadcast
Reynolds's Ill. News	National splits	Labour replies to Snowden's broadcast	Interview with Henderson
Sunday Dispatch	Henderson meets Lloyd George	Snowden's broadcast	Statement by Snowden
Sunday Express	National splits	Lloyd George: secret pact with Labour	Dewar's propaganda
News of World	Henderson meets Lloyd George	Snowden's broadcast	MacDonald's broadcast
People	Confusion of election	Nominations	All parties ready
Sunday Chronicle	Henderson meets Lloyd George	Snowden's broadcast	MacDonald's broadcast
Sunday Graphic	[Great turf record]	[Society wedding]	[Society wedding]
Sunday Pictorial	Baldwin at Birmingham	Snowden's broadcast	[Society wedding]
Sunday Referee	Need for National victory	Lloyd George's broadcast	Vote National

speeches, heavily biased reports from the constituencies, appeals to help National candidates and, on polling day, to resist apathy and vote National. Perhaps *The Times*'s campaign was best summed up by its reprinting of a virulent *Daily Mail* article by Snowden on 21 October. If the bastion of British journalism was working at such a level, there was little hope of moderation from the rest of the press.

The best-selling quality daily was the *Daily Telegraph*. Its editorial line was similar to *The Times*'s, in that it felt a Labour victory would mean 'ruin, swift and sure'; but, while urging National unity, it was more pro-Conservative, and criticized the Liberals and free trade.[52] News reporting followed the editorial line very closely, especially in the accounts of constituency campaigns. The *Telegraph* was less guarded about the result, however, telling its readers on 22 October that the Government would win comfortably, although it did not fail to stress, on polling day, the duty of supporting National candidates. Lest anyone had any doubts, it had already summed up its view on 23 October, saying in a display caption that the choice was between 'The NATIONAL WAY: through strict and necessary ECONOMY to increased employment, assured national prosperity and imperial economic unity' and 'The SOCIALIST WAY: through loose and lavish EXPENDITURE to increased unemployment, debt, devastation, ruin and imperial disruption'. Its conclusion was straightforward: 'VOTE NATIONAL'. This, it should be remembered, was simply an insertion in the news coverage, on the main news page, not an advertisement paid for by the Government parties. It also printed copies of National election posters, again as news rather than as paid advertising.

There could be little doubt where the third quality daily, the *Morning Post*, stood; again, its news coverage was often indistinguishable from its editorial line. The paper gave partisan support to the Conservatives, attacking free trade and Liberal extremists while making no criticism of Conservative extremists, doubtless because it would not have believed a Tory could be too extreme. Labour—or the 'Anti-Nationalists' as they were dubbed in both editorial and news columns—was seen as the main danger, though, for a Labour victory would see Britain unable to pay for food imports, and 'the spectre of famine would soon be stalking through our great cities'.[53] It was 'a matter of life or death'.[54] While stressing the dangers of over-

[52] *Daily Telegraph*, 13, 9, 10, 12 Oct. 1931.
[53] *Morning Post*, 23 Oct. 1931.
[54] Ibid. 19 Oct. 1931.

confidence, the paper was predicting a sweeping Government victory as early as 21 October. The *Post* carried a number of interesting features, such as a series by the political correspondent on 'The Men Who Misruled Us', which damned an ex-minister a day. It also printed copies of National election posters.

All the popular dailies were highly selective in their news coverage and strident in their editorial comments; and with the quality press portraying the election with such unashamed bias, it was hardly surprising that the more sensational titles made no attempt at balance. The *Daily Express* had long been a propaganda vehicle for Beaverbrook, and during the 1931 campaign his views influenced its editorial line and the selection of news coverage considerably, first by giving bloated coverage to his own activities, and secondly by giving news a Beaverbrookian slant. Thus MacDonald's manifesto, intended as an appeal for a totally free hand, was presented as 'The Premier's Imperial Call', and the editorial argued that MacDonald had 'realised the urgent need of Empire Free Trade'.[55] The manifesto of Baldwin, whose speeches received scant coverage due to the clashes earlier in the year, was presented as showing 'strict adherence to [the] Beaverbrook–Chamberlain letters' which had ended the feud.[56] Editorially, the *Express* criticized Labour, though eschewing strong personal attacks on the party's leadership. Labour's manifesto would lead to 'chaos' and on polling day it hoped that 'the mad Moscow policy' of Labour would be 'destroyed for ever'.[57] But the paper's main offensive concentrated on the free-trade Liberals, who were seen as the main danger to a protectionist Government. A week before polling it was predicting that Labour would lose 105 seats and that '[f]ull-blooded Protection [was] sweeping the country'.[58]

The Rothermere newspapers, the *Daily Mail* and the *Daily Mirror*, had, unlike the *Express*, been opposed to an election until the last moment, and they continued to behave as though there were a serious chance of a Labour victory. The news coverage in the *Mail* was, like that in the *Express*, highly selective but not insubstantial, and corresponded closely to its editorial line. The main themes were anti-Labour virulence; hostility to 'wrecking' candidates, who were seen as 'un-English' in that they might let in Labour by splitting the National vote; and near adulation of MacDonald as a national saviour, 'the man

[55] *Daily Express*, 9, 8 Oct. 1931.
[56] Ibid. 9 Oct. 1931.
[57] Ibid. 10, 27 Oct. 1931.
[58] Ibid. 9, 20, 19 Oct. 1931.

of destiny' whose hour had come.[59] A Labour Government would mean national ruin and inflation *à la* Weimar Germany. Upon the result of the election 'depend[ed] not only the whole future of Britain, but also whether her 45,000,000 people have wages on which to live and bread to buy'; there would be deaths from starvation if Labour won.[60] A number of feature articles also led voters towards the same conclusions, for example by Snowden (a virulent piece entitled 'Labour's Little Lenins') and Rothermere (arguing that the British Empire would collapse as surely as had the Roman, if Labour won the election, for 'within a very few years' Britain would fall 'into collapse and chaos from which there may be no recovery for centuries').[61] The *Mail* also offered, in conjunction with the *Sunday Dispatch*, £5,000 for the most accurate forecast of the result.

There were no prizes for guessing that the *Daily Mirror* would follow its stable-mate's line. As a picture paper, it devoted little space to the election, preferring instead its usual fare of crime, gossip, sport, and 'society'. Such election coverage as there was, however, showed heavy bias. On 12 October the editorial argued that there was 'no shadow of a doubt that a return to Socialism [would] bring about sudden and irreparable anarchy' under 'some variant of the Bolshevist tyranny'.[62] The paper's news coverage reflected this line. Its pictorial front page was used to what the *Mirror*'s proprietor undoubtedly thought was good effect, especially on Monday, 19 October when, in the aftermath of Snowden's 'Bolshevism Run Mad' broadcast, the *Mirror* covered its front page with a picture of people running in a street, and an explanatory caption, which quoted from the Chancellor's speech and continued that the picture, 'reprinted from the "Daily Mirror" of 1917 shows the terrible and unforgettable scene in the Nevsky Prospect, Petrograd's famous thoroughfare, when the Leninites opened fire on the crowd with machine guns during the Russian Revolution'. A week later, the page was filled with a 1922 photograph of starving children in the Volga region under the headline 'Bolshevism Run Mad'. If electors wanted to avoid such an outcome in Britain, they should support the National Government. This was scurrilous nonsense, but doubtless had an effect in reinforcing the determination of the bulk of the paper's readership to vote National. Thus the

[59] *Daily Mail*, 7, 15, 24 Oct. 1931
[60] Ibid. 12, 14 Oct. 1931.
[61] Ibid. 20, 24 Oct. 1931.
[62] *Daily Mirror*, 12 Oct. 1931.

breathtaking stridency of the *Mirror* compensated for the limited extent of its coverage; no wonder MacDonald expressed gratitude to the Rothermere press.[63]

The *Daily Sketch* had similarly light coverage of the campaign, but, unlike its rival, did not compensate with gutter journalism: indeed, its lack of attention accorded ill with the paper's assertion that the country was going through 'perhaps the most momentous General Election in [British] history'.[64] Nevertheless, it stood firmly behind the Government. It also offered a £5,000 prize for the best prediction of the result.

The two remaining London dailies were less enthusiastic about the Government; indeed one, the *Daily Herald*, was as hostile as the above titles were favourable. The control of the TUC, and especially of Bevin, made this so. But if its line was different, its journalism was very much of the same ilk, with news reporting indistinguishable in tone from editorial comment. Its news coverage was heavily weighted towards Labour politicians, although there was extensive—and disparaging—reportage of MacDonald and National Labour. Editorially the *Herald* stressed free trade and attacked the 'free hand' as a tariff ramp. News coverage reflected this line, for example with stories of prominent Liberals who were backing Labour because of free trade. A series of 'scoops' tried to discredit MacDonald—alleging, for example, that he was being financed by the Conservatives—but these could not be proved after the premier's denials.[65] On 26 October it came closer to the mark, printing a facsimile of a slip found in pay packets at a London factory, which read: 'PLEASE NOTE SHOULD THE NATIONAL GOVERNMENT NOT COME IN WITH A WORKING MAJORITY, WE SHALL BE COMPELLED TO CLOSE DOWN THE BEST PART OF OUR MANUFACTURING DEPARTMENTS.' This, it went on, was a widespread occurrence. It was a good story. Clearly such employers were interfering unjustifiably with the democratic process. But it might have had more impact had people like Greenwood and Cramp not been saying that workers who voted National were 'backlegs'; and besides, in so prominently featuring the 'warning', the *Herald* added to the circulation thereof.

Perhaps it was a belief in the effectiveness of such revelations and appeals to 'the Liberal vote' that led the *Herald* into presenting Labour's prospects in a hopelessly over-optimistic and idealized manner. The fact that such reports tended to stand alongside

[63] MacDonald to Harmsworth, 30 Oct. 1931 (MacDonald papers, PRO 30/69/677).
[64] *Daily Sketch*, 27 Oct. 1931.
[65] *Daily Herald*, 13, 17, 22 Oct. 1931.

increasingly desperate appeals to electors not to be panicked or stampeded, however, suggests they were an attempt to boost flagging morale rather than to report the news accurately. At the time headquarters was grimly urging starry-eyed party agents to send in more realistic analyses of Labour's prospects, for example, the *Herald* was trumpeting that at Transport House there was 'no fuss, worry or rush, but . . . the confidence that comes of conviction in victory'.[66] In addition, the overstatement of Liberal support for Labour in the constituencies led to ridiculous predictions of Labour successes in certain seats. (Some examples are given in Table 9.8.) Under the circumstances, it was hardly surprising that, after the election, the *Herald* had to excuse its wild inaccuracy by recourse to the myth that Labour had been defeated by last-minute scares. In fact, the *Herald* was every bit as ready as the pro-National press to use scares and smears. Its editorials took an increasingly shrill line, culminating in a polling day crescendo of whose tone even the Rothermere press might have been proud:

> The idea of a Dictatorship with himself as Dictator, of the Conversion of Parliament into a 'Council of State' on the Fascist model, of the destruction of that Party system which springs naturally from free institutions, appears to have been much in the mind of Mr MacDonald himself. . . . A vote for the 'Nationals' is a vote against democracy, a vote against political freedom, a vote for the pinchbeck Fascism of a bunch of pinchbeck Mussolinis.[67]

Subsequent claims that the *Herald* had fought an honourable campaign came only from the Labour side.[68] It had, in fact, been at least as bad as the other popular dailies, even to the extent of carrying an election competition, although, perhaps significantly, the prize was for predicting, not the result, but the total number of votes cast.

The Liberal *News Chronicle*, in close contact with Liberal headquarters, was also more critical of the Government than the Conservative dailies. Its editorial line stressed the twin evils of reckless expenditure under Labour, and high and permanent tariffs under the Tories. Thus it urged as many Liberals to stand as possible. The *Chronicle* also claimed to agree with both the Liberal manifesto and Lloyd George's election address, although feeling it could not 'wholly

[66] *Daily Herald*, 13 Oct. 1931.
[67] Ibid. 27 Oct. 1931.
[68] See e.g. Labour Party, *The Power of the Press* (London, 1936), 1: 'the *Daily Herlad* alone among the newspapers of the world told the truth of what was going on behind the scenes'.

Table 9.8. Daily Herald *predictions of Labour gains* (%)

		1929	1931
Watford	Con	45.9	78.3
	Lib	30.3	–
	Lab	23.8	21.7
	CON MAJ	15.6 (6,295)	56.6 (24,653)
Eastbourne	Con	49.9	85.3
	Lab	22.5	14.7
	Lib	21.4	–
	CON MAJ	27.4 (9,953)	70.6 (25,861)
Winchester	Con	44.8	69.7
	Lab	36.6	30.3
	Lib	18.6	–
	CON MAJ	8.2 (3,234)	39.4 (17,602)

Source: *Daily Herald*, 24, 27, 22 Oct. 1931.

endorse' the latter's advice to vote Labour.[69] Instead, a questionnaire on 19 October aimed to identify moderate Labour and Conservative candidates. For much of the following week, reaction to it dominated the paper's news and editorial content. On polling day, the editorial, with acknowledged reluctance, urged its readers to support the National Government, because Labour's programme was 'a menace', but that if the choice in a particular constituency lay between an extreme protectionist and a moderate Labourite, Liberals should help strengthen 'the saner Labour element'. The *Chronicle*'s news coverage was less heated than that of the *Herald* and the bulk of the Conservative press, but it took its lead very much from the editorial column and was strongly Liberal in bias.

The final London daily also had a rather distinctive view of the campaign. The *Daily Worker* attacked 'the three capitalist parties', stressed marches and demonstrations against the cuts, and highlighted Communist and fellow-travelling candidates.[70] Items such as the CPGB manifesto, and appeals for funds, figured prominently. Its news reporting was sheer propaganda, and vitriol the order of the day, with

[69] *News Chronicle*, 10, 16 Oct. 1931.

[70] *Daily Worker*, 7 Oct. 1931.

attacks on the 'unspeakable' 'scum politician', Thomas; on 'the grovelling Henderson'; on Baldwin, 'this impudent liar' and 'outspoken enemy of every worker'; and on Snowden, referred to deliciously as 'Capitalism's barking dog'.[71] Still, it was not above using the Chancellor's revelations against the Labour leaders, while attacking also 'the National Starvation Government'.[72] Its polling day advice was to vote Communist and, where no CPGB candidate was standing, to write 'Communist Party' across the ballot paper.

It seems that only one title out of the 3 London evening, 31 provincial morning, and 79 provincial evening newspapers supported Labour—the prestigious *Manchester Guardian*. The Liberal stalwart had welcomed the National Government at first, but soon changed its tune. Bassett criticized this switch, but it had a straightforward explanation. The increasingly pro-Labour editor, Ted Scott, was on holiday at the time of the Government's formation. From his return on 28 August, the paper shifted towards opposition to an election and the Government, a line which lost it much revenue due to advertisers' objections.[73] During the campaign, the *Guardian*'s editorials had a strongly anti-election, anti-Conservative, pro-free trade tone. Thus MacDonald's manifesto was condemned as an attempt to conceal the Government's intention of introducing protection. Meanwhile, the paper stressed that there was 'hardly a Conservative candidate in the country who [was] not preaching full-blooded Protection', which was only slightly an exaggeration and which tended to disprove subsequent claims that the Tories had deceived people as to their true intentions.[74] Scott accepted Labour's free-trade protestations, and so on 21 October he finally came out with the uninspiring advice that Liberals should prefer 'even the weakness of a Labour government to the certain and positive mischiefs that a Tory Government [would] ensure'. Since a Labour victory was impossible, he argued on polling day, Liberals should support Labour in order to offset the danger of a National/Protectionist landslide. The paper's news coverage, though, was both extensive and reasonably independent of the editorial line, a refreshing change from the London dailies.

The Sunday newspapers, on the whole, were less concerned about the election. The heaviest coverage came from the two quality papers. *The Observer* had extracts from speeches and extensive analysis of the

[71] *Daily Worker*, 8, 22, 15, 10 Oct. 1931.
[72] Ibid. 16, 9 Oct. 1931.
[73] Bassett, *Nineteen Thirty-One*, 198–203, 304; D. Ayerst, *Guardian: Biography of a Newspaper* (London, 1971), 468–75.
[74] *Manchester Guardian*, 20 Oct. 1931.

campaign's progress. Its news coverage was not especially biased, but Garvin's editorials were unequivocal, defining the issue starkly. The choice, he wrote, lay 'between National Government and a programme of national downfall and disgrace such as our public life ha[d] never seen. This [was] the first General Election in which Britain's fate [was] as strictly staked as ever it was in war.'[75] The *Sunday Times* also had a solid news coverage of the campaign. Its reporting was somewhat more tainted by the editorial line; the latter was firmly pro-National and heavily critical of Labour and the TUC.

At the other end of the market, most of the popular Sundays carried little election news or comment. The *Sunday Chronicle*, *Sunday Graphic*, *Sunday Pictorial*, and *News of the World* all stressed the duty of voting National. The *Sunday Referee* supported the Government but stated that '[t]he fundamental patriotism of all the Parties [could] not be doubted'.[76] Finally, the *People*—Odhams's other paper—took a very neutral line editorially and in news terms almost ignored the election. Its editorials were vague, even on 25 October when it urged the need to return a strong Government in order to secure the return of prosperity. Doubtless the desire to avoid a head-on clash with its stable-mate, the *Herald*, made the *People* so disguise its National preferences.

Finally, in the middle of the market, the *Sunday Dispatch*, the *Sunday Express*, and *Reynolds's Illustrated News* all had rather more coverage of the campaign. The *Dispatch*'s line was similar to that of its sister paper, the *Mail*, and dominated its news coverage. The 25 October edition saw thirty-three questions and answers designed to help electors to decide how to vote. The objectivity of the advice offered can be judged by the following:

> How do the Parties stand?
> On the one side there is the National Government, led by Mr Ramsay MacDonald and consisting of the best elements in the Conservative, Liberal and Labour Parties. On the other side, there is the Socialist Party, led by Mr Arthur Henderson and the men who ran away from the country's crisis, taking their orders from the TUC.[77]

This was a sustainable view of the situation, but it was also highly contentious, and to pass it off as fact was a deplorable exercise, debasing any journalistic standards to which the paper might have laid

[75] *Observer*, 25, 11 Oct. 1931.
[76] *Sunday Referee*, 11 Oct. 1931.
[77] *Sunday Dispatch*, 25 Oct. 1931.

claim. The editorial line and news reporting of the *Sunday Express*, meanwhile, were the same as its daily counterpart. *Reynolds's Illustrated News*, on the other hand, supported Labour, editorially and in its news coverage, although less vehemently than the *Daily Herald*. But *Reynolds's*, with its small circulation, could hardly compete with the massed ranks of the pro-National press on Sundays.

Did it matter? The Labour Party claimed, at the time and subsequently, that the press had played a large part in its defeat. A number of factors could be cited in support of this hypothesis. First, the National Government enjoyed the support of almost every newspaper in the country. Only the *Daily Herald* and *Reynolds's* of the national papers, and the *Manchester Guardian* of the regional papers, opposed the Government; the *News Chronicle* gave it reluctant support, and the *Daily Worker* damned everyone. Among the lesser provincial titles it is doubtful whether any supported Labour. Thus in terms of titles alone the Government enjoyed an overwhelming majority. This is reinforced when looked at in terms of circulation (see Table 9.9). Secondly, the papers which opposed Labour were heavily biased. They rarely attempted to provide a balanced view in their news reporting, a fact which was almost as true of *The Times* as it was of the *Daily Mirror*. Their editorials were still more anti-Labour. Thirdly, a number of thoroughly scurrilous attacks were made on Labour and its leaders, a process which probably reached its apogee in the 19 October edition of the *Daily Mirror* with its appalling implication that a Labour victory would mean machine guns in the streets.

However, these criticisms need to be tempered. The *Daily Herald* was as biased and as scurrilous as most of its competitors. Its personal attacks on MacDonald, culminating in its polling day characterization of him as a 'pinchbeck Mussolini' were as strong as any attacks launched by the rest of the press, with the possible exception of the *Daily Worker*. As in the campaign itself, it was simply not true that an honourable Labour Party, keen to discuss the issues on their merits, was jostled aside by a scaremongering and unscrupulous National Government campaign. The pro-National press often was scaremongering and unscrupulous, but the Labour press was at least equally so, as the Labourite *New Statesman* accepted.[78] As a whole, the press coverage of the 1931 election was not such as to arouse pride in

[78] *New Statesman*, 24 Oct. 1931.

Table 9.9. *London newspapers: circulation and views of the election*

	National	Labour
Daily Morning	8,806,000	1,130,000
Evening	1,700,000	–
Sunday	12,278,000	283,000

British journalism, and was to be unrivalled in its scurrility for fifty-two years.

The central proposition, that newspapers were a major factor in Labour's defeat, is more difficult to assess. The impact of the press on elections today is still a matter of debate despite masses of opinion poll evidence. As has been seen, even without the press there were ample reasons for the electorate to turn against Labour in 1931. It must be remembered that to win the election, even to hold onto its 1929 parliamentary strength, Labour needed to increase its vote in 1931; and there was no reason why, after two dismal years in office, having lost some of its best-known leaders, and with a less convincing programme, it should have won the allegiance of either the new voters or voters who had felt unable to vote Labour in 1929. In that sense, Labour's defeat was inevitable. At most, the pro-National press, in keeping up the pressure on its readership to vote for the Government, ensured a high turn-out instead of allowing apathy and complacency to take hold, and so, perhaps, meant Labour lost a few more seats than it would have done otherwise. But to blame the press for Labour's defeat, or even to cite it as a major factor, was to blame the messenger for the message and to seek to evade unpleasant political realities, or else to explain why hopelessly over-optimistic predictions of Labour success had come to naught.

III

Modern elections are fought largely on television, but the first TV election did not come until 1959. The thirty years up to then had seen radio grow to prime importance amongst the mass communications media. In 1931, certainly, radio had a greater impact than ever before.

Until the First World War, radio was generally known only as a means of communicating between ships at sea. However, the 1920s saw a vast increase in the number of people who could listen to the programmes of the British Broadcasting Company, formed in 1923 and a public corporation from 1 January 1927 (see Table 9.10). At the 1924 general election, there had been one broadcast by each party leader; in 1929 there were six Conservative broadcasts, three Labour, and three Liberal. This 2:1:1 ratio was 'justified' on the grounds that the Conservatives were the Government party; not surprisingly, the Labour Party especially was incensed.[79]

In 1931 matters were hardly likely to be more easily settled. There were few indications that the allocation would favour Labour inordinately. After the formation of the National Government, there were a number of pro-Government or pro-Government policy talks broadcast, by, for example, MacDonald and Snowden, with no opportunity for the Opposition to reply. In addition, MacDonald broadcast on 7 October to announce the dissolution of Parliament; although not formally considered an election broadcast, its content suggested that it was just that.

Sir John Reith, director-general of the BBC, decided at an early stage that he wanted no more than a dozen party broadcasts in all, and that only parties nominating 50 or more candidates would be eligible. This meant the rejection of requests from the CPGB, the Scottish National Party, Plaid Cymru, and the ILP. The New Party was told that if it nominated 50 candidates it 'would have a claim', although it is interesting to speculate whether Reith would really have contemplated breaching the press boycott on the Mosleyites; in the event, of course, they only put up 24, so the question did not arise. Requests from Beaverbrook and Churchill were also rejected.[80]

The manner in which the broadcasts were finally allocated was little short of disgraceful. On 6 October, Reith was called to the House of Commons to meet three Conservatives, Ralph Glyn (MacDonald's PPS), Sir Bolton Eyres-Monsell (the chief whip), and Sir William Ormsby-Gore (Postmaster-General). Dismissing Reith's suggestion that Samuel and the Labour chief whip should be represented, they finally agreed that there should be broadcasts by one Liberal of each

[79] M. Pegg, 'British Radio Broadcasting and its Audience, 1918–1939', D.Phil. thesis (Oxford, 1979), 32.

[80] Hollins, 'Presentation', 409; Reith diary, 6 Oct. 1931, in *The Reith Diaries*, ed. C. Stuart (London, 1975), 107; Beaverbrook to Reith, 8 Oct. 1931 (Beaverbrook papers B/188); Churchill to Reith, 10 Oct. 1931 (Churchill papers 2/183, in Gilbert, *Churchill*, Vol. 5: *Companion 2*).

Table 9.10. *Radio licences, 1922–32*

Year ending 31 Dec.	Total Licences	Estd. No. of People Able To Listen	Approx No. Per 100 households
1922	36,000	149,000	1
1923	595,496	2,465,000	5.5
1924	1,129,578	4,676,500	10
1925	1,645,207	6,811,000	15
1926	2,178,259	8,713,000	19
1927	2,395,183	9,581,000	21
1928	2,628,392	10,513,000	23
1929	2,956,736	11,827,000	26
1930	3,411,910	13,648,000	30
1931	4,330,735	16,327,000	35
1932	5,263,017	19,841,500	43

Source: M. Pegg, 'British Radio Broadcasting and its Audience, 1918–1939', D.Phil. thesis (Oxford, 1979), 32.

persuasion, and two Conservatives, Labourites, and National Labourites.[81] Unremarkably, this cosy arrangement angered Samuel and Henderson. However, apart from the concession of one further broadcast to Labour, the list was implemented unchanged (see Table 9.11). Reith believed that it 'seem[ed] to create equal discontent in every party and hence [was] perhaps as satisfactory as it could be'.[82]

How fair was this allocation? Labour was vociferous in its protests, but Churchill bemoaned the fact that while there would be five 'socialist' speakers, there would be only one Conservative, Baldwin.[83] Many Tories believed the BBC had a left-wing bias.[84] Yet the allocation was indefensible in any argument about balance. First, the allocation of broadcasts—six for the Government and four for the Opposition—did not reflect the contest in the country. In most constituencies the fight was between a Government and an Opposition candidate. Translated onto constituency level, therefore, the broadcasts

[81] Reith diary, 6 Oct. 1931, in Stuart (ed.), *Reith Diaries*, 10; Hollins, 'Presentation', 408.

[82] Reith diary, 7, 8, 16 Oct. 1931, in Stuart (ed.), *Reith Diaries*, 107–8.

[83] *The Times*, 14 Oct. 1931.

[84] Lord Henry Scott to Stonehaven, 4 Oct. 1931; Reith to Stonehaven, 12 Oct. 1931; Ball to Geoffrey Fry, 3 Nov. 1931 (Baldwin papers, vol. 45 (v), ff. 198–203).

Table 9.11. *Party election broadcasts, 1931*

1.	Baldwin	Con	Tu	13 Oct.	9.20–9.40 p.m.
2.	Clynes	Lab	We	14 –	9.05–9.25 p.m.
3.	Lloyd George	Ind Lib	Th	15 –	9.20–9.40 p.m.
4.	Simon	Lib Nat	Fr	16 –	9.20–9.40 p.m.
5.	Snowden	Nat Lab	Sa	17 –	9.20–9.40 p.m.
6.	Graham	Lab	Tu	20 –	9.20–9.40 p.m.
7.	Samuel	Lib	We	21 –	9.05–9.25 p.m.
8.	Baldwin	Con	Th	22 –	9.20–9.40 p.m.
9.	Henderson	Lab	Fr	23 –	9.20–9.40 p.m.
10.	MacDonald	Nat Lab	Sa	24 –	9.20–9.40 p.m.

produced a 6:4 imbalance in favour of the Government. Secondly, the broadcasts were allocated not on a party, but on a Government–Opposition basis; the allocation of a broadcast each to MacDonald and Snowden would have been indefensible, since National Labour had fewer than half the number of candidates originally designated by Reith as the entitlement to one broadcast. Their broadcasting could only be justified on the grounds of their position as Government spokesmen. Finally, the fact that three Liberals—albeit of differing views—were allowed to broadcast was ludicrous. Neither Simon nor Lloyd George met the original stipulation of 50 candidates; and altogether the three Liberal groups had fewer than one-third as many candidates as the Labour Party, which also had only three broadcasts.

In a sense, though, this inequality probably helped Labour, in that its speakers did not do well on air. Clynes's performance was rated as especially unsuccessful, both in content and presentation. The latter also let Henderson down. The strongest impact was made by Snowden, who in a bloodcurdling talk on 17 October described Labour's programme as 'Bolshevism run mad': perhaps no other political broadcast in British history has achieved such immediate and lasting fame or notoriety. The generally acknowledged master of the medium, Baldwin, had an indifferent first broadcast, but was better second time around.[85]

In its twice-nightly news bulletins, the BBC, forbidden from editorializing, was reasonably objective for most of the campaign. For

[85] A. Briggs, *The History of Broadcasting in the United Kingdom, Vol. 2: The Golden Age of Wireless* (London, 1965), 139; Gower to Baldwin, 21 Oct. 1931 (Baldwin papers, vol. 45 (v), ff. 88–9).

example, the amount of coverage given to the parties' manifestos was roughly equal.[86] However, this impression was shattered on the eve of polling, in an announcement made after the main bulletin at 9.40 p.m. After stressing that the ballot was secret, the announcer continued that everyone should vote because '[o]n your action, or your failure to act, may depend your own and your children's future and the security and prosperity of your country'.[87] As Reith expected, this aroused Labour hostility, because it was clearly a call to vote for the Government.[88] The BBC's campaign coverage was completed on election night, when it broadcast the results until 4 a.m.

The coverage afforded by film newsreels could not rival the kind of immediacy achieved by radio and the press. Nevertheless, film's impact, albeit somewhat marginal, was greater than at any previous election. The first sound newsreels in Britain were produced in 1929, and by 1931 the five major companies (British Movietone, Gaumont British, Paramount, Pathé, and Universal) were all producing them, and soon they were a feature of all cinema programmes. Audience interest was great, less because of the content of the reels than because, for the first time, the public was being presented with the news in sound and moving pictures.[89] These developments coincided with large cinema attendances. It is difficult to obtain reliable figures, but it seems likely that at least half the adult population saw at least one newsreel during the campaign.[90]

The owners of the newsreel companies tended to be Conservative but this bias could not be too blatantly apparent in the newsreels themselves. Cinema proprietors and managers did not like having their (mostly working-class) audiences upset by contentious political material. With a choice of five companies and a circulation war getting under way, the 79 per cent of cinemas which were independent of the big chains could afford to be choosy.[91] But it is also worth remembering that politics was just one of many subjects covered by the reels. One

[86] Hollins, 'Presentation', 412.

[87] Quoted in *New Statesman*, 31 Oct. 1931.

[88] Reith diary, 26 Oct. 1931, in Stuart (ed.), *Reith Diaries*, 109.

[89] A. Aldgate, *Cinema and History: British Newsreels and the Spanish Civil War* (London, 1979), 18.

[90] S. Rowson, 'A Statistical Survey of the Cinema Industry in Great Britain in 1934', *Journal of the Royal Statistical Society*, 49 (1936), 67–119; N. Pronay, 'British Newsreels in the 1930s: 1. Audience and Producers', *History*, 56 (1971), 411–18.

[91] Gower to Beaverbrook, 23 Oct. 1931 (Beaverbrook papers, B/197).

estimate places the political content of Paramount's reels at 17 per cent; Movietone, 11 per cent; Gaumont, 10 per cent; Pathé, 7 per cent; and Universal at only 3.5 per cent. At election times, of course, these figures might have been higher, though in 1931 Universal ignored the campaign completely.[92]

The coverage given by the other four newsreels to the election campaign is shown in Table 9.12. Broadly speaking, Movietone gave it the heaviest treatment, and supported the Government. It was the only company to stress the recovery in trade and employment which was taking place, and quick to imply that the National administration should be given the credit. Its attempts to help the Government were not helped by a typically over-sensitive MacDonald, who refused to be filmed electioneering with Thomas in Derby.[93] The premier also refused to give Movietone an eve-of-poll interview, which resulted, ironically, in their giving the last words on the campaign to a fierce attack on the 'old gang' by Mosley.[94] The other reels gave the campaign less coverage; Pathé was the least objective, giving no coverage at all to Labour's leaders and declaring joyously after the election: 'Now—Let us all pull together for prosperity.'[95]

What impact did the newsreels have? From the scanty evidence available, it seems that MacDonald was well received by audiences by the end of the campaign, even if he had not been at the start, and that Simon was seen by pro-National observers to have come across well. On the other hand, neither Henderson nor Lloyd George seems to have made a very good impression.[96] It would seem that, once again, any obstructions placed in Labour's way in presenting its case in the media did it less harm than good. Overall, in any case, the newsreels made no decisive impact. Their coverage was too slender, both in individual reels and overall, to form opinions, especially when many in the audience—like the disgruntled person switching on his or her TV today—considered themselves as viewers rather than electors.

It would be foolish to argue that the newsreels and radio were wholly without impact. Interest was aroused by their very novelty. And in

[92] Hollins, 'Presentation', 634.

[93] *Derby Daily Telegraph*, 22 Oct. 1931.

[94] L. Landau to R. Rosenberg, 25 Oct. 1931 (MacDonald papers, PRO 30/69/1176).

[95] Hollins, 'Presentation', 665.

[96] G. F. Sanger (editor, British Movietone News) to L. Landau, 22 Oct. 1931 (MacDonald papers, PRO 30/69/1176).

Date	British Movietone	Paramount
8 Oct.	Prime Minister's National Appeal	
12 Oct.	Post Office workers' parade, Aeroplane propaganda of Government, Kid Lewis (boxer) spkg. for New Party, Trade revival	Prime Minister's National Appeal, Baldwin's mass meeting
15 Oct.	Henderson interview, Lloyd George interview, Pictures of nomination day, Samuel, Churchill, women candidates, MacDonald at Seaham	Simon speaks to nation, Electioneering in Birmingham
19 Oct.	Baldwin interview, Pictures of electioneering, heckling, Maxton, and other candidates, Sir John Simon, exclusive	MacDonald electioneering, Lloyd George interview
22 Oct.		Henderson interview
26 Oct.	Mosley at Stoke	Baldwin interview

Date	Pathé	Gaumont
8 Oct.		
12 Oct.	Prime Minister's National Appeal, Baldwin's mass meeting	Prime Minister's National Appeal, Baldwin's mass meeting
15 Oct.	Simon speaks to nation	Simon speaks to nation
19 Oct.	Lloyd George interview	Henderson interview, Lloyd George interview
22 Oct.	Baldwin interview	[No political item]
26 Oct.	[No political item]	[No political item]

Source: Hollins, 'Presentation', 634.

some cases, most notably Snowden's broadcast, the new media could be of decided influence on the electors, if not in changing, then at least in reinforcing, voting intentions. But the press remained the main news medium, while the efforts of party candidates and activists also played a significant part. Electioneering and the media coverage of the election were changing, then, but it would be wrong to exaggerate the extent of the change, or to claim that the 1931 election campaign was 'modern'. If its style was very different from that of 1900 it was no less different from that of 1964.

10

THE ISSUES AT STAKE

THE election campaign of 1931 has long been regarded as, at best, a rather unfortunate and distasteful affair; at worst, as '[t]he shortest, strangest, and most fraudulent election campaign of our times'.[1] For years, Labourites in particular felt they had been cheated. 'Never had a more poisonous campaign been waged. Never had fouler depths been plunged. Never has a political party faced so extensive a barrage of lies: never had an electorate been so panicked by fear as they were in 1931.'[2] Thus spoke a 1935 Labour pamphlet; but non-Labour notables also subscribed to this view. Snowden, resigning from the Cabinet in 1932, was adamant in retrospect that the election had been a Tory tariff ramp, and this idea has found implied acceptance among some historians.[3] An extensive survey of the campaign, with special reference to the contents of the election addresses issued by the main parties' candidates (see Table 10.1), however, shows that Labour was beaten fairly and squarely, that the use of 'dirty tricks' was not the monopoly of any party, and that the National victory was largely, though not exclusively, a victory for the Conservatives. Their claim that it provided a mandate for tariffs is also largely borne out because the Tories were, on the whole, (although not without qualification in some cases), frank about their protectionism because they believed it to be a vote-catcher.

I

National politicians placed great stress, of course, on the need to defeat Labour decisively in order to secure the stability of sterling. A hefty majority would mean a mandate to deal with the trade deficit, and so increase confidence. Lord Grey, for example, saw this as 'the great issue' beside which others paled, and hoped that there would be no Labour MPs at all after the election.[4] This was an extreme version of

[1] *Manchester Guardian*, 28 Oct. 1931.
[2] F. R. West, *Trickery and Treachery of the 'National' Government* (London, 1935), 3.
[3] See e.g. Stevenson and Cook, *Slump*, 101.
[4] Grey, National Liberal Club, 12 Oct., *The Times*, 13 Oct. 1931; Dewsbury, 23 Oct., *The Times*, 24 Oct. 1931.

Table 10.1. *Issues in candidates' election addresses, 1931* (%)

Issue	Con	Lib	LibN	NLab	Lab
Trade					
Tariffs openly advocated	61	–	3	6	–
'Baldwin formula' on tariffs	18	–	–	–	–
Imperial preference	74	–	3	22	–
Full acceptance of free hand	19	52	91	89	–
Pledge against food taxes	–	21	3	11	–
Free trade, anti-tariff	–	44	–	–	93
Public economy, taxation					
Need for economy	68	61	53	72	–
Taxation	48	32	35	39	48
Unemployment benefit cut	25	37	35	39	96
Public servants' salary cuts	11	25	24	22	75
Means test	3	3	3	–	21
Nationalization, socialism					
Nationalization generally	6	14	–	–	15
of Bank of England	7	4	6	–	76
of coal	1	–	–	–	50
of iron and steel	1	–	–	–	46
of transport	1	–	–	–	48
of land	1	–	6	–	40
Socialism, anti-socialism	11	1	3	6	34
Crisis					
Most critical in history	4	3	6	–	2
Issues as vital as World War One	7	3	9	–	–
Labour win means national bankruptcy	74	38	74	56	–
Labour unfit to govern	7	–	–	–	–
German inflation 1923	6	2	9	–	–
Russia, Bolsheviks	3	–	–	–	–
TUC	9	4	6	6	–
General Strike, 1926	2	1	–	–	–
Starvation if opponents win	9	4	6	6	6
Bankers' ramp	4	2	6	–	62
Election unnecessary, a Conservative ramp	–	49	3	–	66
National Government 'reactionary'	–	–	–	–	42

Record of second Labour Government					
Record of second Labour Government	76	23	26	11	34
Personalities					
MacDonald	65	59	79	78	22
Snowden	21	13	24	28	8
Thomas	15	6	15	11	–
Baldwin	32	13	9	17	25
Simon	12	1	9	6	1
Samuel	6	6	3	6	3
Lloyd George	3	1	–	–	8
Henderson	12	6	9	17	14
Ex-ministers' actions in August	70	30	35	72	14
General domestic issues					
Employment, unemployment	71	57	41	39	71
General wage level, standard of living	23	17	18	–	67
Agriculture	47	28	21	17	56
Education	5	10	–	6	34
Housing	4	7	9	6	54
Local issues	8	7	3	–	8
House of Lords	–	–	–	–	14
Electoral reform	–	8	–	–	1
Trade Disputes Act, 1927	–	–	–	–	4
Foreign and Imperial policy					
League of Nations	9	19	9	6	40
Disarmament	14	28	6	28	25
World disarmament conference	2	19	3	11	43
War debts and reparations	20	63	18	33	61
War in Manchuria (started Sept.)	–	–	–	–	1
No mention of foreign affairs	54	22	68	33	14
India	8	17	3	11	15
TOTAL NUMBER AVAILABLE FOR STUDY	480	107	34	18	483

Note: This table is based upon an analysis of every address issued, and any mention, however brief, of an issue qualifies.

Source: Candidates' election addresses (Conservative Party papers).

what other National spokesmen were saying. For Baldwin, the election was the 'acid test of democracy' since Labour's policies would lead to 'chaos and catastrophe' and a 'wild panic' in sterling meaning that 'the poor [would] starve'.[5] Snowden defined the issue as being 'between prosperity and ruin', while Hilton Young saw a Labour victory as leading to 'starvation, misery and rage'.[6]

Such comments might seem melodramatic, but for many electors in 1931 they undoubtedly rang true. The experience of Europe since 1914 had been miserable, with the Great War, revolution, civil war, and famine in Russia, abortive revolutions across east-central Europe, fascism in Italy, hyperinflation in Germany, and fairly general depression since 1929. Why should Britain be immune, especially given its need to import food? Some National candidates laid special stress on the German inflation of 1923. MacDonald told one meeting of his experience in seeing workers at Krupps' works in Essen being paid in great piles of near-worthless paper and added that '[n]ation after nation had gone through this kind of thing during the past year or two'. He did not add that starvation had been a serious problem in none of them.[7] Underpinning these often contentious arguments were the realities of the adverse trade balance and the need for a stable currency with which to pay for essential food imports.

Some non-Labour politicians took a less hostile line. This was true of Samuel, who after all was generally seen as quite pro-Labour and who was now most concerned about blocking protection. But even he stressed that a Labour victory would be damaging. Lloyd George went further, denying the validity of the 'one great issue'. On 15 October he broadcast a fierce attack on the Conservatives and their 'malarial swamp' of protectionism, which posed the real danger to the nation.[8] But most Liberals agreed with their National cohorts that it was imperative that Labour should be defeated.

Labour's leaders had to meet such arguments as best they could; and their manifesto did little to help. For example, Graham said a Labour victory would not mean national ruin because the party

[5] Baldwin, broadcast, 13 Oct., *The Times*, 14 Oct. 1931; Middlemas and Barnes, *Baldwin*, 648, 651; Baldwin, Liverpool, 21 Oct., *Liverpool Post*, 22 Oct. 1931; Newcastle, 23 Oct., *The Times*, 24 Oct. 1931.

[6] Snowden, 'Letter to Electors on the Eve of Poll', 25 Oct. 1931, in id., *Autobiography*, ii. 1065; Young, Oundle, 13 Oct. *The Times*, 14 Oct. 1931.

[7] MacDonald, Easington, 12 Oct., *The Times*, 13 Oct. 1931.

[8] Lloyd George, broadcast, 15 Oct., *The Times*, 16 Oct. 1931.

'guarantee[d] a balanced Budget on sound lines and no inflation'.[9] The difficulties experienced in August, and the commitment to restore the cuts, suggested that this was a fairly complacent attitude, while Labour could not deny that its victory would lead to at least a dip in the value of sterling, if only because the latter, having been predicted by so many National politicians, had taken the air of a self-fulfilling prophecy. This in turn showed that the Government's leaders had little doubt as to the outcome of the campaign.

II

The proposal to nationalize the Bank of England posed particular problems. While it owed its presence in the manifesto to socialist doctrine, it owed its salience to the myth of the bankers' ramp. That it was a myth had been admitted by Henderson on 8 September, but confusion and wilful misrepresentation remained, especially as many candidates were eager to use anything to help alleviate their difficulties. Two-thirds of Labour candidates mentioned the 'ramp'; three-quarters, bank nationalization. Addison, Clynes, Greenwood, and Lansbury were especially assiduous in speaking of financiers' 'dictation'.[10] In short, Labourites felt this was an issue upon which they could capitalize.

National spokesmen responded with two lines of counter-attack. First, they denied all suggestions of impropriety on the part of the bankers. MacDonald laid great emphasis on the correctness of their conduct, while Baldwin, somewhat intriguingly, told a meeting that it was 'just about as much a ramp as a hippopotamus at the zoo'.[11] Secondly, Labour's proposals for the nationalization of the banks, and especially the Bank of England, came under constant fire, and were acknowledged subsequently by the national agent to have been a serious electoral liability.[12] Cripps claimed Labour had 'a complete scheme ready', but the manifesto spoke only of 'national ownership and control' without giving further details.[13] The only full proposals

[9] Graham, broadcast, 20 Oct., *The Times*, 21 Oct. 1931.

[10] Addison, election address, Swindon (Conservative Party papers); Clynes and Greenwood, Liverpool, 22 Oct., *Liverpool Post*, 23 Oct. 1931; Lansbury, Stratford, 25 Oct., *Daily Herald*, 26 Oct. 1931.

[11] MacDonald, broadcast, 7 Oct., *The Times*, 8 Oct. 1931; Easington, 12 Oct., *The Times*, 13 Oct. 1931; Baldwin, Finsbury Park, 17 Oct., *The Times*, 19 Oct. 1931.

[12] G. R. Shepherd to H. E. Rogers, 17 Nov. 1931 (East Bristol DLP papers, Acc. 39035/60).

[13] Cripps, Hull, 8 Oct., *News Chronicle*, 9 Oct. 1931.

which existed were those which Frank Wise, of the ILP, had presented to the Macmillan committee in 1930. For the Bank of England he had proposed an expert executive board, free from day-to-day political control, but working under the aegis of an appointive banking council comprising representatives of Government and various interest groups including labour. On joint stock banks he had been less clear, especially as to the extent of competition which would remain after nationalization.[14]

Thus Labour's opponents could have a field day in attacking its banking policy. They could deride it for having, contrary to Cripps's claim, no detailed plans at all: as Chamberlain said, if Labour had a 'complete scheme', why did it not produce it for the electors' judgement?[15] Wise's retort, that his proposals could be gleaned from the pages of the Macmillan report, hardly helped the average elector—or hard-pressed Labour candidate.[16] It was for Labour's leaders to declare their policy, and this they signally failed to do.

National politicians could also, though, make political capital out of the Wise scheme. This was the tactic adopted by Snowden in his broadcast of 17 October, when he derided national ownership as meaning the banks would be 'run by a joint committee of the Labour Party and the Trade Union Council' and investments 'ordered by some board'. Three days later, he went so far as to say that a Labour victory would see the City's business transferred to Transport house.[17] This was certainly unjust, and repeated old Conservative slanders. But given that Labour had been unable, despite great efforts and numerous denials by Citrine, to disprove charges of TUC dictation, it was sure to have an impact. And Labour's responses to Snowden's charges lacked conviction. Morrison explained that banking would not be a state department, 'but a public corporation run by men with a knowledge of finance and industry'.[18] But public corporations were not as familiar in 1931 as they were later to become, and Morrison could not give his best answer to Snowden—that trade unionists would not, *per se*, be represented on the boards—because this had been a source of great dispute with Bevin, and would only have opened

[14] Committee on Finance and Industry, *Minutes of Evidence* (Cmd. 3897; London, 1931), 134–7, 145.

[15] Chamberlain, Wakefield, 18 Oct., *Wakefield Express*, 19 Oct. 1931.

[16] Letters from J. Walton Newbold and Wise, *The Times*, 16, 17 Oct. 1931.

[17] Snowden, broadcast, 17 Oct., *The Times*, 19 Oct. 1931; 'Labour's Little Lenins', *Daily Mail*, 20 Oct. 1931.

[18] Morrison, South Hackney, 23 Oct., *The Times*, 24 Oct. 1931.

Labour's wounds if given during the campaign. If Labour could not answer electors' misgivings, though, it could hardly blame them for voting National.

Finally, the proposals for bank nationalization could be linked with the issue of the national credit and the stability of sterling. MacDonald claimed that an attempt to socialize the Bank of England would destroy confidence, while Simon condemned the plan as 'preposterous moonshine'.[19] The Conservative candidate for Eastbourne stated bluntly that '[t]he Socialist leaders wish[ed] to take control of the Banks; so [did] the Burglars'.[20] Thus on a central issue of its own choosing Labour laid itself open to heavy, vehement, and, it must be said, largely justified criticism from its opponents, and failed, not only to get its message across, but also adequately to define what its message was.

III

Problems also stemmed from Labour's purported pride in the record of the second Labour Government. A fifty-page eve-of-campaign pamphlet, *Two Years of Labour Rule*, showed this tendency at its most bizarre. The Government's foreign policy was trumpeted, with some justification. There was far less reason to make exaggerated claims for domestic policy. Public works had been on the way to solving unemployment, the pamphlet argued, before the world slump hit Britain in early 1930. There was no suggestion that Labour could have done anything to insulate Britain from some of the slump's worst effects. Sceptics were met with the 'explanation' that even MPs had been so busy carrying useful reforms that they had 'found it difficult to realise how much was actually being accomplished'. Because of press hostility it had been 'almost impossible for the average citizen fully to appeciate the extent of Labour's worthwhile services to the nation'. Only now, with the benefit of hindsight, could 'its full range and significance be perceived'.[21] During the campaign this frankly ridiculous line was followed by Labour spokesmen, especially Henderson, who on one notable occasion remarked, in a somewhat

[19] MacDonald, Seaham, 13 Oct., *The Times*, 14 Oct. 1931; Runciman, National Liberal Club, 12 Oct., *The Times*, 13 Oct. 1931; Simon, Cleckheaton, 12 Oct., *Manchester Guardian*, 13 Oct. 1931.

[20] Edward Marjoribanks, election address, Eastbourne (Conservative Party papers).

[21] Labour Party, *Two Years of Labour Rule* (London, 1931), 1.

unfortunate turn of phrase, 'that '[t]he Labour Government did more for unemployment than any previous Government'.[22] It was inevitable that Labour would have to defend the record of its late administration, but such an approach, verging on braggadocio, was unwise. Quite apart from increased unemployment, the second Labour Government had been a miserable experience for many workers, especially in textiles, coal, and iron and steel; it had also failed to fulfil promises to the unions. To boast of the Government's fine record to such people suggested either a tenuous grip on reality or sheer desperation. Labour candidates were rather more wary, only 34 per cent mentioning the subject in their election addresses.

The Liberals also found difficulty here. Few of their candidates mentioned the Labour Government. After all, the Liberals had given general support to the administration throughout its life, and Samuel had been in the van of those advocating co-operation. Thus orthodox Liberals made little of Labour's failings in office, although right-wingers like Grey, and many, though not all, Simonites could be less circumspect, since Simon, at least, had never really approved of co-operation. The Conservatives suffered none of the Liberals' inhibitions, and in attacking the Labour Government found a rich vein none of the other parties could easily tap. Most of their candidates mentioned it. Amery accused it of 'fiddl[ing] while Rome was burning', wasting time on trade-union legislation instead of tackling urgent economic problems; Chamberlain condemned its 'reckless folly and extravagance'.[23]

But how could National supporters condemn the Government when they were now supporting its two leading figures, MacDonald and Snowden? In fact, one of the more impressive features of the campaign was the way in which the National Labourites were absolved from responsibility. This could only be justified to a very limited extent. For example, Baldwin pointed to Snowden's warning to the House of Commons in February 1931 that drastic steps would be needed to restore the nation's finances. But MacDonald and Snowden, it could be argued, should have given a stronger lead; and when Baldwin continued that '[i]f that were not sufficient the Budget which was introduced about that time failed to balance', he seemed to be

[22] Henderson, Burnley, 15 Oct., *Manchester Guardian*, 16 Oct. 1931.
[23] Amery, Birmingham, 14 Oct., *Birmingham Post*, 15 Oct. 1931; Chamberlain, Hull, 21 Oct., *Manchester Guardian*, 22 Oct. 1931.

forgetting that it had been Snowden's budget.[24] However, such inconveniences tended to be lost in the clamour of adulation for the 'courage' of the two men. In addition, many Conservatives had no concern about consistency, and simply switched from criticism to praise. The candidate for Blackpool, who in May had been condemning MacDonald's war record and praising the Moray golf club for expelling him in 1916, now posed as a firm supporter of the premier.[25] For themselves, the National Labour ministers differentiated themselves from the late ministry, MacDonald saying on one occasion that it had 'shirked the unpleasant duty of carrying out what it admitted to be its duty', which suggested that he had not been a member of it, let alone its leader.[26]

The sad record of Labour could be contrasted, increasingly as the campaign proceeded, with the better performance of the new Government (see Table 10.2). Unemployment had been rising for most of 1931, to stand at 2,733,782 on the day Labour left office. This figure rose and fell before rising to 2,825,772 on 28 September. The latter figure was announced on 7 October, the day Parliament was dissolved. But it then fell steadily, at a time of the year when it customarily rose. Indeed, during the last decade, only 1921 and 1925 had seen a fall in the autumn.[27] This was due to a number of factors: devaluation, which made British exports more competitive; increased business confidence due to the formation and continuation of the National Government; and, in the case of cotton textiles, the outbreak in September of the Sino–Japanese dispute in Manchuria, which increased Chinese demand for British, as opposed to Japanese, products. It was not, at this stage, due to the enforcement of legislation preventing certain classes of people from claiming unemployment

[24] Baldwin, Finsbury Park, 17 Oct., *The Times*, 19 Oct. 1931.

[25] Cuttings from *Lancashire Daily Post*, n.d. [May 1931]; *Blackpool Evening Gazette*, 12 Oct. 1931 (Lancashire Record Office, Blackpool CA papers, PLC 5/14/2). The contest in Blackpool in 1931 was almost incredible. Sir Walter de Frece, the retiring MP, had decided not to stand and had gone to live in Monaco. Bolst, a fiercely reactionary Conservative who was married to the daughter of a United States senator, was opposed by the crime writer Edgar Wallace, standing as a Lloyd George Liberal. Wallace travelled between meetings in a yellow Rolls-Royce, and most of the campaign was spent in arguments between the candidates regarding how much they had paid for their cars, and where they had been made; how much they paid in taxes; whether Bolst was a British citizen; and whether Wallace would be spending most of 1932 in Hollywood and so be unable to represent the constituency. Ultimately Bolst won.

[26] MacDonald, broadcast, 7 Oct., *The Times*, 8 Oct. 1931.

[27] *The Times*, 15 Oct. 1931.

benefit.[28] The decrease was not spectacular, but helped the Nationals, first by giving an air of returning prosperity and still further discrediting Labour as a party of depression, and, secondly, because the increases in employment tended to be concentrated in specific regions with a large number of marginal seats, like the Midlands (hosiery, lace, motors, and boot and shoe all showing signs of returning prosperity) and the textile belt of Yorkshire and Lancashire. In addition, coal picked up in the Midlands and the North, although there was no marked improvement in south Wales and Scotland. National spokesmen were not slow to capitalize. MacDonald spoke, with a degree of relief, of collieries reopening in his constituency, and Thomas stated on 20 October that in the past three weeks 150 'definite' applications had been received from foreign firms for factory sites in Britain and that generally trade was improving, 'proof' that the Government was a success. (These factors undoubtedly helped Thomas retain Derby.) Meanwhile, the London and North-Eastern and the London, Midland and Scottish railways announced that they were to spend £5,000,000 and £2,000,000 respectively on improvements that winter.[29]

In individual constituencies, the prospects of a trade revival could have a significant impact in drawing support to the National candidate. In Barrow, for example, there was a 12.8 per cent swing from Labour to the Conservatives, which was at least partly due to the announcement on 21 October by the town's largest employer, Vickers-Armstrong, that if the Government won the election a £1,500,000 overseas shipbuilding order would be placed with the firm. Barrow was suffering from heavy unemployment, and the announcement had 'a profound effect' on the town. Labour's cause was not helped by the fact that its candidate was Mayor of Newcastle-upon-Tyne, Barrow's chief rival in the industry.[30] Fortunately for the Government, the other possible corollary of devaluation—increased retail prices—had made no appreciable impact before the election was over (see Table 10.3).

All this, plus Labour's heavy emphasis on the level of unemployment benefit, tended to confirm that party's 'depression' image. *The Times*'s correspondent in Leicester found unemployed men 'more concerned

[28] Sir Henry Betterton (Minister of Labour), Rushcliffe, 14 Oct., *The Times*, 15 Oct. 1931; *The Times*, 18, 25 Nov., 23 Dec. 1931.

[29] *The Times*, 14, 21, 28 Oct., 4, 11 Nov. 1931; MacDonald, Blackhall, 14 Oct., *The Times*, 15 Oct. 1931; Thomas, Derby, 20 Oct., *Manchester Guardian*, 21 Oct. 1931; *Daily Express*, 23 Oct. 1931.

[30] *Morning Post*, 24 Oct. 1931.

Table 10.2. *Unemployment, August to November 1931*

Date	Figure	Up (+) or Down (−)	Announced
24 Aug.	2,733,782	(increase)	1 Sept.
31	2,762,219	+28,437	8
7 Sept.	2,800,631	+38,412	15
14	2,789,080	−11,551	22
21	2,811,615	+22,535	29
28	2,825,772	+14,157	6 Oct.
5 Oct.	2,791,520	−34,252	13
12	2,766,746	−24,774	20
19[a]	(2,736,700)	(−30,046)	(26)
19	2,737,878	−28,868	27
26	2,726,092	−11,786	3 Nov.
2 Nov.	2,710,944	−15,148	10
9	2,683,924	−27,020	17
16	2,648,429	−35,495	24
23	2,615,115	−33,314	1 Dec.
30	2,622,027	+ 6,912	8

[a] The approximate figure for 19 October was issued a day early by the Ministry of Labour, in time for inclusion in the polling day newspapers.

Source: The Times, Tuesdays, 2 Sept. to 9 Dec. 1931.

Table 10.3. *Official cost of living index figure*

1914	(July)	100	1931	May	129
1928	(Mean)	157		June	127
1929	(Mean)	154		July	130
1930	(Mean)	145		Aug.	128
1931	Jan.	138		Sept.	128
	Feb.	136		Oct.	128
	Mar.	134		Nov.	130
	Apr.	129		Dec.	132

Source: Statistical Abstract, No. 82, 137.

with finding work than with complaining about their benefit'.[31] This theme was hammered in particular by Baldwin, who said the Government's 'main object' would be '[t]o make our factories busy once more, to bring back work on the land, to substitute wages for doles'.[32] Samuel stressed that '[f]or the unemployed to get back to work [was] ... infinitely more important than any question of the dole'.[33]

Thus Labour's concentration on its record in office was counter-productive and, as the campaign proceeded, the signs of returning prosperity helped confirm Labour's image as one of depression and failure.

IV

Another comparison made by National spokesmen and candidates also worked to the detriment of Labour; the supposed contrast between the courage and patriotism of MacDonald, Thomas, and Snowden on the one hand and the cowardice and opportunism of the ex-ministers on the other (see Table 10.1). It was an unfair comparison, but it took hold.

MacDonald never attained greater prestige than during the period of the first National Government, and during the campaign he was accorded much praise by National candidates of whatever hue. Twice as many Conservatives mentioned MacDonald as mentioned Baldwin, and between three- and four-fifths of the candidates of each of the National parties used his name. National spokesmen were also keen to laud the premier. Much was made of his services to Labour, not least by MacDonald himself when telling, for example, of when his flat had been the Labour Representation Committee's headquarters.[34] For him, the issue remained simple: the national credit, upon which working-class living standards depended, had to be defended against Labour's 'irresponsible' Opposition. He continued to stress that he was a socialist and a Labour candidate, but added that socialism must have 'foundations' in a sound financial system.[35] He seems not to have given up hope that he might return to lead Labour.[36]

[31] *The Times*, 19 Oct. 1931.

[32] Baldwin, Leeds, 20 Oct., *Birmingham Post*, 21 Oct. 1931; broadcast, 23 Oct., *The Times*, 24 Oct. 1931.

[33] Samuel, broadcast, 21 Oct., *The Times*, 22 Oct. 1931.

[34] MacDonald, interview, *Daily Express*, 13 Oct. 1931.

[35] MacDonald, Wingate, 24 Oct., *Manchester Guardian*, 26 Oct. 1931.

[36] MacDonald, Easington, 12 Oct., *The Times*, 13 Oct. 1931; Seaham, 13 Oct., ibid., 14 Oct. 1931; Blackhall, 14 Oct., ibid., 15 Oct. 1931; Derby, 22 Oct., *Manchester Guardian*, 23 Oct. 1931; Seaham 26 Oct., *Manchester Guardian*, 27 Oct. 1931.

This cut little ice with dedicated Labourites, who attacked him vigorously. In the forefront, of course, were the attempts of the *Daily Herald* to smear MacDonald and his followers; but Labour speakers generally were very hostile, and even Henderson and Morrison lost some of their previous restraint. On 19 October Henderson said it was 'a most pathetic tragedy' that MacDonald was leading the anti-Labour fight.[37] Morrison attacked his erstwhile hero for hiding his socialist principles, and added that the premier's 'thinking apparatus had gone wrong, and it was time he took a walking tour in the Highlands'.[38] Some Labourites had been less sympathetic from the outset, and when Citrine stated late in the campaign that the breach was 'final and irrevocable', he was in a position to ensure the accuracy of his prediction.[39]

If MacDonald provided an object for National admiration, Snowden provided the entertainment. Having announced his retirement from the Commons, and being in indifferent health, he spent the duration of the campaign at 11 Downing Street, but he had no intention of taking a back seat, and in an astonishing series of statements made a great and unexpected impact on the campaign. On 16 October he published a letter to National Labour candidates ridiculing Labour's claims to be a free-trade party, revealing that the late Cabinet had voted for a tariff. Next day, in a broadcast, he condemned Labour's programme as 'not Socialism' but 'Bolshevism run mad'.[40] Then, in an article entitled 'Labour's Little Lenins', published in the *Daily Mail* on 20 October, he launched a fierce attack on the ex-ministers and the 'sheer bunkum' of the Labour manifesto. That evening, in a broadcast, Graham tried to answer some of Snowden's charges; five minutes later the Chancellor was consulting P. J. Grigg at the Treasury about a reply to Graham's countercharges, which was published the following day.[41] In the last weekend, he wrote another strongly worded article for the *Sunday Pictorial*, supplemented Runciman's comments about the Post Office savings bank, and in an eve-of-poll message attacked Labour as 'the Party that ran away'.[42]

[37] Henderson, Birmingham, 19 Oct., *Manchester Guardian*, 20 Oct. 1931; Thorpe, 'Arthur Henderson'.

[38] Morrison, South Hackney, 10 Oct., *The Times*, 12 Oct. 1931.

[39] Citrine, Seaham, 23 Oct., *Daily Herald*, 24 Oct. 1931.

[40] Snowden, broadcast, 17 Oct., *The Times*, 19 Oct. 1931.

[41] Gertrude Grigg to Thomas Jones, 21 Oct. 1931 (Jones papers, Z/1931, 58); *Manchester Guardian*, 22 Oct. 1931.

[42] Snowden, 'Letter to Electors on the Eve of Poll', 25 Oct. 1931, in id., *Autobiography*, ii. 1065.

These attacks were far more virulent than anything produced by MacDonald, and aroused great Labour bitterness. The *New Leader* called him 'the star "stunt" journalist of the "Daily Mail" ', while Henderson said the Chancellor 'ought to be ashamed of himself'.[43] Alexander expressed grief, referring to Snowden romantically as 'a man that I loved'.[44] Less restrained was Cripps, who denounced Snowden's allegations as 'a tissue of falsehoods'.[45] Some non-Labourites also disliked his conduct. Sankey, his Cabinet colleague, thought the Chancellor's campaign 'a great mistake', while the Conservative *Spectator* commented that the Government's case was 'strong enough to make resort to this kind of vituperation between old colleagues unnecessary'.[46]

Labour's attempts to answer Snowden's charges were often inadequate. For example, over the tariff question, Graham's sole available response—that they had only voted for a revenue tariff—left it open to Snowden to argue that this was still a clear interference with free trade. The best answer Labour could find was to argue that Snowden, who claimed never to have read the 1928 policy document, *Labour and the Nation*, on which the 1931 manifesto was supposedly based, had been in fact its part author, and that, as Henderson put it, he was accusing them of 'being mad Bolshevists because [they] still [stood] for what he used to stand for'.[47] However, such refutations could only have a limited effect, for Snowden hurled charge upon charge on the basis that some of the mud would stick. In doing so he helped to keep the Labour campaign on a very unfavourable defensive.

Naturally, controversy surrounded Snowden's behaviour. Henderson could 'only suppose that his once great mind [had] become warped by bitterness', and the *Manchester Guardian* also referred to his judgement being 'warped' by his all-consuming and 'unreasoning' resentment against Labour.[48] Bitterness undoubtedly played a part. But it was not the whole story. First, he felt that Labour had shown itself unfit for office; its victory now would mean a sterling collapse which would hit

[43] *New Leader*, 23 Oct. 1931; Henderson, Burnley, 21 Oct., *The Times*, 22 Oct. 1931.
[44] Alexander, Sheffield, 19 Oct., *Daily Herald*, 20 Oct. 1931.
[45] Cripps, Gloucester, 19 Oct., *Daily Herald*, 20 Oct. 1931.
[46] Sankey diary, 20 Oct. 1931 (Sankey papers, MSS Eng. hist. e. 285); *Spectator*, 24 Oct. 1931.
[47] Henderson, West Bromwich, 19 Oct., *Manchester Guardian*, 20 Oct. 1931; Burnley, 21 Oct., ibid., 22 Oct. 1931.
[48] Henderson, interview, *Reynolds's Illustrated News*, 25 Oct. 1931; *Manchester Guardian*, 20 Oct. 1931.

no one harder than the workers. As he repeated, he did 'not want to see the work of a lifetime brought to rack and ruin'.[49] In this way, his conduct was consistent with his lifelong concern for the interests of the working people. Beside their interests, those of the post-1918 Labour Party, a creation of which he had never been especially enamoured, were of little importance. Secondly, Snowden realized that a National victory would mean a Conservative attempt to force through protective tariffs, which might succeed if—as many Tories were expecting—he was excluded from the post-election Cabinet. Thus he set out to make his exclusion unthinkable. The praise loaded on him by Nationals of all parties, and the widespread use made of his revelations, by Chamberlain among many others, meant that he had succeeded.[50] The belief voiced by Runciman, that Snowden was 'the man who above all others [had] given them their majority', meant he could be certain of a place in the Cabinet despite the hostility of many Conservatives.[51]

Most of Snowden's charges had been directed at the ex-ministers, and indeed this group's conduct was a major bone of contention during the campaign. In his opening speech, Baldwin said that the ex-ministers had agreed to 90 per cent of the cuts and then 'ratted' on MacDonald; the latter attacked them for running away from the supposed unpopularity of the economies.[52] This set the scene for National spokesmen to stress the ex-ministers' commitment to the cuts and their supposed insincerity in promising now to restore them.[53]

Exception could be taken to the tone in which many of these charges were made. For example, Snowden described their behaviour as 'an instance of political depravity without parallel in party warfare'.[54] But apart from Baldwin's claim that the Conservatives had promised Labour their full support in implementing their economy programme, the substantial charges made against the ex-ministers were broadly

[49] Snowden, broadcast, 17 Oct., *The Times*, 19 Oct. 1931.

[50] See e.g. Chamberlain, Wakefield, 18 Oct., *Wakefield Express*, 19 Oct. 1931; Baldwin, Leeds, 20 Oct., *Birmingham Post*, 21 Oct. 1931.

[51] Runciman to his wife, 2 Nov. 1931 (Runciman papers, WR 303); for hostility, see Bridgeman journal, Oct. 1931, reporting the views of 'many people' (Bridgeman papers); Thomas Jones diary, 29 Oct. 1931, reporting the views of Stonehaven, the Chamberlains, Hailsham, Hoare, Cunliffe-Lister, Sassoon, and Kingsley Wood (Jones papers, Z/1931, 59).

[52] Baldwin, Birmingham, 9 Oct., *The Times*, 10 Oct. 1931; MacDonald, Easington, 12 Oct., *The Times*, 13 Oct. 1931.

[53] Chamberlain, Birmingham, 12 Oct., *Birmingham Post*, 13 Oct. 1931.

[54] Snowden, 'Labour's Little Lenins', *Daily Mail*, 20 Oct. 1931.

accurate. They had accepted the £56,000,000 cuts, and many had been more heavily committed. It was only left to Baldwin to return to one of his favourite themes to complete these efforts: 'They quailed, they lost their nerve; they forgot they were Englishmen, and only remembered that they were Socialists'.[55] In short, the ex-ministers were pilloried from start to finish of the campaign.

They tried to counter these accusations of cowardice and lack of patriotism. But in the midst of the bafflingly complex cross-currents of the election campaign, it was very difficult to do so. Henderson claimed that he had reserved his position until he could see 'the complete picture', and said the Opposition's insistence on larger cuts, not TUC dictation, had made him resign, but this was rather recondite at the side of the taunt that Labour had 'run away'; and, since most Labour candidates knew little of the inner workings of the August crisis, and received no detailed guidance from Transport House, it found little echo in the country. Instead, each candidate was alone against a fierce barrage of allegations regarding the Labour leadership.

The less than veracious comments of ex-ministers gave further openings for National criticism. Clynes's comment that it was 'untrue' that they had accepted 'sweeping reductions' sat ill beside Henderson's 8 September speech in which he had referred to '£56 millions of economies, provisionally accepted'.[56] Their performance over tariffs also confused many and helped erode public belief in Labour's free-trade commitment.

Inevitably, the ex-ministers ceased denying allegations and tried instead to counter them in kind, saying they had been the brave ones for resigning. This might appeal to activists but it would do little to convince the uncommitted voters whom Labour needed to win over. Graham stressed that they had been ready to balance the budget, but said it was 'incredible' that British credit had depended on a cut in unemployment benefit.[57] The point was, though, that by the weekend of 22–23 August it had. Henderson, on the other hand, emphasized what a wrench it had been for him to leave office; this could easily be misrepresented as self-pity and office-seeking.[58]

Towards the end of the campaign, some ex-ministers began to make statements regarding their past conduct which were, frankly, untruthful.

[55] Baldwin, Liverpool, 21 Oct., *Liverpool Post*, 22 Oct. 1931.
[56] Clynes, broadcast, 14 Oct., *The Times*, 15 Oct. 1931.
[57] Graham, broadcast, 20 Oct., *The Times*, 21 Oct. 1931.
[58] Henderson, Burnley, 21 Oct., *Manchester Guardian*, 22 Oct. 1931.

Snowden alleged that Alexander had agreed to cuts in naval pay so long as there was a concomitant cut in unemployment benefit. The former First Lord of the Admiralty denied the charge, telling a meeting that '[f]rom the beginning he had opposed the cuts in naval pay'. But it was Snowden who was telling the truth. On 20 August, in a memorandum to the Cabinet, Alexander had stated: 'I think the personnel of the Navy as a whole will loyally accept the sacrifice that is demanded of them in pay if equivalent reductions are made throughout the Public Service, and if the unemployment [benefit] rates are reduced.' He had been more concerned, in fact, with averting reductions in the shipbuilding programme, which would mean Britain's 'prestige as a Naval Power . . . be[ing] heavily damaged'.[59] Similarly Greenwood, who as a member of a small Cabinet committee had recommended various expedients including higher unemployment insurance contributions and a 'needs test' for transitional benefit, condemned allegations that he had 'agreed to tamper with unemployment benefits' as 'one of the foulest lies in our political history'.[60] In the absence, of course, of the Cabinet minutes, it was one man's word against another. No wonder many Labour candidates were confused by it all.

A number of results can be discerned from this controversy. First, it helped to discredit the ex-ministers, and suggested they were indeed 'unfit to govern'. Secondly, it rattled the Labour leadership, rendering it less effective and keeping it on the defensive throughout the campaign. Finally, it helped to destroy the Labour case on two of the issues upon which it had hoped to capitalize during the campaign, trade policy and the National Government's economies.

V

Trade policy and public economy would have been salient issues at a party election in the autumn of 1931. In 1929 there had been a balance of trade surplus of £103,000,000, but in 1930 the figure had fallen to £28,000,000, and by mid-1931, a considerable deficit was inevitable;

[59] *The Times*, 27 Oct. 1931; Alexander, Sheffield, 26 Oct., *Daily Herald*, 27 Oct. 1931; 'Reductions in Naval Expenditure 1932: Memorandum by the First Lord of the Admiralty', 20 Aug. 1931 (Cabinet papers, NE (31) 34).

[60] Greenwood, Halifax, 23 Oct., *Yorkshire Observer*, 24 Oct. 1931; Cabinet committee on unemployment insurance finance, report (Cabinet papers, CAB 27/458).

the final figure for 1931 was £104,000,000.[61] In response to this, before the crisis the Conservatives had been stressing their protectionism; the Liberals had been campaigning in May and June for free trade; and Labour, thanks to a mixture of gut reaction and Snowden's obduracy, had also remained committed to the free-trade cause.

Events since the start of August had scarcely diminished the electoral importance of the issue. It was widely known that the Labour Cabinet and the general council had discussed a 10 per cent revenue tariff, and Henderson had admitted publicly that he would have preferred it to the benefit cut. In addition, a number of Liberal MPs had shown they were no longer unqualified free traders; Simon had called for an emergency tariff and Runciman for the prohibition of luxury imports. Thus the case for free trade as against protection, already faltering, had been weakened still further. It was bound to be a bitter and bruising struggle.

Labour believed that opposition to tariffs could win it votes, especially from people who had supported the Liberals in 1929. The problem, however, was that the Government, in MacDonald's manifesto, had only asked for a free hand, not exclusively a mandate for tariffs. Labour's task was to discredit the 'doctor's mandate', and so it described the election as a Conservative 'ramp' to obtain surreptitiously a mandate for tariffs. The point was made by two-thirds of the party's candidates, and by most of its major spokesmen, Henderson saying that the only purpose of the Tories' National allies was 'to give the so-called National Government a cloak of respectability under which the country could be stampeded into a scheme of general tariffs'.[62] Graham, in his broadcast, made the most explicit charge of Conservative duplicity. They would, he said, readily drop MacDonald and the Liberals if they rejected protectionism: '[t]he country would then by an electoral trick be saddled with a Tory and tariffist Government'.[63]

National spokesmen were quick to deny such allegations. MacDonald faced the charge squarely, saying that he was ready to adopt any measures necessary to restore the balance of trade, and his very presence at the head of the Government, well known not only as a long-time socialist but also a free trader, tended to discredit Labour's attacks. His call to voters over the heads of constituency Conservative

[61] *Statistical Abstract*, No. 82, 438.
[62] Henderson, Bolton, 16 Oct., *Manchester Guardian*, 17 Oct. 1931.
[63] Graham, broadcast, 20 Oct., *The Times*, 21 Oct. 1931.

and Liberal associations to vote for the National candidate regardless of his or her attitude towards fiscal policy also had a reassuring effect.[64] He was helped in these efforts by the leading Conservative spokesmen. First, they frequently couched their—often stridently protectionist—appeals within the terms of the free hand. Secondly, they ridiculed the idea that they had benefited from the crisis. In July, Baldwin said, they had been expecting a landslide election victory in their own right; now they were merely part of a coalition.[65] Chamberlain was still more forthright, referring to the 'sacrifices' the Tories had made in joining the National Government.[66]

The Liberals also defended the free hand against Labour attacks. However, many of their candidates feared that the election was a Conservative 'ramp', and on 12 October Samuel made the point that a National victory must not lead inexorably and without serious consideration to the adoption of protection. On 21 October, though, he said that he trusted Baldwin and his colleagues and felt confident that they could continue to work together while the 'emergency' lasted.[67] Given this expressed spirit of co-operation, it seems doubtful whether Labour's attacks on the free hand did it much good or its National opponents much harm. It remains, however, to look at the broader debate on trade policy; and what emerges clearly is that, for many candidates, it was the central issue.

Among the four National parties, the centre ground was occupied by the Liberal Nationals and National Labour, with the marked exception of Snowden. Almost all their candidates supported the free hand fully. Simon said he would be ready to accept tariffs if they were found necessary, and ridiculed Labour's free-trade protestations. Runciman, however, advocated the prohibition of luxury imports rather than protective duties, about which he clearly had serious reservations.[68] The leading National Labour candidates, MacDonald and Thomas, also pledged firm allegiance to the free hand. The premier said they had 'open minds to explore the whole question', but he would never agree to any tariff 'which mean[t] a lowering of the standard of life of

[64] MacDonald, Easington, 12 Oct., *The Times*, 13 Oct. 1931.
[65] Baldwin, Birmingham, 9 Oct., *The Times*, 10 Oct., 1931.
[66] Chamberlain, Birmingham, 12 Oct., *Birmingham Post*, 13 Oct. 1931.
[67] Samuel, Darwen, 12 Oct., *Manchester Guardian*, 13 Oct. 1931; broadcast, 21 Oct., *The Times*, 22 Oct. 1931.
[68] Simon, Spen Valley, 15 Oct., *Manchester Guardian*, 16 Oct. 1931; Runciman, National Liberal Club, 12 Oct., *The Times*, 13 Oct. 1931.

the people'.[69] Thomas stood closer to the Conservatives, calling especially for the stimulation of empire trade. Even his rhetoric approached that of a *bona fide* member of the EIA, as for example when he said that '[t]he return of the National Government would be a warning to the foreigner. . . . We intend to show the foreigner that the men and women of this country are behind the National Government.'[70] Clearly, Thomas was quite ready to accept full and permanent protection in the aftermath of the election. MacDonald, characteristically, was wavering a little more, but he would clearly accept it if it was done without unseemly haste and with a display of Conservative humility. This would be represented by the promised enquiry into trade policy, which was to precede action. In reality, of course, it was well known that this would recommend protection, and although the details were somewhat obscure it could be expected to follow the lines set out in Conservative speeches based on the recommendations of the Cunliffe-Lister committee of the CRD, which had reported in June.

Snowden wanted to remain in the Government but, as an adamantine free trader, was in a more difficult position. Therefore he set out, first, to discredit Labour as a free-trade party. He did this by emphasizing the late Cabinet's vote in favour of a tariff, and was highly successful in embarrassing his former colleagues. Secondly, he denied that protection was the issue at the election, although he went too far in his broadcast of 17 October in stating that there must be another election before any permanent change in the fiscal system could be made. Chamberlain responded swiftly that this infringed the free hand—as indeed it did—and Snowden was forced to retract. He had gambled and failed. Even so, on 26 October he was still prepared to tell Liberal readers of the *News Chronicle* that there was 'no danger of general Protection'. This can only be seen as sheer arrogance—based on Snowden's belief that he would be able to block any proposal of general protection from a non-departmental post and the House of Lords—verging on dishonesty, for Chamberlain's response to his broadcast had made it perfectly clear that the Conservatives would consider the imposition of protective tariffs a legitimate possibility if the Government won the election.

The Samuelite Liberals were as keen as Snowden on the

[69] MacDonald, broadcast, 7 Oct., *The Times*, 8 Oct. 1931; Shotton, 19 Oct., *Manchester Guardian*, 20 Oct. 1931.

[70] Thomas, Derby, 14 Oct., *Manchester Guardian*, 15 Oct. 1931.

maintenance of free trade; it was the issue upon which many of their candidates, especially the more radical and those fighting against Conservative candidates, campaigned. Almost half declared unequivocally for free trade in their election addresses. The candidate in Liverpool, East Toxteth, facing a straight fight against the sitting Conservative, stood as 'an uncompromising Free Trader in opposition to the Tory Tariff ramp'.[71] Other Liberals, including Samuel, said they accepted the free hand but also pledged themselves to oppose the taxation of food. The Liberal leader's speeches tended to concentrate on the fiscal issue, refusing to be committed in advance on tariffs, criticizing imperial preference, and calling for international action to reduce tariff barriers. This made him popular among fundamentalist Liberals even if it did nothing to ingratiate him with the majority of his Cabinet colleagues. In the final week of the campaign, though, he tended to move away from the trade issue and towards emphasis on the need for a Government victory to ensure financial stability.

Despite Conservative allegations, Samuel's emphasis on the virtues of free trade was not mere perversity. He and his followers felt that to abandon free trade totally, on top of remaining in the Government, would drive many Liberals towards Labour. Secondly, there was a genuine belief that protection might lead to serious social divisions; even Grey let slip on one occasion that a tariff should only be an emergency measure.[72] And of course, the influence of Lloyd George, now posing as a staunch Cobdenite, was a threat no Liberal leader could ignore. To gain Liberal votes for the Government, therefore, the Samuelites felt they had to stand up for their free-trade principles. However, they stood for little else. The grandiose schemes of 1929 were forgotten, and the Liberals fought on the most negative lines of any party.

The debate on trade policy was met with no less gusto by the Conservatives. It has been claimed, most notably by Mowat that, as he put it, the election 'gave no mandate for the tariff which the Conservatives later claimed as the price of victory'.[73] This reads quite well, and also fits conveniently with Mowat's analysis of the 1931 crisis as a whole. It is also somewhat at variance with the facts. The clear implication in this argument is that the Conservatives slipped their tariff policy past the electorate while distracting the latter with the

[71] A. S. Doran, election address, Liverpool, East Toxteth (Conservative Party papers). [72] Grey, South Shields, 17 Oct., *The Times*, 19 Oct. 1931.
[73] Mowat, *Britain between the Wars*, 409.

argument that the only issue at stake was defeating Labour and preserving the nation's finances intact. Certainly, Tories made much of the supposed danger presented by Labour. However, what is equally clear is that most were completely open about their preference in fiscal policy.

A survey of Conservative election addresses proves this to be the case. Protection was openly and unequivocally advocated by 61 per cent of Tory candidates. A further 18 per cent said that they would consider any expedient but believed that tariffs would be found to be the best. This reflected the line of Baldwin, who was less keen than most of his senior colleagues to push protection to the forefront of the Tory campaign; thus it is referred to here as the 'Baldwin formula'. In addition, 74 per cent came out for imperial preference, which clearly implied protection. Only 19 per cent declared themselves unequivocally in favour of the free hand. Against these 19 per cent, perhaps, could be levelled the charge of dishonesty; yet on the other hand, they might have earned praise as helping non-Conservatives to support the National Government.

A regional survey of election addresses tends further to undermine the Mowat theory (see Table 10.4). Taking both those who baldly advocated protection and those who espoused the 'Baldwin formula', a high level of open protectionism covered the entire country, with only Wales, Severn, and the Western Peninsula having fewer than 60 per cent of Conservative candidates advocating it. The fact that these were traditional free-trade areas might be a partial explanation, which would suggest a degree of Conservative sleight-of-hand; however, in other traditional free-trade areas, like Lancashire and the West Riding, nearly 80 per cent of Tory candidates favoured tariffs openly. In many areas well over four-fifths of candidates did so. This hardly suggests general dishonesty on the part of Conservative candidates.

When attention is switched from the regional to the occupational background of seats, it is again apparent that there was no deception (see Table 10.5). It is clear that although more Conservatives were openly protectionist in middle-class and low-unemployment divisions, three-quarters of candidates in working-class, textile, and agricultural seats were, too. There was a noticeably lower figure only in the mining areas, where the Conservatives fared worst anyway, so hardly lending credence to the view that the election offered no mandate for protection.[74]

[74] Figures for the constituencies are based on the 1931 *Census*.

Table 10.4. *Regional survey of protectionist election addresses*

% of Conservative candidates advocating protection or 'Baldwin formula'					
A.	London	94	L.	Salop/Staffs	89
B.	Outer London	87	M.	W. Midlands	90
C.	SE England	86	N.	W. Lancastria	77
D.	S. Central England	85	O.	E. Lancastria	78
E.	The Severn	55	P.	West Riding	80
F.	Wessex	77	Q.	Rest of Yorkshire	89
G.	Western Peninsula	55	R.	Cumbria	60
H.	East Anglia	85	S.	NE England	66
I.	Lincoln & Rutland	75	T.	Wales	57
J.	E. Midlands	78	U.	Scotland	71
K.	NW Midlands	72			

Table 10.5. *Conservative protectionism and the occupational background of constituencies* (%)

No.	Type	Open advocacy/ Baldwin formula	Complete free hand	Imperial Preference
50	Middle Class	88	9	84
50	Low Unemployment	83	15	87
25	Textile	77	23	59
50	Agricultural	76	24	76
50	Working Class	75	19	69
50	High Unemployment	73	24	76
50	Mining	64	29	57

Note: Social basis of constituencies worked out from 1931 *Census*. The constituencies referred to are those with the heaviest concentrations of particular types of occupational group: e.g. 'Agricultural' refers to the 50 seats with the highest percentage of agricultural workers resident therein.

Of course, elections were not fought by election addresses alone. But most leading Conservative spokesmen were also frank on the subject. Neville Chamberlain sounded like a salesman in saying that while all expedients should be investigated he was 'convinced' that there would be found 'no weapon so rapid in its action or as easy to apply or so effective for all purposes as a carefully designed system of duties upon foreign imports'.[75] Protection over the last year would have meant 750,000 extra jobs for British workers at wages of £3 per week; 'the only hope' for Britain's future was 'Imperial economic unity'.[76] Meanwhile, Cunliffe-Lister stated baldly that a tariff was 'necessary' to restore the trade balance, improve efficiency, help agriculture, and promote imperial unity. There was 'no substitute'.[77] Hilton Young was even more explicit, demanding a 33 per cent tariff with imperial preference, while Churchill, the erstwhile free trader, boasted that 'the new House of Commons [would] be absolutely free to set up a permanent general tariff' if it saw fit.[78] Amery, a long-time protectionist, went even further, telling meetings that tariffs would drastically improve living standards, and that any tariff worth having must be permanent.[79] Even Baldwin, who tended to be more cautious and could be criticized with some justice for trying to keep protection off the campaign agenda, was far from silent: on 9 October, opening his election tour, he said that he believed and 'cherish[ed] the hope' that tariffs would be found necessary. He was to reiterate this nationwide throughout the campaign.

The truth of the matter was that the Conservatives had no reason to hide their protectionism. Labour purported to believe differently. As Henderson said:

> Every time . . . tariffs had [*sic*] been submitted to the British electorate since the days of the Hungry Forties the electorate have seen what it involved, and have refused to go that road. If only the issue is put plainly to the electorate in 1931 the same verdict will be given as has been given before.[80]

Many Labour candidates concentrated heavily on free trade in the belief that it would be their salvation, and by the end of the campaign it was practically the sole issue for many. The day before polling, Henderson, in a message to the *Daily Herald*, stated that '[t]o-morrow we go over the top to meet the tariff enemy', as though no other issue

[75] Chamberlain, Wakefield, 18 Oct., *Wakefield Express*, 19 Oct. 1931.

[76] Chamberlain, Birmingham, 19 Oct., *Birmingham Post*, 20 Oct. 1931; Birmingham, 12 Oct., ibid. 13 Oct. 1931.

[77] Cunliffe-Lister, election address, Hendon (Conservative Party papers); Cunliffe-Lister, Hampstead Garden Suburb, 13 Oct., *The Times*, 14 Oct. 1931.

[78] Hilton Young, Carlisle, 9 Oct., *The Times*, 10 Oct. 1931; Romford, 19 Oct., ibid. 20 Oct. 1931; Churchill, Epping, 13 Oct., *Manchester Guardian*, 14 Oct. 1931.

[79] Amery, Birmingham, 14 Oct., *Birmingham Post*, 15 Oct. 1931.

[80] Henderson, Leeds, 22 Oct., *Yorkshire Observer*, 23 Oct. 1931.

existed.[81] In truth, many candidates, including Henderson, disliked or were unsure of the Labour manifesto; and, again like him, many had been weaned on Cobdenism as Liberals. Hence the stress on free trade.

But tariffs were not the electoral liability they had been in 1906 and 1923. Under the impact of the slump public opinion had moved towards protection, or at least away from the perceived sterility of free trade. Labour argued that tariffs would not cure unemployment, and that they would drive down wages, increase the cost of living, perpetuate inefficiency, and corrupt public life. But what had been the experience of large sections of the working class under free-trade Labour? Unemployment among insured workers had more than doubled. Wage cuts had been suffered widely, especially in textiles, hosiery, building, baking, and the furniture trades. Efficient industries such as lace-making had had to lay off workers because the Labour administration had refused to protect them from the most blatant foreign dumping. The ailing iron and steel industry, vital to Britain's Great Power status, was denied the protection it craved. Labour's commitment to efficiency merely seemed to mean 'rationalization' and redundancies; and its commitment to low prices was a sure way of losing what rural support it had, since it was only through higher prices that agriculture could regain prosperity. All in all, Labour's condemnation of tariffs tended merely to show up in still sharper relief the failings of the second Labour Government, and its lack of a credible alternative.

The Conservatives did not, on the whole, hide their protectionism, because they felt they had nothing to hide. As before the crisis, they saw it as a vote-winner, and could claim with some justice after the election that they had been proved right. The fact was that many sections of public opinion had been moving towards the idea of some form of protection. There were a number of reasons for this. The key factor, of course, was the impact of the slump on Britain. During the two-year tenure of the Labour Government insured unemployment had risen from 1.1 to 2.8 million. This was so large and so fast an increase as to shock many people out of the free-trade beliefs of a lifetime. At least, it was argued, protection was *an* answer, and should

[81] *Daily Herald*, 26 Oct. 1931; see also Henderson, interview, *Reynolds's Illustrated News*, 25 Oct. 1931. For concentration on free trade, see e.g. Noel-Baker's notes for his speeches at the end of the campaign and at his eve-of-poll rally in Coventry (Noel-Baker papers, NBKR 1/32 and 1/35); cf. *The Times*, 24 Oct. 1931, showing him going hard for Liberal votes.

be given a chance. This was especially so given that the raising of foreign (and most spectacularly American) tariffs against British goods, and the failure of international action to reduce tariff barriers generally, undercut the free-trade argument that tariffs would impair international relations. They were already damaged, it was argued: it was time for Britain to look after her own interests as other countries were looking after theirs. This new mood could be seen amongst politicians of all parties, be it the old Conservative free traders like Derby or Churchill, now reconciled to a measure of protectionism; Liberals like Simon, Runciman, and the Liberal Nationals as a whole; or Labour men like Addison. Business opinion had been moving in the same direction: as already mentioned, the Associated Chambers of Commerce had come out for extensive safeguarding in August 1930, while two months later the Federation of British Industry had stated that 96 per cent of its members favoured protection with as much imperial preference as could be negotiated with the dominions. Many trade unionists had moved in the same direction; the iron and steel workers, under Pugh, were the most notable example, but there were others in industries like lace-making. Citrine himself had come to favour some form of tariff. It is more difficult to be certain as to how far these views had penetrated the consciousness of ordinary voters, particularly since for this period the evidence of opinion polls or even Mass-Observation is lacking. Nevertheless, it seems unlikely that, if large sections of business and, to a lesser extent, trade-union opinion were moving that way, sections of the electorate would not follow suit. And during the campaign Labour candidates who began as ardent free traders often found themselves moderating their stance in a protectionist direction; that was the experience of, among many others, the candidates in Derby. It is perhaps also worth noting that Arthur Henderson, in his confidential post-mortem of the campaign for Labour's NEC, was to explain, if somewhat grudgingly, the National victory partly in terms of the appeal of tariffs 'to large numbers of people who had come to believe that it was better to try any policy to cure unemployment than to go on with unemployment at its present level'.[82] Coming from a lifelong free trader, that would seem reasonably convincing evidence that there had indeed been considerable popular support for the Tories' tariff policy.

[82] Labour Party NEC minutes, 10 Nov. 1931, 'Report on the General Election by the Secretary' (Labour Party papers); for Derby, see A. J. Thorpe, 'The British General Election of 1931', Ph.D. thesis (Sheffield, 1988), 579.

The only remaining question is whether the stress placed by some people on the 'one great issue' precluded a mandate for permanent protective tariffs. This was the line of Snowden and the Samuelites. However, it was mostly Liberals like Grey, Liberal Nationals, and National Labourites who argued that the only issue was the defeat of Labour, the reason being that they had few positive proposals. Few if any Conservatives took this stance, although it is only fair to point out that Baldwin was sometimes close to it. Generally, they had ideas and policies, and put them before the electorate. If some of their allies tried to convince themselves that the Conservative Party, most of whose candidates and leaders were screaming of the need for protection, was not protectionist and would not want to see tariffs introduced after the election, it was hardly the Conservative Party's fault. Even Baldwin's speeches cannot be quoted to support such a view, for although he stressed the need to beat Labour as the primary need and made play with the 'doctor's mandate' he always mentioned his belief in the desirability and necessity of protection.

VI

The issue of public economy had been growing in importance throughout 1931 and would have been a major issue whenever and however the election had come. The actual conditions of the 1931 election did nothing to diminish its significance. The need for economy was stressed heavily in National election addresses, although the individual cuts made by the Government tended to be played down. Labour candidates unanimously denied the need for economy, and attacked the specific measures involved, especially the reduction in unemployment benefit, where Labour policy was the immediate restoration of the old rates. Fewer, although still the great majority, also mentioned public servants' salary and wage cuts, on which policy was a little more circumspect, promising restoration as soon as possible.

The general position of the Government was that its supporters should stress the need which had existed for public economy in order to avert the collapse of sterling, and candidates were ordered to make no pledges regarding restoration.[83] Within this framework, the Conservatives, with long experience in the rhetoric of retrenchment, were the least restrained in defending the cuts. Sir Austen Chamberlain

[83] Cabinet committee on emergency business, 1931, first meeting, 15 Oct. 1931 (Cabinet papers, CAB 27/463).

argued quite simply that they were essential because taxation was far too high, depressing industry and blunting the nation's competitive edge.[84] Sir Kingsley Wood pointed out that the TGWU had been forced to take steps earlier in the year to balance its unemployment fund and that the Government was merely following suit, while Baldwin stressed the need for the unemployed to contribute like others.[85] Great play was made of the ex-ministers' commitment to economies. As Chamberlain pointed out, the Government had made no cut in excess of 10 per cent, whereas Labour had agreed to wage cuts of 12 per cent for the police, 15 per cent for teachers, and no less than 25 per cent for certain members of the armed forces.[86] As to restoration, Baldwin would only promise that the cuts would be reconsidered when the position was more stable.

The Liberals abandoned ideas of high expenditure on national development and concentrated on the need to curtail spending. Grey was unequivocal, saying the economies had prevented far larger cuts in real terms, but Samuel was rather more circumspect, and said that the cuts would be reconsidered if prices rose appreciably due to the devaluation of sterling.[87] However, it was only in exceptional cases, like G. L. Mander, defending the strongly working-class seat of East Wolverhampton, that a Liberal candidate expressed his hostility to the benefit cut.[88] Liberal National spokesmen adopted a similar line to that of the Samuelite leadership, Simon, for example, stressing the dangers of a much larger cut in real terms.[89] National Labourites, whose main *raison d'être* was their belief in the necessity of economy, were very keen to stress it. Their spokesmen made four points: that the Labour Cabinet had agreed to nine-tenths of the cuts; that the only alternative was a far larger cut in real terms; that taxation must be kept down to liberate capital for 'more productive' uses; and that the benefit cut would be as short-lived as possible, but that it would be dishonest to promise its immediate restoration.[90]

[84] Sir Austen Chamberlain, Birmingham, 13 Oct., *Birmingham Post*, 14 Oct. 1931.

[85] Wood, Eltham, 22 Oct., *The Times*, 23 Oct. 1931; Baldwin, Birmingham, 9 Oct., *The Times*, 10 Oct. 1931.

[86] Chamberlain, Bolton, 20 Oct., *Birmingham Post*, 21 Oct. 1931.

[87] Grey, South Shields, 17 Oct., *The Times*, 19 Oct. 1931; Samuel, Darwen, 12 Oct., *Manchester Guardian*, 13 Oct. 1931; Darwen, 20 Oct., ibid. 21 Oct. 1931.

[88] G. L. Mander, election address, East Wolverhampton (Conservative Party papers).

[89] Simon, broadcast, 16 Oct., *The Times*, 17 Oct. 1931.

[90] Thomas, Derby, 14 Oct., *The Times*, 15 Oct. 1931; see also MacDonald, Horden, 16 Oct., *Manchester Guardian*, 17 Oct. 1931.

Labour saw this issue as a vote-winner, since its manifesto promised restoration of the cuts, which National candidates were not allowed to do. The party believed that most of the two million-plus unemployed were probably already Labour voters. Even so, to promise to increase their benefit should consolidate their support; while many of the half a million public servants, who might not normally vote Labour, should also be attracted. Labour attacked the cuts on humanitarian grounds; on the grounds that they were false economies which would increase unemployment and so unbalance the budget; legalistically, as being executed in breach of contract; and as the prelude to a general wage-cutting campaign. (The last argument provided a means of relating the cuts to people in work.) The perceived potential of this issue could be seen in the high proportion of candidates mentioning it. However, a number of factors made it less of a winning issue than seemed likely at first.

A major problem was that the extent of the ex-ministers' commitment to the cuts soon became known; but other factors were also operative. First, Labour's commitment to restoration was somewhat equivocal. Benefits would be restored immediately, but the other cuts would be lifted only 'as rapidly as the claims of the unemployed . . . permit[ted]'.[91] This, and the fact that Labour rhetoric concentrated on the iniquities of the benefit cut but ignored the very real difficulties of public servants—most of whom were not part of the unemployment insurance scheme in any case—did little to impel public servants to switch to Labour. The Government, after all, was offering reconsideration as soon as the economic and financial position permitted.

Labour's case was also spoiled by its failure convincingly to show how it would maintain its promised balanced budget while restoring the cuts. This is not to say that Snowden's was the only way of balancing the books, but Labour had now ruled out many alternatives, such as the revenue tariff. To claim now, as did Henderson, that numerous simple expedients, such as adjusting the 'scandal' of the 'Derating' Act, would balance the budget was, frankly, ridiculous.[92] Unable to convince people that it could match up income and expenditure, the party was exposed to the charge that it would face a budget deficit, depreciate the currency, and so render any increase in the money values of benefits and salaries nugatory. Finally, much of the rhetoric with which some Labourites surrounded the issue was not

[91] 'Labour's Call to Action', in Craig, *Election Manifestos*, 94–8.
[92] Henderson, Bradford, 18 Oct., *Yorkshire Post*, 19 Oct. 1931.

calculated to bring over those electors who had not supported the far more moderate Labour programme of 1929. For example, Cripps praised the Invergordon mutineers for opposing the cuts, and added gratuitously that it had 'served the Government right'.[93] Thus an issue, perhaps the issue, on which Labour had had high hopes of success in 1931, was far less beneficial than had been hoped. In consolidating existing voters it was useful, but in obtaining the new supporters Labour needed, it probably had very little impact.

VII

Controversy on most of the more general domestic and foreign issues tended either to be drowned out by the larger issues or absorbed into them. Thus unemployment was debated mainly within the context of trade and nationalization policy. Agriculture was also absorbed in the question of trade, the Government as a whole promising to adopt any measure likely to help, the Conservatives offering protection, and Labour suggesting import and export boards in its manifesto, although little was heard of these as Labour candidates tried to present themselves as free traders. The Liberals had very little to offer except opposition to tariffs and a few suggestions as to economies of scale and improved marketing methods. Labour promised that agricultural workers would be included in the unemployment insurance scheme, the creation of wage boards, and the abolition of tied cottages, but these pledges had been made in 1929, and probably did little more than remind such rural labourers as had supported the party then of how Labour had let them down. Other domestic issues like housing were mentioned by few candidates in detail, although Labour tried to capitalize on Greenwood's work on slum clearance and candidates in Scotland called for rent restriction. It seems unlikely that the issue made much impact.

Education, however, did have something of an impact, as Roman Catholics gained their revenge for Trevelyan's bill, which had been seen as antipathetic towards church schools. The Catholic vote, a mainstay of Labour in many areas, had been tending to defect at recent by-elections, and in May 1931 this problem had been compounded by the promulgation of Pope Pius XI's anti-socialist encyclical, which gave great scope to clergymen to instruct their flocks to oppose

[93] Cripps, Devonport, 19 Oct., *Morning Post*, 20 Oct. 1931.

Labour.[94] There was not a total withdrawal of support, but some candidates had great difficulties. In Dartford, for example, Catholics issued a leaflet pointing to the encyclical and urging their co-religionists to vote Conservative.[95] There were also reports of widespread Catholic defections in Leeds, Burnley, Preston, Linlithgowshire, and Harrow.[96] Priests at three of Manchester, Platting's five Catholic churches instructed their congregations to withdraw support from Clynes, and hinted strongly that they should support the Conservative. He lost the seat.[97]

In addition, the Church of England hierarchy came out more firmly for the National Government than it might have done for a single party. On 19 October, the Archbishop of Canterbury said party issues were not at stake, praised the Prime Minister for his courage, and stressed the need to find 'the men whom [they] could trust . . . not to look upon some vague and uncertain future, but to deal forcibly and courageously with the immediate issues'.[98] The clear message was that Anglicans should support the National Government. The Bishop of Winchester called for the re-election of the Government with a large majority.[99] Labour was weaker among Anglicans than among other denominations, but the involvement of religion to this extent was an interesting sidelight on the difficulties the party had to face and, conversely, the great stock of goodwill which existed for the National Government.

Imperial affairs were largely ignored, except in so far as the Conservatives advocated closer economic links within the empire. Foreign affairs were mentioned widely in Labour and Liberal manifestos, but, interestingly (given that their leaders would be conducting foreign policy for the rest of the decade) most Conservatives and Liberal Nationals made no mention of the subject, and hardly any mentioned the forthcoming world disarmament conference. Labour made what it could of Henderson's foreign policy and disarmament, while the Liberals also showed a greater commitment to better international relations. But there were very few votes in foreign affairs in 1931.

[94] *The Times*, 25 May 1931. [95] *The Times*, 27 Oct. 1931.

[96] *The Times*, 17 Oct. 1931; *Daily Express*, 26 Oct. 1931; *The Times*, 20 Oct. 1931; Conservative agent, Linlithgow, to Baldwin (Baldwin papers, vol. 45 (v), f. 32); *The Times*, 14 Oct. 1931.

[97] *Morning Post*, 26 Oct. 1931.

[98] Archbishop of Canterbury, Canterbury, 19 Oct., *The Times*, 20 Oct. 1931.

[99] *Morning Post*, 27 Oct. 1931.

VIII

Some people claimed subsequently that the electorate had not been faced with the real issues at all, but had been panicked by a series of stunts into supporting the National Government. This was long the prevalent view within the Labour Party.[100] However, as is clear from the evidence presented above, the electors did not need to be terrorized into opposing Labour; and although there were 'dirty tricks' they were not the sole preserve of either side.

A number of the tactics used by National spokesmen were somewhat discreditable. For example, a number of them, including MacDonald and Steel-Maitland, displayed German banknotes from 1923 to show what might happen if the currency were devalued, while Simon said that a box of matches would have cost £20 in Germany in 1923 before waving various notes around.[101] This was gimmickry at its worst, and did its perpetrators little credit. They were doing well enough overall (although both MacDonald and Simon were worried about losing their seats) to avoid demeaning themselves in this way. It should be noted, however, that neither Samuel nor his close colleagues, nor the Conservative leadership, participated; they were already arguing about the policies the re-elected National Government should implement.

The Nationals' use of the threat of starvation in the event of a Labour victory was also discreditable. It was based on the premiss that Britain could only feed herself for two days in every seven: a depreciated currency would leave her unable to buy essential imports. But less than one in ten Tories mentioned it, although those who did did so in bloodcurdling terms, the candidate for Newport claiming a Labour victory would mean 'ULTIMATE STARVATION'.[102] The basic assumptions were tenuous, the language alarmist. But some Labour candidates spoke in similar terms—a broadsheet in Colchester, for example, said a National victory would mean 'thousands' would 'surely starve' because 'Conservatism [would] starve them at the dictates of foreign bankers'.[103] Labour also complained that, over the weekend before the poll, workers were pressurized by their employers into

[100] See e.g. Labour Party, *Annual Report, 1932*, 3.

[101] Steel-Maitland to F. Duckitt, 24 Oct. 1931; Steel-Maitland to B. Pontifex, 21 Oct. 1931 (Steel-Maitland papers, GD 193/2828/2/87 and 90); Simon, Birkenshaw, 19 Oct., *Yorkshire Observer*, 20 Oct. 1931.

[102] R. G. Clarry, election address, Newport (Conservative Party papers).

[103] Quoted in *The Times*, 21 Oct. 1931.

voting for National candidates. This did take place, but it is doubtful whether it was any more reprehensible than the comments of the NUR general secretary, Cramp, or of Greenwood, that any trade unionist who voted for the National Government was a 'blackleg'.[104]

But the most notorious 'stunt' was the scare regarding the Post Office savings bank. In his broadcast of 23 October, Henderson defended Labour's proposal to nationalize the banks by saying that the money would remain safe, as safe indeed as the deposits in the Post Office bank. Next day, Runciman set out to discredit this argument by claiming that in April and August the Labour Cabinet had been worried because 'a substantial part' of the deposits in the bank had been lent to the unemployment insurance fund, making them realize the 'difficulties' they would face 'if serious distrust of British credit set in'.[105] Snowden then issued a statement praising Runciman and adding that while the danger to small savings had passed because the budget had been balanced, it would return if Labour won the election. Henderson, in reply, dismissed the allegations as a scare, stressed that the money had never been in any danger and argued that Runciman, by impugning the safety of the deposits, had jeopardized British credit. Snowden's statement, he concluded, did not really corroborate Runciman's, since the former referred to the depreciation of the currency while the latter called into question the creditworthiness of the fund. The following evening (26 Oct) Runciman stated that 'a very large amount' of the bank's deposits had been lent to the fund.[106] By this time MacDonald had also lent his weight to the story. Two questions arose from all this: were Runciman's allegations valid, and did they have a significant impact on the outcome of the election?

The practice of raising sums of money from the Post Office savings bank for Treasury use dated back at least as far as 1888, and after the election Churchill freely admitted that he had borrowed money from it for the unemployment insurance fund during his period as Chancellor.[107] Inevitably, given the increasing demands on the fund, the net loans had increased over the years, and during the whole of

[104] Cramp, no location given, 23 Oct., *Daily Telegraph*, 24 Oct. 1931; Greenwood, Liverpool, 22 Oct., *Liverpool Post*, 23 Oct. 1931; for a predictable reaction, see Baldwin, Glasgow, 25 Oct., *The Times*, 26 Oct. 1931.

[105] Runciman, South Shields, 24 Oct., *Manchester Guardian*, 26 Oct. 1931.

[106] Runciman, North Paddington, 26 Oct., *Morning Post*, 27 Oct. 1931.

[107] *Parl. Deb.*, 5th ser., 259, cols. 669–70, Chamberlain, 17 Nov. 1931; col. 130, Churchill, 11 Nov. 1931; all figures taken from *Statistical Abstract*, No. 77 (London, 1934), 147.

1931 the outstanding debt rose from £38,950,000 to £75,390,000. The total assets of the savings bank, meanwhile, were £290,235,000 at the end of 1930 and £289,441,000 at the end of 1931. In other words, there had been plenty more scope for loans. Indeed, during 1932, with only £16,000,000 more deposited at the bank, the Government of which Runciman was a member was to increase the loan to the unemployment fund to £115,000,000. So, really, Runciman's argument was that Labour had led Britain to the verge of bankruptcy, since otherwise the Treasury would have been able to meet its obligations if required. The argument that the deposits themselves and in isolation had been in danger was, as Lansbury later described it to Runciman's face, 'a lie, and a putrid lie at that'.[108]

But if Lansbury was right on that point, he and many other Labourites were wrong to attribute their defeat or even the scale thereof to the Post Office savings scare. Certainly, many people had accounts: 9,538,515 at the end of 1931, with an average of £30 5s 2d in each. But the idea that Labour would otherwise have won the election is almost too bizarre for words. At the outset of the campaign, Labour had been pessimistic, and little had happened during the campaign to lift its gloom. The editor of the pro-Labour *Railway Service Journal*, in the middle of the campaign, felt a National triumph highly likely.[109] Many of the statements made by Labour's leaders radiated pessimism, while the party press and publicity department issued a model election address which spoke of electing enough Labour MPs to help to resist protection.[110] The Webbs expected to lose 100 seats.[111] Thus by the time Runciman raised the 'scare', Labour candidates all over the country were on the defensive, clinging increasingly to free trade as a lifebelt.

By that time all the predictions were pointing to a National victory. On 20 October the *Daily Express* had expected Labour to lose 105 seats; National politicians had no doubt whatever that the Government would win a handsome victory; and the stock market prediction of the National majority started the campaign at 150 and rose steadily to 205 on polling day.[112] Indeed, some National politicians had become so

[108] *Parl. Deb.*, 5th ser., 259, col. 540, Lansbury, 16 Nov. 1931.

[109] *Railway Service Journal*, Nov. 1931.

[110] Labour Party press and publicity department, 'Model Election Address' (Passfield papers).

[111] Estorick, *Cripps*, 102.

[112] Bridgeman journal, Oct. 1931 (Bridgeman papers); Lord Lothian to E. F. C. Lance, 27 Oct. 1931 (Lothian papers, GD 40/17/258/366); stock exchange figures

certain of victory by the last week of the campaign that they began to worry lest complacent electors would not bother to vote, and Baldwin and Stonehaven led the way in attacking apathy.[113]

The Post Office scare, therefore, had little impact on the result. But some Labour spokesmen had been predicting a scare with such vigour that they had seemed almost to be hoping for one; and, it filled a useful role for Labourites.[114] For, like the equally non-decisive Zinoviev Letter in 1924, it enabled Labour, and its leadership especially, to try to explain away the party's defeat as the result of a conspiracy of lies and falsehoods. This was to be the argument of the *Daily Herald* and Henderson, in particular. Both had made outrageously optimistic predictions: 'the reports which come to me from every part of the country are amazingly good', Henderson said on 24 October, while Clynes had suggested that there were 'very cheerful indications of a widespread Labour victory'.[115] And the *Herald* had been making predictions that Labour would capture what were, in fact, hopeless seats.[116] Stressing the scurrility of the campaign and the salience of the savings bank scare gave them an excuse, and helped the parliamentary leaders by obscuring the fact that it was largely their mistakes and failings over the years, and especially in recent weeks and months, which had brought the party to the sorry state in which it was soon to find itself.

Even before the August crisis, it had seemed impossible that Labour could win the next general election. Everything that had happened since then had merely served to confirm that impression. As it entered the 1931 election campaign, Labour was perceived to be divided. Electors could believe that they were upholding the best Labour values by supporting the candidate endorsed by MacDonald, until recently the undisputed leader of the Labour Party. In addition, Labour had few issues on which it could attack. As the party of Government between 1929 and August 1931, it was in the unenviable position of

given occasionally in *Daily Herald*, *Manchester Guardian*, *Morning Post*, *Daily Express*, *Daily Telegraph*.

[113] Baldwin, broadcast, 22 Oct., *The Times*, 23 Oct. 1931; letter from Stonehaven, *The Times*, 24 Oct. 1931.

[114] See e.g. Lord Arnold, Bethnal Green, 23 Oct., *Daily Herald*, 24 Oct. 1931.

[115] Henderson, Blackburn, 24 Oct., *Manchester Guardian*, 26 Oct. 1931; Henderson, interview, *Reynolds's Illustrated News*, 25 Oct. 1931; Clynes, Manchester, 19 Oct., *Manchester Guardian*, 20 Oct. 1931.

[116] See *Daily Herald*, 22, 27 Oct. 1931.

being seen as responsible for many of the ills faced by the country. Yet at the same time it lacked the benefits it might have had by fighting as the governing party—the most recent experience in office, the prestige of the Prime Minister, the help of the civil service, perhaps some backing from 'the establishment', as well as somewhat fairer treatment in the media. Even on the issues it felt were favourable, trade policy and the expenditure cuts, its position was hopelessly compromised and it misjudged the national mood. When it moved onto more positive proposals, its policies were ill-defined, ill-thought out, and worse explained. And the record of the second Labour Government—the first to be in office for more than a few months—was a millstone around the party's neck, contrasting sharply with the National Government's apparent restoration of prosperity, with the first sustained—although, as it transpired, temporary—fall in unemployment for over two years coinciding conveniently with the election campaign.

The National Government made the most of its opportunities, enjoying great success in highlighting the compromised position of the Labour leadership, and in showing the failings of the second Labour Government while exempting the National Labourites from blame. The Liberals were in an unhappy position, and it showed, but most Conservatives advocated their policies with gusto. The country, shaken by the slump, was ready to elect the National Government to face the difficult future which lay ahead and as an insurance against the troubled times just past, doubtless as, albeit on a slightly lesser scale, they would have elected the Conservatives in a party election. The mass of electors were not only reacting against Labour; they were also voting for a better future, although whether they got it is a matter of debate.

Finally, it was ludicrous to claim that the electorate had been panicked by National scares. The charge was an insult to the intelligence of the voters; that it had to be resorted to was an indictment of the recent performance of the Labour Party and its leaders. Just how much of an indictment began to be revealed on the night of 27 October.

11

THE OUTCOME

AT the dissolution of Parliament, the National Government had a majority of around 60, and few sober observers on any side expected that it would fail to increase that, at the very least to 100. Many felt the figure would be much larger, but were often reticent in voicing their feelings, Conservatives because they feared appearing complacent, Samuelites because they were hoping that somehow a huge Tory preponderance could be avoided, and Labourites because they too were hoping for little short of a miracle. Even privately, however, few people would have predicted that the result would give the Government a record majority, reduce Labour to a rump of 46 MPs, and see the consolidation of an electoral realignment which would disadvantage Labour for years to come. But such was to be the outcome.

As the declarations began on the night of 27 October, however, facts could be dodged no longer. The first result, at Hornsey, showed a fall in the Labour vote, despite the withdrawal of the Liberals, and an increase in the Conservative majority from 9,511 (19.0 per cent) to 33,609 (69.0 per cent). Soon afterwards, it was declared that Labour had lost all three Salford seats to the Tories in straight fights. In each case its number of votes (or *vote*, as opposed to the percentage of the total votes gained, which will be referred to as *poll share*) had fallen, and in Salford South, where there had also been a straight fight in 1929, there was a swing to the Conservatives of 13.5 per cent. The three had been Labour's 181st, 192nd equal, and 279th equal safest seats after the 1929 election. Their loss did not presage disaster, but it did—unless they were total freaks—point to a sharp set-back. That night's remaining results made it clear that Labour had been routed, and the results declared from the county areas the following day merely emphasized the point (see Table 11.1).

Labour did not gain a single seat; the Tories did not lose one. Labour lost some of its safest constituencies, for example Bermondsey, Rotherhithe (1929 majority 42.3), Sheffield Attercliffe (40.8), and Morpeth (39.2). The failure to unseat MacDonald or Thomas, or indeed any of the National Labourites, meant the Government was saved even that slight embarrassment. In addition, scarcely any of

Table 11.1. *Result of the 1931 general election* (Turnout 76.4%)

	Votes	% share	MPs
Conservative	11,905,925	55.0	470
Liberal National	809,302	3.7	35
Liberal	1,372,595	6.5	33
National Labour	341,370	1.5	13
National	100,193	0.5	3
[TOTAL GOVERNMENT]	[14,529,385]	[67.2]	[554]
Labour	6,324,737	29.3	46
Lloyd George Liberal	103,528	0.5	4
ILP	260,344	1.2	3
Unendorsed Labour	64,549	0.3	3
CPGB	74,824	0.3	—
Irish Nationalist	123,053	0.4	2
New Party	36,377	0.2	—
Others	139,576	0.6	3
TOTAL	21,656,373	100.0	615

Labour's leaders were spared from the holocaust. People like Henderson at Burnley and Addison at Swindon had been widely expected to lose; more spectacular were the defeats of Clynes at Manchester, Platting, which he had held since 1906 (on a swing of around 15 per cent), Graham at Central Edinburgh, Morrison at South Hackney, and Alexander at Sheffield, Hillsborough. Only Lansbury of the late Cabinet held his seat—Poplar, Bow and Bromley—and even he suffered a swing to the Conservative of 11.1 per cent. Of the former junior ministers only two survived: Clement Attlee, the late Postmaster-General, with a majority of 551 at Stepney, Limehouse, and Cripps, with a majority of 429 at East Bristol. Thus the leadership of the rump PLP was dictated from the outset.

I

The scale of the result had come as a surprise to everyone except the lucky few who had predicted it correctly in newspaper competitions and who now won large cash prizes for their audacity. Politicians' reactions generally expressed surprise. The Conservative leaders were especially pleased. Baldwin, aiming to moderate the mood of his followers in Parliament, stressed the extent to which it had been a National rather than a party victory, and called for continued co-operation because '[t]he magnitude of the defeat [made] it all the more imperative that [they] should be faithful to [their] trust'.[1] In short, he was not prepared to throw over the National Government or MacDonald for a purely party administration, which would be more right-wing and so less congenial. Chamberlain was equally committed to existing arrangements. He felt the result showed the world that Britain was ready to sort herself out; in particular, 'something [would] have to be done to control foreign imports'. And Chamberlain—who despite MacDonald's preference for Runciman was to succeed Snowden at the Treasury—looked to the future with optimism. The recent trade revival and the 'remarkable' drop in unemployment, he said, gave them 'hope that a movement ha[d] been started which w[ould] . . . spread far beyond the confines of this country. Recovery [was] in the air, and the new Government w[ould] set about its work with confidence and hope.'[2] Privately, he looked forward to the fusion of the Conservatives, National Labour, and the Liberal Nationals into a National party.[3] Thus there was no chance of a Conservative rebellion strangling the Government at birth.

This should have reassured MacDonald, but the premier remained suspicious of 'the Conservative wirepullers'.[4] He clearly felt the large majority weakened his own position within the Government, and had severe misgivings. In a public statement he said that the majority 'must convince the whole world' that in a crisis Britain could always depend on a hearty response from 'willing hands and devoted minds'. 'The very emphasis of the response [was] embarrassing, but [he] appeal[ed] for forbearance as well as confidence.'[5] In other words, he did not want to become merely another Conservative Prime Minister, a fact which probably did little to strengthen the Government or make it more coherent over the next three-and-a-half years. Certainly, many Conservatives felt at the time that a party Government would have been more purposeful in a number of areas of policy.[6]

[1] Middlemas and Barnes, *Baldwin*, 652.
[2] *Birmingham Post*, 29 Oct. 1931; for MacDonald's preference, see Hankey diary, 28 Oct. 1931 (Hankey papers, HNKY 1/7).
[3] K. Feiling, *Life of Neville Chamberlain* (London, 1946), 197.
[4] MacDonald diary, 29 Oct. 1931 (MacDonald papers, PRO 30/69/1753).
[5] *Manchester Guardian*, 29 Oct. 1931.
[6] For early misgivings, see e.g. Bridgeman journal, Oct. 1931 (Bridgeman papers).

Such Conservatives were most disgruntled by the continuing presence of free-trade Liberals in the Government. The feeling was largely mutual. The huge Tory majority was the last thing the Samuelites had wanted. So an official myth was provided, courtesy of the *Liberal Magazine*, to the effect that 'in something like three hundred constituencies there was no Liberal candidate chiefly because the Liberal party unexpectedly found itself without the necessary funds at the very last moment, when it was too late adequately to repair the defect.'[7] This was simply untrue, for the Liberals had in any case anticipated fighting on a far narrower front than in 1929, and the *News Chronicle* had stated during the campaign that ample funds were available to finance candidates. The piece went on with even less regard for reality:

> [I]t is important to remember that in 375 constituencies those electors who desired to support the National Government had no means of doing so except by voting for the Conservative candidate. It is not disputed that about three million Liberals without surrendering a shred of their disapproval of the Conservative Party policy, for once in their lives and for this time only screwed themselves up to this unfamiliar form of discharging a patriotic duty.[8]

In fact, Samuel himself punctured this myth, admitting that even if the Liberals had put up far more candidates, 'probably most of them would not have been elected'.[9]

It was generally recognized among Samuelites that only through unity would the Liberals have any chance of holding up protectionism and maintaining Liberalism as a credible independent force in British politics.[10] But it soon became clear that such unity was unattainable. Within a week, Lloyd George withdrew from all offices in the LPP.[11] Meanwhile, overtures to the Liberal Nationals were met with hostility.[12] After all, the one advantage which the official Liberals had had over the Simonites before the election had been their monopoly of Liberal appointments in the administration. Now that was no longer true, as Simon (Foreign Secretary) and Runciman (President of the Board of Trade) entered the Cabinet, and Brown and Hore-Belisha became junior ministers. When the Liberal Nationals did finally unite with someone it would be with the Conservatives, in 1966. In the mean

[7] *Liberal Magazine*, Nov. 1931.
[8] Ibid.
[9] *Manchester Guardian*, 29 Oct. 1931.
[10] *Liberal Magazine*, Nov. 1931.
[11] Lloyd George to Samuel, 3 Nov. 1931 (Samuel papers, A/84, f. 8).
[12] Samuel to Fisher, 4 Nov. 1931 (Fisher papers, 69, f. 69).

time, it seemed extremely unlikely that the Samuelites would be able to remain long in the Government.[13] Indeed, they almost left on the introduction of protection in February 1932, and finally did so over the adoption of imperial preference seven months later. By contrast, no great matter of principle would arise to separate the Liberal Nationals or National Labour from their Conservative colleagues. Sufficient will always existed between the representatives of those three parties to avoid any split.

II

Labour reactions varied. Maxton and Trevelyan, on the left, had expected Labour to lose, though not so heavily. For Maxton, one stage in the development of the Labour movement had come to a bitter end. Gradualism must now be abandoned and socialists be ready to take power, for the National Government would hasten the collapse of capitalism.[14] This line was to lead the ILP out of the Labour Party within a few months. Other left-wingers would remain, especially within the PLP, to argue the case for fundamental changes from within. On the other hand the TUC, and especially Bevin and Citrine, also wanted changes in the party, especially in terms of its relationship with the wider Labour movement.

There was resistance to any great changes, however, and naturally enough it came from the unreconstructed gradualist who was to remain party leader (with Lansbury as leader of the PLP) until October 1932, Henderson. The latter set about formalizing the conspiracy theory of 1931 with a view to obstructing radical changes in the party's structure, outlook, or policy. Thus his initial reaction to the result stated that the Conservatives' 'manœuvre' had succeeded 'beyond [their] most optimistic expectations'. The electorate had been 'duped', as it had been on previous occasions, and although Labour had suffered a 'severe setback' its total vote was a bedrock upon which to build. Even in this somewhat petulant outburst, however, his moderation shone through, as when he referred to Labour as 'the only effective bulwark against reaction and revolution'.[15] Henderson continued in this vein in the report on the election which he wrote, in his capacity as party secretary, for the NEC on 10 November.

[13] Lothian to Judge Richard Feetham, n.d. [Nov. 1931] (Lothian papers, GD 40/17/256/250–1).
[14] Maxton, 'What Next', *New Leader*, 6 Nov. 1931.
[15] *Manchester Guardian*, 29 Oct. 1931.

Once again, the conspiracy theories were laid on thick. After outlining the organizational problems Labour had faced, dismissing the notion that there had been any cooling off in the spirits of Labour activists, and protecting himself from attacks on his leadership by stating that some losses would have been inevitable whenever and however the election had been fought, he suggested reasons for Labour's reverse. First, he stressed that the defeat had not been as bad as it appeared; Labour had won only one-twelfth of the seats, but had obtained almost one-third of the votes cast; and to obtain so many votes under such adverse conditions was 'an achievement which rightly call[ed] for the pride and admiration of the Movement'. Ten factors, he argued, had helped the Government. These were: the ability to appeal to patriotism; the prestige of MacDonald and Snowden and the discrediting of the ex-ministers; extensive co-operation between the National parties in the constituencies; 'the most formidable press attack ever made at a General Election'; bias in the allocation of broadcasts; the threat of inflation if Labour won; attacks on the Labour administration's record on unemployment and expenditure; the appeal of tariffs as a policy 'to large numbers of people who had come to believe that it was better to try any policy to cure unemployment than to go on with unemployment at its present level'; the Post Office savings scare; and also, '[m]isrepresentation, false accusations of the most blatant and despicable kind, scare predictions, personalities—indeed, anything that was calculated to stir up panic fears and frighten the electorate was resorted to.' In short, the result was due to the unique nature of the election. Under the circumstances, Labour had done well, and if it persevered along the old lines it would be victorious next time. There was nothing to be gained by 'exaggerating [their] set-back or by allowing [them]selves to be stampeded into making false or ill-considered moves'. They had 'to prepare for the time when the nation w[ould] have recovered from its . . . hysteria and [be] prepared to give proper consideration to [their] policies and programme'.[16]

Many of these arguments were tendentious, to say the least. Many Labourites, whether the extreme left, the new PLP leadership, or the corporatists of the general council, were reluctant to brush aside Labour's defeat so deftly. And even Henderson had conceded that the record of the second Labour Government had been an electoral handicap to the party. It was Citrine, at a joint meeting of the general

[16] Labour Party NEC minutes, 10 Nov. 1931, 'Report on the General Election by the Secretary' (Labour Party papers).

council and the NEC on 10 November (from which Henderson was absent, ill), who shattered any idea that Labour could go on as it had since 1918. He stated bluntly that the party must examine how three men they had trusted could have turned on Labour and driven it to disaster. 'The feeling of the General Council', he added, 'was that they did not wish these men to return.' In reality, there had been very little prospect of their return anyway; but then Citrine really laid the law down:

They [the general council] did not seek in any shape or form to say what the Party was to do, but they did ask that the primary purpose of the creation of the Party should not be forgotten. It was created by the Trade Union Movement to do those things in Parliament which the Trade Union Movement found ineffectively performed by the two-Party system.[17]

For all the disclaimers, this was the declaration of the general council's attempt to take over the direction of the party. Citrine had been biding his time; now he struck, to good effect. Within a year the party was to be in some ways unrecognizable from the MacDonald–Henderson–Webb party of 1918–31.

III

'The most romantic side of the General Election is the statistical side,' opined the *Liberal Magazine* whimsically in November 1931. With due deference to that periodical, it must be stressed that beauty is in the eye of the beholder; and, for all the romance, it was not until 1982 that any systematic analysis of the election results was undertaken. Of necessity, this section must cover much the same ground as Close's article of that year, even though it is the result of original research and not derived from Close as such.[18]

The first point to be made is the obvious one—that the result, in terms of seats, was a massive triumph for the National Government, which won 554 of the 615 seats, and especially the Conservatives (470). It was also a horrendous set-back for Labour, which collapsed to 46 seats from its pre-dissolution 265. This huge disparity was unprecedented in modern British electoral history. Even if the Government were to collapse, the Conservatives had enough seats to

[17] Minutes of joint meeting of NEC and TUC general council, 10 Nov. 1931 (Labour Party papers, NEC minutes).

[18] D. H. Close, 'The Realignment of the British Electorate in 1931', *History*, 67 (1982), 393–404.

form a comfortably-based party administration for the duration of the 1931 Parliament. And, given the determination of Baldwin and Chamberlain to preserve the existing regime, there was no prospect even of that accession to Opposition strength. Only the secession of the 33 Samuelites—which came about over trade policy in 1932–3—could be expected to add any ballast to the non-ministerial benches.

Many observers, however, argued that Labour had been unfairly treated by the electoral system. Certainly the result under a national system of proportional representation would have been somewhat different (see Table 11.2). However, Labourites had been less keen on such arguments in 1929, when winning more seats than the Conservatives with fewer votes; and, over the following two years, when resisting Liberal demands for electoral reform. And even under PR, the Conservatives would have won a comfortable overall majority of 61, and the Government one of 211. Also, many more National—and Tory—voters were prevented from voting by unopposed returns than Labour supporters. Thus it was a conclusive result, however viewed, and especially when seen in comparison with the other great

Table 11.2. *Comparison of actual and PR results*

	Actual	PR	Discrepancy
Government			
Conservative	470	338	+132
Liberal	33	40	− 7
Liberal National	35	23	+ 12
National Labour	13	10	+ 3
National	3	2	+ 1
TOTAL	554	413	+141
Opposition			
Labour	46	180	−134
ILP	3	7	− 4
Unendorsed Labour	3	2	+ 1
Lloyd George Liberal	4	3	+ 1
CPGB	–	2	− 2
New Party	–	1	− 1
Other	5	7	− 2
TOTAL	61	202	−141

Table 11.3. *Twentieth-century electoral landslides*

	Leading party	% of total votes	Seats
1900	Con	51.1	402
1906	Lib	49.0	400
1918	Coaln	47.1	473
1924	Con	46.2	412
1931	Nat G	67.2	554
1935	Nat G	53.3	429
1945	Lab	48.0	393
1959	Con	49.4	365
1966	Lab	47.9	363
1983	Con	42.4	397

electoral landslides of the century (see Table 11.3). Thus even in terms of votes, Labour was heavily defeated. A closer analysis of comparable results bears out this verdict still further. This anaysis will be conducted primarily by looking at the parties' respective *votes* rather than their *poll shares* since the former gives a better indication of what actually happened.

In 49 seats there was a Conservative–Labour straight fight in both 1929 and 1931 (2/2 seats). In these divisions, the Tory vote increased by an average of 42.9 per cent, while that of Labour fell by 24.2 per cent. This reflected substantial Labour defections and a positive move of the electorate towards the Government and/or the Conservatives in a wide variety of constituencies.

Also in 49 seats there was a Conservative–Labour–Liberal clash in both years (3/3 seats). In these divisions, the Conservative vote increased by a mean of 47.6 per cent. Labour's vote fell by 22.9 per cent; significantly the Liberal decrease, 23.3 per cent, was even sharper, suggesting that within the National camp there was a positive move away from the Liberals and towards the Conservatives. Thus the Liberals' claim that it was no party victory was placed heavily in doubt. The pattern of movement from Liberal to Conservative was also reflected in the three Conservative–Liberal 2/2 seats, where the former rose by 49.5 per cent and the latter fell by 25.0 per cent, although it would be rash to make much of so small a sample.

Meanwhile, there were 236 seats where the Liberals stood against Labour and the Tories in 1929 but not in 1931 (3/2 seats). This meant that there were 1929 Liberal votes to be picked up; often it would have been necessary for one of the remaining two parties to add a substantial proportion of these to its vote in order to win the seat. Yet, even here, the Labour vote fell, on average, by 10.2 per cent, while the Conservatives increased by 79.7 per cent. Thus in seats where Labour needed to gain new votes to be successful, it was unable even to poll its 1929 strength.

It is profitable to pursue this line of investigation further by breaking these figures down according to the social-occupational and regional types of seats involved. Both the 2/2 and 3/3 seats were small samples and should therefore be treated with caution, but in so far as they confirm the patterns which will be drawn from the 3/2 seats, they are worthy of discussion.

The figures in Table 11.4 show a number of significant points. The Conservative increase was highest in mining, textile (one only), and high-unemployment seats. This suggests that they were starting from a lower base, but also, first, that in the conditions of 1931 a normally apathetic and residual anti-Labour vote in strongly Labour areas felt it had a chance of turning the socialists out; and secondly, that these areas were particularly attracted by programmes perceived as offering a return to prosperity. The Conservative increase was also large in the working-class seats, where the same factors probably applied. In middle-class, low-unemployment, and agricultural seats the rise was also marked, although, since these were already pro-Conservative anyway, less spectacular.

Table 11.4. *Vote changes in 2/2 seats*

		Percentage	
	Number	Con Increase	Lab Decrease
Average 2/2 Seat	49	42.9	24.2
Middle Class	6	43.6	32.3
Working Class	14	48.0	15.6
Agricultural	2	30.8	29.0
Mining	11	56.1	10.3
Textile	1	57.7	26.2
High Unemployment	18	58.3	31.8
Low Unemployment	2	31.1	42.7

The Labour vote can be seen to have fallen heaviest in the areas where its gains in 1929 had been most tentative, and where the loss of the 'respectable' image afforded by MacDonald and Snowden would have done it the greatest harm—middle-class, low-unemployment, and agricultural seats. However, defections were also heavy in high-unemployment seats, suggesting that in those areas Labour was held at least partly responsible for economic distress, and also that the Government's proposals had positive attractions. The Labour decrease was lowest in the working-class and mining seats. However, it must be remembered that many seats fell into both categories; and if the five non-mining working-class seats are taken alone, the Labour decrease was 21.5 rather than 15.6 per cent. The results *in seats* tend to bear out the view that it was in mining areas that the Labour support was at its most solid in 1931—not surprisingly, given bitter mining memories of the last Conservative Government—though even there, the party's vote slipped from the heady heights of 1929 and many seats were lost.

The 3/3 seats bore out many of these conclusions (see Table 11.5). The Conservative vote rose sharpest in the mining seat (one only) and the middle-class seats. This, it seems, was at the expense of both the other parties, but especially the Liberals. The Tory vote also increased

Table 11.5. *Vote changes in 3/3 seats*

	Percentage			
	Number	Con Increase	Lab Decrease	Lib Decrease
Average 3/3 seat	49	47.6	22.9	23.3
Middle Class	18	63.0	21.1	39.1
Working Class	10	37.1	23.1	12.8
Agricultural	15	30.5	21.7	16.6
Mining	1	83.8	15.6	33.6
Textile[a]	4	31.8	29.3	1.1
High Unemployment	12	45.7	23.7	15.2
Low Unemployment	11	37.4	20.1	25.1

[a] One of these seats was Darwen, where there was special pressure on National voters to vote for the Liberal leader, Sir Herbert Samuel. If Darwen is excluded as exceptional, the other three seats showed an average Tory increase of 43.7, and an average Liberal fall of 8.2 per cent.

heavily in areas of high unemployment, and substantially in the others. The Labour vote fell heavily. The average was exceeded in the textile, high-unemployment, and working-class seats, suggesting large-scale defections as a result of Labour's economic failure and the attractions of Conservative economic policies. The fact that Labour did almost as badly as average in the middle-class and agricultural seats, in which it was starting from a very low base, was very discouraging for future efforts in those areas. In the mining seat the Labour vote held up better, but even so a fall of nearly one-sixth and the loss of the seat (Penistone) could hardly be welcomed. The Liberals' fortunes fluctuated widely. They fared especially badly in mining and middle-class seats, and best in working-class, high-unemployment, and agricultural divisions. Even excluding Darwen, the Liberal vote held up better in textile seats than in others.

Most of these impressions can be confirmed by reference to the 236 3/2 seats (see Table 11.6). The increases in the Conservative vote were ubiquitous and in many constituencies exceeded 100 per cent. The average in itself was very high. Below it were low-unemployment, agricultural, and middle-class divisions, in all of which the Tory vote would have been quite high in 1929. The rise was above average in the other types of seat, probably because of the attractiveness of the National Government and protectionism, and the lower base from

Table 11.6. *Vote changes in 3/2 seats*

	Percentage			
	Number	Con Increase	Lab Decrease	Average poll share 1929
Average 3/2 seat	236	79.7	10.2	22.4
Middle class	79	73.9	11.0	22.8
Working class	43	96.4	7.3	21.7
Agricultural	32	64.8	+1.3	28.5
Mining	25	118.9	7.9	20.0
Textile	5	90.1	13.3	26.6
High Unemployment	52	86.2	12.2	18.9
Low Unemployment	45	71.8	4.5	26.3

which the Tories were starting. Dole cuts, on this and all the other evidence, did little electoral damage, the implication being either that the unemployed voted Labour already or that they were more interested in finding work than having cuts restored.

The Labour vote fell on average by just over 10 per cent, a poor performance considering that to gain any seats, and to retain many they had won in 1929 on a minority vote in three-cornered contests, they had needed an increase in their vote. Labour did best in the agricultural seats, marginally increasing its vote, starting from a very low base indeed. This suggested some rural Liberals were less ready than their urban counterparts to vote Tory: of course, in many such areas the battle was still primarily one between Conservatives and Liberals. Indeed, it is possible that in these areas some 1929 Labour voters either abstained or voted Conservative, with their places being taken in the Labour ranks by Liberals who were more determined to oppose the Tories. Similar considerations probably applied also in the low-unemployment seats, where Labour also performed better than average. In the working-class and mining seats, Labour also bettered its mean, suggesting a greater degree of loyalty in those areas. Even so, its vote fell. The heaviest falls came in middle-class seats, where Labour's perceived moderation and respectability of 1929 had been replaced by images of extremism and irresponsibility; in high-unemployment seats, where Labour was damaged by its image as a party of depression; and finally, in textile seats, where it was damaged by its record in office and the misfortunes of that industry and its workers since 1929, as well as the desire for tariff protection and the apparent start of a return to prosperity during the campaign.

But of course, regional variations also had significance. As in all social types of constituencies, so in all regions, Labour did badly; even in its best, Wales, where it retained 15 of the 35 seats, it fell back heavily from its *annus mirabilis* of 1929, when it had won 25. In that year nine regions had accounted for 226 of Labour's 287 seats (see Table 11.7). Although some of these areas remained Labour's least weak, and indeed, with Wales, accounted for all but two of the party's seats in 1931 (the 46th was Cripps's at East Bristol), the massacre of Labour MPs in these, its strongest areas, was a terrific blow. Many of the regions of fresh advance in 1929, such as the West Midlands, saw a terrible set-back, and in most Labour would only be able in 1935 to recover its disappointing position of 1924.

Again, the blow—and conversely, the Conservative success—came

Table 11.7. *Labour in selected regions, 1923–1935*

Region		No. of Seats	Seats won by Labour 1923	1924	1929	1931	1935
A.	London	62	22	19	36	5	22
B.	Outer London	41	14	8	19	4	11
J.	East Midlands	31	12	8	19	3	8
M.	West Midlands	33	5	5	17	–	4
N.	Western Lancastria	31	6	6	13	1	5
O.	Eastern Lancastria	41	16	11	28	4	12
P.	Yorkshire, West Riding	42	24	24	34	7	25
S.	North-Eastern England	31	14	17	24	2	14
U.	Scotland	71	34	26	36	3	20
TOTAL		383	147	124	226	29	131
TOTAL SEATS WON BY LABOUR			191	151	287	46	154

in terms of votes as well as seats (see Table 11.8). In all cases this was bad news for Labour. Even so, the decreases varied in scale. They were heaviest in London, the West Midlands, western Lancastria, and Scotland, and lightest in north-eastern England and the East Midlands. The Conservatives rose especially in the areas where they had been weakest in 1929. Thus even in terms of votes, the story made miserable reading for Labourites. They were operating in a new electoral landscape, where straight fights were the norm, and their failure even to maintain the levels of 1929, which in themselves would not have been sufficient to retain many seats, meant disaster. It was no longer enough to keep the 1929 vote. Labour had to advance, and this it failed signally to do. The increasingly obvious long-term debility of the Liberals also meant that the straight fights which characterized 1931 would become the norm in years to come. In 1935 there were 389 straight fights—only 20 less than in 1931—as opposed to only 98 in 1929. Thus when in 1935 Labour slightly exceeded its 1929 poll share in 1935, it won nothing like as many seats. The electoral landscape had undergone an earthquake which had left Labour at the wrong side of a cavernous ravine.

The news for the official Liberals was at least as bad as for Labour. They had become, due to the scale of the administration's victory, irrelevant to the fate of the National Government. They added a

Table 11.8. *Vote changes in 3/2 seats in selected regions (%)*

	Con Increase	Lab Decrease	Average Lib poll share 1929
National average, 3/2 seats	79.7	10.2	22.4
London	80.4	23.8	20.0
Outer London	81.7	12.2	21.3
East Midlands	98.1	8.2	24.4
West Midlands	61.0	18.9	17.7
Western Lancastria	74.6	27.2	20.0
Eastern Lancastria	81.8	15.7	20.0
Yorkshire, West Riding	103.6	15.8	21.8
North-Eastern England	100.2	5.1	19.8
Scotland	83.8	17.7	18.0

veneer of National unity, true, which greatly reassured MacDonald; it was for that reason that they would be allowed to differ from the Cabinet's decision to implement protection, without having to resign. But it was only a veneer; few Government supporters were sorry when they resigned in September 1932. The election result itself had left the Samuelites with only 33 seats, 2 less than the Simonites; and, as the analysis of 3/3 seats showed, their candidates fared badly when exposed to the icy blast of Conservative opposition. Indeed, 9 seats were lost to the Tories; although that figure was offset by 16 gains (14 from Labour), the implications for the future were bleak, especially if at the next election the Tories opposed them in all seats and Labour staged a recovery.

The Liberal Nationals and National Labour were in a stronger position, in so far as they were prepared to support protectionism and so able to remain in alliance with the Conservatives. However, they were both consigned to a greater or lesser degree to the role of client parties; they would never be able to expand into mass parties in their own right or, in the case of National Labour, anything more than a personal following for successive MacDonalds.

For the extremist parties there was even less cheer in the results. Of 26 Communist candidates, two of whom spent the campaign in prison, 21 lost their deposits. Their largest poll share was won by the leading south Wales mining Communist, Arthur Horner, but even he could gain only 31.9 per cent of the poll in a straight fight with Labour at

East Rhondda. On average, each CPGB candidate received only 8.2 per cent of the votes cast. Even in their secondary objective of keeping Labour MPs out of Parliament, they had only slightly more success; they were probably decisive in Labour's loss of two apparently safe seats, at Sheffield, Attercliffe, and West Fife. In the latter case, the Conservative took the seat of Adamson, the former Scottish Secretary; and in 1935 the same Communist candidate, William Gallacher, was to capture the seat. But the failure of 'class against class' to benefit even at the depths of Labour's difficulties in 1931 suggested to some that a new line would soon have to be taken.

Mosley's New Party fared even worse, 22 of its 24 candidates losing their deposits and none of those 22 obtaining one vote in twenty cast: their average poll share was 2.0 per cent. This was increased to an overall figure of 4.1 per cent by the more creditable performance of Sellick Davies at Merthyr (30.6 per cent in a straight fight with Labour) and Mosley himself at Stoke (24.1 per cent, but coming third). It was little wonder that Mosley soon began to move on other lines.

What of the future? Many Labourites felt the election had been an aberration; next time they would win. But this was to ignore the disastrously weak base offered to Labour for further electoral advance by the 1931 result. The state of the Liberal Party suggested—as was to be the case—that there would be almost as many straight fights at the next election: Labour could expect no great help from third-party interventions. And in many areas its opponents had built up substantial leads which would be very difficult to overcome. As Table 11.9 shows, there would have to be a general swing of over 17.5 per cent to Labour for it even to regain its 1929 position of 287 seats; and of 20.0 per cent for it to have a bare overall majority of 5. That would involve a massive turnaround, and Labour, as might have been predicted in the aftermath of 1931, was to do little during the rest of the decade to suggest that it was capable of such a transfiguration. Indeed, by the time of the 1935 election the economy was performing better than for some years; there were areas of severe depression but they were never extensive enough, and often not pro-Labour enough in themselves, to furnish the party with a majority. True, there were occasionally heavy swings against the Government at by-elections, but the trend was never sufficiently sustained to throw the Government from office at a general election. By 1939–40 the economy, spurred on by rearmament,

Table 11.9. *Electoral prospects post–1931*

Party	% Lead over Labour						
	0.0–10.0	10.1–15.0	15.1–20.0	20.1–25.0	25.1–30.0	30.1–35.0	35.1–40.0
Conservative	39	32	36	27	27	27	26
Liberal	6	3	1	3	1	5	1
Liberal National	4	1	3	2	4	–	1
National Labour	2	1	2	–	2	1	2
Other	3	1	–	–	–	1	–
TOTAL	54	38	42	32	34	34	30
CUMULATIVE TOTAL	54	92	134	166	200	234	264
CUMULATIVE TOTAL[a]	100	138	180	212	246	280	310

[a] including 46 seats, 1931.

was doing still better; there was little to suggest a Labour victory then, either, with by-elections often showing swings towards the Government. The realignment of 1931 had set a new electoral mould which was only broken by the ferment of the Second World War. Thus far from being, as Henderson claimed, in any way a triumph for Labour, the general election of 1931 was a National, and especially a Conservative, victory of a profundity scarcely realized at the time.

CONCLUSION

THE 1931 general election and its outcome were not a huge confidence trick, a Conservative protectionist ramp, or the result of any kind of capitalists' or bankers' conspiracy; not the result of wilful treachery on the part of MacDonald; and not the result of a conspiracy on the part of Labour's enemies to deprive the party of office or to discredit it. These points are not novel; they have been made by many historians before; but they need to be reiterated for the record. Most of these arguments were sheer mythology, conspiracy theory little elevated from the level of the *Protocols of the Elders of Zion*, designed to excuse the failings of Labour in office and to explain the decisive rejection of 'socialism' at the polls. For neither the first nor the last time, Labour used such excuses to avoid facing harsh realities.

The Labour Party had had, in fact, little prospect of maintaining its current position of 287 seats, let alone of winning an overall majority, since the end of 1929. The slump meant it was saddled with the image of a party of depression, especially since its own efforts to improve matters were so feeble. Divisions within the Labour movement and the increasing debility of the leadership, allied to mounting financial and organizational difficulties, had merely emphasized the party's poor prospects. Not for nothing did some Labourites welcome the demise of the Government in August 1931. But two things soon became clear. First, the party's problems had not been due solely or even mainly to MacDonald and Snowden. Henderson was little improvement, yet he was the best the party could do. And, in addition, the issues on which Labour now hoped to capitalize—'socialist' rhetoric, opposition to the economies, and defence of free trade—were insufficient to hide the record of the late ministry, the lack of real policies, or the perceivedly bad behaviour of the ex-ministers. In July 1931 Labour had been heading for conclusive defeat; the events of the next couple of months merely worsened its position. By the time the campaign opened on 7 October, Labour had no chance whatever of victory.

By contrast, the Conservatives had been expecting victory on the scale of 1924, and the events of August to October merely confirmed the impression. Problems of leadership, policy, and organization, faced in the aftermath of defeat in 1929, had been resolved; Baldwin was ready to lead a united, protectionist party Government whenever the chance might come. Ultimately, he had to take second place to MacDonald, but the 'free hand', accepted with reluctance by the Conservatives, meant they were still free to impose tariffs after the election. Given that they formed over three-quarters of the new House of Commons, and that they had mostly fought on frankly protectionist lines, there was no reason why they should not have done so. The existence of the National Government might have increased the number of seats they won, but did not make a decisive difference.

For the Liberals, 1929–31 had been a disastrous time. Neither the split with the Simonites nor the small number of candidates nominated in 1931 was unpredictable after the events of those years. The size of the secession, and the departure of Lloyd George, were perhaps less to have been expected. But the collapse of the Liberal Party in 1931 was the logical consequence of recent events within the party. However, the true impact of this collapse could be disguised for a time by Liberal participation in the National administration.

But the 1931 general election was not just a crushing victory for the National Government. It also represented an electoral realignment on a significant scale, as the three-party system of the 1920s was very largely buried. This was not only because the Liberal Nationals and National Labour moved closer and closer towards the Conservatives. For the foreseeable future the official Liberals, even after their departure from the Cabinet in September 1932 and from the Government benches the following year, would be unable to force a large number of three-cornered fights (from which Labour had benefited so much in 1929). The 1920s had seen Labour in problems when trying to get extensive middle-ground support; now it was to find it even more difficult. By contrast, the Government seemed moderate, competent, and could long claim to be made up of the best of all parties. Thus in the less fraught conditions of 1935 Labour could recover its vote of 1929, and even slightly exceed it (38.0 as opposed to 37.1 per cent), but, under the changed circumstances, win only 154 seats as opposed to 287. In addition, the question of whether Labour could advance beyond that level of support was unanswered. Labour seemed to be condemned to Opposition for the foreseeable future. It is probable that the peacetime election due by 1940 would have confirmed this. The Second World War and its consequences were the factors which enabled Labour to win parliamentary majorities.

Prior to that, the realignment of 1931, allied to Liberal demise and Labour's perceived unfitness to govern, made its position very weak. Even if everyone did not realize this at the time, it is clear in retrospect.

The result of the 1931 general election had a number of implications for the rest of the decade. First, it was clear that protective tariffs of some kind would be introduced with a degree of imperial preference, as indeed they were in 1932. In the light of this fact the presence of the Samuelite Liberals in the Government for the first year of its existence was anomalous, wasting Government time and energy, and discrediting the official Liberals even further. And after their departure, it must be questioned whether some of the Tories' other allies—the ailing MacDonald as premier, Simon performing poorly as Foreign Secretary, Runciman being awkward over tariffs at the Board of Trade, and Thomas leaking budget secrets—did much to strengthen the administration. One need not be a Conservative partisan to conjecture that a purely Tory Government might have served the country as well if not better, especially since then there might have been a somewhat more sizeable parliamentary Opposition to keep it up to the mark. However, this is not to subscribe to the 'Devil's decade' view that the National Governments were massively incompetent. While it is important not to forget that for many people the 1930s were indeed a decade of searing poverty, unemployment, and even hunger, much of the country was far from depressed. After the peak of unemployment had been reached in late 1932, the economy and the bulk of the population outside the depressed areas like south Wales and north-eastern England became more prosperous. The cuts of 1931 were restored in 1934, and the National Governments could point, if not to spectacular success, then, at least, to a record of consistent, moderate achievement, while avoiding the extremes to which most of Europe was falling prey. For many people that was an agreeable contrast to the frequent upheavals of 1918–31.

Labour could have drawn numerous conclusions from 1931. Henderson was especially keen to avoid any great change in the power-structure or outlook of the Labour movement, so his report on the election stressed that it had been a freak necessitating no new departures. The TUC, however, had long wanted change. The revivification of the national joint council (later the national council of labour) provided the instrument through which it could exert greater control, and the experience of the second Labour Government and the cataclysmic defeat in 1931 meant people of Henderson's outlook could do little to prevent their taking over. However, things did not go all the general council's way; the PLP in 1931–5 was far to the left of its former position. Hence the corporatist/fundamentalist split of August to October 1931 was perpetuated and institutionalized, which did the party little good. One clear benefit of 1931 was that the party began to realize the need for detailed policy research, which was carried out to a greater extent than ever before, even if some aspects—for example, drawing up blueprints for nationalized industries—were somewhat neglected.

The pattern for the leadership of the parties during the decade was set by the events of 1931. Baldwin was now almost unassailable at the head of the Conservative Party, partly because most of the new intake of Tory MPs (over 200) would feel gratitude and loyalty to him, and partly because he was now cushioned against the right-wingers who had caused him such difficulties in 1929–31. This is not to say that he would never again have problems; but he was able to stay on until he wanted to retire, in 1937, after a further spell (1935–7) as Prime Minister. Chamberlain, installed at the Treasury after the election in place of Snowden, was now the clear heir apparent, with his only real rival earlier in the year, Hailsham, a long way behind (he became War Secretary). MacDonald was head of National Labour for as long as he wanted to be; indeed, the main question which was to trouble it for the rest of its existence, that is, until 1945, was to find a role other than that of support for him and, subsequently, his son, Malcolm. The Liberal National Party was a less artificial body; even so, Simon's position at its head was never seriously challenged as he went from major office of state to major office of state for the rest of the decade. In the absence of Lloyd George, who formally resigned the leadership after the election, Samuel remained at the head of the official Liberal Party, a thankless task and one he performed with little panache or adeptness. As Labour in Parliament moved to the left, the chimera of Lib–Lab co-operation, upon which he had been so keen, disappeared. And what of Labour? Lansbury, as the only remaining ex-Cabinet Minister, became leader of the PLP, and, in October 1932, party leader, following the resignation of Henderson, who was still out of Parliament, ill, preoccupied with the disarmament conference at Geneva and upset about the direction in which the party was going. When Lansbury resigned shortly before the 1935 election, Attlee, who had deputized for the leader on previous occasions, was elected in his place, ostensibly as a stopgap. When this was confirmed after the election, it became clear that Labour had learnt one wrong lesson from 1931: one of Attlee's attractions was that he did not seem much of a leader, in contrast to MacDonald. Men who might have proved more effective in the 1930s—if not the 1940s—like Greenwood, Morrison, or even Dalton and Alexander, were kept from the leadership largely by Attlee's seeming mediocrity and the fact that he had managed to save his seat in 1931.

Another clear implication for Britain in the 1930s emanating from the 1931 election was that it would not, unlike the rest of Europe, suffer unduly from political extremism. Both the Communists and the proto-fascist New Party polled derisorily, despite offering clear alternatives to a system apparently in crisis. If they could not profit at a time like that, it was unlikely that they could never do so. A country in search of solutions preferred a new mixture of the old faces and ideas.

The events of 1931 remain fascinating to this day. The election was not 'just another general election'; many of its central features were unusual, even unique. Yet despite that, most of its features and consequences were logical results of political developments in Britain since the First World War. The general election of 1931 was by no means as aberrant as has often been alleged.

APPENDIX 1. BRITISH GENERAL ELECTION RESULTS 1918–1945

1918 (Turn-out 57.2%)

	Votes	% share	Candidates	MPs	Unopposed
Coaln Con	3,472,738	32.5	362	332	41
Coaln Lib	1,396,590	12.6	145	127	23
Coaln Lab	53,962	0.4	5	4	1
Coaln Ind	9,274	0.1	1	1	–
Coaln NDP	156,834	1.5	18	9	–
[TOTAL COALN]	[5,089,398]	[47.1]	[531]	[473]	[65]
Con	671,454	6.1	83	50	–
Lab	2,245,777	20.8	361	57	11
Lib	1,388,784	13.0	276	36	4
Co-op	57,785	0.6	10	1	–
Irish Natst	238,197	2.2	60	7	1
Nat Pty	94,389	0.9	26	2	–
Sinn Fein	497,107	4.6	102	73	25
Others	503,927	4.7	174	8	1
TOTAL	10,786,818	100.0	1,623	707	107

1922 (Turn-out 73.0%)

	Votes	% share	Candidates	MPs	Unopposed
Con	5,502,298	38.5	482	344	42
Lab	4,237,349	29.7	414	142	4
Lib	2,668,143	18.9	333	62	6
Nat Lib	1,471,317	9.9	152	53	4
CPGB	33,637	0.2	5	1	–
Irish Natst	102,667	0.4	4	3	1
Others	376,919	2.4	51	10	–
TOTAL	14,392,330	100.0	1,441	615	57

1923 (Turn-out 71.1%)

	Votes	% share	Candidates	MPs	Unopposed
Con	5,514,541	38.0	536	258	35
Lab	4,439,780	30.7	427	191	3
Lib	4,301,481	29.7	457	158	11
CPGB	39,448	0.2	4	–	–
Irish Natst	97,993	0.4	4	3	1
Others	154,452	1.0	18	5	–
TOTAL	14,547,695	100.0	1,446	615	50

1924 (Turn-out 77.0%)

	Votes	% share	Candidates	MPs	Unopposed
Con	7,854,523	46.8	534	412	16
Lab	5,489,087	33.3	514	151	9
Lib	2,928,737	17.8	339	40	6
CPGB	55,346	0.3	8	1	–
Constitutionalist	185,075	1.2	12	7	–
Irish Natst	–	–	1	1	1
Sinn Fein	46,457	0.2	8	–	–
Others	81,054	0.4	12	3	–
TOTAL	16,640,279	100.0	1,428	615	32

1929 (Turn-out 76.3%)

	Votes	% share	Candidates	MPs	Unopposed
Con	8,656,225	38.1	590	260	4
Lab	8,370,417	37.1	569	287	–
Lib	5,308,738	23.6	519	59	–
CPGB	50,634	0.2	25	–	–
Irish Natst	24,177	0.1	4	3	3
Others	238,184	0.9	29	6	–
TOTAL	22,648,375	100.0	1,730	615	7

1931 (Turn-out 76.4%)

	Votes	% share	Candidates	MPs	Unopposed
Con	11,905,925	55.0	518	470	49
Lib	1,372,595	6.5	111	33	5
Nat	100,193	0.5	4	3	–
Lib Nat	809,302	3.7	41	35	7
Nat Lab	341,370	1.5	20	13	–
[TOTAL NAT]	[14,529,385]	[67.2]	[694]	[554]	[61]
Lab	6,324,737	29.3	491	46	5
Lloyd George Lib	103,528	0.5	6	4	–
ILP	260,344	1.2	19	3	–
Unendorsed Lab	64,549	0.3	6	3	1
CPGB	74,824	0.3	26	–	–
Irish Natst	123,053	0.4	3	2	–
New Party	36,377	0.2	24	–	–
Others	139,576	0.6	23	3	–
TOTAL	21,656,373	100.0	1,292	615	67

1935 (Turn-out 71.1)%

	Votes	% share	Candidates	MPs	Unopposed
Con	10,496,300	47.8	515	387	23
Nat	53,189	0.3	4	1	–
Lib Nat	866,354	3.7	44	33	3
Nat Lab	339,811	1.5	20	8	–
[TOTAL NAT]	[11,755,654]	[53.3]	[583]	[429]	[26]
Lab	8,325,491	38.0	552	154	13
Lib	1,443,093	6.7	161	21	–
ILP	139,577	0.6	17	4	–
CPGB	27,117	0.1	2	1	–
Irish Natst	101,494	0.3	2	2	–
Others	204,628	1.0	31	4	1
TOTAL	21,997,054	100.0	1,348	615	40

1945 (Turn-out 72.8%)

	Votes	% share	Candidates	MPs	Unopposed
Con	9,101,099	36.2	559	197	1
Nat	133,179	0.5	10	2	–
Lib Nat	737,732	2.9	49	11	–
[TOTAL NAT]	[9,972,010]	[39.6]	[618]	[210]	[1]
Lab	11,967,746	48.0	603	393	2
Lib	2,252,430	9.0	306	12	–
CPGB	102,780	0.4	21	2	–
Common Wealth	110,634	0.5	23	1	–
ILP	46,769	0.2	5	3	–
Irish Natst	148,078	0.4	3	2	–
Others	494,748	1.9	104	17	–
TOTAL	25,095,195	100.0	1,683	640	3

APPENDIX 2. REGIONS USED

THE following are regions of Britain as defined in T. Stannage, *Baldwin Thwarts the Opposition: The British General Election of 1935* (London, 1980), 249–58. While they are open to objections, I have kept to his format to make comparison easier.

A. London (61 constituencies, 62 seats)

All the London boroughs, i.e. those within the London County Council area.

B. Outer London (41)

All Middlesex county seats (10)
Essex county seat: Romford (1)
Kent county seats: Chislehurst, Dartford, Gravesend (3)
Surrey county seats: Epsom, Mitcham (2)
Boroughs: Bromley, Croydon N & S, Ealing, East Ham N & S, Edmonton, Hornsey, Kingston-upon-Thames, Leyton E & W, Richmond, Rochester, Chatham, Rochester, Gillingham, Tottenham N & S, Walthamstow E & W, West Ham Plaistow, West Ham Silvertown, West Ham Stratford, West Ham Upton, Willesden E & W, Wimbledon (25)

C. South-East England (22 constituencies, 23 seats)

Kent county seats: Ashford, Canterbury, Dover, Faversham, Isle of Thanet, Maidstone, Sevenoaks, Tonbridge (8)
Surrey county seats: Chertsey, Eastern, Farnham, Guildford, Reigate (5)
All Sussex county seats (6)
Boroughs: Brighton (2), Hastings, Hythe (3/4)

D. South-Central England (15)

Both Oxfordshire county seats (2)
All Berkshire county seats (3)
All Buckinghamshire county seats (3)
All Hertfordshire county seats (5)
Boroughs: Oxford, Reading (2)

E. The Severn (24)

All Somerset county seats (6)
Devon county seats: Honiton, Tiverton (2)
All Gloucestershire county seats (4)
Wiltshire county seats: Chippenham, Westbury, Swindon (3)
Boroughs: Bath, Bristol C, E, N, S, & W, Cheltenham, Exeter, Gloucester (9)

F. Wessex (18 constituencies, 19 seats)

All Dorset county seats (4)
All Hampshire county seats (7)
Wiltshire county seats: Devizes, Salisbury (2)
Boroughs: Bournemouth, Portsmouth C, N, & S, Southampton (2), (6)

G. Western Peninsula (13)

All Cornwall county seats (5)
Devon county seats: Barnstaple, South Molton, Tavistock, Torquay, Totnes (5)
Boroughs: Plymouth Devonport, Drake & Sutton (3)

H. East Anglia (29 constituencies, 30 seats)

All Norfolk county seats (5)
All Suffolk county seats (5)
All Bedfordshire county seats (3)
Cambridgeshire (1)
Huntingdonshire (1)
Isle of Ely (1)
Essex county seats: Chelmsford, Colchester, Epping, Harwich, Maldon, Saffron Walden, South-Eastern (7)
Boroughs: Cambridge, Great Yarmouth, Ilford, Ipswich, Norwich (2), Southend-on-Sea (6/7)

I. Lincoln & Rutland (9)

All Lincolnshire & Rutland county seats (7)
Boroughs: Grimsby, Lincoln (2)

J. East Midlands (30 constituencies, 31 seats)

All Derbyshire county seats (8)
All Leicestershire county seats (4)
All Northamptonshire county seats (4)
All Nottinghamshire county seats (5)
Boroughs: Derby (2), Leicester E, S, & W, Northampton, Nottingham C, E, S, & W (9/10)

K. North-West Midlands (11)

Cheshire county seats: Altrincham, Chester, Crewe, Eddisbury, Knutsford, Macclesfield, Northwich (7)
Boroughs: Newcastle-upon-Lyme, Stoke-on-Trent Burslem, Stoke-on-Trent Hanley, Stoke-on-Trent Stoke (4)

L. Salop/Staffs. (10)

All Shropshire county seats (4)
Staffordshire county seats: Burton, Cannock, Leek, Lichfield, Stafford, Stone (6)

M. West Midlands (33)

Boroughs: all Birmingham seats (12), Coventry, Dudley, Smethwick, Walsall, Wednesbury, West Bromwich, Wolverhampton E, W, & Bilston, Worcester (22)
Herefordshire county seats: Hereford, Leominster (2)
Staffordshire county seat: Kingswinford (1)
Warwickshire county seats: Nuneaton, Rugby, Tamworth, Warwick & Leamington (4)
All Worcestershire county seats (4)

N. Western Lancastria (30 constituencies, 31 seats)

Cheshire county seat: Wirral (1)
Lancashire county seats: Chorley, Fylde, Lancaster, Lonsdale, Newton, Ormskirk, Waterloo, Widnes (8)
Boroughs: Barrow, Birkenhead E & W, Blackpool, Bootle, all Liverpool seats (11), Preston (2), St Helens, Southport, Wallasey, Warrington (21/22)

O. Eastern Lancastria (37 constituencies, 41 seats)

Cheshire county seat: Stalybridge & Hyde (1)
Lancashire county seats: Clitheroe, Darwen, Farnworth, Heywood & Ratcliffe, Middleton & Prestwich, Mossley, Royton, Stretford, Westhoughton (10)
Boroughs: Accrington, Ashton-under-Lyne, Blackburn (2), Bolton (2), Burnley, Bury, Eccles, Leigh, all Manchester seats (10), Oldham (2), Rochdale, Rossendale, Salford N, S, & W, Stockport (2), Wigan (26/30)

P. West Riding Area (42)

Yorkshire WR county seats: Colne Valley, Doncaster, Don Valley, Elland, Hemsworth, Keighley, Normanton, Penistone, Pontefract, Pudsey & Otley, Rother Valley, Rothwell, Shipley, Skipton, Sowerby, Spen Valley, Wentworth (17)
Boroughs: Barnsley, Batley & Morley, all Bradford seats (4), Dewsbury, Halifax, Huddersfield, all Leeds seats (6), Nelson & Colne, Rotherham, all Sheffield seats (7), Wakefield (25)

Q. Remainder of Yorkshire (13)

Yorkshire ER county seats: Buckrose, Holderness, Howdenshire (3)
Yorkshire NR county seats: Richmond, Scarborough & Whitby, Thirsk & Malton (3)
Yorkshire WR county seats: Barkston Ash, Ripon (2)
Boroughs: All Hull seats (4), York (5)

R. Cumbria (6)

All Cumberland county seats (4)
Westmorland (1)
Borough: Carlisle (1)

S. North-East England (30 constituencies, 31 seats)

All Durham county seats (11)
All Northumberland county seats (3)
Yorkshire NR county seat: Cleveland (1)

Boroughs: Darlington, Gateshead, Hartlepools, Middlesborough E & W, Morpeth, all Newcastle-upon-Tyne seats (4), South Shields, Stockton-on-Tees, Sunderland (2), Tynemouth, Wallsend (15/16)

T. Wales (35)

All seats in Wales (35)

U. Scotland (70 constituencies, 71 seats)

All seats in Scotland (70/71)

V. Northern Ireland (9 constituencies, 12 seats)

All seats in Northern Ireland (9/12)

W. Universities (7 constituencies, 12 seats)

Cambridge (2), Combined English (2), Combined Scottish (3), London, Oxford (2), Queen's Belfast, Wales (12)

SELECT BIBLIOGRAPHY

Manuscript Collections

Public Records

Cabinet: CAB 23 (Cabinet conclusions, 1929–31)
CAB 27 (Cabinet committees)
CP 203(31)
CP 203(31) (Revise)
CP 243(31)
CP 247(31)
NE (31)
Prime Minister's office: PREM 1
Treasury: T 171

Private papers

Addison papers (Bodleian Library, Oxford).
Alexander papers (Churchill College, Cambridge).
Altrincham papers [Sir Edward Grigg] (Microfilm at Bodleian Librar Oxford).
Amulree papers (Bodleian Library, Oxford).
Astor papers (Library, University of Reading).
Attlee papers (Churchill College, Cambridge).
Baldwin papers (Library, University of Cambridge).
Ballard, Albert papers (Sheffield Archives Office).
Beaverbrook papers (House of Lords Record Office).
Bevin papers (Churchill College, Cambridge, and Modern Records Centr University of Warwick).
Bridgeman papers (Shropshire Record Office, Shrewsbury).
Butler papers (Trinity College, Cambridge).
Chamberlain, Sir Austen papers (Library, University of Birmingham).
Chamberlain, Neville papers (Library, University of Birmingham).
Citrine papers (British Library of Political and Economic Science).
Cripps papers (Nuffield College, Oxford).
Croft papers (Churchill College, Cambridge).

Cunliffe-Lister, Sir Philip—see Swinton papers.
Dalton papers (British Library of Political and Economic Science).
Davies, Lord of Llandinam papers (National Library of Wales, Aberystwyth).
Dawson papers (Bodleian Library, Oxford).
Denman, R.D.—see Staffield House papers.
Dynevor Muniments [C.A.U. Rhys] (Dyfed Archives Office, Carmarthen).
Elliot papers (National Library of Scotland, Edinburgh).
Fisher, H. A. L. papers (Bodleian Library, Oxford).
Gilmour, Sir John papers (Scottish Record Office, Edinburgh).
Glyn, R. C. G. papers (Berkshire Record Office, Reading).
Graham Pole, David papers (Borthwick Institute of Historical Research, York).
Griffiths, James papers (National Library of Wales, Aberystwyth).
Grigg, Sir Edward—see Altrincham papers.
Hankey papers (Churchill College, Cambridge).
Haydn Jones, Henry papers (National Library of Wales, Aberystwyth).
Headlam, Cuthbert papers (Durham County Record Office, Durham).
Henderson papers (Labour Party Library, London).
Heneage, A. P. papers (Lincolnshire Archives Office, Lincoln).
Hoare, Sir Samuel—see Templewood papers.
Johnston papers (National Library of Scotland, Edinburgh).
Jones, Thomas papers (National Library of Wales, Aberystwyth).
Lansbury papers (British Library of Political and Economic Science).
Layton papers (Trinity College, Cambridge).
Lewis, Walter papers (Warwickshire Record Office).
Lloyd George papers (House of Lords Record Office and National Library of Wales, Aberystwyth).
Lothian papers (Scottish Record Office, Edinburgh).
Mabane W. M. papers (Kirklees District Archives Office, Huddersfield).
MacDonald papers (Public Record Office, Kew).
Maclean papers (Bodleian Library, Oxford).
Mathers, George papers (National Library of Scotland, Edinburgh).
Middleton, J. S. papers (Labour Party Library, London, and Ruskin College, Oxford).
Morris-Jones, J. H. papers (Clwyd Record Office, Hawarden).
Morrison papers (Nuffield College, Oxford).
Muirhead, R. E. papers (National Library of Scotland, Edinburgh).
Noel-Baker, Philip papers (Churchill College, Cambridge).
Passfield papers [Lord Passfield and Beatrice Webb] (British Library of Political and Economic Science).

Pethick-Lawrence papers (Trinity College, Cambridge).
Phillips, Marion papers (Labour Party Library, London).
Ponsonby, Lord papers (Bodleian Library, Oxford).
Reading papers (India Office Library, London).
Rhys, C. A. U.—see Dynevor Muniments.
Runciman papers (Library, University of Newcastle).
Samuel papers (House of Lords Record Office).
Sankey papers (Bodleian Library, Oxford).
Selborne, 3rd Earl of papers [Viscount Wolmer] (Bodleian Library, Oxford).
Simon, E. D. papers (Central Library, Manchester).
Simon, Sir John papers (Bodleian Library, Oxford).
Sinclair, Sir Archibald—see Thurso papers.
Staffield House papers [R. D. Denman] (Bodleian Library, Oxford).
Stansgate papers (House of Lords Record Office).
Steel-Maitland papers (Scottish Record Office, Edinburgh).
Swinton papers [Sir Philip Cunliffe-Lister] (Churchill College, Cambridge).
Templewood papers [Sir Samuel Hoare] (Library, University of Cambridge).
Thomas papers (Kent Archives Office, Maidstone).
Thurso papers [Sir Archibald Sinclair] (Churchill College, Cambridge).
Trevelyan papers (Library, University of Newcastle).
Webb, Beatrice—see Passfield papers.
Whiteley, Wilfrid papers (Borthwick Institute of Historical Research, York).
Wolmer, Viscount—see Selborne, 3rd Earl of.

Records of Political Parties and Associations

(i) Conservative

Conservative Central Office and Research Department (Conservative Party Archive, Bodleian Library, Oxford).
National Society of Conservative Agents (Victoria Library, London).

Birmingham Conservative and Unionist Association (Reference Library, Birmingham).
Bradford CA (West Yorkshire Archive Service, Bradford).
Sheffield City CA (Sheffield Archives Office).

Accrington CA (Library, University of Manchester).
Barkston Ash CA (West Yorkshire Archive Service, Leeds).
Bath CA (Bath Record Office).
Birmingham Ladywood CA (Reference Library, Birmingham).

Blackpool CA (Lancashire Record Office, Preston).
Bodmin CA (Cornwall Record Office, Truro).
Bradford Central CA (West Yorkshire Archive Service, Bradford).
Bradford East CA (West Yorkshire Archive Service, Bradford).
Bradford South CA (West Yorkshire Archive Service, Bradford).
Chelmsford CA (Essex Record Office, Chelmsford).
City of London CA (Victoria Library, London).
Clitheroe CA (Lancashire Record Office, Preston).
Cornwall North CA (Cornwall Record Office, Truro).
Crosby CA [Waterloo CA] (Lancashire Record Office, Preston).
Darwen CA (Lancashire Record Office, Preston).
Derby CA (Derbyshire Record Office, Matlock).
Derbyshire West CA (Derbyshire Record Office, Matlock).
Dorset West CA (Dorset Record Office, Dorchester).
Ealing CA (Greater London Record Office).
Falmouth and Camborne CA (Cornwall Record Office, Truro).
Flintshire CA (Clwyd Record Office, Hawarden).
Fylde CA (Lancashire Record Office, Preston).
Harborough CA (Leicestershire Record Office, Leicester).
Horncastle CA (Lincolnshire Archives Office, Lincoln).
Keighley CA (West Yorkshire Archive Service, Leeds).
Lambeth Kennington CA (British Library of Political and Economic Science).
Leeds West CA (West Yorkshire Archive Service, Leeds).
Maidstone CA (Kent Archives Office, Maidstone).
Middleton and Prestwich CA (Lancashire Record Office, Preston).
Newcastle West CA (Tyne and Wear Record Office, Newcastle).
Northwich CA (Cheshire Record Office, Chester).
Rushcliffe CA (Nottinghamshire Record Office, Nottingham).
Sheffield Central CA (Central Library, Sheffield).
Sheffield Ecclesall CA (Central Library, Sheffield).
Stockton CA (Durham County Record Office, Durham).
Stone CA (Staffordshire Record Office, Stafford).
Wandsworth Clapham CA (British Library of Political and Economic Science).
Warwick and Leamington CA (Warwickshire Record Office, Warwick).
Waterloo CA—see Crosby CA.
Westminster St George's CA (Victoria Library, London).
Wood Green CA (Greater London Record Office).
Wrexham CA (National Library of Wales, Aberystwyth).
York CA (York Archives Office).

(ii) Labour

Labour Party national executive committee minutes and subject files (Labour Party Library, London).

Birmingham BLP (Microfilm at Reference Library, Birmingham).
Bristol BLP (City Record Office, Bristol).
Glasgow BLP (Microfilm at Reference Library, Birmingham).
Leeds City LP (West Yorkshire Archive Service, Leeds).
Woolwich BLP (Microfilm at Reference Library, Birmingham).

Batley and Morley DLP (West Yorkshire Archive Service, Bradford).
Bristol East DLP (City Record Office, Bristol).
Broxtowe DLP (Nottinghamshire Record Office, Nottingham).
Cambridge TCLP (Cambridgeshire Record Office, Cambridge).
Cambridgeshire TCLP (Cambridgeshire Record Office, Cambridge).
Canterbury DLP (Kent Archives Office, Maidstone).
Colne Valley DLP (Microfilm at West Yorkshire Archive Service, Kirklees [Huddersfield]).
Derby DLP (Local Studies Library, Derby).
Derbyshire West DLP (Derbyshire Record Office, Matlock).
Doncaster DLP (Archives Department, Doncaster).
Durham DLP (Durham County Record Office, Durham).
East Anglia ILP (British Library of Political and Economic Science).
Edinburgh South DLP (National Library of Scotland, Edinburgh).
Glasgow ILP Federation (Microfilm at Reference Library, Birmingham).
Gloucester TCLP (Microfilm at Reference Library, Birmingham).
Greenwich DLP (Local History Library, Greenwich).
Hamilton DLP (Microfilm at Reference Library, Birmingham).
Houghton-le-Spring DLP (Shotton papers, Durham County Record Office, Durham).
Jarrow DLP (Durham County Record Office, Durham).
Lambeth North DLP (British Library of Political and Economic Science).
Leeds Central DLP (West Yorkshire Archive Service, Leeds).
Newport DLP (South Wales Coalfield Archive, University College Swansea).
Nottingham South DLP (Nottinghamshire Record Office, Nottingham).
Nuneaton DLP (Warwickshire Record Office, Warwick).
Paddington South DLP (British Library of Political and Economic Science).
Penistone DLP (M[illegible]film at Reference Library, Birmingham).
Peterborough DLP (Microfilm at Reference Library, Birmingham).
Pontypridd TCLP (Microfilm at Reference Library, Birmingham).

Roxburgh and Selkirk DLP (National Library of Scotland, Edinburgh).
Sowerby DLP (West Yorkshire Archive Service, Calderdale [Halifax]).
Stockport TCLP (Microfilm at Reference Library, Birmingham).
Wansbeck DLP (Northumberland Record Office, Newcastle).
York DLP (York Archives Office).

(iii) Liberal

Lancashire and Cheshire and North-Western LF (Central Library, Manchester).
Leeds LF (West Yorkshire Archive Service, Leeds).
Manchester LF (Central Library, Manchester).
Midland LF (Library, University of Birmingham).
Scottish LF (Library, University of Edinburgh).
Yorkshire LF (West Yorkshire Archive Service, Leeds).

Altrincham LA (Cheshire Record Office, Chester).
Chester LA (City Record Office, Chester).
Flintshire LA (Clwyd Record Office, Hawarden).
Lincoln LA (Lincolnshire Archives Office, Lincoln).
Manchester Exchange LA (Central Library, Manchester).
Sutton-in-Ashfield LA (Nottinghamshire Record Office, Nottingham).

(iv) Trade Unions, etc.

Trades Union Congress (Modern Records Centre, University of Warwick).

Amalgamated Association of Operative Cotton Spinners and Twiners (Lancashire Record Office, Preston).
Amalgamated Engineering Union (Modern Records Centre, University of Warwick).
Amalgamated Society of Locomotive Engineers and Firemen (Modern Records Centre, University of Warwick).
Amalgamated Society of Woodworkers (Modern Records Centre, University of Warwick).
Amalgamated Union of Building Trade Workers (Modern Records Centre, University of Warwick).
Ayrshire Miners' Union (National Library of Scotland, Edinburgh).
Fife, Clackmannan and Kinross Miners' Union (National Library of Scotland, Edinburgh).
Iron and Steel Trades Confederation (Modern Records Centre, University of Warwick).
Lanark Miners' County Union (National Library of Scotland, Edinburgh).

Mid and East Lothian Miners' Association (National Library of Scotland, Edinburgh).
Miners' Federation of Great Britain (South Wales Coalfield Archive, University College, Swansea).
National Society of Operative House and Ship Painters and Decorators (Modern Records Centre, University of Warwick).
National Union of Foundry Workers (Modern Records Centre, University of Warwick).
National Union of Railwaymen (Modern Records Centre, University of Warwick).
Railway Clerks' Association (Modern Records Centre, University of Warwick).
South Wales Miners' Federation (South Wales Coalfield Archive, University College, Swansea).
Transport and General Workers' Union (Modern Records Centre, University of Warwick).
West Lothian Mineworkers' Union (National Library of Scotland, Edinburgh).

Edinburgh Trades Council (Microfilm at Reference Library, Birmingham).
Leeds Trades Council (West Yorkshire Archive Service, Leeds).
Llanelli Trades Council (Dyfed Archives Office, Carmarthen).
Sheffield Trades Council (Central Library, Sheffield).

Printed Sources

Government Publications

Census of England and Wales, 1931.
Census of Scotland, 1931.
First Report of the Royal Commission on Unemployment Insurance (Cmd. 3872; (London, 1930–1).
Hansard, *Parliamentary Debates*, fifth series.
Report of the Committee on Broadcasting (Cmd. 5091; London, 1935–6).
Report of the Committee on Finance and Industry (Cmd. 3920; London, 1930–1).
Report of the Committee on National Expenditure (Cmd. 3920; London, 1930–2).
Report of the Royal Commission on the Press, 1947–1949 (Cmd. 7700; London, 1949).
Return of the Expenses of each Candidate at the General Election of May, 1929 (PP 114; London, 1929–30).
Return of the Expenses of each Candidate at the General Election of October, 1931 (PP 109; London, 1931–2).
Statistical Abstract of the United Kingdom, 1913 and 1924–37 (Cmd. 5903; London, 1938–9).

Yearbooks, etc. (1929–1932)

Annual Register
Labour Party, *Annual Report*
Labour Yearbook
Liberal Yearbook
TUC, *Annual Congress Report*

Newspapers

(i) National Daily

Daily Express
Daily Herald
Daily Mail
Daily Mirror
Daily Sketch
Daily Telegraph
Daily Worker
Morning Post
News Chronicle
The Times

(ii) National Sunday

News of the World
Observer
People
Reynolds's Illustrated News
Sunday Chronicle
Sunday Dispatch
Sunday Express
Sunday Graphic
Sunday Pictorial
Sunday Referee
Sunday Times

(iii) Regional

Birmingham Post
Lancashire Daily Post
Liverpool Post
Manchester Guardian
Scotsman
Western Daily Press
Western Mail and South Wales News

Western Morning News
Yorkshire Observer
Yorkshire Post

(iv) Local

Blackpool Evening Gazette
Colne Valley Guardian
Cornish Evening Tidings
Cornishman
Derby Daily Express
Derby Daily Telegraph
Edinburgh Evening News
Evening Dispatch
Evening News
Evening Standard
Glamorgan Free Press and Rhondda Leader
Grimsby Daily Telegraph
Huddersfield Daily Examiner
Kentish Independent and Kentish Mail
Kentish Mercury
Louth Standard
Pontypridd Observer
South Wales Echo and Evening Express
Staffordshire Sentinel
Star
Wakefield Express
West Briton and Cornwall Advertiser

(v) Other Periodicals

Co-operative Review
Economist
Forward
Gleanings and Memoranda
Labour Organiser
Liberal Magazine
Locomotive Journal
Ministry of Labour Gazette
Monthly Journal (Amalgamated Society of Woodworkers)
Monthly Journal of the National Society of Painters
New Dawn
New Leader
New Statesman
Political Quarterly

Railway Service Journal
Spectator
Town Crier

Memoir and Biography

ALLEN, LORD, *Plough my own Furrow: The Story of Lord Allen of Hurtwood as Told through his Writing and Correspondence*, ed. M. Gilbert (London, 1965).
AMERY, L. S., *My Political Life* (3 vols.; London, 1953–5).
—— *The Empire at Bay: The Leo Amery Diaries 1929–1945*, ed. J. Barnes and D. Nicholson (London, 1988).
ANGELL, N., *After All: The Autobiography of Norman Angell* (London, 1951).
ATTLEE, C. R., *As It Happened* (London, 1954).
BALDWIN, A. W., *My Father: The True Story* (London, 1955).
BALDWIN, O., *The Questing Beast: An Autobiography* (London, 1932).
BELLAMY, J., and SAVILLE, J. (eds.), *Dictionary of Labour Biography* (8 vols.; London, 1972–87).
BLAXLAND, G., *J. H. Thomas: A Life for Unity* (London, 1964).
BONDFIELD, M. G., *A Life's Work* (London, n.d. [1948]).
BOOTHBY, R., *I Fight to Live* (London, 1947).
—— *Recollections of a Rebel* (London, 1978).
BOWLE, J., *Viscount Samuel: A Biography* (London, 1957).
BOYLE, A., *Montagu Norman: A Biography* (London, 1967)
—— *Only the Wind will Listen: Reith of the BBC* (London, 1972).
BRITTAIN, V., *Inside the Left: Thirty Years of Platform, Press, Prison and Parliament* (London, 1942).
—— *Socialism over Sixty Years: The Life of Jowett of Bradford, 1864–1944* (London, 1946).
—— *Bermondsey Story: The Life of Alfred Salter* (London, 1949).
BROWN, W. J., *So Far . . .* (London, 1943).
BULLOCK, A., *The Life and Times of Ernest Bevin* (3 vols.; London, 1960–83).
BUTLER, J. R. M., *Lord Lothian (Philip Kerr), 1882–1940* (London, 1960).
CAMPBELL, J., *Lloyd George: The Goat in the Wilderness, 1922–1931* (London, 1977).
CARLTON, D., *Anthony Eden: A Biography* (London, 1981).
CARPENTER, L. P., *G. D. H. Cole: An Intellectual Biography* (London, 1973).
CHURCHILL, R. S., *Lord Derby, 'King of Lancashire': The Official Life of Edward, Seventeenth Earl of Derby* (London, 1959).
CITRINE, LORD, *Men and Work: An Autobiography* (London, 1964)
—— *Two Careers* (London, 1967).
CLAY, H., *Lord Norman* (London, 1957).
CLYNES, J. R., *Memoirs* (2 vols.; London, 1937–8).

COOKE, C., *The Life of Richard Stafford Cripps* (London, 1957).
COOPER, A. D., *Old Men Forget: The Autobiography of Duff Cooper, Viscount Norwich* (London, 1953).
COOTE, C., *A Companion of Honour: The Story of Walter Elliot* (London, 1965).
CROFT, LORD, *My Life of Strife* (London, n.d. [1948]).
CROSS, C., *Philip Snowden* (London, 1966).
CROSS, J. A., *Sir Samuel Hoare: A Political Biography* (London, 1977).
—— *Lord Swinton* (Oxford, 1982).
DALTON, H., *Call Back Yesterday: Memoirs, 1887–1931* (London, 1953).
—— *The Political Diary of Hugh Dalton, 1918–40, 1945–60*, ed. B. Pimlott (London, 1986).
DAVIDSON, J. C. C., *Memoirs of a Conservative: J. C. C. Davidson's Memoirs and Papers, 1910–37*, ed. R. Rhodes James (London, 1969).
DENMAN, R. D., *Political Sketches* (Carlisle, 1949).
DONOUGHUE, B., and JONES, G. W., *Herbert Morrison: Portrait of a Politician* (London, 1973).
DUTTON, D., *Austen Chamberlain: Gentleman in Politics* (Bolton, 1985).
ELTON, LORD, *Among Others* (London, 1938).
ESTORICK, E., *Stafford Cripps: A Biography* (London, 1949).
FEILING, K., *The Life of Neville Chamberlain* (London, 1946).
FOOT, M., *Aneurin Bevan: A Biography* (2 vols.; London, 1962–73).
GALLACHER, W., *Revolt on the Clyde: An Autobiography*, new edn. (London, 1949).
GILBERT, M., *Winston S. Churchill, Vol. 5: 1922–1939* (London, 1976), and companion volume of documents, part 2 (London, 1981).
GRAHAM, T. N., *Willie Graham: The Life of the Rt. Hon. W. Graham* (London, n.d. [1948]).
GRIGG, P. J., *Prejudice and Judgment* (London, 1948).
HAMILTON, M. A., *Arthur Henderson: A Biography* (London, 1938).
—— *Remembering my Good Friends* (London, 1944).
HANNINGTON, W., *Unemployed Struggles, 1919–1936: My Life and Struggles amongst the Unemployed* (London, 1936).
HARRIS, K., *Attlee* (London, 1982).
HARROD, R. F., *The Life of John Maynard Keynes* (London, 1951).
HEUSTON, R. F. V., *Lives of the Lord Chancellors, 1885–1940* (Oxford, 1964).
HYDE, H. M., *Lord Reading: The Life of Rufus Isaacs, First Marquess of Reading* (London, 1967).
—— *Strong for Service: The Life of Lord Nathan of Churt* (London, 1968).
—— *Baldwin: The Unexpected Prime Minister* (London, 1973).
JENKINS, E. A., *From Foundry to Foreign Office: The Romantic Life Story of the Rt. Hon. Arthur Henderson, MP* (London, 1933).
JOHNSTON, T., *Memories* (London, 1952).
JONES, T., *Lloyd George* (London, 1951).
—— *A Diary with Letters, 1931–1950* (London, 1954).

JUDD, D., *Lord Reading: Rufus Isaacs, First Marquess of Reading, Lord Chief Justice and Viceroy of India, 1860–1935* (London, 1982).

KENWORTHY, J. M., *Sailors, Statesmen—and Others: An Autobiography* (London, 1933).

KIRKWOOD, D., *My Life of Revolt* (London, 1935).

KNOX, W. (ed.), *Scottish Labour Leaders, 1918–39: A Biographical Dictionary* (Edinburgh, 1984).

LANSBURY, G., *Looking Backwards—and Forwards* (London, 1935).

LAYBOURN, K., *Philip Snowden: A Biography, 1864–1937* (Aldershot, 1988).

LEE, J., *This Great Journey: A Volume of Autobiography, 1904–45* (London, 1963).

LEWENTHAL, F. M., *Arthur Henderson* (Manchester, 1989).

LLOYD GEORGE, F., *The Years that are Past* (London, 1967).

MCALLISTER, G., *James Maxton: Portrait of a Rebel* (London, 1935).

MACDONALD, M., *People and Power: Random Reminiscences* (London, 1969).

MCGOVERN, J., *Neither Fear nor Favour* (London, 1960).

MACLEOD, I., *Neville Chamberlain* (London, 1961).

MACMILLAN, H., *Winds of Change, 1914–1939* (London, 1966).

MCNAIR, J., *James Maxton, the Beloved Rebel* (London 1955).

MCSHANE, H., and SMITH, J., *Harry McShane: No Mean Fighter* (London, 1978).

MAHON, J., *Harry Pollitt: A Biography* (London, 1976).

MANNING, E. L., *A Life for Education: An Autobiography* (London, 1970).

MARQUAND, D., *Ramsay MacDonald* (London, 1977).

MARWICK, A., *Clifford Allen, the Open Conspirator* (London, 1964).

MIDDLEMAS, R. K., and BARNES, J., *Baldwin: A Biography* (London, 1969).

MORGAN, A., *J. Ramsay MacDonald* (Manchester, 1987).

MORGAN, K. O., and MORGAN, J., *Portrait of a Progressive: The Political Career of Christopher, Viscount Addison* (Oxford, 1980).

MORRIS, A. J. A., *C. P. Trevelyan, 1870–1958: Portrait of a Radical* (Belfast, 1977).

MORRIS-JONES, J. H., *Doctor in the Whips' Room* (London, 1955).

MORRISON, H., *An Autobiography: By Lord Morrison of Lambeth* (London, 1960).

MOSLEY, N., *Rules of the Game: Sir Oswald and Lady Cynthia Mosley, 1896–1933* (London, 1982).

MOSLEY, O., *My Life* (London, 1968).

NICOLSON, H., *King George the Fifth: His Life and Reign* (London, 1952).

—— *Diaries and Letters, 1930–1939*, ed. N. Nicolson (London, 1966).

OWEN, F., *Tempestuous Journey: Lloyd George, his Life and Times* (London, 1954).

PARMOOR, LORD, *A Retrospect: Looking Back over a Life of more than Eighty Years* (London, 1936).

PELLING, H., *Winston Churchill* (London, 1974).

PETHICK-LAWRENCE, F. W., *Fate Has Been Kind* (London, n.d. [1943]).
PIMLOTT, B., *Hugh Dalton* (London, 1985).
POLLITT, H., *Serving my Time: An Apprenticeship to Politics* (London, 1940).
POSTGATE, R., *The Life of George Lansbury* (London, 1951).
RADICE, E. A., and RADICE, G. H., *Will Thorne, Constructive Militant: A Study in New Unionism and New Politics* (London, 1974).
READING, SECOND MARQUESS OF, *Rufus Isaacs: First Marquess of Reading* (2 vols.; London, 1945).
REITH, J. C. W., *Into the Wind* (London, 1949).
—— *The Reith Diaries*, ed. C. Stuart (London, 1975).
RHODES JAMES, R., *Churchill: A Study in Failure, 1900–1939* (London, 1970).
—— *Victor Cazalet: A Portrait* (London, 1976).
—— *Anthony Eden* (London, 1986).
ROSE, K., *King George V* (London, 1983).
ROSKILL, S., *Hankey, Man of Secrets* (3 vols.; London, 1970–2).
ROWLAND, P., *Lloyd George* (London, 1975).
SAMUEL, VISCOUNT, *Memoirs* (London, 1945).
SEXTON, J., *Sir James Sexton, Agitator: The Life of the Dockers' MP* (London, 1936).
SHAKESPEARE, G. H., *Let Candles Be Brought In* (London, 1949).
SHINWELL, E., *Conflict without Malice* (London, 1955).
—— *I've Lived through It All* (London, 1973).
SIMMONS, C. J., *Soap-Box Evangelist* (Chichester, 1972).
SIMON, VISCOUNT, *Retrospect: The Memoirs of the Rt. Hon. Viscount Simon* (London, 1952).
SKIDELSKY, R., *Oswald Mosley* (London, 1975).
SNELL, LORD, *Men, Movements and Myself* (London, 1936).
SNOWDEN, P., Viscount, *An Autobiography* (2 vols.; London, 1934).
SWINTON, VISCOUNT, *I Remember* (London, n.d. [1948]).
—— *Sixty Years of Power: Some Memories of the Men who Wielded It* (London, 1966).
SYLVESTER, A. J., *Life with Lloyd George: The Diary of A. J. Sylvester, 1931–1945*, ed. C. Cross (London, 1975).
TAYLOR, A. J. P., *Beaverbrook* (London, 1972).
TEMPLEWOOD, VISCOUNT, *Nine Troubled Years* (London, 1954).
THOMAS, J. H., *My Story* (London, 1937).
THURTLE, E., *Time's Winged Chariot: Memoirs and Comments* (London, 1945).
WEBB, B., *Beatrice Webb's Diaries*, ed. M. I. Cole (2 vols.; London, 1956).
—— *The Diary of Beatrice Webb*, ed. N. and J. MacKenzie (4 vols.; London, 1979–85).
—— and WEBB, S., *The Letters of Sidney and Beatrice Webb*, ed. N. MacKenzie (3 vols.; London, 1978).
WEDGWOOD, J. C., *Memoirs of a Fighting Life* (London, 1941).
WEIR, L. M., *The Tragedy of Ramsay MacDonald* (London, n.d. [1938]).

WILLIAMS OF BARNBURGH, LORD, *Digging for Britain* (London, 1965).
WINTERTON, EARL, *Orders of the Day* (London, 1953).
WRENCH, J. E., *Geoffrey Dawson and our Times* (London, 1955).
YOUNG, G. M., *Stanley Baldwin* (London, 1952).

Other Books

ALDCROFT, D. H., *The British Economy, Vol. 1: The Years of Turmoil, 1920–1951* (Brighton, 1986).
ALDGATE, A., *Cinema and History: British Newsreels and the Spanish Civil War* (London, 1979).
AYERST, D., *Guardian: Biography of a Newspaper* (London, 1971).
BALL, S., *Baldwin and the Conservative Party: The Crisis of 1929–1931* (London, 1988).
BASSETT, R., *Nineteen Thirty-One: Political Crisis* (London, 1958).
BERKELEY, H., *The Myth that will not Die* (London, 1978).
BLAKE, R., *The Conservative Party from Peel to Churchill* (London, 1970).
BLANSHARD, P., *Communism, Democracy and Catholic Power* (London, 1952).
BLEWETT, N., *The Peers, the Parties and the People: The General Elections of 1910* (London, 1972).
BOOTH, A., and PACK, M., *Employment, Capital and Economic Policy in Great Britain, 1918–1939* (Oxford, 1985).
BOOTH, A. H., *British Hustings, 1924–1950* (London, 1956).
BOYLE, A., *The Climate of Treason*, rev. edn. (London, 1980).
BRAND, C. F., *The British Labour Party*, 2nd edn. (Stanford, 1974).
BRANSON, N., *History of the Communist Party of Great Britain, 1927–1941* (London, 1985).
BRIGGS, A., *The History of Broadcasting in the United Kingdom, Vol. 2: The Golden Age of Wireless* (London, 1965).
BUTLER, D. E. (ed.), *Coalitions in British Politics* (London, 1978).
—— and KAVANAGH, D., *The British General Election of 1983* (London, 1984).
—— and BUTLER, G., (eds.), *British Political Facts, 1900–1985*, 6th edn. (London, 1986).
BUTLER, LORD (ed.), *The Conservatives: A History from their Origins to 1965* (London, 1977).
CAPIE, F., *Depression and Protectionism: Britain between the Wars* (London, 1983).
CARBERY, T. F., *Consumers in Politics: A History and General Review of the Co-operative Party* (Manchester, 1969).
CARLTON, D., *MacDonald versus Henderson: The Foreign Policy of the Second Labour Government* (London, 1970).
CLEGG, H. A., *A History of British Trade Unions since 1889, Vol. 2: 1911–1933* (Oxford, 1985).

CLINE, C. A., *Recruits to Labour: The British Labour Party, 1914–1931* (Syracuse, 1963).
COLE, G. D. H., *A History of the Labour Party from 1914* (London, 1948).
—— and COLE, M. I., *The Condition of Britain* (London, 1937).
COOK, C., *A Short History of the Liberal Party, 1900–1976* (London, 1976).
—— and RAMSDEN, J. (eds), *By-Elections in British Politics* (London, 1973).
CRAIG, F. W. S. (ed.), *British Parliamentary Election Results, 1918–1949* (Glasgow, 1969).
—— *British Parliamentary Election Statistics, 1918–1970*, 2nd edn. (Chichester, 1971).
—— *British General Election Manifestos, 1900–1974*, rev. edn. (London, 1975).
—— *Minor Parties at British Parliamentary Elections* (London, 1975).
CURRAN, J., and SEATON, J., *Power without Responsibility: The Press and Broadcasting in Britain* (Glasgow, 1981).
DEWAR, H., *Communist Politics in Britain: The CPGB from its Origins to the Second World War* (London, 1976).
DIVINE, D., *Mutiny at Invergordon* (London, 1970).
DOUGLAS, R., *The History of the Liberal Party, 1895–1970* (London, 1971).
DOWSE, R. E., *Left in the Centre: The Independent Labour Party, 1893–1940* (London, 1966).
FREEDEN, M., *Liberalism Divided: A Study in British Political Thought, 1914–1939* (Oxford, 1986).
GARSIDE, W. R., *The Durham Miners, 1919–1960* (London, 1971).
GOODHART, P., and BRANSON, U., *The 1922: The Story of the Conservative Backbenchers' Parliamentary Committee* (London, 1973).
GWYN, W. B., *Democracy and the Cost of Politics* (London, 1962).
HOWELL, D., *British Social Democracy: A Study in Development and Decay* (London, 1976).
HOWSON, S., and WINCH, D., *The Economic Advisory Council, 1930–1939: A Study in Economic Advice during Depression and Recovery* (London, 1979).
HUTT, A., *A Post-War History of the British Working Class* (London, 1937).
JOHNSTON, R. J., *The Geography of English Politics: The 1983 General Election* (London, 1985).
JOHNSTON, T., *The Financiers and the Nation* (London, 1934).
KINNEAR, M., *The British Voter: An Atlas and Survey* (London, 1968).
KOSS, S., *The Rise and Fall of the Political Press in Britain* (2 vols.; London, 1981–4).
KUNZ, D. B., *The Battle for Britain's Gold Standard in 1931* (London, 1987).
LABOUR PARTY, *Two Years of Labour Rule* (London, 1931).
—— *The Power of the Press* (London, 1936).
MCHENRY, D. E., *The Labour Party in Transition, 1931–1938* (London, 1938).
MIDDLEMAS, K., *The Clydesiders: A Left-Wing Struggle for Parliamentary Power* (London, 1965).

MIDDLEMAS, K., *Politics in Industrial Society: The Experience of the British System since 1911* (London, 1979).

MILIBAND, R., *Parliamentary Socialism: A Study in the Politics of Labour* (London, 1961).

MILLER, W. L., *Electoral Dynamics in Britain since 1918* (London, 1977).

MITCHELL, B. R., and DEANE, P., *Abstract of British Historical Statistics* (Cambridge, 1962).

MORGAN, K. O., *Consensus and Disunity: The Lloyd George Coalition Government, 1918–1922* (Oxford, 1979).

—— *Rebirth of a Nation: Wales, 1880–1980* (Oxford, 1981).

MOWAT, C. L., *Britain between the Wars, 1918–1940* (London, 1955).

MUGGERIDGE, M., *The Thirties: 1930–1940 in Great Britain* (London, 1940).

PAGE ARNOT, R., *The Miners in Crisis and War: A History of the Miners' Federation of Great Britain* (London, 1961).

PEELE, G., and COOK, C. (eds.), *The Politics of Reappraisal, 1918–1939* (London, 1975).

PELLING, H., *The British Communist Party: A Historical Profile* (London, 1958).

—— *A History of British Trade Unionism*, 2nd edn. (London, 1963).

—— *A Short History of the Labour Party*, 4th edn. (London, 1972).

PEP, *Report on the British Press: A Survey of its Current Operations and Problems with Special Reference to National Newspapers and their Part in Public Affairs* (London, 1938).

PIMLOTT, B., *Labour and the Left in the 1930s* (Cambridge, 1977).

—— and COOK, C. (eds.), *Trade Unions in British Politics* (London, 1982).

PINTO-DUSCHINSKY, M., *British Political Finance, 1830–1980* (Washington, DC, 1981).

POLLARD, S. (ed.), *The Gold Standard and Employment Policies between the Wars* (London, 1970).

POLLOCK, J. K., *Money and Politics Abroad* (New York, 1932).

PRONAY, N., and SPRING, D. W., *Propaganda, Politics and Film, 1918–45* (London, 1982).

RAMSDEN, J., *A History of the Conservative Party, Vol. 3: The Age of Balfour and Baldwin* (London, 1978).

—— *The Making of Conservative Party Policy: The Conservative Research Department since 1929* (London, 1980).

RAYMOND, J. (ed.), *The Baldwin Age* (London, 1960).

RHODES JAMES, R., *The British Revolution: British Politics 1880–1939* (2 vols.; London, 1977).

RICHARDSON, W., *A Union of Many Trades: The History of USDAW* (Manchester, n.d.).

ROSS, J. F. S., *Parliamentary Representation* (London, 1943).

SAYERS, R. S., *The Bank of England, 1891–1944* (3 vols.; Cambridge, 1976).

SCANLON, J., *Decline and Fall of the Labour Party* (London, n.d. [1932]).

SKIDELSKY, R., *Politicians and the Slump: The Labour Government of 1929–1931* (London, 1967).

SMOUT, T. C., *A Century of the Scottish People, 1830–1950* (London, 1986).

SOUTHGATE, D. (ed.), *The Conservative Leadership, 1832–1932* (London, 1974).

STANNAGE T., *Baldwin Thwarts the Opposition: The British General Election of 1935* (London, 1980).

STEVENSON, J., *British Society, 1914–45* (Harmondsworth, 1984).

—— and COOK, C., *The Slump: Society and Politics during the Depression* (London, 1977).

STUTTERHEIM, K. VON, *The Press in England* (London, 1934).

THORPE, A. J. (ed.), *The Failure of Political Extremism in Interwar Britain* (Exeter, 1988).

TURNER, J. (ed.), *Businessmen and Politics: Studies of Business Activity in British Politics, 1900–1945* (London, 1984).

WERTHEIMER, E., *Portrait of the Labour Party*, 2nd edn. (London, 1930).

WEST, F. R., *Trickery and Treachery of the 'National' Government* (London, 1935).

WILLIAMS, F., *Fifty Years' March: The Rise of the Labour Party* (London, 1949).

WILLIAMS, J. E., *The Derbyshire Miners: A Study in Industrial and Social History* (London, 1962).

WILSON, T., *The Downfall of the Liberal Party, 1914–1935* (London, 1966).

WINTER, J. M. (ed.), *The Working Class in Modern British History: Essays in Honour of Henry Pelling* (Cambridge, 1983).

Articles

BALL, S., 'The Conservative Party and the Formation of the National Government: August 1931', *Historical Journal*, 29 (1986), 159–82.

—— 'Failure of an Opposition? The Conservative Party in Parliament, 1929–1931', *Parliamentary History*, 5 (1986), 83–98.

CALLCOTT, M., 'The Nature and Extent of Political Change in the Interwar Years: The Example of County Durham', *Northern History*, 16 (1980), 215–37.

CAPIE, F., and COLLINS, M., 'The Extent of British Economic Recovery in the 1930s', *Economy and History*, 23 (1980), 40–60.

CAREW, A., 'The Invergordon Mutiny, 1931: Long-Term Causes, Organization and Leadership', *International Review of Social History*, 24 (1979), 157–89.

CLOSE, D. H., 'The Realignment of the British Electorate in 1931', *History*, 67 (1982), 393–404.

CULLEN, S., 'The Development of the Ideas and Policy of the British Union of Fascists, 1932–40', *Journal of Contemporary History*, 22 (1987), 115–36.

DARE, R., 'British Labour, the National Government and the "National Interest", 1931', *Historical Studies* (Melbourne), 18 (1979), 345–64.

DUNBABIN, J. P. D., 'British Elections in the Nineteenth and Twentieth Centuries, a Regional Approach', *English Historical Review*, 95 (1980), 241–67.

FAIR, J. D., 'The Conservative Basis for the Formation of the National Government of 1931', *Journal of British Studies*, 19 (1980), 142–64.

—— 'The Second Labour Government and the Politics of Electoral Reform, 1929–1931', *Albion*, 13 (1981), 276–301.

HARRISON, B., 'Women in a Men's House: The Women MPs, 1919–1945', *Historical Journal*, 29 (1986), 623–54.

HASTINGS, R. P., 'The Birmingham Labour Movement, 1918–1945', *Midland History*, 5 (1980), 78–92.

HOLLINS, T. J., 'The Conservative Party and Film Propaganda between the Wars', *English Historical Review*, 96 (1981), 359–69.

MCKIBBIN, R. I., 'Arthur Henderson as Labour Leader', *International Review of Social History*, 23 (1978), 79–101.

—— 'The Economic Policy of the Second Labour Government, 1929–1931', *Past and Present*, 68 (1975), 95–123.

MALAMENT, B. C., 'Philip Snowden and the Cabinet Deliberations of August 1931', *Bulletin of the Society for the Study of Labour History*, 41 (1980), 31–3.

MARTIN, K., 'Public Opinion: The Sunday Newspapers', *Political Quarterly*, 6 (1936), 111–15.

PRONAY, N., 'British Newsreels in the 1930s: 1. Audience and Producers', *History*, 56 (1971), 411–18.

—— 'British Newsreels in the 1930s: 2. Their Policies and Impact', *History*, 57 (1972), 630–72.

ROWSON, S., 'A Statistical Survey of the Cinema Industry in Great Britain in 1934', *Journal of the Royal Statistical Society*, 49 (1936), 67–119.

THORPE, A. J., 'Arthur Henderson and the British Political Crisis of 1931', *Historical Journal*, 31 (1988), 117–39.

—— ' "I am in the Cabinet": J. H. Thomas's Decision to Join the National Government in 1931', *Historical Research* (forthcoming).

WADSWORTH, A. P., 'Newspaper Circulations, 1800–1954', *Transactions of the Manchester Statistical Society*, 1954–55, 1–40.

WEBB, S., 'What Happened in 1931: A Record', *Political Quarterly*, 3 (1932), 1–17.

WEBSTER, C., 'Healthy or Hungry Thirties?', *History Workshop*, 13 (1982), 111–25.

—— 'Health, Welfare and Unemployment during the Depression', *Past and Present*, 109 (1985), 204–29.

WILLIAMS, D., 'London and the 1931 Financial Crisis', *Economic History Review*, 15 (1962–3), 513–28.

WILLIAMSON, P., 'A "Bankers' Ramp"? Financiers and the British Political Crisis of August 1931', *English Historical Review*, 99 (1984), 770–806.
—— ' "Party First and India Second": The Appointment of the Viceroy of India in 1930', *Bulletin of the Institute of Historical Research*, 61 (1983), 86–101.
—— ' "Safety First": Baldwin, the Conservative Party, and the 1929 General Election', *Historical Journal*, 25 (1982), 385–409.
WRENCH, D. J., ' "Cashing In": The Parties and the National Government, August 1931–September 1932', *Journal of British Studies*, 23 (1984), 135–53.

Unpublished Theses

HOLLINS, T. J., 'The Presentation of Politics: The Place of Party Publicity, Broadcasting and Film in British Politics, 1918–1939', Ph.D. thesis (Leeds, 1981).
MCEWAN, J. M., 'Unionist and Conservative MPs, 1914–1939', Ph.D. thesis (London, 1959).
PEGG, M., 'British Radio Broadcasting and its Audience, 1918–1939', D.Phil. thesis (Oxford, 1979).
ROBERTS, J. A., 'Economic Aspects of the Unemployment Policy of the Government, 1929–1931', Ph.D. thesis (London, 1977).
ROLFE, K. W. D., 'Tories, Tariffs and Elections: The West Midlands in English Politics, 1918–1935', Ph.D. thesis (Cambridge, 1974).
ROWE, E. A., 'The British General Election of 1929', B.Litt. thesis (Oxford, 1959).
SELF, R. C., 'The Conservative Party and the Politics of Tariff Reform, 1922–1932', Ph.D. thesis (London, 1982).
SHORTER, P. R., 'Electoral Politics and Political Change in the East Midlands of England, 1918–1935', Ph.D. thesis (Cambridge, 1975).
THORPE, A. J., 'The British General Election of 1931', Ph.D. thesis (Sheffield, 1988).
WILLIAMSON, P., 'The Formation of the National Government: British Politics, 1929–31', Ph.D. thesis (Cambridge, 1987).

INDEX